CLEEVE SCHOOL
HISTORY DEPARTMENT

28

AQA
A-level
History

Germany 1871–1991

The Quest for Political Stability

Steve Ellis
Alan Farmer

DL DYNAMIC LEARNING

HODDER
EDUCATION
AN HACHETTE UK COMPANY

Acknowledgements

The Publishers would like to thank the following for permission to reproduce copyright material.

Photo credits

p.v *l* © Bettmann/CORBIS, *r* © INTERFOTO/Alamy; **p.vi** © Berliner Verlag/Archiv/dpa/Corbis; **p.vii** © Berliner Verlag/Archiv/dpa/Corbis; **p.viii** © imageBROKER/Alamy; **p.1** © Klaus Niermann/ullstein bild via Getty Images; **p.4** © Klaus Niermann/ullstein bild via Getty Images; **p.23** Punch; **p.31** © Library of Congress Prints and Photographs Division Washington, D.C. 20540 [LC-D16-ggbain-16692]t; **p.33** © INTERFOTO/Alamy; **p.70** © Popperfoto/Getty Images; **p.73** © ullstein bild/Getty Images; **p.84** © Berliner Verlag/Archiv/dpa/Corbis; **p.115** © DIZ Muenchen GmbH, Sueddeutsche Zeitung Photo/Alamy; **p.118** © DIZ Muenchen GmbH, Sueddeutsche Zeitung Photo/Alamy; **p.128** © imageBROKER/Alamy; **p.147** © DIZ Muenchen GmbH, Sueddeutsche Zeitung Photo/Alamy; **p.154** © Hulton-Deutsch Collection/CORBIS; **p.158** © DIZ Muenchen GmbH, Sueddeutsche Zeitung Photo/Alamy; **p.172** © Hulton-Deutsch Collection/CORBIS; **p.183** The Weiner Library/REX; **p.188** © ITAR-TASS/TopFoto; **p.189** © Bettmann/CORBIS; **p.190** © ITAR-TASS/TopFoto; **p.197** © Keystone Pictures USA/Alamy; **p.201** bpk; **p.213** © philipk76/Fotolia; **p.223** © ullsteinbild/TopFoto; **p.230** © ullsteinbild/TopFoto; **p.232** picture-alliance/dpa; **p.236** *tl* Keystone Pictures USA/Alamy, *tc* Pictorial Press Ltd/Alamy, *tr* Owen Franken/Corbis, *bl* Hulton-Deutsch Collection/Corbis, *br* Martin Lengemann/ullstein bild/Getty Images; **p.245** © ullstein bild/ullstein bild/Getty Images; **p.247** © MINGAM/Gamma-Rapho/Getty Images; **p.254** bpk/Hanns Hubmann; **p.256** bpk/Hanns Hubmann; **p.267** © epa european pressphoto agency b.v./Alamy.

Text credits

p.40 Figures 3 & 4 Source: Kennedy, Paul (1987) *Rise and Fall of the Great Powers: Economic Change and Military Conflict from1500 to 2000*, Fontana Press; **p.63** Source I: Questions on German history: ideas, forces, decisions from 1800 to the present: historical exhibition in the Berlin Reichstag: catalogue (1984) German Bundestag; **p.87** Figures 1 & 2 Source: Collier, Martin & Pedley, Philip (2000) *Heinemann Advanced History: Germany 1919–45*. Heinemann Publisher; **p.88** Figure 3 Source: Farmer, Alan & Stiles, Andrina (2007), *The Unification of Germany*, Hodder Education; **p.98** Figure 5 Source: Collier, Martin & Pedley, Philip (2000) *Heinemann Advanced History: Germany 1919–45*. Heinemann Publisher; **p.101** Source: Collier, Martin & Pedley, Philip (2000) *Heinemann Advanced History: Germany 1919–45*, Heinemann Publisher; **p.119** Figures 1 & 2 Source: Collier, Martin & Pedley, Philip (2000) *Heinemann Advanced History: Germany 1919–45*, Heinemann Publisher; **p.126** Figure 3 Source: Collier, Martin & Pedley, Philip (2000) *Heinemann Advanced History: Germany 1919–45*, Heinemann Publisher; **p.151** Source A: Welch, David (1995), 'Hitler: Who voted for him?', *History Review* Issue 2, History Today Ltd.; **p.171** Source D: *The Memoirs of Hans Kehrl*, 1973 (retrieved from: http://germanhistorydocs.ghi-dc.org); **p.192** Source A: Habbe, Christian, 'A Time of Retribution: Paying with Life and Limb for the Crimes of Nazi Germany' 27 May 2011, *Der Spiegel* online International; **p.222** Extract A: Schlauch, Wolfgang (1945) 'American policy towards Germany', *Journal of Contemporary History*. Used by permission from Sage Publications, Extract B: Adapted from Leffler, Melvyn (1996) *The Struggle For Germany And The Origins Of The Cold War*, German Historical Institute, Extract C: Adapted from Ranieri , Ronald J., October (2005) 'Building A Social Democratic Hall Of Fame', Humanities & Social Sciences Online; **p.243** Figure 4 Source: Kirk, Tim (2003) *Cassell's Dictionary of Modern German History*, Cassell; **p.258** Source A: Adapted from an interview of Helmut Schmidt: Britain's empire has gone, though you think it still exists, 22 December 2013, *The Guardian*; **p.271** Source: Interview with Kohl's Top Aide on German Reunification: 'It Was Practically a Miracle', March 2009, *Der Spiegel* online International.

AQA material is reproduced by permission of AQA.

Every effort has been made to trace all copyright holders, but if any have been inadvertently overlooked, the Publishers will be pleased to make the necessary arrangements at the first opportunity.

Although every effort has been made to ensure that website addresses are correct at time of going to press, Hodder Education cannot be held responsible for the content of any website mentioned in this book. It is sometimes possible to find a relocated web page by typing in the address of the home page for a website in the URL window of your browser.

Hachette UK's policy is to use papers that are natural, renewable and recyclable products and made from wood grown in sustainable forests. The logging and manufacturing processes are expected to conform to the environmental regulations of the country of origin.

Orders: please contact Bookpoint Ltd, 130 Milton Park, Abingdon, Oxon OX14 4SB. Telephone: (44) 01235 827720.
Fax: (44) 01235 400454. Email education@bookpoint.co.uk Lines are open from 9 a.m. to 5 p.m., Monday to Saturday, with a 24-hour message answering service. You can also order through our website: www.hoddereducation.co.uk

© Steve Ellis and Alan Farmer 2015
First published in 2015 by
Hodder Education,
An Hachette UK Company
Carmelite House
50 Victoria Embankment
London EC4Y 0DZ

www.hoddereducation.co.uk

Impression number   10 9 8 7 6 5 4 3 2 1

Year   2019 2018 2017 2016 2015

Cover photo Alamy CPY 801: Wilhelm II

Illustrations by Integra Software Services Pvt. Ltd., Pondicherry, India

Typeset in 10.5/12.5pt ITC Berkeley Oldstyle Std Book by Integra Software Services Pvt. Ltd., Pondicherry, India

Printed in Italy

A catalogue record for this title is available from the British Library.

ISBN 978 1 4718 3776 0

Contents

Part 2: The Impact of Nazism, War and Division, 1929–91

Author: Steve Ellis

Section 1: The Nazi experiment, 1929–49

Section 2: Division to unity: the Federal Republic of Germany, 1949–91

Introduction

This book on modern German history is written to support the 'Germany' option of AQA's A-level History Breadth Study specification. It covers a traumatic and extraordinary period of European history, encompassing two World Wars, the Holocaust and the Cold War, in all of which the German state played a key role. It is also a study about the making and breaking of a nation, and about a people whom the British love to stereotype: organised, efficient and humourless; a nation whose footballers and cars are routinely 'world class'; a country where everything works and everything has its place. Above all, modern German history has Adolf Hitler, about whom more has been written and said than about almost any other historical figure. However, beyond the stereotypes, and beyond the almost obsessive and dark fascination with Hitler, is a nation of huge social, linguistic and religious diversity, of great beauty and with a rich cultural heritage.

This is ultimately a story of great tragedies. A German male born in 1900, who lived into his eighties, would have grown up under the Kaiser, fought in the Great War, seen his family grapple with the economic misery of **hyperinflation** and the Great Depression, endured Hitler's terroristic Third Reich, experienced the barbarities of the Second World War and the Holocaust, lived through the Allied occupation and spent his older adulthood in a divided nation. The period covered by this book, therefore, is not only about a quest for political stability, but it is also about a quest for national identity.

▲ Trümmerfraven, or 'rubble-women', who cleared the streets after the Second World War.

v

The key content

'The Quest for Political Stability: Germany, 1871–1991' is one of the breadth studies offered by AQA, and as such covers over 100 years. The content is divided into two parts.

Part 1 (1871–1929) is studied by those taking the AS examination.

Parts 1 and 2 (1871–1991) are studied by those taking the full A-level examination.

Each part is subdivided into two sections.

PART 1: EMPIRE TO DEMOCRACY, 1871–1929

Part 1 begins with the creation of a new nation, which experienced great contrasts and tensions in subsequent decades: between autocracy and democracy, socialism and elitism, traditional and new cultural forms. It is a period fractured by a catastrophic defeat in 1918, ushering in a new democracy which literally had to fight for its very existence.

The *Kaiserreich*, 1871–1914

The new *Kaiserreich*, built on Prussian 'blood and iron', fostered an attitude that German culture and morals were superior to all others, and that discipline and unquestioning obedience were essential German values. A study of political and social developments in the Wilhelmine era, therefore, is essential for understanding not only the events that led inexorably to the First World War, but also in understanding the criticisms hurled at the new post-war democracy. It is also a period in which key individuals, notably Otto von Bismarck and Kaiser Wilhelm II, have attracted enormous conflicting historical interpretation.

Empire to democracy, 1914–29

The political impact of the First World War not only brought an end to the Second *Reich* and the Hohenzollern monarchy, it also provided a legacy which the new Republic was never able to overcome, and which set the conditions for much of the history of Germany in the twentieth century. Though it survived a political onslaught from the right and the left in the years 1919–23, the Weimar Republic could not throw off the shackles of an unanticipated, psychologically devastating defeat and a peace settlement viewed by Germans as humiliating and vindictive. It is also a period of fascinating cultural experimentation, challenging traditional forms of expression and thinking.

PART 2: THE IMPACT OF NAZISM, WAR AND DIVISION, 1929–91

Part 2 covers the events which shaped both German and wider European history into the twenty-first century. It begins with the collapse of Weimar democracy and its replacement by a one-party Nazi dictatorship, through to Germany's defeat in the Second World War and the post-war Allied occupation, which condemned the nation to a forty-year period of division into West and East Germany.

The Nazi experiment, 1929–49

This period covers morally challenging issues and events. The Weimar Republic was shamelessly undermined by right-wing political elites who 'levered' Hitler into power with the intention of securing their own power. However, the 'puppet' turned the tables on his 'masters' in a matter of months, unleashing an unprecedented terroristic, ideologically and racially motivated regime determined to impose its own narrow vision of what was 'normal' on the rest of Europe.

You may already know some of the 'popular' history of the Nazis and the Second World War, but this section explores not only the main events of the period, but also the underpinning ideas and ideology that 'justified' its excesses.

Defeat in 1945 was utter and total. The destruction of the German state through Hitler's calculated war of conquest led to a new European and world order, placing Germany at the centre of the Cold War, and Berlin at its front line. By 1949, one Germany had become two.

Division to unity: the Federal Republic of Germany, 1949–91

The West German state confounded the many doubters who believed the Germans incapable of, or temperamentally unsuited to, democratic forms of government. Under chancellor Adenauer, West Germany quickly established itself at the forefront of European affairs and as a fundamental part of the Western anti-Communist alliance. The 1950s' 'economic miracle' set the foundations for West Germany to emerge as a dominant world economic power. Though the 1960s and 1970s saw extra-parliamentary challenges to the state, particularly over its reluctance to acknowledge its Nazi past, by the end of the 1980s West Germany, under the direction of Chancellor Kohl, was able to lead the reunification process as the East German state crumbled. On 3 October 1990, Germany once again became one state and 'one people'.

Key concepts

The study of history does not just include narrative – interesting though the stories often are! There are four concepts which steer our thinking and our understanding of the past. These are important in your study, and questions are likely to involve assessing these concepts.

- Change and continuity: To what extent did things change? What are the similarities and differences over time?
- Cause and consequence: What were the factors that led to change? How did the changes affect individuals and groups within society, as well as the country as a whole?

In relation to these concepts, the essay questions you will face will be asking you to assess, for example:

- the extent you agree with a statement
- the validity of a statement
- the importance of a particular factor relating to a key question
- how much something changed or to what extent something was achieved.

In addition, you will be learning about different interpretations: how and why events have been portrayed in different ways over time by historians. In the first section of both the AS and A-level examination you will be tested on this skill with a selection of contrasting extracts.

The key questions

The specification lists six key questions around which the study is based. These are wide-ranging in scope and can be considered across the whole period. They reflect the broadly based questions (covering twenty years or more) that will be set in the examination.

1 How was Germany governed and how did political authority change and develop?
You will study the political tensions between the Reichstag and the Emperor and his chancellors in the Second Reich; following this you will consider how authoritarian elites and groups undermined Weimar democracy leading to one-party Nazi rule. Finally, you will examine the development of the new West German state through to its reunification with East Germany in 1990.

2 How effective was opposition?
This key question complements your study of political authority. You will consider the nature and limitations of the political opposition to Imperial and authoritarian control in Wilhelmine Germany. You will learn about how, in the inter-war period, opposition groups succeeded in undermining Weimar democracy, but failed to limit the ambitions of the Nazis. Finally, you will study how the relatively stable West German parliamentary consensus was challenged by extra-parliamentary opposition from the 1960s onwards.

3 How and with what results did the economy develop and change?
Germany was an economic powerhouse fuelling the political ambitions of its leaders. You will examine Germany's rapid economic growth during the Second Reich and the severe economic consequences of fighting and losing the First World War. You will study the contribution of economic factors to the collapse of the Weimar democracy, and follow this up by analysing two so-called 'economic miracles': the recovery under the Nazis in the 1930s and under Adenauer in the 1950s. Finally, you will consider how West German governments coped with turbulent global economic conditions from the 1970s and the economic challenges of reunification.

4 What was the extent of social and cultural change?
You will cover an astonishing diversity of social and cultural change throughout a period when human technology advanced at a greater rate than ever before, and when social and cultural norms changed almost beyond recognition. Yet, Germans alive in 1871 would have recognised continuing elements of German culture in 1991, notably the notions of Heimat (nation) and 'identity'. What it was, socially and culturally, to be 'a German' is a continuing theme throughout the study.

5 How important were ideas and ideology?
These are concepts fundamental to an understanding of German social, cultural and political development throughout the period of this study. There are some key continuities, particularly the geo-political ambitions of the Second and Third Reichs, intent on creating a larger, more self-sufficient German empire. Your study of Nazi Germany inevitably focuses on a state driven by its ideological beliefs; the creation of two Germanys in the 1940s, and the reunification process in 1989–91, also owe as much to ideas and ideology as to political and economic considerations.

6 How important was the role of key individuals and groups and how were they affected by developments?
The impact of 'great' individuals and groups is a key fascination of historical study, and this period of German history is rich in its opportunity to study extraordinarily influential leaders such as Bismarck, Kaiser Wilhelm II, Hitler, Adenauer and Brandt. It is no less rich in its diversity of significant groups, religious, social, cultural or generational.

How this book is designed to help your studies

1 With the facts, concepts and key questions of the specification

At the beginning of each chapter the book flags up the elements of the specification and the key questions that are being covered.

Activities are provided, helping you to create notes, and enabling you to consider the main areas of interpretation throughout the period.

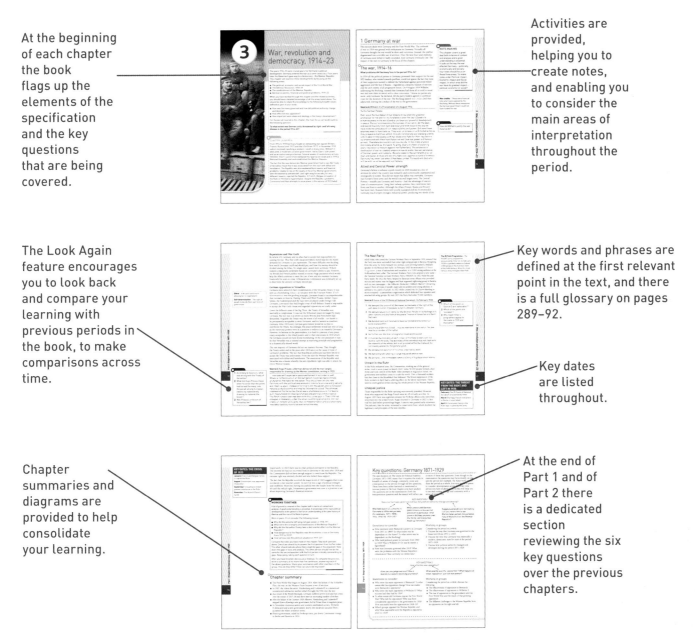

The Look Again feature encourages you to look back and compare your learning with previous periods in the book, to make comparisons across time.

Key words and phrases are defined at the first relevant point in the text, and there is a full glossary on pages 289–92.

Key dates are listed throughout.

Chapter summaries and diagrams are provided to help consolidate your learning.

At the end of Part 1 and of Part 2 there is a dedicated section reviewing the six key questions over the previous chapters.

2 With the skills needed to answer examination questions

The book provides guidance in answering examination questions in the form of a separate skills section at the end of each chapter.

Interpretation skills are developed through the analysis of extended pieces of writing by leading academics.

3 With the skills in reading, understanding and making notes from the book

Note-making

Good note-making is really important. Your notes are an essential revision resource. What is more, the process of making notes will help you understand and remember what you are reading.

How to make notes

Most note-making styles reflect the distinction between key points and supporting evidence. Below is advice on a variety of different note-making styles. Throughout each section in the book are note-making activities for you to carry out.

The important thing is that you understand your notes. Therefore, you don't have to write *everything* down, and you don't have to write in full sentences.

While making notes you can use abbreviations:

Full text	Abbreviation
Government	Govt
Weimar Republic	WR
Red Army Faction	RAF

You can develop your own abbreviations. Usually it is only you who has to understand them!

You can use arrows instead of words:

Full text	Abbreviation
Increased	↑
Decreased	↓

You can use mathematical notation:

Equals	=
Plus, and	+
Because	∵
Therefore	∴

Note-making styles

There are a large number of note-making styles. However you prefer to make notes, by hand or on a laptop or tablet, the principles are the same. You can find examples of three popular styles below. All of them have their strengths; it is a good idea to try them all and work out which style suits you.

Style 1: Bullet points

Bullet points can be a useful method of making notes:

- They encourage you to write in note form, rather than in full sentences.
- They help you to organise your ideas in a systematic fashion.
- They are easy to skim read later.
- You can show relative importance visually by indenting less important, or supporting points.

Usually it is easier to write notes in bullet points after you have skim-read a section or a paragraph first in order to get the overall sense.

Style 2: The 1–2 method

The 1–2 method is a variation on bullet points. The method is based on dividing your page into two columns: the first for the main point, the second for supporting detail. This allows you to see the structure of the information clearly. To do this, you can create a chart to complete, as follows:

Main point	Supporting detail

Style 3: Spider diagrams

Spider diagrams or mind maps can be a useful method of making notes:

- They will help you to categorise factors: each of the main branches coming from the centre should be a new category.
- They can help you see what is most important: often the most important factors will be close to the centre of the diagram.
- They can help you see connections between different aspects of what you are studying. It is useful to draw lines between different parts of your diagram to show links.
- They can also help you with essay planning: you can use them to quickly get down the main points and develop a clear structure in response to an essay question.
- You can set out the spider diagram in any way that seems appropriate for the task, but usually, as with a spider's web, you would start with the title or central issue in the middle with connecting lines radiating outwards.

Bismarck's Germany 1871–90

This chapter covers the years 1871–90 – a period when Otto von Bismarck dominated the newly created German Empire. The chapter deals with a number of areas:

- The 1871 German constitution
- The role of the Chancellor
- The role of the *Reichstag*
- Bismarck's domestic policies
- Bismarck's fall

When you have worked through the chapter and the related activities, you should have a detailed knowledge of all the areas listed above. You should be able to relate this knowledge to the following two breadth issues defined as part of your study:

- How was Germany governed and how did political authority change and develop?
- How important was the role of a particular individual (in this case Bismarck) in Germany's political development?

For the period covered in this chapter the main focus can be phrased as a question:

How successful was Bismarck in managing the political situation in Germany between 1871 and 1890?

The focus of the question is on the problems Bismarck faced in controlling the German Empire (which his actions before 1871 had brought about) and in managing the 1871 German constitution (for which he was largely responsible).

CHAPTER OVERVIEW

The Second German Empire, which came into existence in 1871, had a complex constitution which tried to ensure Prussian dominance over the rest of Germany and Bismarck's dominance over both Prussia and Germany. The German political system is hard to classify. Germany was not ruled by an all-powerful monarch, but nor was it a parliamentary democracy.

Bismarck dominated Germany for nearly two decades after 1871. While he had great success in foreign policy, ensuring Europe remained at peace, he faced some problems on the domestic front. His clash with the Catholic Church (the *Kulturkampf*) and his efforts to suppress socialism were far from successful. His welfare measures in the 1880s are often regarded as his greatest domestic achievement. While William I was emperor, Bismarck's position was secure. However, William's death in 1888, followed almost immediately by the death of his son Frederick, resulted in Wilhelm II becoming emperor. Wilhelm dismissed Bismarck in 1890.

William I and Wilhelm II

This book, like most books on this period, will call Germany's first Emperor (or *Kaiser*) William I. This will differentiate him from Kaiser Wilhelm II – William II's traditional name in Britain.

NOTE-MAKING

Use the headings in this section to make brief notes as you work through it. Set these notes out clearly using the main headings, sub-headings and sub-points.

For example:

Main heading: The German constitution

Sub-heading 1: Autocratic or democratic?

Sub-heading 2: Prussian domination?

Sub-heading 3: Bismarck as Imperial Chancellor

When you have completed your notes on the first few pages, review the process and then devise your own sub-headings for the remainder of the section, using the headings and questions in the text to help you.

Second German Empire – The first German Empire (or Reich) was the Holy Roman Empire, established in AD800. Napoleon Bonaparte brought the Holy Roman Empire – described by the writer Voltaire as neither holy, nor Roman, nor an empire – to an end in 1806. The Second German Empire was the one established by Bismarck. It lasted until 1918.

Federal – A government in which several states, while independent in domestic affairs, combine for general purposes.

Veto – The power or right to reject or forbid a proposed measure.

Secede – To leave or quit.

1 The German Empire in 1871

The Second German Empire – or *Kaiserreich* – was proclaimed on 18 January 1871 in the Palace of Versailles following Prussian–German success in the war against France (1870–71). King William I of Prussia, the strongest state in Germany, became the new German Emperor (*Kaiser*) with Otto von Bismarck as his Imperial Chancellor.

The German constitution

How democratic was the *Kaiserreich*?

The constitution of the new German Empire incorporated the main provisions of the constitution of the North German Confederation, drawn up by Bismarck in 1867. Germany was to be a **federal** state. Powers and functions were divided between the central government and 25 state governments (see Figure 1).

The King of Prussia was the Emperor of Germany. He had the power to appoint and dismiss the Chancellor and to dissolve the *Reichstag*. He controlled foreign policy, could make treaties and alliances, commanded the army and could declare war and make peace. He supervised the execution of all federal laws. He also possessed the right to interpret the constitution.

The Chancellor was the chief minister of the *Reich*. He was responsible to the Emperor, not the *Reichstag*. He chaired sessions of the *Bundesrat* (see below) and could appoint and dismiss state secretaries responsible for the various government ministries. He could ignore resolutions passed by the *Reichstag*.

The *Reichstag* was the national parliament. It was elected by all males over 25 years of age. It could accept or reject legislation but had only limited powers to initiate new laws. State secretaries were excluded from membership of the *Reichstag* and were not responsible to it. Its members were unpaid, and were elected every five years unless the *Reichstag* was dissolved by the *Kaiser*.

The *Bundesrat*, or Federal Council, comprised 58 members, nominated by the state assemblies. Its consent was required in the passing of new laws. Theoretically, it had the power to change the constitution. However, a vote of fourteen members constituted a **veto**. Prussia had seventeen members on the *Bundesrat*, Bavaria six members and the smaller states one each. In theory, the *Bundesrat* had extensive powers. In practice, it usually rubber stamped the Chancellor's policies.

The federal or national government had specific responsibilities for the *Reich* as a whole, including matters such as defence, foreign affairs, civil and criminal law, customs, railways and the postal service.

While no longer sovereign or free to **secede**, the various states which comprised the *Reich* preserved their own constitutions, rulers, parliaments and administrative systems. State governments retained considerable powers over taxation, education, police, local justice and transport. The kings of Bavaria, Saxony and Wurttemberg even retained their own armies.

Emperor

- Always the king of Prussia
- Could appoint and dismiss the Chancellor
- Could dissolve the *Reichstag*
- Controlled foreign policy
- Could make treaties and alliances
- Commanded the army
- Could declare war and make peace
- Supervised the execution of all federal laws
- Possessed the right to interpret the constitution

Chancellor

- Chief Minister of the *Reich*
- Not responsible to *Reichstag*, only to the Emperor
- Decided upon *Reich* policy outlines
- Chaired sessions of the *Bundesrat*
- Could 'hire and fire' state secretaries responsible for the various government ministries
- Could ignore resolutions passed by the *Reichstag*
- Office was normally combined with the Minister-Presidency of Prussia

Federal

Centralised government with specific responsibilities for the *Reich* as a whole, e.g. foreign affairs, defence, civil and criminal law, customs, railways, postal service

State

Regional government with specific responsibilities for individual states, e.g. education, transport, direct taxation, police, local justice, health

Bundesrat

- The Federal Council
- Comprised 58 members nominated by state assemblies
- Consent was required in the passing of new laws
- Theoretically able to change the constitution
- A vote of 14 against a proposal constituted a veto
- Prussia had 17 of the 58 seats
- Bavaria had six seats and the smaller states one each
- In theory, it had extensive powers. In practice, it usually rubber stamped the Chancellor's policies

Reichstag

- The national parliament
- Elected by all males over 25 years of age
- Could accept or reject legislation, but its power to initiate new laws was negligible
- State secretaries were excluded from membership of the *Reichstag* and not responsible to it
- Members were not paid
- Could approve or reject the budget
- Elected every 5 years (unless dissolved)

▲ **Figure 1 How Germany was ruled.**

The North German Confederation

This had been created in 1867, following Prussia's success against Austria in the Seven Weeks' War of 1866. Bismarck might have pressed for the unification of all Germany in 1866. However, as well as the threat of French intervention, he feared that if Prussia absorbed too much too soon, this might be more trouble than it was worth. The four southern states of Bavaria, Wurttemberg, Baden and Hesse-Darmstadt thus retained their independence. All other German states were formed into a North German Confederation under Prussian leadership.

Autocratic or democratic?

The German political system, designed by Bismarck, defies easy classification. Some see it as essentially autocratic, with power residing ultimately with the Emperor. But it is also possible to argue that the system was remarkably democratic, certainly by nineteenth-century standards, with the *Reichstag* having considerable potential power (see pages 6–7). The complex system can be seen (positively) as creating a delicate equilibrium with the key institutions keeping each other in check. It can also be seen (negatively) as creating major tensions, not least between monarchical and parliamentary claims to power, and between federal and state power.

Prussian dominance?

Bismarck intended that Prussia should dominate the new *Reich*. To a large extent, he succeeded in his aim:

1 Prussia possessed 60 per cent of Germany's population and two-thirds of its territory. Prussia returned 235 deputies out of a total of 397 in the *Reichstag*. The fact that it had seventeen seats in the *Bundesrat* meant it could block any unwelcome constitutional amendments.
   – As German Emperor, the Prussian King was head of the imperial executive and civil service and supreme warlord of the *Reich's* armed forces.
   – Except from the periods 1872–73 and 1892–96, the Imperial Chancellor was always simultaneously prime minister of Prussia.
2 Prussian and imperial institutions were so intertwined that they could hardly be distinguished. The Prussian minister of war was also the imperial minister of war. Imperial secretaries of state worked closely with Prussian ministers.
3 Not surprisingly, Prussia's aristocracy enjoyed a dominant position in the political, military and administrative structure of the Empire.
4 The Prussian state parliament, elected by a three-class system, was dominated by the aristocracy, the rich, the military and a conservative civil service. This hindered the development of parliamentary democracy in Germany as a whole.

However, for all the complaints about a 'Prussianisation' of Germany, the identity of 'old Prussia' was significantly diluted by its integration into the *Reich*. Prussia could no longer be governed without consideration of the wider interests of Germany. Prussian influence was slowly undermined by the need to make concessions to the states. Non-Prussians soon held important posts in government both in the *Reich* as a whole and in Prussia. It was the new *Reich*, not Prussia, which now engaged the loyalties of most Germans.

The Prussian state government

Prussian voters were divided into three classes, according to the amount of taxes they paid. This ensured that the rich had far more electoral power than the poor and power remained in the hands of the conservatives. Most of the other state assemblies were elected by universal suffrage (the right of most people to vote).

Otto von Bismarck in 1871. ▶

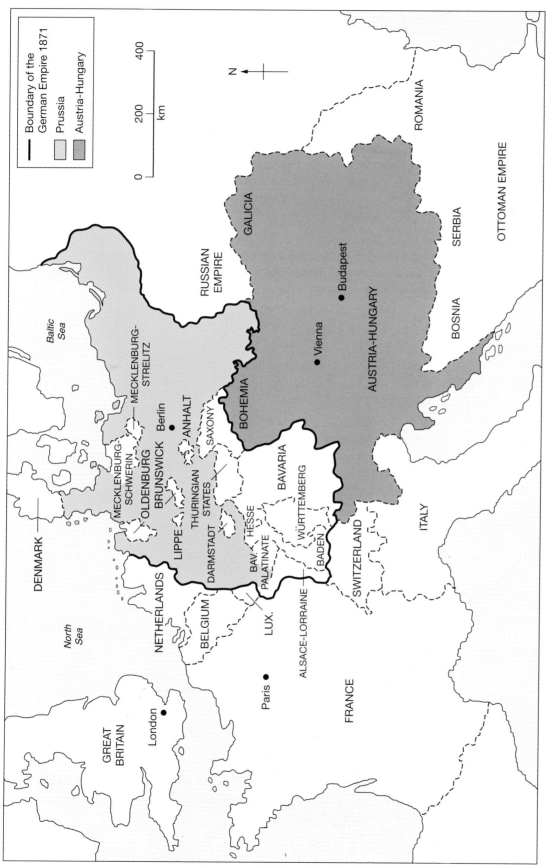

▲ **Figure 2** Map of the German Empire – the *Kaiserreich* – in 1871. What does this suggest about Prussia's power within the *Kaiserreich*?

Bismarck as Imperial Chancellor

After 1871 Bismarck was Prussian Prime Minister and Foreign Minister and Imperial Chancellor. As such, he exercised most of the powers ascribed to the Crown in the constitution. His reputation as the man who had brought about German unification coupled with his influence over Emperor William I gave him an immensely strong position, which he exploited.

Loathing the existence of any rival authority, Bismarck ensured that other ministers were little more than senior clerks, carrying out his orders. There was nothing that resembled an imperial cabinet. Bismarck dominated the secretaries of state and made sure that they did not confer with the *Kaiser* without his permission. His mistrust of potential rivals encouraged him to rely increasingly on his son Herbert, who was **Secretary of State** of the Foreign Office from 1886.

Nevertheless, while Bismarck exerted a tight grip over all aspects of policy, foreign and domestic, in the *Reich* and in Prussia, there were practical and theoretical limitations to his power, especially in domestic affairs:

- The fact that Germany was a federal state reduced his influence.
- The *Reichstag* was a major constraint (see below).
- Bismarck's long absences from Berlin (he liked to spend time on his country estates) and his poor health (often stomach troubles arising from over-eating and over-drinking) reduced his control of day-to-day decision-making.

Many contemporaries viewed Bismarck with awe – a legend in his own lifetime. Recent historians have often been less impressed. They have represented him as more a lucky opportunist than a master-planner. They have also drawn attention to his less desirable attributes: his vindictiveness, his intolerance of criticism and his frequent use of bullying to get his way. It should be said that these methods did not always succeed. After 1871 he was persistently thwarted in his efforts to shape the domestic developments of the *Reich*.

The *Reichstag*

Bismarck was anxious for political power in Germany to remain in traditional hands – in those of the Emperor, his army officers, his ministers – and particularly in his own. Arguably the constitution gave little opportunity for the exercise of democracy. The *Reichstag*, for example, could censor the Chancellor but not secure his dismissal. It could itself be dismissed at any time and new elections called. Bismarck regarded the *Reichstag* with some disdain – as a collection of squabbling politicians who did not reflect popular opinion.

Characteristically, he was ready to work with the *Reichstag* only on condition that it accepted his proposals or some compromise acceptable to him. If agreement could not be reached, he usually dissolved the *Reichstag* and called for fresh elections. He was prepared to use all the means at his disposal, not least the exploitation of international crises, to swing public opinion in elections to secure the passage of contentious legislation.

Secretary of State – The German equivalent of Foreign Secretary.

Reichstag politicians have often been criticised by historians for failing to do more to exploit their potential power. However, they faced a difficult task. The balance of power was tilted sharply in favour of the monarchy and most Germans remained deeply respectful of authority, believing that it was right and proper that the Emperor, or his Chancellor, should rule. There was no widespread conviction that power should be in the hands of the political party which happened to have a majority of seats in the *Reichstag*. Even members of left-wing parties did not expect the *Reichstag* to exercise much control over government. The most that they hoped for was that it would have some influence on government decisions.

Source A Bismarck speaking to the *Reichstag* in July 1879.

I cannot, and the government cannot, be at the beck and call of particular parties. It must go its own way that it regards as correct; these courses are subject to the resolutions of the Reichstag; the government will require the support of the parties but it can never submit itself to the domination of any single party!

> What does Source A reveal about Bismarck's view of the 1871 constitution?

Socialist leader August Bebel claimed that the *Reichstag* was the 'fig-leaf of despotism'. However, in reality, the *Reichstag* had more power than Bebel suggested and Bismarck had envisaged:

- The Second Empire needed a vast number of new laws and no bill could become a law until it passed the *Reichstag*. The government also needed more money, which only the *Reichstag* could provide. Bismarck, therefore, was forced to negotiate deals and grant concessions.
- The *Reichstag* was an open forum of debate whose members enjoyed parliamentary immunity. Debates were widely reported in the press. The Chancellor and the ministers of state could be questioned and embarrassed.
- For many Germans, the *Reichstag* – not the *Kaiser* – was the focus of national attention.
- No parliament in the world in the 1870s was elected on a broader franchise.
- Universal male suffrage promoted the development of mass political parties with popular appeal (see Figure 4, page 14). While these parties were in no position to form governments, Bismarck could not afford to ignore them. Although under no constitutional obligation to adopt policies approved by the *Reichstag*, he did need to secure support for his own legislative proposals.
- What is striking is how troublesome the *Reichstag* was for Bismarck, criticising and often thwarting his plans. Indeed, historians may have overemphasised the way that the *Reichstag* bowed to Bismarck and not emphasised enough the way that he bowed to *Reichstag* pressure. On several occasions in the 1880s he explored the possibility of changing the constitution – proof of the *Reichstag*'s influence.

> **Franchise** – The right to vote for a representative in a national election.

The *Reichstag* was thus neither an all-powerful parliament nor simply a pliant instrument under Bismarck's control. It was something in between. It certainly acquired a genuine popular legitimacy and became a focal point for those whom Bismarck saw as 'enemies of the state': Poles, Catholics and socialists.

The role of the army

The army played an important role in the *Reich*, as it had done in Prussia. It was essentially Prussian. The Prussian army was by far the largest of the four armies that comprised the German army. The three other contingents, from Bavaria, Saxony and Wurttemberg, all came under the Emperor's command in time of war and followed the Prussian lead in organisation, instruction and weaponry.

Prussian–German officers owed personal loyalty to the King/Emperor, not the state. The system of conscription ensured that all German men served for two to three years in the army. This gave officers ample opportunity to build on the values already inculcated at school: discipline, pride in military institutions and love of the Fatherland.

As the creator of the *Reich*, the army had a special place in the minds of most Germans. After 1871 it was taken for granted that the army's needs must always come first and that the highest virtues were military ones. Uniforms encouraged respect and obedience and both Bismarck and the *Kaiser* always wore military uniform in public.

Given that the military budget was not subject to annual approval, the army was virtually independent of *Reichstag* control. It was not bound to consult any civilian authority before acting. Many army officers were hard-line conservatives. They had little time for the *Reichstag* and even less for liberals and socialists. Indeed, some army officers were as much concerned with the 'enemy' within as they were with Germany's enemies beyond the *Reich's* borders. If called upon, they were ready to disperse demonstrations, break strikes and crush any attempt at revolution.

Emperor William I

In many respects, the key man in the 1871 constitution was the Emperor. Yet Emperor William I is often the forgotten man of Bismarck's Germany. He became King of Prussia in 1861 and viewed his kingship of Prussia as more important than the title of German Emperor which he received in 1871. Despite possessing considerable powers as *Kaiser*, William was generally content to leave the task of governing Germany (and Prussia) to Bismarck and limited himself to embodying the dignity of the new state. William, conservative in most matters, had reservations about some of Bismarck's measures, including the *Kulturkampf* (see page 15) and his Chancellor's tough handling of subordinates. But he appreciated Bismarck's ability. Bismarck appreciated William's support. He described William in his memoirs as a polite, gentlemanly, courteous man with the attitude and manners of a Prussian army officer. William, despite several assassination attempts on his life, seems to have been genuinely popular in his later years – a man who personified the values of 'old Prussia'. Many Prussians approved of William's rather austere and simple lifestyle.

Interpretations: the German political system

The exact nature of the German political system after 1871 continues to be debated. Historians have variously described it as a military monarchy, a Prussian autocracy, a semi-autocracy or a constitutional monarchy. So who exactly held power in Germany? Was it the *Kaiser*, the Imperial Chancellor (that is, Bismarck from 1871 to 1890) or the *Reichstag*?

> ***Kulturkampf*** – This translates as a struggle for culture or a struggle for civilisation. In Germany, after 1871 the struggle was essentially between the state and the Catholic Church.

Source B Adapted from *Bismarck* by B. Waller, (Blackwell), 1985.

It is absurd to argue that the government of Imperial Germany was absolute or even semi-absolute. The Emperor, not Bismarck, held ultimate power; the strength of parliament was considerable and gradually growing; freedom of speech and freedom of the press were marked and their champions increasingly numerous; the law was sensible and respected.

ACTIVITY

Source B provides one interpretation of the way Germany was ruled after 1871.

- In what way do you agree with the source?
- In what way do you disagree with the source?
- Using material from the source and your own knowledge, to what extent was Germany post-1871 a parliamentary democracy?

Alsace-Lorraine

Germany seized the provinces of Alsace and (half of) Lorraine from France after victory in the Franco–Prussian War. A good case could be made for including Alsace in the German *Reich*, but Lorraine was mainly French-speaking. The loss of the two provinces sharpened the edge of French resentment at losing the war.

German disunity

How united was Germany?

The new *Reich* was born in a mood of national euphoria. Germans were proud of their victory over France, proud that their new country was the strongest military state in Europe, proud that Germany was strong economically, and proud that its economic strength was growing.

Nevertheless, the new *Reich* was far from united:

- Each state had its own traditions. Each also had powers over education, justice, agriculture, religious matters and local government.
- Over 60 per cent of the population were Protestant, but Catholicism was strong in Alsace-Lorraine, in south-west Germany, in the Rhineland and among the Poles.
- Ten per cent of the *Reich*'s population were non-German minorities – Poles, Danes and French.
- There were economic and social divisions – between rich and poor, and between the industrialising north and west and the predominantly rural south and east.

Thus, a major problem was to unite Germany in fact as well as in theory. Pre-1871 nationalism had been generally seen as a progressive force which aimed to sweep away the old regime and introduce liberal and representative government. After 1871 German nationalism became more conservative. The German nation was now identified with the new *Reich*, any criticism of which was denounced as unpatriotic. A distinct national identity developed that transcended that of the member states. Arguably non-Prussian Germans became more Prussian while Prussians became more German.

German economic development

The results of the war against France stimulated the German economy. Alsace-Lorraine, for example, contained Europe's largest deposits of iron ore, and production increased rapidly after 1871. The injection of huge French indemnity payments into the German economy, following the Franco–Prussian War, helped to cause a spectacular, if short-lived, boom. The boom assisted German banks, which,

The Franco–Prussian War 1870–71

In 1870 France and Prussia went to war. The Prussian army, allied with troops from four southern German states – Bavaria, Wurttemberg, Baden and Hesse-Darmstadt – easily defeated French forces. Historians remain divided about what to call the war: should it be Franco–Prussian (the usually accepted name) or Franco–German? The war was so dominated by Prussian military expertise that, in many ways, it was essentially a Prussian enterprise. Nevertheless, the war was also the first genuinely German war in which all the German states fought. By 1871, when the war ended, all Germans were proud of, and wished to be associated with, the Prussian–German victory.

Proletariat – The proletariat comprised the growing numbers of industrial workers – men and women who worked in factories, mills and mines. Those belonging to political left-wing parties claimed the proletariat were exploited by the factory, mill and mine owners. The German philosopher Karl Marx (who is usually regarded as the founder of Communism) claimed that the proletariat'would eventually rise up and seize power.

in turn, provided capital for new railways and new industries such as electricity and chemicals. Between 1871 and 1890 coal production soared, steel production increased by some 700 per cent and the railway network doubled in size.

Growing industry swelled the ranks of the German industrial working class. In 1871 only five per cent of Germans lived in urban areas. By 1900 nearly twenty per cent did so. This had political as well as economic consequences. Many of the proletariat were attracted to socialism. The peasantry, declining in numbers, tended to be more conservative.

	1870		1890
Population (millions)	41	Germany	49
	32	Britain	38
	36	France	38
Coal (millions of tonnes)	38	Germany	89
	118	Britain	184
	13	France	26
Steel (millions of tonnes)	0.3	Germany	2.2
	0.6	Britain	3.6
	0.08	France	0.6
Iron ore (millions of tonnes)	2.9	Germany	8
	14	Britain	14
	2.6	France	3.5

▲ **Figure 3** German population and production compared with Britain and France: 1870–90.

German society

German society, despite all the economic changes, remained divided along traditional class lines. What mobility there was tended to be within a class rather than between different classes. The higher levels of the civil service and the army remained predominantly the preserve of the nobility. The most direct threat to the nobility's supremacy came from wealthy industrialists who tried to emulate, rather than supersede, the nobles.

While the middle classes were expanding, most Germans were agricultural or industrial workers. For many farm labourers, life was hard and industrial employment seemed an attractive option. Thus, there was a drift to the cities, even though the living and working conditions of the proletariat remained poor.

WORKING TOGETHER

Divide into groups. Each group should discuss who actually held power in the German Empire after 1871. Below are a number of suggestions. Rank the list in order and present your findings to the rest of the class. Compare the order given by each group. Can you reach a consensus opinion as a class?

- The Imperial Chancellor
- The Emperor (or *Kaiser*)
- The *Bundesrat*
- The *Reichstag*
- The German army
- The state governments
- Prussia

KEY DATES: THE GERMAN EMPIRE IN 1871
1870 Start of the Franco–Prussian (or Franco–German) War.
January 1871 The Second German Empire was proclaimed at the Palace of Versailles in France.
January 1871 End of Franco–Prussian War. France paid a heavy indemnity and surrendered Alsace-Lorraine to Germany.

2 Bismarck in power, 1871–90

This section will examine the way that Bismarck ruled Germany from 1871 to 1890. He dominated most aspects of German policy – foreign and domestic. In foreign policy he acted alone. German diplomacy was very much a one-man affair, even if at times he had to fight tooth and nail with Emperor William I in order to get his way. But in domestic affairs, Bismarck took advice, listened to suggestions and seized upon the ideas of others.

Otto von Bismarck (1815–98)

How effectively did Bismarck handle political matters from 1871 to 1890?

Bismarck's father was a moderately wealthy *Junker*. Bismarck was proud of this and all his life liked to present himself as a *Junker* squire. However, he was too clever, too enterprising and too non-conformist to be a typical *Junker*. His mother came from a middle-class family of merchants. Many of her relatives were civil servants, university professors or lawyers. Bismarck did not get on well with his mother, but from her he inherited his intelligence and determination.

At university he developed a reputation as a duellist (fighting 25 duels in one particular year). He was a crack shot and an expert fencer. Passing his law examinations, Bismarck won entry to the Prussian civil service. A year of military service followed, and then on his mother's death in 1839, he retired to help run the family estates.

In 1847 two events occurred to change the direction of his life. First he married Johanna von Puttkamer who provided a stable background to his life, bringing up their numerous children and overlooking his repeated infidelities. Secondly he was elected to the Prussian United *Diet*. Seemingly an arch-conservative, he declared: 'Only two things matter for Prussia: to avoid an alliance with democracy and to secure equality with Austria'. He soon became Prussian envoy to the *Bundestag* at Frankfurt, where, apart from a short time in Vienna as Prussian ambassador, he remained until 1859. During his years in Frankfurt, it became his overriding concern to oppose Austria.

The appeal of German nationalism

Until the mid-1850s Bismarck had shown little but contempt for nationalism. However, by the late 1850s his views had changed. Aware of the popular appeal of German nationalism, he realised that the nationalist movement might be manipulated in the interests of enhancing Prussian power and aid the creation of a united Germany under Prussian control. In 1859 Bismarck was moved from the *Bundestag* to become Prussian ambassador in Russia. In September 1862, he returned to Prussia to become Chief Minister. He only accepted the post on condition that he could do as he saw fit so that he could (as he himself put it) 'make his own music'. His appointment was one of the most momentous occasions in Prussian, German and European history.

In 1862 he had a reputation as a tough, ambitious and ruthless politician. Although viewed (mistakenly) as a conservative reactionary and (correctly) as a loyal supporter of the monarchy, he was also seen (with some justification) as an unpredictable maverick. His appointment as Chief Minister was seen as a deliberate affront to the liberals who regarded him as a bigoted reactionary. Given that Bismarck had no ministerial experience, he was not expected to last long in power.

NOTE-MAKING

Your notes should focus on Bismarck's successes and failures. Use the headings and questions to help you create sub-headings and select material. Decide at the end of each major issue faced by Bismarck whether he had been successful or not. It may be that you are undecided with regard to some issues, if so, make a note that he succeeded in part and failed in part. (This is what happens to most politicians in most periods in history!) Conclude with an evaluation of Bismarck's success in ruling Germany from 1871 to 1890. Do remember that he remained in power for over two decades. He must have been doing something right!

Junker(s) – *Junkers* were the land-owning nobility in Prussia. They had their own rules of conduct based on an elaborate code of honour, devotion to the military life, a strong sense of service to the Prussian state and an even stronger sense of their own importance. Most were deeply conservative.

Diet – An assembly or parliament.

Bundestag – The Federal German Council which was a conference of representatives from all the states within the German Confederation from 1815 to 1866.

On 30 September, in his first speech to the Prussian Parliament, he declared:

Germany does not look to Prussia's liberalism, but to its power … It is not through speeches and majority decisions that the great questions of the day are decided … It is by iron and blood.

This phrase, afterwards reversed to 'blood and iron', became almost synonymous with Bismarck. Convinced that great issues are decided by might not right, he was determined to make Prussia as mighty as possible. Prussian leadership in Germany would ensure Prussian might. In the 1860s he was essentially a Prussian patriot rather than a German nationalist: his loyalty was to the Prussian King – not to the German people. By brilliant diplomacy and a series of wars against Denmark (1864), Austria (1866) and France (1870–71) he brought about German unification and the creation of the Second Reich.

Realpolitik characterised Bismarck's political career from first to last. He had contempt for idealism and idealists. While he was a sincere Protestant, he was able to divorce personal from political morality. What was good for Prussia (and then Germany) was good. In his view, the end justified the means. He recognised that a conservative regime could no longer operate without popular support, not least that of the liberal middle class whose power was growing. He hoped to achieve conservative ends by means that were far from conservative. His unscrupulous methods occasionally brought him into conflict with William I and the Prussian military and political élites. But while many distrusted his tactics, most respected his judgement.

By 1871 Bismarck was a man of imperious and dominating temperament with an unquenchable thirst for power. He saw himself as a man of destiny, convinced that he would have a great impact on the world. Nevertheless, he once admitted: 'I am all nerves; so much so that self-control has always been the greatest task of my life and still is'. He smoked heavily, consumed huge amounts of alcohol and ate enormous meals. In 1883 his weight reached 114 kilograms. Given to melancholy, he suffered from periods of laziness. He was also an inveterate womaniser and gambler. Aggressive and emotional, his relations with Emperor William I were stormy; their meetings sometimes degenerated into slanging matches, followed sometimes by tears. Ruthless, unpredictable, vindictive and unscrupulous, Bismarck could also be charming and witty, a delightful companion and entertaining conversationalist.

Bismarck's motives and methods

Historians continue to argue over Bismarck's achievements, his motives and his methods. Innumerable books have been written about him. By 1895 there were already 650 biographies available. Twenty years later there were 3,500 and the number has continued to increase ever since.

When it comes to primary evidence the problem is not a lack of material but an excess, much of it conflicting. Bismarck left a wealth of letters, articles, speeches and official reports. There were also his voluminous *Reminiscences* which are of questionable accuracy: he increased the drama around every event, sometimes embroidering fact with a little fiction, and always presented himself favourably.

While in office, Bismarck frequently made totally contradictory statements at the same time about the same events. Historians interpret this differently. Some see it as symptomatic of Bismarck's perversity of mind, a desire to confuse or mislead friends and enemies alike. Some see it as a lack of settled purpose and an inability to think clearly and coherently in abstract terms. And there are others who see it simply as Bismarck's way of 'reasoning out loud', rehearsing a number of different arguments before reaching a decision.

Realpolitik – The term is used to describe the ruthless and cynical policies of politicians who are willing to use whatever means are available to them to achieve their aims.

Whatever the reason, it means that Bismarck's own evidence needs to be used with caution. A single letter or speech is not necessarily a true reflection of his policies or intentions at any given time. Therefore it is difficult to disentangle with any certainty Bismarck's motives, or to decide how far he planned ahead. 'Politics', he said, 'is not an exact and logical science but is the capacity to choose in each fleeting moment of the situation that which is least harmful or most opportune'. He was the supreme opportunist, both before and after 1871. Accordingly, his policies can best be described as flexible.

In 1850 Bismarck declared that the only sound foundation for a great state is not idealism but 'state egoism' (national self-interest). Thirty years later, his beliefs had not changed. Defending himself against critics who accused him of sudden changes of policy, he said:

I have always had one compass only, one lodestar by which I have steered: the welfare of the state … What is useful, advantageous and right for my Fatherland and – as long as this was only Prussia – for my dynasty, and today for the German nation.

Source C From *A History of Modern Germany 1800–2000,* by Martin Kitchen, (Blackwell), 2006, p. 175.

… [Bismarck's] power-hungry brutality, his lust for confrontation rather than compromise, and his inability either to delegate authority or to tolerate anyone who even approached being his equal, left a fatal legacy. He was a man of profound and even pathological contradictions, and the ambivalence and inconsistency of his own imperious [domineering] personality was deeply embedded in the structure of the Reich of which he was the architect.

Source D From *European Alliances and Alignments 1871–90* by William L. Langer, (Vintage Books), 1950, p. 479.

[Bismarck's] had been a great career, beginning with three wars in eight years and ending with a period of twenty years during which he worked for the peace of Europe, despite countless opportunities to embark on further enterprises with more than an even chance of success … No other statesman of his standing had ever before shown the same great moderation and sound political sense of the possible and desirable … Bismarck at least deserves full credit for having steered European politics through this dangerous transitional period without serious conflict between the great powers.

1 How do Sources C and D differ?
2 Historians Kitchen and Langer are writing about different aspects of Bismarck's policies. Why might this explain the difference in emphasis of the two extracts?

The liberal era, 1871–79

After 1871 Bismarck, who claimed to stand above party or sectional interest, needed a parliamentary majority. Although he was by no means a true liberal, he had little alternative but to work with the National Liberals – the strongest party in the *Reichstag* for most of the 1870s (see Figure 4 on page 14). In some respects the National Liberals were ideal allies. Most of them applauded Bismarck's success in creating a united Germany and were eager to help him consolidate national unity. In the early 1870s, a great deal of useful legislation was passed:

- A national system of currency was introduced.
- A *Reichsbank* was created.
- All internal tariffs were abolished.
- There was much legal standardisation.

Reichsbank – A national German bank, similar to the Bank of England.

Party	Number of seats in *Reichstag*							
	1871	**1874**	**1877**	**1878**	**1881**	**1884**	**1887**	**1890**
The National Liberals	125	155	128	99	47	51	99	42
	The main support for this party came from the Protestant middle class. The party had two principal aims: (a) the creation of a strong nation-state and (b) the encouragement of a liberal constitutional state; the former in practice being the priority. Until 1878 the National Liberals were Bismarck's most reliable *Reichstag* allies.							
The Centre Party	58	91	93	94	100	99	98	106
	This party defended the interests of the Catholic Church							
The Social Democratic Party	2	9	12	9	12	24	11	35
	Having close links with the trade unions, this was predominantly a working-class party. It fought for social reforms.							
The German Conservative Party	57	22	40	59	50	78	80	73
	This party was mainly composed of Prussian landowners. Sceptical about the unification of Germany, it came to support Bismarck after 1878.							
The Free Conservatives	37	33	38	57	28	28	41	20
	Drawn from a wider geographical and social base than the German Conservatives, the party contained not just landowners, but also industrialists and professional and commercial interests. It offered Bismarck steady support.							
The Progressives	47	50	52	39	115	74	32	76
	A liberal party, but one which, unlike the National Liberals, remained opposed to Bismarck's pursuit of a powerful nation-state at the expense of liberal constitutional principles.							
National Groups	14	30	30	30	35	32	29	27
	Reichstag members representing Alsatians, Poles and Danes.							
Guelphs	9	4	10	4	10	11	4	11
	Hanoverians who were supporters of the deposed King George.							

▲ **Figure 4** Germany's political parties 1871–90.

The National Liberals and Bismarck also united against the Catholic Church. Nevertheless, relations between Bismarck and the National Liberals were always uneasy. Politically Bismarck did not agree with their hopes for the extension of parliamentary government. He became increasingly irritated as they opposed a number of his proposals.

The army budget

The army budget was a particular bone of contention. In 1867 Bismarck and the National Liberals agreed that the military budget should remain at a fixed level outside *Reichstag* control until 1872. During the Franco–Prussian War the fixed budget was extended until 1874. In 1874 Bismarck presented a law proposing that an army of over 400,000 men should be automatically financed by federal expenditure.

> **Septennates** – The arrangement whereby military spending was agreed in the *Reichstag* for seven years. This greatly reduced the *Reichstag*'s financial power because it could only vote on military spending, the main government expense, every seven years.

Given that 80 per cent of all federal expenditure was spent on the army, this threatened seriously to reduce the *Reichstag*'s monetary powers. The measure – the 'Eternal Law' – was thus opposed by the National Liberals. Accusing them of trying to undermine German military strength, Bismarck threatened to call new elections. The National Liberals shrank from a constitutional conflict. A compromise was eventually reached. The military budget was fixed for seven years at a time (the **Septennates**), rather than voted for annually or fixed permanently.

KEY DATES: OTTO VON BISMARCK

1871 The National Liberals became the strongest party in the *Reichstag*.

1874 The military budget was fixed for seven years.

The *Kulturkampf*

How successful was the *Kulturkampf*?

Much of the 1870s was dominated by Bismarck's clash with the Catholic Church – the *Kulturkampf*. There were a number of reasons for this clash:

- Two-thirds of Germans, mainly those in Prussia and the north, were Protestant. One-third were Catholic.
- In the late nineteenth century Church and State came into conflict in several countries. In 1864 Pope Pius IX's *Syllabus of Errors* had condemned as erroneous every major principle for which liberals stood. In 1870 the Vatican Council laid down the doctrine of papal infallibility. This ruled that papal pronouncements on matters of faith and morals could not easily be questioned.
- These papal measures aroused great alarm in liberal circles. Many of Germany's most enlightened men believed that the future of mankind was at stake. It seemed certain that militant Catholicism would interfere in the *Reich*'s domestic affairs and support reactionary causes. The National Liberals, in particular, were determined to do battle with the Catholic Church in what they saw as a life and death struggle for freedom and progress against the forces of backwardness.

Bismarck's foreign policy, 1871–90

Bismarck's diplomatic skills had helped bring about the *Kaiserreich* in 1871: he continued to display the same masterly skills for the next two decades. After 1871 Germany was the strongest power on the continent. Aware that Germany was surrounded by resentful and anxious neighbours, Bismarck made it clear that Germany was now a 'satiated power', with no more territorial ambitions. He believed that any attempt to extend Germany's frontiers would unite the other powers against it. Convinced that further wars could only threaten the *Reich*'s security, his central aim was to maintain peace.

France seemed the main threat to peace. Many French people, resenting their defeat in 1870–71 and the loss of Alsace-Lorraine, wanted revenge. However, France without allies did not pose a serious danger: Bismarck was confident that Germany could defeat France again if necessary. His main fear was that France might ally with either Russia or Austria. Germany might then have to fight a war on two fronts. He was determined to avoid this possibility by isolating France and remaining on good terms with both Russia and Austria. His main problem was that there was always the possibility of friction between Austria and Russia over the Balkans, where their interests were at variance.

In 1879 he signed the Dual Alliance with Austria. In 1882 Italy joined the German–Austrian alliance which thus became the Triple Alliance. Determined to maintain good relations with Russia, Bismarck signed the Reinsurance Treaty with Russia in 1887. Most historians praise Bismarck for his successful efforts in maintaining European peace from 1871 to 1890.

The Centre Party

German Catholics formed their own party, the Centre Party, in north Germany in 1870 to defend their interests. After the creation of the Empire, it joined forces with south Germans, Poles and the people of Alsace-Lorraine, becoming the second largest party in the *Reichstag* in 1871. It was unique among German parties in drawing its support from all social strata. It favoured greater self-rule for the component states of the *Reich*. It also objected to state interference in the Church's traditional sphere of influence: the education system.

Bismarck and Catholicism

Bismarck, a sincere Protestant, had little affection for Catholicism and viewed the Catholic minority with suspicion. His greatest concern in domestic policy was to unify and consolidate the new *Reich*. Suspicious of those who opposed his creation, he saw plots and subversive activities everywhere. Many of the national minorities – the French in the west and the Poles in the east – who had no wish to be within the *Reich* were Catholic. So were Germans in the southern states, many of whom still tended to identify with Austria rather than with Prussia. So too were the Rhinelanders, some of whom still resented being 'Prussian' (despite being part of Prussia since 1815).

Bismarck saw the success of the Centre Party in 1871 as a grave danger to the Empire's unity. He thought that Centre politicians would encourage civil disobedience among Catholics whenever the policies of the state conflicted with those of the Church. His suspicions deepened when he observed how rapidly the Party became a rallying point for opponents of the Empire.

Whether he really believed that the anti-Prussian political alignment in the *Reichstag* was a papal-inspired conspiracy of malcontents bent on destroying the *Reich* is debatable. But the *Kulturkampf* was widely understood at the time to be a war against internal opponents of unification. It may be that the *Kulturkampf* was also a calculated political ploy on Bismarck's part to put himself at the head of a popular, Protestant crusade. It certainly enabled him to work closely with the National Liberals in the 1870s.

The 'Old Catholics'

Some 5,000 Catholics – they were known as 'Old Catholics' – refused to accept the decree on papal infallibility and broke with the Church. When Old Catholic teachers and professors were dismissed by Catholic bishops, Bismarck had an excellent excuse to attack the Catholic Church. Maintaining that the Prussian government was committed to the principle of religious toleration, he condemned the Catholic Church's actions in a series of newspaper articles in 1872. This marked the start of the *Kulturkampf*.

Actions against the Catholic Church

While the *Kulturkampf* was centred on Prussia and directed against the Catholics of the Rhineland and Poland, its effects were felt throughout the *Reich* and legislation against the Church was passed in Prussia, by other state governments and by the *Reichstag*.

In 1872 Catholic schools were brought directly under the supervision of the state. In 1872 the *Reichstag* forbade the Jesuit order, a Catholic order of priests whose members had always been supporters of Papal authority, to set up establishments in Germany and empowered state governments to expel individual Jesuits. In May 1873 Dr Adalbert Falk, the Prussian Minister of Religion and Education, introduced a package of measures known as the May Laws. These aimed to bring the Catholic Church under state control:

- All candidates for the priesthood now had to attend a secular (non-religious) university before commencing training.
- All religious appointments became subject to state approval.
- In 1874 obligatory civil marriage was introduced in Prussia.

In 1875 the *Kulturkampf* reached a climax:

- Laws empowered Prussia to suspend subsidies to the Church in parishes where the clergy resisted the new legislation.
- All religious orders, except nursing orders, were dissolved.

Clergy could be fined, imprisoned or expelled if they failed to comply with the legislation which was vigorously enforced in Prussia by Falk. By 1876 all but two of the twelve Prussian Catholic bishops were in exile or under house arrest and more than a thousand priests were suspended from their posts.

The results of the *Kulturkampf*

The results of the *Kulturkampf* were not what Bismarck had hoped. Attempts to repress Catholicism met with considerable opposition. Pope Pius IX counter-attacked, threatening to excommunicate those who obeyed the oppressive laws. Only 30 out of 10,000 Prussian Catholic priests submitted to the new legislation. Catholic communities sheltered defiant priests and fiercely maintained their religious culture and identity.

Bismarck's hope of destroying the Centre Party backfired: the *Kulturkampf* strengthened rather than weakened his political opponents. In 1871 the Centre won 58 seats: in 1874 it won 91 seats. Bismarck's hope of leading a popular Protestant crusade also failed to materialise. Protestants opposed some of the *Kulturkampf* legislation because it limited the influence of the Protestant – as well as the Catholic – Church in education. Many on the left disliked the violation of fundamental civil rights, not least freedom of conscience.

The end of the *Kulturkampf*

By 1878 Bismarck accepted that the *Kulturkampf* had failed. He had underestimated the enemy; the Catholic Church had more popular support than he had expected. By opening up a rift between the *Reich* and its Catholic subjects, the *Kulturkampf* had increased disunity, not removed it. Moreover, he was now anxious to have the Centre Party on his side against a potentially worse enemy: socialism.

Bismarck was thus ready to cut his losses and end the *Kulturkampf*. His opportunity came with the death of Pope Pius IX in 1878. His successor Leo XIII was conciliatory, and direct negotiations led to improved relations between Bismarck and the Church. Falk was symbolically dismissed in 1879 and some of the anti-Catholic measures were repealed: exiled clergy, for example, were allowed to return. However, the Catholic Church did not win a complete victory. Many of the May Laws remained in force: for example, civil marriage remained compulsory, Jesuits were forbidden to enter Germany, and the state continued to oversee all permanent Church appointments.

Bismarck withdrew from a dangerous battlefield. Typically, he sought to turn failure to advantage, by henceforward harnessing Catholic political power in the *Reichstag* to the support of conservative, protectionist and anti-socialist measures.

Treatment of the national minorities

Bismarck regarded the national minorities – the Danes, French and Poles – as potential 'enemies of the state'. He thus sought to reduce their influence:

- The Polish language was outlawed in education and law courts.
- Alsace-Lorraine was not granted full autonomy. Instead it became a special region under direct imperial rule with a governor and Prussian civil servants. The German language was imposed in schools and local administration.

However, Bismarck did not rely solely on repression. Those French people who disliked German rule were allowed to leave (400,000 had done so by 1914). The German governors of Alsace-Lorraine made great efforts to conciliate the French-speaking provinces.

It does seem that the national minorities' alienation from the *Reich* probably lessened over the years. School, conscription and everyday experience 'Germanised' many minorities.

Economic protectionism

Why did Bismarck come to support protectionist policies?

In the early 1870s Bismarck left economic matters in the hands of Rudolf Delbruck, a capable administrator who continued the **free trade** policies of the *Zollverein*. Support for free trade was an essential principle of most National Liberals. In 1879, however, Bismarck ditched both free trade and the National Liberals. Aligning himself with the Conservative and Centre parties, he supported the introduction of tariffs to protect German industry and farming. What were his motives?

Economic and financial factors

There were strong economic and financial reasons for introducing protective tariffs. In the late 1870s German agriculture suffered from the effects of a series of bad harvests and from the importation of cheap wheat from the USA and Russia. As the price of wheat fell, German farmers suffered. As a landowner himself, Bismarck understood the dangers of a prolonged agrarian depression. He also feared that if Germany was reliant on foreign grain, it would be seriously weakened in time of war. Protectionism would aid German self-sufficiency.

A slowdown in industrial growth after 1873 helped to produce a crisis of confidence in free trade. Industrialists and workers looked to the government to protect their interests and alleviate their distress. The adoption of protective tariffs by France, Russia and Austria in the late 1870s seemed to make it all the more desirable to follow suit.

Finally, the federal government's revenue, raised from customs duties and **indirect taxation**, was proving woefully inadequate to cover the growing costs of armaments and administration. In order to make up the deficit, supplementary payments were made by individual states, a situation that Bismarck found distasteful. He hoped that new tariffs would give the federal government a valuable extra source of income, ensuring that it was financially independent of both the states and the *Reichstag*.

Political factors

Bismarck realised there were political advantages in abandoning free trade. By the late 1870s landowners and industrialists were clamouring for protective tariffs. By espousing protectionist policies, Bismarck could win influential support.

KEY DATES: THE KULTURKAMPF

1872 The (traditional) start of the *Kulturkampf*.

1873 The May Laws were introduced in Prussia.

1879 The (traditional) end of the *Kulturkampf*.

Free trade – Unrestricted trade without protective import duties. Protective duties – or tariffs – are levied in order to protect a nation's own industries and/or farming from cheap foreign competition. Free trade allows people to purchase goods cheaply but it can endanger a country's industrial and agricultural production.

Zollverein – This was a free trade union which had been established by Prussia in 1834. By 1844 it included most German states – with the important exception of Austria. It had done much to unify both the currency and system of weights and measures across Germany before unification in 1871.

Indirect taxation – Taxation placed on the sale of goods rather than collected directly from the taxpayer.

Although he had worked with the National Liberals, he had never been particularly friendly with them. Their insistence on parliamentary rights and refusal to pass anti-socialist legislation irritated him. Moreover, in the 1878 elections, the National Liberals lost some 30 seats. The combined strength of the two Conservative parties was now sufficient to outvote them in the *Reichstag*. In pursuing the protectionist case, popular with the Conservatives, Bismarck saw his chance to break with the National Liberals and broaden his political support.

The 1879 Tariff Act

By 1879, protectionists, made up mostly of Conservatives and Centre Party members, had a majority in the *Reichstag*. Bismarck now introduced a general tariff bill.

Source E Part of Bismarck's address to the *Reichstag* in May 1879.

The only country [which persists in a policy of free trade] is England, and that will not last long. France and America have departed completely from this line; Austria instead of lowering her tariffs has made them higher; Russia has done the same ... Therefore to be alone the dupe of an honourable conviction cannot be expected from Germany for ever ... Since we have become swamped by the surplus production of foreign nations, our prices have been depressed; and the development of our industries and our entire economic position has suffered in consequence. Let us finally close our doors and erect some barriers ... in order to reserve for German industries at least the home market, which because of German good nature, has been exploited by foreigners ... I see that those countries which have adopted protection are prospering, and that those countries which have free trade are deteriorating.

> 1 What arguments did Bismarck use in support of the Tariff Act (see Source E)?
> 2 What arguments might his National Liberal opponents have used against the measure?

In July 1879 a tariff bill passed through the *Reichstag* and duties were imposed on imports. The political results were far-reaching. Bismarck had now firmly committed himself to the Conservative camp. The National Liberal Party splintered. Those who still believed in free trade and parliamentary government broke away, eventually uniting with the Progressives to form a new radical party in 1884. Other National Liberals remained loyal to Bismarck but he was no longer dependent on their backing. In that sense the 'liberal era' was effectively at an end.

Historians continue to debate the economic effects of the abandonment of free trade. Arguably, protective tariffs consolidated the work of unification by drawing north and south Germany closer together and accelerated the growth of a large internal market. Protection might have meant higher bread prices, but this did not mean that workers had lower living standards. Tariffs did serve to protect German jobs.

The Centre Party and the National Liberals determined to frustrate Bismarck's attempt to make the government less dependent on the states and *Reichstag*. A Centre Party deputy, Count George von Frankenstein put forward a scheme whereby all revenues coming to the federal government in excess of 130 million marks were to be divided up among the states, and would then be returned as part of the state payments. As a result of the 'Frankenstein Clause' the budgetary rights of the *Reichstag* and the state parliaments were preserved. Bismarck thus failed to secure the financial independence he sought.

KEY DATES: ECONOMIC PROTECTIONISM

1878 The National Liberals lost seats in the *Reichstag* elections.

1879 Bismarck introduced the Tariff Act which introduced protective import duties in Germany and led to the splintering of the National Liberals.

Bismarck and socialism

How successful was Bismarck in tackling the socialist threat?

In 1875 moderate and revolutionary socialists united to form the Social Democratic Party (or SPD). The Party's declared aim was the overthrow of the existing order. But it also declared that it would use only legal means in the struggle for economic and political freedom. The new Party called for nationalisation of banks, coal mines and industry, and for social equality.

The socialist threat

Bismarck was hostile to socialists, regarding them as dangerous revolutionaries. Rather than underestimating the enemy, as with the *Kulturkampf*, it may be that he overestimated the socialist threat. Socialists were not as strong or as revolutionary as he feared and they liked to appear. However, Bismarck's fears were rational. Socialism was a threat to the kind of society he intended to maintain. Socialists did preach class warfare and did talk of the dictatorship of the proletariat. Moreover, as Germany became more industrialised, swelling the ranks of the proletariat, socialist support increased. In 1877 the SPD won nearly 500,000 votes giving them twelve seats in the *Reichstag*.

Assassination attempts

In 1876 Bismarck tried to pass a bill preventing the publication of socialist propaganda. It was defeated. Other measures to prosecute the SPD also failed to get through the *Reichstag*.

In May 1878 an anarchist tried to assassinate Emperor William I. The would-be assassin had no proven association with the SPD, but Bismarck, like many of his contemporaries, drew no clear distinction between anarchism and socialism and saw the murder attempt as part of a 'red' conspiracy. However, his efforts to push through a bill against socialism were defeated by National Liberal members, concerned about civil liberties.

A week later there was a second attempt on William's life that resulted in the Emperor being seriously wounded. Again the failed assassin had no direct SPD link, but Bismarck criticised the National Liberals for failing to pass the anti-socialist bill that might have protected the Emperor. Scenting political advantage, he dissolved the *Reichstag*.

His manoeuvre succeeded. The electorate, deeply shocked by the murder attempts, blamed the SPD and the National Liberals. The SPD vote fell from 493,000 in 1877 to 312,000 while the National Liberals lost 130,000 votes and 29 seats.

Source F Tiedemann, Bismarck's secretary, writing about Bismarck's reaction to the second assassination attempt on William.

As I stepped out of the park, I saw the Chancellor walking slowly across the field in the bright sunshine, with his dogs at his heels. I went to meet him and joined him. He was in the best of tempers. After a little while I said, 'Some urgent telegrams have arrived.' He answered jokingly; 'Are they so urgent that we have to deal with them out here in the open country?' I replied: 'Unfortunately they are. The Emperor has again been fired at and this time he has been hit. His Majesty is seriously wounded.' With a violent start the Prince [Bismarck] stopped dead. Deeply agitated, he thrust his oaken stick into the ground in front of him and said, breathing heavily, as if a lightning flash of revelation had struck him: 'Now we will dissolve the Reichstag!' Only then did he enquire sympathetically after the Emperor's condition and ask for details of the attempt.

Nationalisation – Government ownership.

Anarchist – A person whose ideal society is one without government of any kind. Late nineteenth-century anarchists often sought to bring about such a condition by terrorism.

1 Why did the author of Source F regard Bismarck's reaction as strange?

2 What value would you place on this source as historical evidence?

Bismarck's actions against socialism

Bismarck now got his way in the new *Reichstag*. An anti-socialist bill, supported by Conservatives and most National Liberals, was passed in October 1878:

- Socialist organisations, including trade unions, were banned.
- Socialist meetings were to be broken up.
- Socialist publications were outlawed.

Between 1878 and 1890 some 1,500 socialists were imprisoned and a great many emigrated. However, the Anti-Socialist Law, far from eliminating socialism, served to rally the faithful and fortify them in their beliefs. Moreover, the law, which was differently implemented in different German states, did not prevent SPD members from standing for election and speaking freely in both the *Reichstag* and state legislatures. After the dip in 1878, the SPD won increasing support. By 1890 it had over a million votes and 35 seats.

In short, Bismarck's attack on socialism was no more successful than his attack on the Catholic Church. His repressive measures may have helped to increase support for the SPD and ensured that moderate and revolutionary socialist factions remained united.

State socialism

Bismarck did not use only repression in his efforts to destroy socialism. He hoped to wean the working classes from socialism by introducing various welfare (state socialism) measures, designed to assist German workers. These measures may not have been as cynical as some of Bismarck's critics have implied. A devout Christian, Bismarck was conscious of a moral obligation to aid those in need. There was a strong tradition in Prussia and other parts of Germany, and a general belief, held by most parties, right and left, that one of the state's most important moral objectives was the promotion of the material well-being of its citizens.

Right (-wing) – In political terms, the right tends to be conservative. Right-wing politicians usually oppose too much change. They also tend to be nationalistic.

Left (-wing) – In political terms, the left is usually in favour of change. Left-wing politicians tend to sympathise with the less wealthy in society. The often incline towards socialism or communism.

Source G Passage from a speech Bismarck made to the *Reichstag* in 1881.

A beginning must be made with the task of reconciling the labouring classes with the state. A remedy cannot be sought only through the repression of socialist excesses. It is necessary to have a definite advancement in the welfare of the working classes. The matter of the first importance is the care of those workers who are incapable of earning a living. Previous provisions for guarding workers against the risk of falling into helplessness through incapacity caused by accident or age have not proved adequate, and the inadequacy of such provisions has been a main contributing cause driving the working classes to seek help by joining the Social Democratic movement. Whoever has a pension assured to him for his old age is more contented and easier to manage than a man who has none.

1 What arguments does Bismarck use to justify his decision to support state socialism (see Source G)?
2 What does Bismarck's line of argument suggest about the values and attitudes of the majority of the *Reichstag*?

In 1883 the first of his proposals for state socialism became law. The Sickness Insurance Act provided medical treatment and up to thirteen weeks' sick pay to three million low-paid workers. The workers paid two-thirds of the contribution and the employers one-third. A worker who was permanently disabled or sick for more than thirteen weeks was given protection by the Accident Insurance Act of 1884. This was financed wholly by the employers. Finally in 1889 came the Old Age and Disability Act which gave pensions to those over 70, and disablement pensions for those who were younger. This was paid for by workers, employers and the state.

How successful was state socialism?

Bismarck's hopes that the working class could be won over by state socialism were not fully realised. Many workers thought the measures a 'sham', particularly as the government still opposed the formation of trade unions. The welfare legislation was not particularly generous. Nor did Bismarck grant unemployment insurance. Moreover, many workers continued to labour under harsh conditions and while such conditions persisted, the SPD was assured of a future. Bismarck, believing that employers must control their factories, opposed demands for state intervention to regulate working hours and limit child and female employment.

Nevertheless, Bismarck's measures laid the foundations of the welfare state in Germany. They were also the first of their kind in the world and became a model of social provision for other countries.

Political developments in the 1880s

In 1881 Bismarck suffered a setback at the polls. The three liberal parties – the National Liberals, the 'Secession' Liberals (who had split from the National Liberals) and the Progressives gained seats from the Conservatives, ensuring that Bismarck could no longer depend on *Reichstag* support. But in the 1884 election Bismarck rallied patriotic support with his colonial policy and the Conservative parties won seats from the Liberal parties.

By 1887 Bismarck was at odds with the *Reichstag* over the renewal of the army grant or Septennates. The current Septennates were not due to expire until 1888, but the international situation alarmed the generals, who pressed for an early renewal. So, in late 1886 Bismarck asked the *Reichstag* to agree to substantial military increases. The *Reichstag* agreed, but only on condition that in future it was allowed to review military expenditure every three years.

Bismarck was furious, declaring:

The German army is an institution which cannot be dependent on short-lived Reichstag *majorities.*

Dissolving the *Reichstag*, he conjured up a picture of a revenge-seeking France, ready for war at any moment. He warned that Germany would remain in danger until the Septennates were passed and only the Conservatives and National Liberals could be relied on to pass them. Bismarck's electoral stratagem worked. The Conservatives and National Liberals won an absolute majority in 1887 and the Septennates were passed.

KEY DATES: BISMARCK AND SOCIALISM

1878 The Anti-Socialist Law was passed, following assassination attempts on Emperor William I.

1883 The Sickness Insurance Act was introduced.

1884 The Accident Insurance Act was introduced.

1889 Old age pensions were introduced.

Bismarck's fall

Why did Bismarck fall from power?

By the late 1880s Bismarck's position seemed in jeopardy. Emperor William I was in his eighties. If William died, Crown Prince Frederick, a man of liberal views, would ascend the throne. It seemed likely that Frederick would dismiss Bismarck and appoint a liberal chancellor.

Wilhelm II and Bismarck

While William I lived, Bismarck's hold on power was never in question. Their meetings were often stormy and emotional. They shouted, threw things and often quarrelled. But they understood each other. 'It is not easy to be the Emperor under such a Chancellor', William remarked, but he managed it successfully, mainly by letting Bismarck have his own way.

When William died (aged 90) in March 1888 he was succeeded by his son Frederick. Frederick, however, died from cancer only three months later. Frederick's 29-year-old son Wilhelm then became Emperor. A convinced German nationalist, Wilhelm was committed to the belief that he ruled by the **divine right of kings**. Wilhelm's character was complex. On the positive side, he was intelligent and energetic. On the negative, he was overbearing, arrogant and erratic.

> **Divine right of kings** – The belief that a monarch rules by the authority of God rather than by the consent of the people.

After Frederick's death, Bismarck's position seemed secure again. He had cultivated Wilhelm's friendship for several years and in public the new *Kaiser* expressed his admiration for Bismarck. But a great gulf separated the two, not least in terms of age. Bismarck, assuming that Wilhelm would not involve himself much in matters of government, tended to treat him in a condescending manner. But Wilhelm was determined to rule as well as to reign. 'I'll let the old boy [Bismarck] potter along for another six months', he told his cronies, 'then I'll rule myself'.

Source H Wilhelm II, writing to his mother in 1898.

For ever and for ever, there is only one real Emperor in the world, and that is the German, regardless of his person and qualities, but by right of a thousand years tradition. And his Chancellor has to obey!

> 1 What does Source H suggest about the character of Wilhelm II?
> 2 Why might the source explain the difficulties that arose between Wilhelm and Bismarck?

Bismarck and Wilhelm in conflict

Wilhelm and Bismarck were soon at odds. Wilhelm questioned the need to maintain the Reinsurance Treaty with Russia (see text box on page 15). The two also disagreed over social policy. Unlike Bismarck, Wilhelm was confident that he could win over the working class by a modest extension of the welfare system, including an end to child labour and Sunday working. Bismarck, by contrast, favoured further repression. Thus, in 1889 he proposed to make the Anti-Socialist Law permanent. Wilhelm was not against renewing the law (he too feared socialism), but he wanted the measure watered down. Bismarck refused. He was then let down by the *Reichstag*, which rejected his entire bill in January 1890. This was a sign that his political power was crumbling.

In February 1890, with new *Reichstag* elections underway, Wilhelm issued a proclamation promising new social legislation. The absence of Bismarck's counter-signature on this proclamation caused a sensation. The election was a disaster for Bismarck. His Conservative and National Liberal allies lost 85 seats while the Radicals gained 46 seats and the Socialists won 24 seats.

Bismarck was trapped between an Emperor bent on having his own way and a hostile *Reichstag*. In an attempt to recover his position, he proposed an extraordinary scheme: the *Reichstag* would be asked to agree to a large increase in the army and a new and extremely repressive anti-socialist law. If, as was probable, they refused, an assembly of German Princes would meet, alter the constitution and drastically curtail the *Reichstag's* powers. Wilhelm refused to support Bismarck's plan and relations between the two men became even worse.

Bismarck dismissed

In March 1890 Wilhelm and Bismarck quarrelled about the right of ministers to advise the monarch. Bismarck had revived an old order first issued in 1852, which forbade ministers to approach the Prussian King except through the Minister-President of Prussia. Bismarck interpreted this to mean that all ministers must obtain permission from him as Chancellor, before they could discuss any government business with the Emperor. Wilhelm was not prepared for such restrictions and commanded that the 1852 order be withdrawn. At a stormy interview Bismarck nearly threw an inkpot at Wilhelm and then enraged him by letting him see a letter from Tsar Alexander III, which was very disparaging of his talents.

Wilhelm now sent Bismarck an ultimatum: resign or be dismissed. Three days later Bismarck sent a letter of resignation in which he justified his actions, claiming (wrongly) that the real difference between Wilhelm and himself lay in the *Kaiser's* pursuit of an anti-Russian policy. This letter was not made public until after Bismarck's death. The official announcement implied that he had resigned for health reasons and that Wilhelm had made every effort to persuade him to change his mind.

KEY DATES: BISMARCK'S FALL

1888 March Death of Emperor William I: Frederick, his son, became emperor.

1888 June Frederick died: Wilhelm II became *Kaiser*.

1890 Kaiser Wilhelm II dismissed Bismarck.

'The Dropping of the Pilot'. An 1890 ▶ cartoon from *Punch*. What does the cartoon suggest was the main reason for Bismarck's dismissal?

In reality Bismarck retired with ill grace to write his memoirs and innumerable newspaper articles, invariably critical of Wilhelm. Failing to exert any influence on policy, he was even heard to speak in favour of republicanism: kings, he said, were dangerous if they had real power. He died in July 1898. On his grave were the words, 'Here lies a true servant of the Emperor William I'.

WORKING TOGETHER

Work in pairs. First compare the notes that you have made on this section. Add anything that you have missed and check anything that you have disagreed on.

Next one of you should identify a difficulty that Bismarck faced. The other should decide to what extent Bismarck contributed to the difficulty he faced and how successfully he tackled the difficulty. Take it in turns to identify difficulties and assess Bismarck's success or failure in tackling the problems.

After you have finished, discuss your findings. In which areas was Bismarck particularly successful? In which areas did he fail?

By doing this you should be in a position to evaluate Bismarck's overall success. To complete the process, you should each write a summary to explain Bismarck's achievements and failures. Which outweighed the other?

Chapter summary

- The Second German Empire was created in 1871, creating a federal state through the German constitution.
- The Emperor, the Chancellor, the *Bundesrat* and the *Reichstag* all held considerable powers in the federal (or central) government, with the 25 state governments also continuing to have powers.
- As Chancellor, Bismarck had great power but he was far from a dictator. He dominated Germany from 1871 to 1890. *Realpolitik* characterised his political actions.
- The powers of the *Reichstag* were limited. Nevertheless, the *Reichstag* was able to cause Bismarck some problems.
- The German economy was strong and growing stronger.
- Initially Bismarck worked with the National Liberals, the largest party in the *Reichstag*. They co-operated against the Roman Catholic Church in a struggle known as the *Kulturkampf*.
- In 1879 Bismarck abandoned free trade and supported protective tariffs for reasons that were partly political and partly economic.
- Bismarck took action against what he perceived to be a socialist threat. Despite his measures, the SPD continued to grow in strength.
- Bismarck introduced measures known as 'state socialism'. These included the Sickness Insurance Act (1883), the Accident Insurance Act (1884) and the Old Age and Disability Act (1889).
- The death of William I in 1888 weakened Bismarck's political position and in 1890 Bismarck was dismissed from power by Wilhelm II.

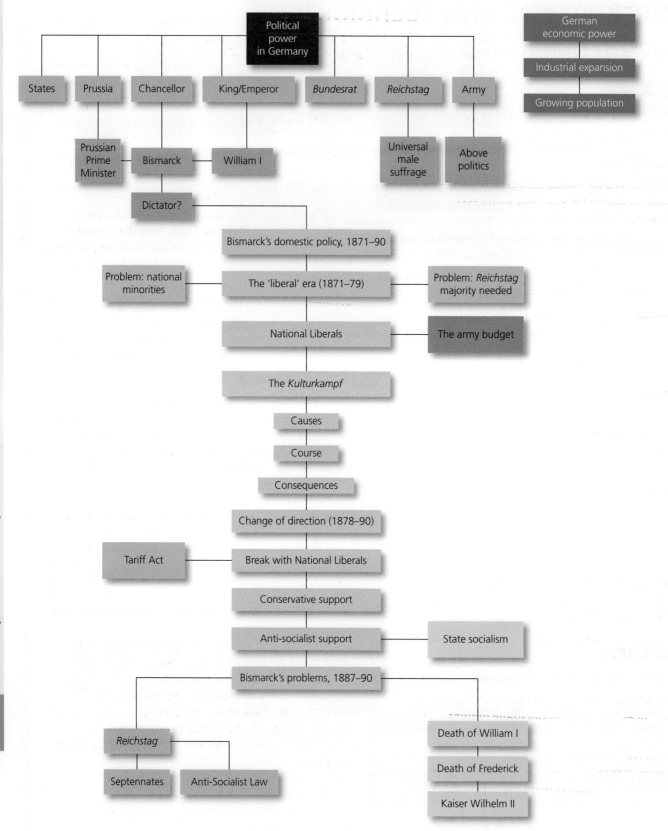

Working on essay technique: focus, structure and deploying detail

As well as learning the facts and understanding the history of Germany in the nineteenth and twentieth century, it is very important to develop skills in answering the types of question that will be set.

Essay focus

Whether you are taking the AS exam or the full A-level exam, Section B presents you with essay titles. Each question is marked out of 25.

AS examination	The full A-level examination
Section B – Answer ONE essay (from a choice of two)	Section B – Answer TWO essays (from a choice of three)

You may come across various question stems, but they all have the same basic requirement. They all require you to analyse and reach a conclusion, based on the evidence you provide.

For example:

- 'Assess the validity (of a quotation)'
- 'To what extent …'
- 'How successful …'
- 'How far …'

The AS titles always give a quotation and then: 'Explain why you agree or disagree with this view'. Almost inevitably, your answer will be a mixture of both. In essence, it is the same task as for the full A-level – just more basic wording.

Each question will reflect, directly or indirectly, one of the breadth issues in your study. The questions will have a fairly broad focus.

EXAMPLE

Look at the following A-level practice question:

How successful was Bismarck in managing political problems in Germany between 1871 and 1890? (25 marks)

This type of question requires you to identify the political problems that faced Bismarck and then to decide how successful he was in tackling them.

Structuring your answer

A clear structure makes for a much more effective essay. In order to structure an answer to the question in the example effectively you need several paragraphs. In each paragraph you will deal with one factor – one problem facing Bismarck.

You will first have to decide the order of your paragraphs. It may be that you will start with the most important problem he faced, then the second – and so on. Or you might wish to deal with the problems in chronological order – in the order that Bismarck faced them.

Remember that you also need a short but clear introduction that briefly explains your argument in relation to the question and a conclusion that provides a summary. This is a useful structure to apply to many questions.

Writing a focused introduction

It is vital that you maintain focus on the question from the beginning of your essay. One way to do this is to use the wording of the question to help write your argument. For example, your first two sentences could look like this:

> Having created the German Empire in 1871, Bismarck had to manage a number of political problems. Inevitably, over the course of nearly two decades, Bismarck tackled some problems more successfully than others.

These opening sentences provide a clear focus on the demands of the question, recognising that you have to highlight the problems Bismarck faced and adjudge his success. They provide a spring-board for the clear essay plan suggested above. Remember, you must learn to apply this approach to other questions you may encounter. You are not just learning how to respond to this question.

Focus throughout the essay

Structuring your answer well will help, but you should also remember to maintain focus throughout the essay. Here are some ideas that will help you to do this.

● Use the wording of the question to help write your answer.

> For example, in response to the practice question on page 27, you could begin your first main paragraph with 'the political situation in 1871'.
>
> *The political situation in 1871 was, in many respects, of Bismarck's own making. Having created the German Empire, he now had to manage it successfully.*
>
> The first sentence begins with a clear point that refers to the primary focus of the question (the political situation). The second sentence links it to the issue of 'success'.

● Write a paragraph for each of the other factors/problems facing Bismarck that you have identified. You may wish to number the factors/problems. This will help to make your structure clear and help you to maintain focus. Later we will look at prioritising factors in order of importance.

Summary

● Work out the main focus of the question.
● Plan your essay with a series of factors focusing on the question.
● Use the words in the question to formulate your answer.
● Return to the primary focus of the question at the beginning of every paragraph.
● Make sure that your structure is clear to the reader.

ACTIVITY

1 Having read the advice on how to write a structured and focused essay, plan and write the first sentence to the following AS-level practice question:

'Bismark failed to control the Reichstag in the years after 1871.' Explain why you agree or disagree with this view.   (25 marks)

Deploying detail

As well as focus and structure, your essay will be judged on the extent to which it includes relevant and accurate detail. Detailed essays are more likely to do well than essays which are vague and generalised.

There are several different kinds of evidence you could use that might be described as detailed. This includes correct dates, views of relevant people, statistics and events. You can also make your essays more detailed by using the correct technical vocabulary. Here you could use words and phrases such as 'Reichstag', 'Bundesrat', 'realpolitik' and 'Kulturkampf' that you have learned while studying this subject.

ACTIVITY

2 Consider the following AS-level practice question:

'Bismarck was successful in controlling the Reichstag after 1871.' Explain why you agree or disagree with this view.   (25 marks)

● Create your own brief essay plan for this question, making a list of points you will include.
● Using your notes from this chapter, find at least three pieces of detail to support each of these points. It is best to use different types of detailed evidence, for example, not just statistics or technical vocabulary, but also dates and specific people.

Working on interpretation skills

Section A of the exam paper is different from Section B (see page 27). Unlike Section B, it contains extracts from the work of historians. Significantly, this section tests different skills. In essence, Section A tests your ability to analyse different historical interpretations. Therefore, you must focus on the interpretations outlined in the extracts. The advice given in this chapter on interpretations is for both the AS and the A-level exams.

- For the **AS exam**, there are two extracts and you are asked which is the more convincing interpretation (25 marks).
- For the **A-level exam**, there are three extracts and you are asked how convincing the arguments are in relation to a specified topic (30 marks).

An interpretation is a particular view on a topic of history held by a particular author or authors. Interpretations of an event can vary, for example, depending on how much weight an historian gives to a particular factor and whether they largely ignore another factor.

The interpretations that you will be given will be largely from recent or fairly recent historians, who may, of course, have been influenced by events in the period in which they were writing.

Interpretations and evidence

The extracts given in the exam will contain a mixture of interpretations and evidence. The mark scheme rewards answers that focus on the *interpretations* offered by the extracts much more highly than answers that focus on the *information or evidence* mentioned in the extracts. Therefore, it is important to identify the interpretations.

- *Interpretations* are a specific kind of argument. They tend to make claims such as 'The Weimar Republic was certain to fail'.
- *Information or evidence* tends to consist of specific details. For example, 'The Weimar Republic's political system was based on proportional representation'.

Analysis of an interpretation

We start by looking at an individual extract and seeing how we can build up skills. This is the essential starting-point for both the AS and the A-level style of question on interpretations. The AS mark scheme shows a very clear progression of thought processes:

Level 5	Answers will display a good understanding of the interpretations given in the extracts. They will evaluate the extracts thoroughly in order to provide a well-substantiated judgement on which offers the more convincing interpretation. The response demonstrates a very good understanding of context. *21–25 marks*
Level 4	Answers will display a good understanding of the interpretations given in the extracts. There will be sufficient comment to provide a supported conclusion as to which offers the more convincing interpretation. However, not all comments will be well-substantiated, and judgements may be limited. The response demonstrates a good understanding of context. *16–20 marks*
Level 3	The answer will show a reasonable understanding of the interpretations given in the extracts. Comments as to which offers the more convincing interpretation will be partial and/or thinly supported. The response demonstrates an understanding of context. *11–15 marks*
Level 2	The answer will show some partial understanding of the interpretations given in the extracts. There will be some undeveloped comment in relation to the question. The response demonstrates some understanding of context. *6–10 marks*
Level 1	The answer will show a little understanding of the interpretations given in the extracts. There will be only unsupported, vague or generalist comment in relation to the question. The response demonstrates limited understanding of context. *1–5 marks*

Now turn to page 30 and study the practice question, which is about Bismarck.

With reference to the extract [A] and your understanding of the historical context, how convincing do you find the extract in relation to Bismarck's authority in Germany between 1871 and 1890? (25 marks)

To help you answer this type of question you need to assess the interpretation in the extract. Carry out activities 1–5 to help you do this.

Extract A

In April 1882, the British ambassador in Berlin referred to Bismarck as 'the German dictator whose power is at its height'. By 1882 the German Chancellor had already enjoyed two decades as a dominant figure and had brought about a major change in German politics in 1878–9. Through the 1880s, Bismarck kept the confidence of the ageing Emperor William I, dominated his own colleagues, browbeat opponents, and pushed government business through the national parliament with backing from one or other coalition of parties.

Adapted from *A History of Germany 1780–1918: The Long Nineteenth Century* by D. Blackbourn, (Oxford University Press), 1997, p. 400.

ACTIVITY

1 What is the argument for the interpretation in Extract A? (Is it arguing that Bismarck had a great deal of power or not?)

2 What evidence can you find in the extract to support the argument? (What details are mentioned to support the argument?)

3 What do you know (what contextual knowledge do you have) that supports these claims?

4 What contextual knowledge do you have to contradict these claims?

5 Using your judgement, are the arguments in support stronger than the arguments against, or vice versa?

Look back at the mark scheme on page 29, and see how your answers might match up to the levels shown there. In relation to Extract A's assertions about Bismarck's power, you should be able to find arguments both to support and to contradict. Remember, you can apply this approach when responding to other, similar, AS-level questions.

Comparing two interpretations

As part of the building up of skills, we move on to comparing two interpretations. This is the format of the AS question, but will also be useful in the process of gaining confidence for A-level students.

ACTIVITY

Consider the AS-level practice question below.

With reference to these two extracts and your understanding of the historical context, which of these two extracts provides the more convincing interpretation of Bismarck's hold on power in Germany after 1871? (25 marks)

6 Follow the same five steps for Extract B as you did for Extract A in activities 1–5, then compare the results of the two and come to a conclusion about which extract provides the most convincing interpretation.

Extract B

There continued to be important practical and theoretical limitations to Bismarck's position. Bismarck himself was all too aware of the potential scope at the *Kaiser*'s court and within the army for independent decision making and, of course, he needed a parliamentary majority for the passage of legislation and approval of the budget. Ultimately the monarch's power of appointment meant that the Imperial Chancellor was as much a royal servant as any Reich Minister.

Adapted from *Bismarck* by K. Lerman, (Routledge), 2004.

The top two levels of the mark scheme refer to 'supported conclusion' (Level 4) and 'well-substantiated conclusion' (Level 5). For Level 4 'supported conclusion' means finishing your answer with a judgement that is backed up with some accurate evidence drawn from the extract(s) and your knowledge. For Level 5 'well-substantiated conclusion' means finishing your answer with a judgement which is very well supported with evidence, and, where relevant, reaches a complex conclusion that reflects a wide variety of evidence.

There is no one correct way to write the answer! However, the principles are clear. In particular, contextual knowledge should be used *only* to back up an argument. None of your knowledge should be free-standing, i.e. in this question, there should not be a paragraph saying what you know about the topic, unrelated to the extracts. All your knowledge should be used in context.

For each extract in turn:

● Explain the evidence in the extract, backed up with your own contextual knowledge. In this example, for Bismarck being a virtual dictator – or not!

● Explain the points in the extract where you have evidence that contradicts Bismarck being a dictator – or not!

Then write a conclusion that reaches a judgement on which is more convincing as an interpretation.

Wilhelmine Germany 1890–1914

This chapter covers the years from 1890 to 1914 – a period when Kaiser Wilhelm II ruled in Germany. The chapter deals with a number of areas:

- The Wilhelmine political system
- Economic, social, cultural and intellectual trends
- German domestic politics, 1890–1914
- The situation in 1914

When you have worked through the chapter and the related activities, you should have a detailed knowledge of all the areas listed above. You should be able to relate the knowledge to the following breadth issues defined as part of your study:

- How was Germany governed and how did political authority change and develop?
- What was the nature and effectiveness of the opposition?
- What were the main economic, social and cultural trends?
- How important were ideas and ideology in Germany's development?

The focus of this chapter can be summarised by the following question:

To what extent did Wilhelm II's personality shape the history of Imperial Germany from 1890 until 1914?

From becoming *Kaiser* in 1888, Wilhelm II was determined to rule as well as reign. His rule was to culminate in the outbreak of the First World War in 1914. Who exerted decisive influence on policy and events in Wilhelmine Germany? What were the objectives of that leadership?

CHAPTER SUMMARY

Wilhelm II's long reign ultimately ended in disaster. It is debateable to what extent he was responsible for that disaster. While he exerted far more influence on German policy than his grandfather William I, he certainly did not control all aspects of German domestic and foreign policy, and neither went according to Wilhelm's – or indeed anyone else's – plan. While Germany's economy continued to expand, this led to the growth of a large proletariat. The German proletariat, like those elsewhere in Europe, tended to support socialism. Accordingly, the Socialist Party in Germany (the SPD) grew in strength, becoming the largest party in the *Reichstag* in 1912. This was anathema to Wilhelm whose views were strongly nationalistic and right wing. He wanted Germany to be a world – rather than just a European – power. By 1914 Germany was thus seriously divided between right and left.

1 Political, economic, social, cultural and ideological trends

This section will examine the main political, economic, social, cultural and intellectual trends that underpinned German development from 1890 to 1914. Under Wilhelm II the *Kaiserreich* developed in ways that Bismarck disapproved of before his death in 1898. (He probably turned in his grave at many of the developments post-1898!) Ironically, Bismarck's 1871 constitution was responsible for some of the developments. Nevertheless, it is hard to blame Bismarck for events that occurred after his fall from power, never mind after his death. Wilhelm II was far more responsible. But to what extent was Wilhelm able to control the changing situation in Germany?

Political trends: the Wilhelmine political system

Who ruled in Wilhelmine Germany?

At the height of the diplomatic crisis in July 1914 which culminated in the First World War, the Austrian Foreign Minister asked in frustration: 'Who actually rules in Berlin?' This was a pertinent question, not just in 1914, but throughout Wilhelm's rule.

The *Kaiser*

According to historian Michael Balfour, Wilhelm was 'the copybook condemnation of the hereditary system'. This view may be over-harsh. Wilhelm did have some talents: a quick mind, an excellent memory and a charming manner. Unfortunately, his understanding of issues was often superficial and distorted by his own prejudices. He lacked powers of steady application and his moods and behaviour were liable to wild fluctuations. 'The Kaiser is like a balloon', said Bismarck, 'If you do not hold fast to the string, you never know where he will be off to'. The British King Edward VII, Wilhelm's uncle, was even more scathing. He described Wilhelm as 'the most brilliant failure in history'.

Arguably, Wilhelm's influence should not be exaggerated. His life was an endless whirl of state occasions, military manoeuvres, cruises and hunting trips. In the first decade of his reign he averaged 200 days per year travelling on official business or private recreation. His social and ceremonial duties meant that he was absent from Berlin for long periods and so he did not have command of the detail of the government's work. Accordingly, it is possible to claim that he did not determine the course of German policy.

However, the German constitution did grant the *Kaiser* extensive powers. He alone had the right to appoint and dismiss the Chancellor and his State Secretaries – completely independent of the *Reichstag*'s wishes. He regarded the *Reichstag* as the 'imperial monkey house'. Wilhelm claimed that 'there is only one Ruler in the *Reich* and I am he'. He believed that his accountability was to God alone. Given his constitutional powers, no major decision could be taken without his agreement. When he spoke, people, in and out of Germany, listened.

NOTE-MAKING

Use the headings in this section to make brief notes as you work through it. Set these notes out clearly using the main headings, sub-headings and sub-points.

For example:

Main heading: The Wilhelmine political system

Sub-heading 1: The *Kaiser*

Sub-heading 2: The German Chancellors

Sub-heading 3: The *Bundesrat*

Sub-heading 4: The *Reichstag*

When you have completed your notes on the first few pages, review the process and then devise your own sub-headings for the remainder of the section, using the headings and questions in the text to help you. As you make your notes, consider these questions: Who ruled in Wilhelmine Germany? Was it the *Kaiser*? Was it his Chancellors? How powerful were the *Bundesrat* and the *Reichstag*? Star or highlight the points which seem important with respect to these questions. By the end of the material on 'Political trends' your notes should enable you to reach a provisional conclusion – which might change as you read on!

The German Chancellors

There were four Chancellors between 1890 and 1914:

- General Leo Caprivi (1890–94)
- Prince Chlodwig Hohenloe (1894–1900)
- Bernhard Bülow (1900–09)
- Theobold Bethmann-Hollweg (1909–17)

These men were essentially civil servants, not seasoned statesmen like Bismarck. They did not dominate the German political scene as decisively as Bismarck had done. They probably lacked Bismarck's talent. They certainly lacked his prestige and independence. William I had usually deferred to Bismarck, but Wilhelm II was determined to participate in the affairs of state. Political survival for the Chancellors was dependent on showing loyalty to Wilhelm and doing his will. This was far from easy when his personal involvement often amounted to little more than whimsical flights of fancy.

Kaiser Wilhelm II (1859–1941)

Wilhelm II was the eldest child of Crown Prince Frederick and Victoria, eldest daughter of British Queen Victoria. He became *Kaiser* in 1888, following the deaths of his grandfather William 1 (in March) and his father Frederick 1 (in June). Most historians are of the view that Wilhelm was arrogant and overtly theatrical – a neurotic braggart, a romantic dreamer, a man who frequently changed his mind. One Austrian wit remarked that Wilhelm wanted to be the bride at every wedding, the stag at every hunt and the corpse at every funeral. Historian John Rohl, who has devoted his life to studying Wilhelm, calls him a 'boastful autocrat, militarist and racist'. Many scholars, convinced that Wilhelm was, at the very least, deeply disturbed, have spent a great deal of time trying to explain his personality.

- Wilhelm's breech birth delivery resulted in the partial paralysis of his left arm and damage to the balance mechanism in his ear. These physical problems, and the dreadful way in which they were treated, have prompted speculation about the possible psychological consequences for the young prince.

- Close attention has been paid to the strained relationship with his parents. During his adolescent years, he grew apart from them, opposing their liberal sympathies and preferring the company of his grandfather. He particularly enjoyed the regimental life of the military garrison at Potsdam. (His love of military ceremonial verged on the pathological.)
- Some have suggested that Wilhelm's self-assertive and erratic behaviour should be seen as symptoms of insanity, megalomania or sadism.
- More recently, he has been depicted as a repressed homosexual or (more likely) a sufferer from attention deficit disorder – a mental condition which reveals itself in volatile and irrational behaviour.

What is indisputable is that Wilhelm proved to be a disaster not only for Germany but also for the rest of Europe. Given his indecision and limited ability, it is perhaps not surprising that, according to historian John Rohl, he surrounded himself with 'a deplorable bunch of advisers'. The result was a lack of progress in domestic affairs combined with an ill-considered and aggressive foreign policy, culminating in the tragedy of the First World War.

Source A Count Eulenburg, a close and influential friend of Wilhelm II, gave this note to Berhard von Bülow in July 1897. Bülow, a protégé of Eulenburg, was about to become Foreign Secretary.

Wilhelm II takes everything personally. Only personal arguments make any impression on him. He likes to give advice to others but is unwilling to take it himself. He cannot stand boredom; ponderous, stiff, excessively thorough people get on his nerves and cannot get anywhere with him. Wilhelm II wants to shine and to do and to decide everything himself. What he wants to do himself unfortunately often goes wrong. He loves glory, he is ambitious and jealous. To get him to accept an idea one has to pretend that the idea came from him ... never forget that H. M. [His Majesty] needs praise from time to time. He is the sort of person who becomes sullen unless he is given recognition from time to time by someone of importance. You will always accomplish whatever you wish so long as you do not omit to express your appreciation when H. M. deserves it. He is grateful for it like a good, clever child. If one remains silent when he deserves recognition, he eventually sees malevolence in it. We two will always carefully observe the boundaries of flattery.

1 What impression of Wilhelm do you obtain from Source A?
2 How reliable is this source as a piece of historical evidence?

The *Bundesrat*

The upper house of the national parliament, comprising men chosen by the various states, was essentially a conservative body. It had been at the centre of Bismarck's system. After 1890 it declined in influence. An increasing number of bills were first discussed by the main political parties and then introduced in the *Reichstag* rather than in the *Bundesrat*.

The *Reichstag*

While the *Reichstag* could discuss, amend, pass or reject government legislation, its power to initiate new laws was negligible. No party or coalition of parties ever formed the government of the day. Even a vote of no confidence in the Chancellor had minimal effect. Thus, although Germany had universal male suffrage, the *Kaiser's* authority in many areas was impervious to popular control.

Right-wing parties

On most issues Wilhelm and his governments could rely on the backing of the right-wing parties: the Conservatives, the Free Conservatives and the National Liberals. However, after 1890 the voting strength of these parties was in decline. In 1887 they won over 50 per cent of the popular vote: by 1912 their share of the vote was down to 26 per cent. Consequently, the imperial government had to find support from other parties if legislation was to be ratified.

The Centre Party

The Centre Party, which consistently won between 90 and 110 seats, was the largest party in the *Reichstag*, until 1912. Representing Catholics, it had a wide spectrum of socio-political views ranging from conservatism to progressive social reform. By 1900 it was the pivotal party, allying with either right or left as the occasion demanded.

The Social Democrat Party (SPD)

The Wilhelmine era saw the meteoric rise of the Social Democrat Party (SPD). Liberated by the lapse of the Anti-Socialist Law in 1890, the SPD appealed to Germany's growing industrial working class. In 1893 it won 11 per cent of the popular vote. Extremely well organised, the Party won 28 per cent of the vote in 1912, becoming the largest party in the *Reichstag*.

The SPD was far from united. In 1891 it adopted an uncompromising Marxist programme to overthrow the Wilhelmine class system. However, many SPD members, who were committed to democratic socialism, favoured the Party's so-called minimum programme. Given that most SPD deputies talked in favour of revolution, the other political parties regarded the SPD as a force for evil.

Marxist programme – Those who supported such a plan supported the ideas of Karl Marx. Marx believed that leaders of the proletariat must work to overthrow the capitalist system by (violent) revolution.

Minimum programme – The name given to the plans of moderate socialists who were opposed to violent revolution. They wanted to bring about government ownership of banks, coal mines and industry, and called for social equality.

Party	1890	1893	1898	1903	1907	1912
German Conservatives	73	72	56	54	60	43
Free Conservatives	20	28	23	21	24	14
National Liberals	42	53	46	51	54	45
Centre	106	96	102	100	105	91
Left Liberals	76	48	49	36	49	42
Social Democrats	35	44	56	81	43	110
Minorities	38	35	34	32	29	33
Right-wing splinter parties	7	21	31	22	33	19
Total	**397**	**397**	**397**	**397**	**397**	**397**

▲ **Figure 1** *Reichstag* election results 1890–1912. The numbers signify the number of seats won.

1 Which were the most extreme measures proposed in Source B?
2 Which Germans were most likely to be attracted by the Erfurt Programme?
3 Use Source B and your own knowledge to explain briefly the significance of the Social Democratic Party in the context of German politics in the 1890s.

Lobby groups – These were people, often belonging to particular organisations, who campaigned to persuade politicians to pass legislation favouring particular interests.

The Pan-German League – Formed in 1893, the League was a powerful right-wing nationalist movement. It supported German expansion both in Europe and worldwide.

Source B Adapted from 'The Erfurt Programme of the Social Democratic Party', 1891.

The Social Democratic Party of Germany fights for the abolition of class rule and of classes themselves and for equal rights and duties for all. The Party makes these demands. The making of new laws and the appointment of high officials to be controlled by the people. All taxes on goods to be abolished as they are an unfair burden on the poor. The costs of the government to be paid from income tax, property tax and inheritance tax, to ensure that the rich pay most.

Interest groups

In the 1890s professionally led interest groups became powerful. Some were economic lobby groups like the Agrarian League. There were a huge variety of trade unions. There were also nationalist pressure groups. These included the Pan-German League, the Navy League and the Colonial Society. These organisations were a symptom of escalating political participation, especially on the part of the middle class.

The states

While the 25 federal states retained control over many domestic matters, imperial authority inexorably gained at the expense of that of the states. This happened not only because of Germany's greater role on the world stage, but because domestically the functions of the *Reich* government expanded, while those of the states remained static. The social insurance schemes (see page 21) were *Reich* measures. Tariffs were *Reich* issues. So were military and naval matters. Urbanisation, better communications, the influence of education and military service eroded provincial isolation and helped to bring about the beginnings of a German identity. The great issues of the day were German, not state, issues.

Prussia

Prussia was easily the *Reich*'s largest state. Its state parliament, the *Landtag*, elected by a three-class male suffrage system which gave disproportionate political weight to the rich, remained a bastion of conservative interests. German chancellors, with the exception of Caprivi, were also prime ministers of Prussia. This dualism meant that, while as imperial chancellors they had often to pursue a liberal policy, as Prussian prime ministers they had to respond to a conservative majority.

The army

Bismarck had fought hard to keep the military under political control. His successors, however, found it hard to stand up to the military chiefs, who frequently had Wilhelm's support. Civilian ministers were not consulted when the General Staff drew up its war plans. War, declared Count Schlieffen, head of the General Staff from 1891 until 1906, was too serious a business to be left to politicians. Most of Germany's civilian leaders agreed: they did not question the expertise of Schlieffen or his master-plan in the event of war (see page 62) – a plan of which most German politicians were unaware.

By 1913 the German army was 800,000 strong; the reserve officer corps was 120,000 strong. The army was no longer so Prussian dominated or aristocratically led as it had been under Bismarck. Most officers were now from the middle class. Nevertheless, in 1913 over half the officers of the rank of colonel and above were aristocrats. Officers were selected not by competitive examination, but by regimental commanders who tended to pick men of like mind and background. Bourgeois officers aped the ways of their aristocratic brothers-in-arms. The army thus remained a right-wing force whose officers often regarded 'mere' civilians with contempt. Most civilians, by contrast, admired military virtues and had great faith in the army as an institution. The special status of the army was a major stumbling block to modernisation of the political system.

The structuralist view

From the 1960s the 'structuralist' school of historiography, led by Hans-Ulrich Wehler, sought to explain history through detailed examination of social, political and economic forces. They believed that the political life of Germany was determined by the economy, by the power structure and by class conflicts played out by various interest groups. Wehler and fellow structuralists claimed that Wilhelm II lacked the strength of character to determine a coherent and co-ordinated policy. He was, in Wehler's opinion, a 'shadow *Kaiser*'. Given the power vacuum, Wehler believed that Prussia's traditional elites – *Junkers*, army officers, leading civil servants and diplomats – exerted a dominating influence over German affairs. According to the structuralists, these elites were determined to maintain their power against the perceived threat of mass democracy. This prompted them to co-operate with the newly emerging leaders of industry and commerce. The structuralists claim that the elites set about imposing anti-democratic and anti-modern values on German society. In Wehler's view, for example, Germany's decision in the 1890s to undertake *Weltpolitik* (see page 54) was 'social imperialism' – an attempt to buttress the position of the elites by diverting the masses away from social and political reform and towards a populist acceptance of the *Kaiser* and the *Reich*.

The anti-structuralist view

While the elites did have a considerable influence in the Wilhelmine era, the structuralist interpretation is far too sweeping:

- It exaggerates the unity of purpose within the elites. The conception of the German nobility – or even the Prussian nobility alone – as a single class is nonsense.
- *Junker* influence was in decline, even in the army.
- *Weltpolitik* had little to do with social imperialism.
- Although most members of the German bourgeoisie – academics, clergymen, doctors, lawyers, engineers, bankers, merchants – feared revolution and opposed full democracy, this does not mean they took their cue from the elite.
- The notion that Wilhelm's personality was irrelevant is mistaken. Historians like John Rohl have shown that the *Kaiser*'s power and influence were considerable when he chose to intervene. He intervened, to disastrous effect, in foreign policy. He also made all the key appointments, surrounding himself with advisors and cronies who bolstered his absolutist ambitions. As well as selecting his chancellors and chief ministers, he also appointed the heads of the civil, military and navy cabinets, who were responsible for all promotions and appointments in their respective departments. Whatever the structuralists may think, it is not for nothing that the period from 1890 to 1914 is called the Wilhelmine era.

Was Wilhelm's Germany authoritarian or democratic?

Structuralist and anti-structuralist historians tend to agree that Wilhelmine Germany was a reactionary state, a state in which (according to the structuralists) the old elites exerted huge influence or a state in which

The elites – The officer class, *Junker* landowners, industrial and business leaders, senior civil servants and judges.

Weltpolitik – This translates as 'world policy'. The term is used to describe Wilhelm's world power ambitions.

(according to anti-structuralists) the *Kaiser* was an authoritarian ruler. However, Germany was rather more democratic than scholars once believed:

- The German press had considerable freedom and criticisms of the *Kaiser* were commonplace. Wilhelm's expressions of autocratic power, in particular, evoked storms of protest.
- By the early twentieth century, the *Reichstag* had an impressive legislative record and a central place in the popular imagination. Remarkable fairness characterised most election campaigns.
- The government needed a *Reichstag* majority in order to push through its legislation. Above all it needed the *Reichstag* to agree both to how money was collected and how it was spent. The budgetary rights of the *Reichstag* were strengthened as the fiscal burden, especially military and naval spending, increased.
- Given the growth in political activity, Germany's leaders often responded to, rather than manipulated public opinion.

Economic trends

Why was Germany so successful economically?

German industry, strong by the mid-nineteenth century, forged ahead after 1871, profiting from political unity. Between 1870 and 1913, while Britain's productive capacity doubled, that of Germany increased eight-fold. Only the USA showed a faster rate of growth. By 1914 Germany had become Europe's industrial superpower. This was partly the result of continued increases in production in 'old' industries: coal, iron, heavy engineering and textiles. However, what really marked out the German economy was the expansion of newer industries: steel, electrical engineering, chemicals and motor construction.

- German steel production increased nearly nine-fold in this period. By 1914 German output was double that of Britain's.
- Two German firms, AEG and Siemens, dominated the world electrical industry. By 1914 nearly half the world's electrical products originated from Germany.
- The German chemicals industry led the way in the production of fertilisers, dyes and pharmaceutical products.
- Daimler-Benz manufactured the world's first marketable automobile.

Reasons for German economic success

There are a number of reasons for Germany's economic success.

- Germany's population continued to grow rapidly, from just under 50 million in 1890 to almost 68 million in 1914. This provided both the market and the labour force for an expanding economy. Internal migration continued unabated as Germans moved from the countryside into towns. In 1871, 64 per cent lived in the countryside: by 1910 this had fallen to 40 per cent.
- Germany possessed huge natural resources: coal from the Ruhr, Saar and Silesia (by 1914 Germany mined a quarter of the world's coal); iron ore from Alsace-Lorraine and the Ruhr.
- Germany had a very good railway system.
- Germany had an excellent education system. Its institutes of higher education led the world. As well as offering study in traditional subjects, they made increasing provision for those with technical skills. Between 1890 and 1914 German university enrolments increased from 28,000 to 60,000. A university degree came within the grasp of the lower middle classes.

- German industry encouraged scientific research. This resulted in many important discoveries.
- German banks pursued an adventurous policy of generous long-term credit facilities for industrial firms. Representatives of banks were often invited onto the board of directors of firms, thus cementing a close partnership between the banking and commercial sectors of the economy.
- The banks were instrumental in the development of a distinctly German feature of industrialisation – cartels. In Britain and the USA the idea of groups of businesses combining together to control prices, production levels and marketing was seen as being against the spirit of free enterprise and against the consumer's interests. In Germany, by contrast, cartels were seen as a sensible means of achieving economic planning, eliminating wasteful competition and promoting efficient large-scale production. In 1875 there were only eight cartels in Germany. By 1905, 366 existed.
- In 1888 agriculture's share of Germany's Gross National Product had been about a half: by 1914 it had shrunk to less than one-quarter. However, German agriculture was in no danger of disappearing. While those employed in agriculture dropped from 42 to 34 per cent between 1882 and 1907, this was still a large proportion: in Britain the proportion was under 10 per cent. German agriculture, protected by government tariffs, was remarkably successful. Yields and output rose steadily – largely as a result of the growing use of machines, artificial fertilisers and scientific methods of stockbreeding. Thus Germany remained largely self-sufficient in terms of food supply.

Cartel – An association of manufacturers who come to a contractual agreement about the level of production and the scale of prices and maintain a monopoly. A monopoly is a situation when someone or a particular firm has total control over something. In industrial terms, this often means a firm has control over the production of a particular product.

Gross National Product – The total value of all goods and services produced within a country.

Year	Population (millions) Total	Per cent in towns over 2,000
1871	41.1	36.1
1880	42.2	41.4
1890	49.4	42.5
1900	56.4	54.4
1910	64.9	60.0

Output of heavy industry (millions of tonnes) Coal		
Year	Germany	Britain
1871	37.7	119.2
1880	59.1	149.3
1890	89.2	184.5
1900	149.5	228.8
1910	222.2	268.7

Output of heavy industry (millions of tonnes) Steel		
Year	Germany	Britain
1871	0.14	0.41
1880	0.69	1.32
1890	2.13	3.64
1900	6.46	4.98
1910	13.10	6.48

Index of industrial production (1913 = 100%)	
Year	Per cent
1871	21.1
1880	49.4
1890	57.3
1900	61.0
1910	86.0
1913	100.0

▲ **Figure 2** The development of the German economy.
(In 1871 Germany produced only a fifth of what it produced in 1913.)

International trade

After 1880 Germany played an important role in the world economy, matched only by Britain and the USA.

- German imports rose from 2.8 to 10.8 billion marks between 1880 and 1913. German exports rose from 2.9 to 10.1 billion in the same period. The greatest rise was in German manufactured goods. By 1914, the trademark 'Made in Germany' had become an international symbol of high quality.
- The trade gap was filled by 'invisible earnings' – profits from investments, services, banks and insurance.
- By 1914 Germany had become the world's third largest creditor nation (after Britain and the USA) and German banks were established worldwide.
- There was a huge rise in the German merchant shipping fleet. In 1880 Germany possessed less steam tonnage than Spain. By 1914, German steam tonnage was three times greater than that of France and second only to Britain. Shipbuilders received state subsidies, enabling them to increase Germany's share of global shipbuilding to 11 per cent.
- By 1914 the value of trade passing through the port of Hamburg was exceeded only in New York and Antwerp.
- Germany's colonies were of almost no economic significance. German trade was mainly with Europe, North and South America and Asia.

Balance of payments (millions of marks)					
Year	Imports	Exports	Visible balance	Invisible balance	Overall
1880	2814	2923	+109	+168	+277
1890	4162	3335	−827	+1249	+422
1900	5769	4611	−1158	+1566	+408
1910	8927	7475	−1452	+2211	+759

▲ **Figure 3** Balance of payments 1890–1910

(Note: Invisible exports relate to services rather than goods. Profits from overseas banking, for example, would be an invisible export.)

	Germany	Austria–Hungary	Central Powers*	France	Russia	Britain	Entente**	USA	Entente and USA
Population (in millions)	66.9	52.1	119.0	39.7	175.1	44.4	259.2	97.3	356.5
Iron and steel production (millions of tonnes)	17.6	2.6	20.2	4.6	4.8	7.7	17.1	31.8	48.9
Per cent of world manufacturing output	14.8	4.4	19.2	6.1	8.2	13.6	27.9	32.0	59.9

*Central Powers: Germany, Austria-Hungary, Turkey and Bulgaria.
**Entente: France, Russia and Britain.

▲ **Figure 4** Material resources in 1913 – a comparison with other major economic powers.

Source for Figures 3 and 4: *Rise and Fall of the Great Powers: Economic Change and Military Conflict from 1500 to 2000* by Paul Kennedy, (Fontana Press), 1987, p. 255.

Organised interests

German economic interests organised themselves as pressure groups, the aim of which was usually to put pressure on the government.

- The cartels (see above) were attempts by particular groups of producers to combine in order to gain an advantage in the market.
- Workers joined trade unions. Membership of the Free Trade Unions rose from 300,000 in 1890 to 2.5 million in 1913. Another 500,000 workers belonged to other trade unions.
- The Central Association of German Industrialists supported heavy industrial interests (like coal, iron and steel).
- The Confederation of Industrialists represented firms who manufactured finished goods.
- The Agrarian League, founded in 1893, campaigned for farmers' interests.
- Alongside these groups there were organisations for every conceivable economic interest including bankers, craftsmen, retailers and white-collar workers.

Economic pressure groups operated at a variety of levels. The best-organised (like the Agrarian League) tried to work directly on public opinion, through newspapers, pamphlets and travelling lecturers. Interest groups also sought to influence government, formally through submissions and evidence to committees, and informally through lobbying ministers or officials. Most of all, however, they worked through the political parties. The Agrarian League worked closely with the Conservative Party, while the SPD represented the working-class trade unions. The two main 'middle parties' – the National Liberals and Catholic Centre Party – tried to perform a balancing act between conflicting economic groups: the National Liberals between heavy industry and agrarian interests, and the Centre Party between the demands of peasants and the claims of the Catholic working class.

Apart from their ability to influence public opinion independently, the interest groups wielded power over political parties because of their importance during elections. They could, for example, threaten to remove their financial support from a party if their demands were not taken into account in the choice of candidate or programme. This might even extend to running or supporting a rival candidate. The activity of the interest groups created a powerful public distaste for the 'system' – a reaction against the deals and horse-trading (the Germans call it 'cow-trading') that went on.

Economic issues, inevitably, became the subject of major political debate. It has been calculated that economic affairs accounted directly or indirectly, for 90 per cent of *Reichstag* business by 1914.

However, there were limits to what governments were prepared to concede to particular interests – limits set by what ministers and officials perceived as the larger needs of society. International prestige, armaments policy, social stability, national efficiency – all required the continuing growth of industry, trade and exports. Any special privileges enjoyed by heavy industry or agrarian interests had to be set against the larger context of government support for the economy as a whole. As historian David Blackbourn writes, 'State and bureaucracy aimed to stand above and harmonize the conflicting interests, not make concessions to any one group that would jeopardize that goal'.

WORKING TOGETHER

It is useful to explain the reasons why Germany was economically successful in the late nineteenth and early twentieth centuries, especially on the industrial front. Below are a number of suggested explanations or factors. Divide into pairs or small groups, with one factor per group. Each pair/group should research and develop its explanation/factor and report back to the rest of the class.

- Germany's growing population
- Germany's natural resources
- Germany's educational system
- German banks
- The system of cartels
- Particular individuals and/or firms, such as Krupps or Siemens

Social trends

What were the main social trends in Wilhelmine Germany?

The German population rose to 68 million by 1914 – 60 per cent higher than in 1871. By 1911 there were more Germans in their late teens than there would be ever again in the twentieth century, and 80 per cent of the population were 45 or younger. This youthfulness perhaps helps explain the mobile and dynamic nature of Wilhelmine society. This dynamism, however, created new divisions as well as reinforcing old ones.

Longer lives

Germans were living longer. Infant mortality fell from around 25 per cent in the 1870s to 15 per cent in 1912, mainly due to improvements in hygiene and medical care. Compulsory immunisation against smallpox had been introduced in 1874. A diphtheria serum, available in the early 1890s, cut the number who died of the disease from one in two to one in six. The impact of medical research and the sharp increase in the number of hospitals, doctors and nurses, as well as improvements in living standards, also ensured that those who survived childhood lived longer. A German man born in the 1870s could expect to live to 36, a woman to 38. Those born in the first decade of the twentieth century could expect to live to 45 and 48 respectively.

An urban society

The movement to the towns that began after 1850 continued at an even faster pace after 1880. By 1910 nearly two-thirds of Germans lived in towns. More than a fifth lived in the 48 big cities with populations exceeding 100,000. By 1907 Berlin had more than 2 million people, of whom 60 per cent had been born outside the city. Even these figures understate the real growth, for many lived in suburbs that would eventually be incorporated in the formal city limits. By 1914 Hamburg had a million people while several other cities – Cologne, Dresden, Leipzig, Munich and Breslau – had more than half a million. Germans moved to towns largely because they expected a better standard of life. Not only Germans moved to the growing towns. In the late nineteenth century, Germany changed from being a net exporter to a net importer of people. Poles made up the largest single group of immigrants but there were also significant numbers of Italians, Dutch and non-Polish Slavs.

Urban tram and train networks, special trains and the coming of the bicycle made getting to work easier. This was also the age of department and chain stores, mail order catalogues and delivery vans, as well as advertising. By the early twentieth century the age of mass consumption had arrived in Germany as in the USA, Britain and other parts of Europe.

Rural society

Urban life seemed attractive to many Germans who lived and worked on the land. Agricultural workers, employed by estate and large farm owners, toiled long hours (a hundred-hour week was the norm) for low wages. Mechanisation came slowly to many areas and farm work was physically hard, especially during haymaking and harvesting. The 'flight' from the land to the city resulted in labour shortages in some areas. This led to high levels of family self-exploitation, including extensive child labour. Despite the harsh conditions, there were still more than 7 million agricultural workers, many on short-term contracts, in 1907.

Rural dwellers were isolated from the rest of society. Around a third of Germany's population had no access to the railways. They were also disadvantaged with regard to education provision and medical care. By the early twentieth century, a rural child was more likely to die before the age of one than an urban child. Compared with the modernity of urban life, the countryside seemed more backward. The constant flow of people from the countryside to the towns was also a source of rural pessimism. Many farmers and agricultural workers felt as though they were outcasts, exploited by the growing cities.

Nevertheless, agricultural prices did pick up at the end of the nineteenth century. By the early twentieth century there is evidence that many rural inhabitants were becoming better dressed and housed. All-in farm houses, where people and animals lived together, became less common. Many peasants who owned between 100 and 300 acres of land became successful commercial farmers.

The standard of living

Between 1885 and 1913 real wages in Germany rose by over 30 per cent. (In Britain, by contrast, real wages sagged in the decade before 1914.) Between 1896 and 1912 the proportion of Prussian taxpayers assessed on incomes of under 900 marks a year (including those with no earnings) fell from 75 to 52 per cent of the total. Those with incomes between 900 and 3,000 marks doubled from 22 to 43 per cent.

As well as having more money, workers also had more leisure time. Working hours in mining and industry were almost a third lower in 1914 than they had been in 1880. The typical working day in the non-agricultural sector was nine and a half hours.

However, by 1914 the mass of the German population remained agricultural and industrial workers. While industrial employment seemed an attractive option to many rural workers, urban living and working conditions remained dismally poor. A third of Germany's population lived at or below the poverty line. Lack of urban housing produced a rising problem of homelessness. The Berlin Homeless Shelter Association accommodated more than 200,000 men a year in the period between 1900 and 1914.

The working class

The working class was far from united.

- There was a gender divide. Men and women rarely did the same work. Even in industries where they worked side by side, such as textiles, women were usually relegated to subordinate 'unskilled' tasks.
- Ethnicity divided workers. Polish and Italian migrants often created their own subculture.
- Catholic and Protestant divisions remained important.
- Skilled workers considered themselves superior to unskilled workers.

Nevertheless, many men and women were bound together by common experiences, problems and attitudes. Workers were ill more often than the better-off, died younger and were smaller in physique. They lived in overcrowded housing and spent much of their income on food. Most working-class families were dependent on the earnings of women and children. Insecurity, particularly with regard to employment, was endemic. Perhaps a third of the workforce experienced some unemployment in a given year. One form of work-loss was rising sharply: the employer's lockout (when employers prevent their employees from working, for example, by shutting their factories). In 1910 nearly 250,000 workers were the victims of almost a thousand separate lockouts. Strikes also became more common. On average 200,000 workers went on strike in each of the years between 1905 and 1913.

Labour movements

Bad conditions encouraged the rise of an organised labour movement. By 1914 there were some 3 million trade union members. The SPD had almost a million members, making it the largest socialist party in the world. The language the party used – exploitation, inequality – made sense to those who heard it. The labour movements, which insisted on the dignity and worth of their members, helped provide workers with a sense of self-respect and fostered a sense of common identity. As well as offering hope for a better world in the future, they sustained workers in the present through a host of worker organisations: not just unions and co-operatives but choral societies, drama groups, lending libraries, educational courses, cycling and gymnastic clubs. They also provided an opportunity for working men to exercise responsibility.

Social mobility

There were material and mental barriers to upward mobility. Even a skilled craftsman's family was hard-pressed to find the money needed to keep children in school – and forego their income. Many working-class families preferred their children to go into skilled jobs rather than pay for an expensive education. There was also widespread scorn for the 'soft' life of the white-collar workers. Strength and manual dexterity continued to be a source of pride for workers – even if most of them hated their jobs!

The likely destination of the upwardly mobile worker was the lower middle class of foremen, clerks and petty officials. Movement straight from the proletariat to the professions was rare but it was often achieved over two generations: a move from the working to the lower middle class and then to the bourgeoisie.

The lower middle class

The number of white-collar workers – minor civil servants, men who held supervisory roles, clerks, small shopkeepers – was growing at a fast rate. Such men were generally better paid than manual workers (though often not by much). This lower middle class often had greater aspirations for their children than working-class families and made use of the educational system to place their children in better positions. The expansion of German universities – enrolments rose from 23,000 in 1875 to 72,000 in 1912 – brought an invasion of students from lower middle class backgrounds. They accounted for nearly a half of all Prussian enrolments by 1914.

The bourgeoisie

The Wilhelmine period was something of a golden age for the so-called bourgeoisie – doctors, high civil servants, professors, merchants, lawyers and businessmen. Such men were increasingly wealthy and this allowed them very comfortable levels of consumption. They could afford fine houses, holidays and servants.

But members of the bourgeoisie often had little in common. There were major differences between industrialists and professionals, between Protestants, Catholics and Jews. While a few great industrialists had far greater wealth than many *Junker* families, most middle-class families did not possess such wealth. Some bourgeoisie families tried to ape the manners of the aristocracy or even inter-marry with *Junker* landowners. But where intermingling occurred, this did not necessarily entail the casting off of bourgeois identity. It was rare for the wealthiest German businessmen to be ennobled – unlike in Britain. Major Ruhr industrialists did not seek and in some cases (for example, the Krupps) declined ennoblement. The bourgeois values remained seriousness, respect, rectitude – perceived to be 'manly' virtues.

The aristocracy and the bourgeoisie tended to share one outlook. Most feared organised labour which they regarded as a threat to domestic stability. Most saw little good in the godless, uncivilised proletariat.

The position of women

While German women were not expected to work after they were married, many working-class married women had no option but to do so in order to provide basic provision for their families. Germany still had 1.25 million female domestic servants in 1907 – about the same as in 1882. But this was a declining share of the labour force. More women were working in better paid industrial or clerical jobs.

There were growing opportunities for unmarried middle-class women.

- Female teacher training expanded from the 1890s.
- Women were prominent in the expanding welfare professions, such as nursing and social work.
- In 1899 German women were finally permitted to acquire medical qualifications after long male resistance.

Male hostility to female emancipation remained deep-rooted. Few women went to university. Women remained formally inferior in law. The husband was the legal guardian of his wife. Abortion was illegal and a double standard persisted in sexual morality. Men could have mistresses. Women were ostracised for committing adultery.

Nevertheless, by 1914 women were becoming more publicly active, at work, in charities, even in politics. This was most obviously true of middle-class women who had by far the greatest opportunities.

Order and discipline

Imperial Germany liked to see itself as an orderly, peaceable society. There was some truth in this view. Germans were not innately docile but they lived increasingly in a world of institutions that sought to discipline them. These institutions might encounter resistance, particularly from the lower classes, but their capacity to shape society was considerable.

Crime

Crime statistics, swollen by the growth of the police and by the addition of many new offences, are hard to unravel. Murder and property crimes seem to have remained constant. Recorded crime rose in urban areas; it declined in rural areas. Working-class districts could be violent places, full of young men with few attachments, who were not averse to carrying clubs, knives and even guns. But by the standards of the time, Germany was not a lawless or violent society. The murder rate stood at around a twentieth of the Italian or Spanish: only the Netherlands in Europe boasted a lower rate. There was far less unrest or 'collective protest' in towns and countryside than elsewhere in Europe. American Ray Stannard Baker observed in 1901 that German cities enjoyed a reputation for being 'safer, perhaps, than any other in the world'. This may have been due to improvements in living standards. But it may also have resulted from a German respect for authority – perhaps, some suggested, too great a respect.

The culture of militarism

The army disciplined Germans. In a sense, German society was militarised. The army's presence was visible everywhere – in barracks, drills and manoeuvres, regimental bands and military parades. Gymnastic clubs promoted soldierly virtues, as did schools. Soldiers had special legal privileges and civilians were expected to step aside to allow an officer to pass in the street. A man in an army officer's uniform was perceived to be powerful. In a famous incident in 1906 a cobbler with a criminal record dressed up in a captain's uniform and led ten soldiers to the Kopenick town hall where he arrested the mayor and stole 5,000 marks.

Not all civilians liked the army. It made enemies through its brutal handling of industrial disputes. Military legal privileges caused resentment among the propertied and educated. The officer corps limited its appeal as a would-be 'school of the nation' in so far as it tried to exclude unwanted elements – Jews, Catholics and middle-class progressives.

But the army, seen as the architect of unification, generally had considerable prestige and military virtues were respected. All German men were expected to undertake military service. It is hard to gauge the impact of the conscript experience. While military discipline was often resented, all who 'got through' the period of service shared an experience that let them take pride in their toughness and bound them in a male – indeed strongly masculine – camaraderie. Some 3 million Germans belonged to ex-servicemen's organisations by 1914.

The harsh, order-giving tones of military routine seeped into civilian life. Many Germans were deferential to figures of authority above them, especially if they wore a uniform. And soldiers were by no means the only men who wore uniforms in Imperial Germany. So did customs officers, postal workers, policemen and railwaymen.

The police

Ex-soldiers often set the tone of German officialdom in its dealings with the public. This tone was especially apparent among the police, who were heavily recruited from former servicemen. The police intervened to an astonishing degree in everyday life. This was partly because so many activities were regulated, resulting in many minor infringements of the law. While sometimes resented, enforcement of regulations had benefits. Strong measures against truancy, for example, created an enviable literacy rate. One police duty was to apprehend the 'work-shy'. Anyone guilty of vagrancy, homelessness or begging could be sent to the workhouse, which functioned as a cross between poorhouse and prison. While many Germans approved of the enforcement of regulations, the police force did not have a reputation for efficiency enjoyed by other branches of Germany's bureaucracy.

The law

Germany was a state based on the rule of law. The great liberal ambition in the mid-nineteenth century to constrain arbitrariness had been largely achieved. Soldiers apart, Germans were equal before the law. Bureaucrats and the police were legally accountable for their actions. The German judiciary enjoyed genuine independence. Demands for tougher punishments emanating from the *Kaiser* and conservative circles had little effect. The German legal system was as good as any in the world at the time.

Conclusion

Largely because of its efficient bureaucracy, Germany was an ordered and disciplined society. The bureaucratic machine, although sometimes resented for its interference, was generally seen as a force for good. Officials in Germany were usually held in high regard.

German culture

Why was German culture so diverse?

Pre-1914 the word 'Kultur' – culture – carried a heavy charge as it had done in the Kulturkampf (see pages 15–18). Infused with growing nationalist sentiment, Kultur supposedly denoted superior German accomplishments in scholarship and the arts. For some it also stood for a greater seriousness and 'depth' than could be found in the 'civilisations' of the Anglo-Saxons and France. But at the same time, culture was starting to acquire its modern sense of 'way of life'. This idea of culture as something that included manners, customs and material artefacts received a powerful stimulus from imperialist encounters with 'native cultures'.

Even if the term is used simply to define the arts, Wilhelmine culture presents a picture of enormous diversity. It included avant-garde art and traditional painting, new drama and pulp fiction, classical and dancehall music. While historians often use the simple distinction between 'high' (or elite) and 'low' (or popular) culture, this is hardly adequate given the complexities involved. The culture wars of the Wilhelmine years, like the previous Kulturkampf, were essentially conflicts about the value of modernity.

> **Avant-garde** – Those who create or support the newest ideas and techniques, especially in art, music, literature, drama and architecture.
>
> **Pulp fiction** – Popular fiction that is often not well written.

High culture

Avant-garde and official, conventional culture were both elitist in their different ways.

Many works musically, artistically and in literature were done within a traditional, established idiom (for example, the novels of Thomas Mann, the paintings of Franz von Lenbach and Anton von Werner, and the music of Brahms and Wagner) and were generally approved. But there were also works by the avant-garde. Literary avant-garde can be traced through successive waves of 'isms' – naturalism, symbolism, expressionism – as shown in the drama of Hauptmann and the poetry of Rilke. Art was even more avant-garde with the emergence of successive new 'movements' – from realism through impressionism to expressionism. Architecture and design were also affected by modernism. The great icons of the modernist movement – Gropius, Mies van der Rohe and Le Corbusier – had served their apprenticeship with Peter Behrens; Gropius had built his famous Fagus shoe factory in glass; the Werkbund exhibition buildings of 1914 in Cologne had predated the ideas of the Bauhaus. In music, regarded by many contemporaries as the quintessential 'German' art form, Richard Strauss and Arnold Schoenberg represented a major break with tradition.

Many elements of what are regarded as 'Weimar culture' (see pages 127–33) were already in place. By 1914 Berlin, a magnet for writers and artists, had a vigorous café culture, abundant theatres, journals and publishers, alongside dealers, galleries and private patrons of avant-garde art. But support for anti-establishment culture also existed elsewhere, especially in Munich – home to a large community of writers and artists. Spanish artist Picasso said in 1897 that if he had a son who wanted to be an artist, he would send him to study in Munich not Paris.

Contemporary culture

Everyday middle-class culture was very influential. By the early twentieth century as many as 100,000 Germans supported themselves from writing, music, the theatre and related activities. Few were avant-garde. While virtually all Germans could read, it is estimated that only about a fifth read journals, magazines or literature of any kind and only about a fifth of these – 4 per cent of the population – read serious German authors like Schiller and Goethe.

The other 16 per cent preferred the immensely popular western novels of Karl May, the sentimental accounts of rural life known as *Heimat* literature and 'light' stories serialised in family magazines and newspapers (16 million copies of daily papers were sold in Germany by 1914).

Highly educated Germans, concerned that cultural standards were being eroded, were critical of mass culture. They expressed concern at the popularity of pulp fiction, new forms of entertainment like the variety show and dancehall, the rise of the cinema (there were 2,500 in Germany by 1914) and the growth of spectator sports, especially football and professional cycling.

Cultural revolt

There was a widespread cultural revolt in these years – and not just in the arts. Many Germans, with time and money to spare, tried to get in touch with their inner selves. Psychology, sexology, 'physical culture', holistic medicine, anthropology, the para-normal, spiritualism and Buddhism were among the intellectually fashionable concerns of Germans in the early twentieth century, with a potential audience stretching down to the lower middle class. This was an age of fads, fashions and instant utopias. Some seemed modern. Others urged the return to the simple life – vegetarianism, wearing sandals and loose clothing, or no clothes at all.

How widespread were anti-modernist attitudes?

In the 1920s and 1930 the Nazis presented themselves as the bitter foes of cultural modernity and demanded a return to the simple German virtues. In so doing, they received much support. It has often been argued that 'anti-modernist' attitudes were similarly widespread in Wilhelmine Germany and that in these attitudes can be found the cultural roots of National Socialism. But this argument does not altogether stand up.

There were certainly critics of almost every aspect of modernity. Many regarded 'Americanisation' and the modern city as a threat to German traditional values. This critique of modernity overlapped with a dislike and hostility towards mass culture and often reflected suspicion of the proletariat. Those who lived in rural Germany particularly resented and feared the changing nature of society. There were also political groups willing to appeal to prejudices against the symbols of modern urban society – socialism, 'deviant' sexuality, avant-garde artists and Jews. While these intellectual currents had their counterparts elsewhere in Europe, anti-modernism in the arts was probably more pronounced in Germany.

However, the responses to the challenge of modernity cannot easily be pigeon-holed in political terms. Radical SPD members, for example, extolled the virtues of hiking or cycling into the countryside or tilling allotments as a way of escaping urban regimentation, thereby embracing anti-modernism. Conversely, many right-wing Germans, albeit loathing modern art, admired modern science and technology, approving of automobile and aircraft developments.

Both pro-modern and anti-modern standpoints were capable of being harnessed to very different political positions. Educated middle-class critics of modernity were invariably selective in practice, accepting the fruits of technology when it suited and using modern communications to convey their message about the virtues of peasant life.

Perhaps all that can be said is that many Germans were uneasy with the established bourgeois order – and with the challenges to it. But contemporary cultural attitudes were far too rich and various to be fitted neatly into a box labelled 'anti-modernism' or 'pro-modernism'.

ACTIVITY

Work in groups. Each group member should choose one of the people mentioned in this section on culture and carry out their own research on them. For your chosen person, you should investigate why the individual was important and their impact on German culture pre-1914. Share your findings with your group.

Ideas and ideology

Why did anti-Semitism develop in Wilhelmine Germany?

While Marxist ideas were enthusiastically supported by the left, right-wing politicians increasingly espoused nationalism and anti-Semitism. Wilhelm II, like many Germans, was both nationalistic and anti-Semitic.

Nationalism

In the mid-nineteenth century, nationalism in Germany had been a progressive force that aimed to promote parliamentary government. By the end of the century this had changed. Most nationalists were now conservative, bent on maintaining the *status quo* in a militarised Germany. Many late nineteenth-century European writers, by no means all German, extolled the virtues of the Germanic race. Militant German nationalists were invariably hostile to – and contemptuous of – other races, especially Slavs. This had some impact on the substantial number of non-Germans – Poles, French and Danes – who lived within the *Reich*. Nationalists wanted to create an ethnically and linguistically homogeneous nation-state. They had little respect for minority languages and culture. There was some discrimination against national minorities – particularly the Poles, who comprised five per cent of Germany's population. Prussia's language legislation in Poland, which decreed that all lessons should be taught in the German language, gave rise to a political crisis of national proportions, including a mass strike by 40,000 Polish schoolchildren in 1906. Repression fuelled rather than dampened Polish nationalism.

Anti-Semitism

By the late nineteenth century many German nationalists were anti-Semitic. Before this time European anti-Semitism was based to a large extent on religious hostility: Jews were blamed for the death of Christ and for not accepting Christianity. While anti-Semitism did not disappear, hostility towards Jews in Germany was politically insignificant by the mid-nineteenth century. In 1871 the German constitution extended total civil equality to Jews.

Throughout the nineteenth century, thousands of Russian Jews, fleeing from persecution, settled in Germany. Many prospered, becoming doctors, bankers, lawyers and academics. Thus, by 1900 Jews played an active and visible part in the cultural, economic and financial life of Germany. Most saw themselves as loyal Germans. Many no longer identified with a separate Jewish community; some inter-married with Germans and converted to Christianity. In 1910 the 600,000 practising Jews who lived in the *Reich* constituted about one per cent of the population.

Belief in race struggle

During the late nineteenth century, anti-Semitism became increasingly racial rather than religious. As early as the 1850s French Count Joseph Arthur de Gobineau argued that races were physically and psychologically different. History, in Gobineau's view, was essentially a racial struggle and the rise and fall of civilisations was racially determined. He claimed that all the high cultures in the world were the work of the Aryan (or Germanic) race and that cultures declined when Aryans interbred with racially 'lower stock'.

Anti-Semitism – A hatred of, or hostility to, Jews.

Aryan – The ideology of Nazism was based on the belief that the Aryan race was the master race. Nazi racial theorists identified the northern European, or Nordic, Aryan racial grouping as superior to all other races.

Social Darwinist – At its simplest, Social Darwinism is a political philosophy which argues that the strong survive at the expense of the weak; it is an idea derived from Charles Darwin's theory of evolution, and used by the Nazis as the cornerstone of their ideological belief in racial hierarchies.

Pacifism – Pacifists are people who are opposed to war. Many socialists were pacifists in 1914.

Absolute monarch – A king or emperor who has virtually absolute or total power and his will and decisions alone make the law.

Charles Darwin's *The Origin of Species*, published in 1859, provided further ammunition for the race cause. Although Darwin said nothing about race, his theory of natural selection as a means of evolution was adopted – and adapted – by many scholars. Social Darwinists soon claimed that races and nations needed to be fit to survive and rule. A number of writers claimed that the Germans had been selected to dominate the earth. They therefore needed more land. This would have to be won from other inferior races, most likely the Slavs. Such visions of international politics as an arena of struggle between different races for supremacy were commonplace by 1914.

The growth of anti-Semitism

Militant German nationalists, who believed that the Germans were indeed the master race, were invariably hostile to – and contemptuous of – other races, especially the Jews. Jews came to stand for all that nationalists loathed: liberalism, socialism and pacifism. Pamphleteers, newspaper editors and politicians presented anti-Semitic views to the German public. So did artists and musicians (like Richard Wagner, the famous composer). Among the most prominent anti-Semitic writers was Wagner's son-in-law Houston Stewart Chamberlain. Son of a British admiral and a German mother, Chamberlain published his most influential work – *Foundations of the Nineteenth Century* – in 1900. He claimed that the Jews were a degenerate race, conspiring to attain world domination and threatening German greatness. His book became a bestseller in Germany, even drawing praise from Wilhelm II.

Economic factors may have encouraged anti-Semitism. Those groups hit by economic and social change (especially peasant farmers and skilled workers) were easily persuaded that Jewish financiers were to blame for their suffering. Anti-Semitic prejudice was also strong in the higher reaches of society: the court, the civil service, the army and the universities. Thus, anti-Jewish feeling permeated broad sections of German society. In the late nineteenth century anti-Semitic politicians contested elections. Right-wing parties, which espoused anti-Semitism, gained a majority in the *Reichstag* in 1893.

However, the strength of political anti-Semitism in Germany should not be exaggerated. The success of the nationalist parties in 1893 had little to do with anti-Semitism. Indeed, no major German political party pre-1914 was dominated by anti-Semites and after 1900 the anti-Semitic parties were in steep decline, running out of voters and money. Respectable opinion in Germany remained opposed to anti-Semitism. In 1914 German Jews seemed in less danger than Jews in France or Russia.

Interpretations: Wilhelm II's 'personal rule'

To what extent was Wilhelm II an absolute monarch?

The exact nature of Wilhelm II's role within the German political system after 1890 continues to be debated. Some historians consider him to have ruled almost as an absolute monarch. Others believe that he was a weak ruler and there was precious little behind his blustering rhetoric. They believe the political life of Germany was determined by the economy, by the power structure and by class conflicts that were played out by interest groups, the bureaucracy and the military.

Source C From *Kaiser Wilhelm II* by J. C. G. Rohl, (Cambridge University Press), 2014, p. xv.

Kaiser Wilhelm II, imperious, impulsive, imbued with antiquated notions of the divine right of kings and of Prussia/Germany's God-given trajectory to greatness, while at the same time insecure and hypersensitive to perceived slights to his imperial dignity or his dynastic mission, was arguably the very last person who should have been entrusted with the immense powers of the Hohenzollern military monarchy at such a critical juncture in Germany's and Europe's history. Nevertheless, he stood at the apex of the *Kaiserreich's* policy-making pyramid for thirty years, from his accession at the premature death from cancer of his father in June 1888 to his ignominious flight into exile in the Netherlands in November 1918. All the generals and admirals, chancellors, ministers and ambassadors who served under him were appointed by him and dependent on his 'All-Highest favour' while in office. Wilhelm followed events at home and abroad with a nervous intensity that on occasions bordered on insanity, issuing orders and covering diplomatic dispatches with often furious diatribes, which have survived in their thousands in the archives. His own words and deeds mark him out as in many respects a forerunner of Hitler, not least in his vitriolic anti-Semitism in exile.

Source D From *A History of Modern Germany 1800–2000* by M. Kitchen, (Blackwell), 2006, p. 177.

There was indeed much tub-thumping [preaching] bombast at court, and the Kaiser was a loud-mouthed poseur with absolutist pretensions, but there was little substance behind all this. On the other hand, he [Wilhelm] was more than a shadow Kaiser since his power and influence were considerable, but only when he chose to intervene. He had certain pet projects that he pushed through and he intervened, usually to disastrous effect, in foreign policy. Most important of all, unlike his grandfather, who left most such decisions to Bismarck, he paid considerable attention to key appointments. Bülow and Tirpitz were the Kaiser's men, key players in his 'personal rule'.

Source E From *The Second Reich: Kaiser Wilhelm II and his Germany* by H. Kurtz, (Macdonald Library), 1970, p. 120.

It was the resurrection of a fake-Kaiser leading the Reich under God and Bismarck that had corrupted him as a human being – the artifice of sham absolute power that, in his case, turned him into an accomplished and very produceable actor. Throughout his reign, he received the thunderous applause of his subjects, while abroad his posturing and oratorical aggressions came to be regarded as political facts of consequence and moment. Critical contemporaries called the whole spectacular and disruptive business his 'personal rule', but the exact applicability of the term may be doubted. The strings in everything that mattered were usually pulled by other people. In the Bülow era particularly, his worst qualities were deliberately pushed into the foreground by that superficial and unscrupulous manipulator of power politics who drove the Kaiser into courses which Wilhelm's instincts told him were false and wrong.

Off-stage, the story was different. Beneath the gorgeous and theatrical apparition of the last German Kaiser, a more human, simple and sensible figure becomes sometimes visible, a more friendly spectre all but stifled under the Imperial purple …

ACTIVITY

Sources C–E give different interpretations of Wilhelm II's 'personal rule' in Germany after 1890. You should begin by reading each one and listing the main points made and the evidence used to support them. Then answer these questions:

- In what way do Sources C and D agree and disagree?
- In what way do Sources D and E agree and disagree?
- Using material from the sources and your own knowledge, consider to what extent was Wilhelm II an absolute monarch?

2 German political developments, 1890–1914

This section will examine the main political developments in Germany from 1890 until the start of the First World War in 1914. Bismarck's departure in 1890 was to have major repercussions in both domestic and foreign policy.

Caprivi's 'new course', 1890–94

How successful was Caprivi's 'new course'?

Leo Caprivi, a middle-aged soldier with a good administrative record but little political experience, became Chancellor in 1890. He hoped to stand above parties and particular interests. Wilhelm had singled out Caprivi because he thought him an amenable character who would do what he was told. In fact, he soon displayed a will of his own. In his first major speech he declared that he was ready to steer a 'new course' that involved a more consultative approach to government and a conciliatory attitude to previously hostile forces.

Social reform

In his first few weeks as Chancellor, Caprivi went out of his way to make concessions to socialists, Poles and Centrists. For example, the anti-socialist laws were allowed to lapse and schools in Polish-populated Prussian areas were allowed to use the Polish language for teaching purposes.

Conciliation proved successful. Caprivi was thus able to rely on *Reichstag* support to push through a number of social measures in 1891:

● Sunday work- was prohibited.
● The employment of children under thirteen was forbidden.
● Women were forbidden to work more than eleven hours a week.
● Courts, with representatives from both sides of industry, were set up to arbitrate in industrial disputes.

Tariff reform

The most important single measure Caprivi put before the *Reichstag* was a bill to reform the 1879 Tariff Act (see page 19). Prompted by wheat shortages that had led to a rise in food prices, Caprivi negotiated a series of commercial treaties with Austria, Italy, Russia and a number of smaller states between 1891 and 1894. Germany agreed to reduce tariffs on agricultural imports in return for favourable rates for German manufactured goods.

The Agrarian League

Although most parties supported tariff reform, the Conservatives opposed it. So did the Agrarian League. Formed in 1893, the League, which soon had 300,000 members, became an effective and well-organised pressure group. An anti-Semitic, rabble-rousing movement, it won widespread support in eastern Prussia. It mounted a virulent anti-Caprivi propaganda campaign, denouncing him as a socialist, bent on ruining wheat producers. It also agitated for subsidies, import controls and minimum prices to protect German farmers.

The army bill

Caprivi angered the right further by reducing the period of military service from three to two years. He also alienated the left by introducing an army bill that increased the peacetime army strength by 84,000 men. When the army bill was defeated, Caprivi dissolved the *Reichstag*. In the 1893 election, the Conservatives and National Liberals improved their position and the new *Reichstag* passed the army bill.

Caprivi's fall

Wilhelm's enthusiasm for social reform barely survived Bismarck's fall. Conservative opposition to the 'new course' reinforced Wilhelm's growing doubts about Caprivi's political suitability. Worried by the SPD's success in 1893 (the party won 44 seats) and frightened by a series of anarchist outrages across Europe (including the stabbing to death of French President Sadi Carnot in 1894), Wilhelm pressed Caprivi to draw up new anti-socialist measures. Aware that the *Reichstag* would not tolerate such a step, Caprivi refused.

Wilhelm and Prussian Minister-President Count Eulenburg now devised a bizarre plan to change the constitution, increasing the *Kaiser*'s power at the expense of the *Reichstag*, and going on to crush socialism. Caprivi managed to talk Wilhelm out of such a course of action. However, having lost the *Kaiser*'s confidence, Caprivi resigned in October 1894.

> ### KEY DATES: CAPRIVI'S 'NEW COURSE', 1890–94
>
> **1890** Caprivi became Chancellor, embarking on a 'new course'.
>
> **1893** The *Reichstag* elections were a success for the Conservatives and the National Liberals.
>
> **1894** Caprivi fell from power.

Prince Hohenlohe, 1894–1900

To what extent did Wilhelm II personally rule Germany from 1894 to 1900?

Prince Chlodwig Hohenlohe-Schillingsfurst, the new Chancellor, was a 75-year-old Bavarian aristocrat of mildly liberal views. Not the man to restrain Wilhelm, he soon became little more than a figurehead. (Hohenlohe admitted that he was a mere 'straw doll' for the *Kaiser*.) The government was dominated by men who were more closely in tune with the direction of policy desired by the *Kaiser* rather than by Hohenlohe.

Reactionary rule

Between 1894 and 1895 the governments in Germany and Prussia took strong action against potential revolutionaries and subversives. SPD offices in Berlin were ransacked and party leaders were put on trial. Prussians suspected of sympathising with socialism lost their jobs. Wilhelm advocated the forcible repression of the SPD. But the *Reichstag* rejected all efforts to pass an anti-socialist law. By 1897 a state of deadlock existed between the government and the *Reichstag*, much as in the last years of Bismarck's rule (see pages 24–5). The government would not introduce legislation acceptable to the *Reichstag* majority, and the majority refused to accept bills presented by the government.

Without the protection of 'ministerial clothes', as Bismarck had warned, the Crown was increasingly exposed to the storm of public criticism (see Source F).

Source F The left liberal, Eugen Richter, denouncing Wilhelm's 'personal rule' in the *Reichstag*, in 1897, to thunderous applause.

Where are the Ministers today? Wherever you look there are only compliant courtiers who agree with every opinion from above, promoted bureaucrats, dashing Hussars turned politicians, lackeys … Germany is a monarchical, constitutional country, but although it may still be possible to rule Russia according to the principles of *sic volo sic jubeo* [a Latin quote: thus I wish, thus I order] or *regis voluntas suprema lex* [the king's will is the supreme law], the German people will not allow themselves to be ruled like that for long.

> Why, according to Source F, was Richter critical of the *Kaiser*'s rule?

In conservative circles in 1897 there was talk of the former chief of the General Staff, General Waldersee, staging a military coup and overthrowing the constitution. Nothing came of this.

Source G Adapted from advice to Wilhelm II by General Alfred Waldersee, 1897.

In view of the tremendous growth of the Social Democrat movement, it appears to me to be inevitable that we are approaching the moment when the State's instruments of power must measure themselves with those of the working masses. If the struggle is inevitable, the State cannot gain anything by postponing it. I feel that it is in the State's interests not to leave it to the Social Democrat leaders to decide when the great reckoning is to begin. For the moment the State is, with certainty, still strong enough to suppress any rising.

Re-organisation of the government

In 1897 there were three new government appointees:

- Admiral Tirpitz became Navy Secretary.
- Count Posadowsky-Wehner became Interior Minister.
- Bernhard Bülow became Foreign Minister.

In addition, two long-serving figures, Friedrich Holstein, a senior official in the Foreign Office and Johannes Miquel, Prussian Finance Minister, began to assume even greater prominence. The emergence of this new team coincided with a new policy: *Weltpolitik*.

Weltpolitik

Bismarck thought of Germany as a continental European power. While he had no objection to overseas colonies, he did not regard them as a priority and had no desire to alienate Britain. Bülow and Tirpitz had a different vision of Germany's future. This vision, supported by Wilhelm and many ordinary Germans, was *Weltpolitik*. The decision to pursue *Weltpolitik* after 1897 was a vital moment in German history.

Structuralist historians (see page 37) think that the ruling class embarked on *Weltpolitik* hoping to rally support around the *Kaiser* and divert attention away from the socialist threat at home. However, the view that *Weltpolitik* was simply a manoeuvre in domestic politics is too simplistic. There were powerful forces at work in Germany that contributed to the new policy:

- Industrialisation had created economic demands for the acquisition of raw materials and markets beyond Europe.
- German nationalists believed that Germany's survival as a leading nation necessitated a more active world policy.
- Pressure groups like the Pan-German League and the Navy League popularised the message of *Weltpolitik* and exerted pressure on the government to pursue the policy to the full.

Weltpolitik was a deliberate attempt to make Germany into a world power on a par with Britain. This meant expanding Germany's navy, creating a large colonial empire and supporting Germany's economic interests across the globe. Wilhelm declared that henceforward no major colonial issue must be decided without Germany having a say in it.

The fact that Wilhelm II was a passionate supporter of *Weltpolitik* was crucial. This may have arisen from his love–hate relationship with Britain. Revenging himself on his mother's native land seems to have become something of an obsession with him. (He loathed his mother.) 'The English', he promised, 'will be brought low someday.'

1 What was Waldersee proposing in Source G and why was he doing so?
2 Why do you think Wilhelm II did not act on Waldersee's advice?

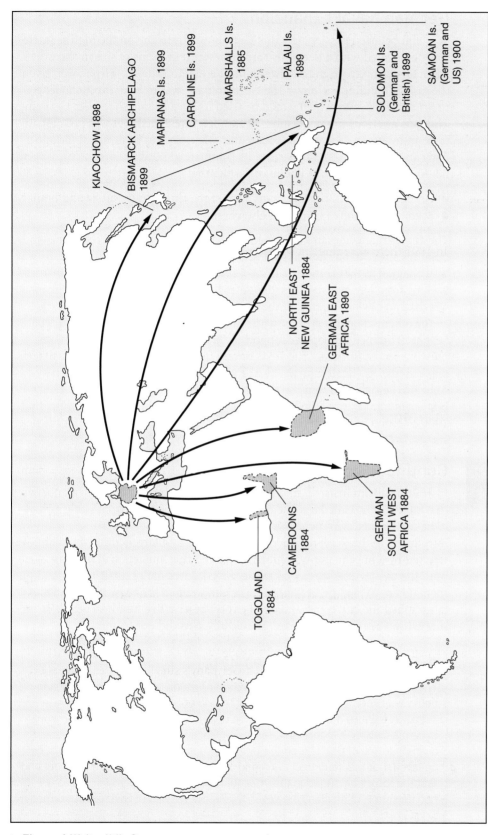

KIAOCHOW 1898

BISMARCK ARCHIPELAGO 1899

MARIANAS Is. 1899

CAROLINE Is. 1899

MARSHALLS Is. 1885

PALAU Is. 1899

SOLOMON Is. (German and British) 1899

SAMOAN Is. (German and US) 1900

NORTH EAST NEW GUINEA 1884

GERMAN EAST AFRICA 1890

GERMAN SOUTH WEST AFRICA 1884

CAMEROONS 1884

TOGOLAND 1884

▲ **Figure 4** *Weltpolitik*: German overseas expansion.

German naval expansion

Wilhelm believed passionately that Germany's future lay on the high seas. He was dissatisfied with a fleet only ranked seventh in terms of size in the world when Germany's foreign trade was almost equal to Britain's. Tirpitz was given the task of building the navy. The German navy was to be a direct challenge to Britain – the lever which would be used to force Britain to respect Germany. This was a serious miscalculation. Britain felt threatened, but was not prepared to be intimidated. Nor would Britain allow Germany to be its equal. Britain's navy and colonies were the basis of its commercial power and security. It seems not to have occurred to Wilhelm or Tirpitz that:

- Germany needed British support against the threat from Russia and France
- Britain might look for support elsewhere.

The anti-parliamentarian Tirpitz needed the *Reichstag* to provide the money to build his ships. In an effort to gain *Reichstag* support for naval expansion, he was instrumental in the creation in 1898 of the Navy League. Supported by financial backing from key industrialists, like Alfred Krupp, a great iron and steel magnate who had an obvious interest in the construction of a big navy, it soon dwarfed all the other nationalist groups, with a membership in excess of 300,000. The League drummed up popular support for naval expansion. This, in turn, put pressure on the *Reichstag*. The 1898 Naval Bill, which proposed building sixteen major ships, was finally carried by 212 votes to 139. The bill was opposed by some on the right and some on the left: the right thought the money would be best spent on the army; the left opposed any increase in military spending. In 1900 a second bill, which proposed building three battleships a year for the next six years, was passed by an even larger majority than the first.

Continued reaction

In 1898 Wilhelm insisted, in a speech made while he was on army manoeuvres, that anyone who called a strike or prevented someone else from working had to be imprisoned with penal servitude. The Hard Labour Bill, subsequently introduced in the *Reichstag* on Wilhelm's orders and largely drafted by him, was rejected by a huge majority. Wilhelm declared that 'matters will not improve until the troops drag the Social Democratic leaders out of the *Reichstag* and gun them down'. When the Berlin tram workers went on strike in 1900 Wilhelm telegraphed the city commandant: 'I expect at least five hundred people to be shot when the troops intervene'. Thankfully, this did not happen.

KEY DATES: PRINCE HOHENLOHE, 1894–1900

1894 Hohenlohe became Chancellor.

1897 Tirpitz became Navy Secretary and Bülow became Foreign Minister.

1897 German began to pursue *Weltpolitik*.

1898 Germany began naval expansion with the passing of a major Naval Bill.

1900 A second Naval Bill increased Germany's battleship-building programme.

German foreign policy 1890–1914

The *Reichstag* had very little influence over foreign affairs. German foreign policy was very much the preserve of the *Kaiser* and his chancellors. After 1890 there was a major re-orientation of policy. Wilhelm II was determined to be his own man in foreign affairs. Convinced that he had been called as an instrument of God to lead the German people into a glorious new era, he believed that the 'feminine' Latin and Slav races had become degenerate and that the future belonged to the 'masculine' Protestant Germanic races. He had no coherent strategy, however, to achieve his aim of German supremacy.

By 1914 Europe was divided into two blocs: the Central Powers (Germany and Austria-Hungary) and the Triple Entente (France, Russia and Britain). German policy-makers over the previous two decades were largely to blame for this state of affairs. They had first driven France and Russia together. Then, by constructing a large fleet, they had driven Britain into the arms of France and Russia. Thus, by 1914 Germany faced the prospect of a war on two fronts.

Chancellor Bülow, 1900–09

How successful was Chancellor Bülow?

Bülow exerted a strong influence as Foreign Minister before becoming Chancellor in 1900. A competent administrator, he had Wilhelm's trust and effectively handled the *Reichstag*. Mainly interested in foreign policy, he refrained from close contact with the various *Reichstag* parties, hoping not to become too involved in domestic issues.

Social reform

By 1900 it was clear that repressive measures had failed to retard the growth of socialism. Interior Minister Posadowsky resumed, in effect, Caprivi's 'new course', introducing a series of measures designed to win working-class support. These included:

- an extension of accident insurance (1900)
- a law making industrial courts compulsory in all large towns (1901). These courts adjudicated in disputes between employers and employees.
- an extension of the prohibition on child labour (1903).

Tariffs

The renewal of Caprivi's commercial treaties was an issue of great controversy. While left-wing parties called for lower tariffs to reduce the price of bread, the Agrarian League demanded higher tariffs. Bülow worked successfully for a compromise. By a huge majority, the *Reichstag* restored tariffs to the pre-1892 level. Popular opposition to higher tariffs helped the SPD to win nearly a million extra votes and 26 extra seats in 1903. The Centre Party remained the largest party and continued to hold the balance of power in the *Reichstag*.

Financial problems

The mounting costs of maintaining the army, expanding the navy and running the empire resulted in a large budget deficit. In 1905 Bülow proposed a two-pronged attack on the deficit by proposing an increase in indirect taxes and an inheritance tax. The Centre Party and the SPD voted down the indirect taxes, which would have hit ordinary Germans hard. The Conservatives and the Centre Party weakened the inheritance tax so as to make it financially insignificant.

The 1907 election

Bülow's government was criticised for its handling of a revolt of the Hottentots and Hereros (rebel tribes) in German South-West Africa in 1904–05. The revolt was crushed but subsequent revelations of brutality, corruption and incompetence in the colony encouraged the Centre Party to ally with the SPD and others in December 1906 to vote against the government's proposal to provide extra money for colonial administration.

In 1907 Bülow, determined to bring the Centre Party to heel, dissolved the *Reichstag*. In the ensuing Hottentot election, pro-government parties did well, campaigning on a nationalistic, anti-socialist and anti-Catholic ticket. While the election was a disaster for the SPD (the Party lost almost

Hottentot election – SPD leader Babel labelled the 1907 election the Hottentot election. The Hottentots were one of the native rebel tribes in south-west Africa.

half its seats), the Centre Party made modest gains due to the fear of many Catholics of another *Kulturkampf* (see pages 15–18). The Conservatives, Free Conservatives, National Liberals and Left Liberals now came together in a coalition known as the 'Bülow Bloc'. Bülow removed ministers objectionable to the Bloc. Posadowsky, nicknamed 'the red count', for example, was dismissed and replaced by Bethmann-Hollweg, a conservative bureaucrat. The Bloc, however, was always fragile. Most Conservatives preferred to co-operate with the Centre Party than ally with the Left Liberals with whom they had little in common.

The Eulenburg affair

In 1906 journalist Maximilian Harden began to publish a series of articles exposing a number of homosexuals who had high positions in the German army. In 1907 Harden made similar insinuations about Wilhelm's best friend Prince Philipp zu Eulenburg. Eulenburg, one of Wilhelm's main advisers and a man who had been particularly influential in government appointments, was accused of using his castle at Liebenberg for regular meetings of homosexuals. Male homosexual acts were an offence of the 1871 criminal code and there were a series of sensational trials. The trials of Eulenburg and Kuno Moltke (another homosexual and close friend of Wilhelm) in July 1908 made it apparent that there was an extensive ring of homosexuals at the German court. As far as is known, Wilhelm never took part in any homosexual acts, but he had often shared a room with Eulenburg and the latter boasted in court that he had had no secrets from Wilhelm during their intimate friendship which had lasted over two decades. Chancellor Bülow was in danger of being dragged into the scandal. He too was homosexual and had Eulenburg to thank for his rapid rise in Wilhelm's favour.

In 1907 Wilhelm broke off all contacts with Eulenburg and Moltke, in effect condemning them in the public eye. He was clearly shaken by the lurid details of their relationship, which were revealed daily in the courts and published widely across Europe. The scandal left Wilhelm severely depressed. It also seriously damaged his reputation both at home and abroad.

The *Daily Telegraph* affair

Another major crisis occurred in the autumn of 1908 following an article in Britain's *Daily Telegraph* newspaper in which Wilhelm expressed his wish for closer relations with Britain. The tone of Wilhelm's remarks were typically ill-considered and tactless. Wilhelm had given the text of the article to Bülow for perusal but he had left the matter to an underling in the Foreign Office who had passed it for publication. The *Kaiser* was savagely attacked in the press, not least by Harden who suggested he should abdicate. *Reichstag* deputies questioned Wilhelm's right to make such important policy statements and there was suddenly clamour for constitutional changes to reduce the *Kaiser's* power. Bülow, who was responsible for clearing Wilhelm's article before publication, was in a difficult position. Caught between loyalty to Wilhelm and the demands of the *Reichstag*, he distanced himself from the views expressed in the article. He secured a promise from the *Kaiser* that constitutional formalities would in future be properly respected. Wilhelm's declaration mollified the *Reichstag* opposition and the crisis ended without leading to constitutional change.

Meanwhile Wilhelm went hunting with his friend Carl Furstenberg. During one evening of 'entertainment', the chief of the Civil Cabinet, Count Dietrich von Hulsen-Haeseler, died of a heart attack while dancing in front of Wilhelm in a ballerina's tutu. When news of the death was made public, the *Kaiser*'s tottering reputation was further damaged.

Source H A letter written by the British ambassador to the British Foreign Secretary in November 1908.

Prince Bülow spoke at some length and in a very depressed tone of the present crisis in Germany. He said that the Emperor meant so well, but the fact was that, as Bismarck had said, there is no longer room for absolutism in Germany. Parliamentary government was, with their countless parties, impossible, but what people clamoured for, and meant to have, was constitutional government. Germany was intensely monarchical and this crisis with its unusually hot outcry against the Sovereign, would, he hoped, pass as other similar crises had passed: but nevertheless, the present feeling against the personal influence of the Emperor in public affairs was very strong, stronger than it had ever been before, and it caused him considerable anxiety. There must in fact be a change; he spoke feelingly on the subject, because, as I had perhaps noticed, his position as things were now, was anything but comfortable.

- Why, according to Source H, was Bülow depressed?
- How reliable is this source in terms of providing evidence about German public opinion in 1908?

Bülow's fall

Wilhelm's trust in Bülow had been fatally weakened by the *Daily Telegraph* affair. He determined to be rid of him and did not have long to wait. As naval and colonial expenditure continued to mount, the budget deficit increased. To cover the deficit, Bülow introduced a finance bill increasing indirect taxation (opposed by the SPD) and the inheritance tax (opposed by Conservatives). The Centre Party, determined to have its revenge on Bülow for his actions in 1906–07, supported the Conservative stand. When the Chancellor's budget proposals were rejected by the *Reichstag* in 1909, Wilhelm secured Bülow's resignation.

KEY DATES: CHANCELLOR BÜLOW, 1900–09

1900 Bülow was appointed Chancellor.

1907 The (so-called) Hottentot election was a success for the Conservative parties.

1908 The Eulenburg affair damaged Wilhelm's reputation.

1908 The *Daily Telegraph* affair weakened Wilhelm's trust in Bülow.

1909 Bülow was forced to resign.

Chancellor Bethmann-Hollweg, 1909–17

To what extent was Germany a parliamentary democracy by 1914?

Theobald Bethmann-Hollweg, a bureaucrat who had worked his way up through the Prussian administration, now became Chancellor, even though he had little support in the *Reichstag*. His essential conservatism aligned him to the right-wing parties. His attempts to broaden his *Reichstag* support (by proposing limited reform of the Prussian constitution) only alienated his natural supporters. The 1912 elections further increased Bethmann-Hollweg's difficulties since there was a distinct shift to the left with the SPD and a group of Left Liberals winning 110 and 42 seats, respectively. The SPD now became the largest party in the *Reichstag*. Given that the new *Reichstag* was no longer dominated by the Conservative–Centre Party alliance, Bethmann-Hollweg had to rely on backroom deals and compromises to get support for government bills. Conservative parties denounced him for his weakness while the SPD demanded more reform.

Budgetary problems

Serious budgetary problems continued. In 1912–13 the problems of imperial finance and defence came to a head. Both the army and navy submitted major expenditure plans. Fortunately for Bethman-Hollweg the inheritance tax was finally accepted. Ironically, the tax was still opposed by the Conservatives – who supported the military measures – and supported by Socialists – who disliked military spending but were keen to set the precedent of a property-based tax.

The new tax did not solve the fiscal crisis. By 1914 the *Reich* debt reached five billion marks. Given that indirect taxes were unpopular with the left and direct taxes unpopular with the right, there was no easy political solution.

The Prussian constitution

Although Conservatives were losing support in the *Reichstag*, in the Prussian *Landtag* (state parliament) their position was virtually unassailable. They controlled the upper chamber and usually had a majority in the lower house, which was still elected by the outmoded three-class system. In 1908 the SPD won 23 per cent of the vote in the Prussian elections but won only seven seats. The Conservatives, with 16 per cent of the vote, won 212 seats. This glaring injustice led to increasing demands for reform.

The SPD

SPD deputies remained divided between orthodox Marxists, who maintained their revolutionary agenda, and moderates who believed that the Party's role was to fight for the improvement of conditions by peaceful means within the framework of capitalism. Significantly, in 1913 SPD deputies supported the new taxes that Bethmann-Hollweg introduced to cover increased defence expenditure. While they might resent the injustice of the Prussian franchise, indirect taxes, which hit the poor proportionately more than the rich, and above all the high price of food, SPD deputies were aware that most SPD voters were patriotic and concerned about the perceived threat from Russia, France and Britain.

Nationalist associations

After 1912 the various nationalist associations (for example, the Pan-German League and the Navy League) became more vocal in their criticism of the German government for what they regarded as its weakness at home and abroad. By 1914 many extreme nationalists were anti-socialist, anti-Semitic and anti-parliamentarian. Many believed in Aryan superiority and dreamed of a new Bismarck who would be strong and ruthless, unafraid to pursue aggressive policies against enemies at home and abroad. 'The political maelstrom of radical ideologies out of which Nazism would eventually emerge was already swirling powerfully well before the First World War', says historian Richard Evans.

The Zabern affair

Relations between Alsace-Lorraine and the rest of Germany were poor. There was considerable friction between the local populace and garrison troops. At Zabern, a small town in Alsace, a young officer made contemptuous remarks about Alsatian recruits that aroused indignation and led to several demonstrations. During one disturbance in November 1913 the commanding officer ordered his men to clear the streets. In the ensuing melee 28 citizens were detained overnight in the barracks. This led to public and official protests: only civilian courts and the police could interfere with the liberty of citizens; the army was acting above the law.

Rather than punish the soldiers concerned, Wilhelm ordered them to be sent away on manoeuvres. The affair rumbled on. The minister of war and Bethmann-Hollweg rejected criticism of the army on the grounds that commanding officers were responsible only to the *Kaiser* and certainly not to the *Reichstag*. The political opposition was so intense that there was a massive vote of no confidence in Bethmann-Hollweg in December 1913 (293 votes to 54). This had little effect: the Chancellor dismissed the vote as an empty gesture. While the Zabern affair underlined the power of the *Kaiser*, it also showed that he could not altogether ignore public opinion.

The political situation in 1914

In 1914 Germany was still in many respects an authoritarian monarchy. Wilhelm's power to appoint the Chancellor enabled him to set the general tenor of government, and he did so, particularly in the period from 1897 to 1908. This coincided with Bülow's political supremacy. Bülow recognised that his own position depended on catering to Wilhelm's personal whims.

However, the *Kaiser*'s political power was within a constitutional framework. German governments could not ignore the *Reichstag* and had to patch up working majorities in order to pass legislation. The *Reichstag*, with its ever-increasing SPD presence, extended its right to debate government policy. Nor was Wilhelm able to take firm action against his critics. All Wilhelm's more repressive schemes were defeated in the *Reichstag*. While he might dream of using his army to strike against the SPD, he did not dare do so in reality.

It may be that Germany was on the way to evolving into a thoroughly democratic state. Certainly many Germans desired the creation of a genuine parliamentary democracy in which the imperial government was responsible to the *Reichstag*. However, Germany was still far from having a parliamentary system by 1914 whereby government was by a parliamentary majority and ministers were responsible to the *Reichstag*. Moreover, the forces of conservatism were strong. The middle classes, backbone of the *Kaiserreich*, were solidly on the side of the establishment. While most *Reichstag* deputies favoured constitutional change, the vast majority had great respect for the monarchy.

The outbreak of the First World War

The assassination of Austrian Archduke Franz Ferdinand, heir to the Habsburg throne, at Sarajevo on 28 June 1914, sparked the crisis that led to war. Austrian leaders, aware that the murder had been planned by a secret society that had links with the Serbian government, believed the time had come to settle accounts with Serbia. Germany agreed. Wilhelm and Bethmann-Hollweg pledged full support for Austria–Hungary on 5–6 July. Hoping to achieve a diplomatic victory, they were prepared to risk, but did not expect, a European war. On 23 July Austria–Hungary presented an ultimatum to Serbia. The terms of the ultimatum were so severe that Serbia, emboldened by promises of Russian support, refused to accept them all.

Austria–Hungary's declaration of war on Serbia on 28 July was followed by Russia's mobilisation of its forces – a decision that made war inevitable. Germany had only one plan to deal with a major war: the Schlieffen Plan. Drawn up in the early twentieth century, it aimed to counteract the threat of a two-front war by launching a rapid all-out assault in the west (via Belgium) in order to defeat France before turning east to face Russia. Thus, as soon as Russia began to mobilise, Germany had to mobilise its own forces. An ultimatum was dispatched to Russia demanding cessation of all mobilisation measures within twelve hours. When Russia refused to comply, Germany declared war on Russia on 1 August. Two days later Germany declared war on France. German violation of Belgium's neutrality brought Britain into the war on 4 August.

While Germany was by no means the only country to blame for the First World War, its leaders must shoulder the major responsibility both for the worsening international atmosphere in the years before 1914 and also for the escalation of the July 1914 crisis.

Had Germany reached a point of crisis by 1914?

By 1914 Germans on the left and right thought Germany was reaching a point of crisis. The left believed that the time might soon be ripe for proletarian revolution. The right feared that this might be about to happen. The 1912 *Reichstag* elections suggested that the SPD was on the rise. Nationalist leaders talked of a military coup to smash the Socialists.

German historians once believed that the domestic crisis drove German rulers to embrace war in 1914. In 1969 historian Fritz Fischer published *War of Illusions*. As well as suggesting that German leaders deliberately planned a war of expansion from 1911, Fischer suggested that the reasons for this aggressive expansionism were to be found less in Germany's international position than in its social, economic and political situation at home. A successful war, the government hoped, 'would resolve the growing social tensions' and consolidate the position of the ruling classes.

But was there a crisis in Germany? There were certainly problems:

- Germany's fiscal position was dire. It had spent too much on its army and navy and not raised sufficient taxes.
- The country was divided between right and left.
- Germany's rulers, none more so than Bethmann-Hollweg, were pessimistic about Germany's future.

However:

- The divisions in 1914 were no greater than previously. Indeed, there is some evidence that the domestic situation was actually improving in 1913 as the 'middle parties' came together and the SPD, for the first time, gave its support to a government finance bill.
- Nationalists had muttered about military coups before but nothing had materialised.
- Germany's economy, if not its government finances, remained strong.
- There is little evidence to support the view that German leaders were actively planning an offensive war policy from 1911 onwards.

- The elites did not pursue war as a means of deflecting political opposition and thereby preserving their own threatened position. If it appeared possible to woo the Social Democrats, why risk a war that – as Bethmann-Hollweg recognised – would increase the chances of revolutionary change?

In short, while there was political tension and frustration in Germany – as elsewhere in Europe in 1914 – revolution seemed less likely in Germany than elsewhere. The notion that Germany went to war because of domestic crisis is mistaken.

Interpretations: To what extent was the *Kaiserreich* a parliamentary democracy by 1914?

Historians have different views about the political situation in Germany on the eve of the First World War and continue to debate whether the *Kaiserreich* was moving in the direction of parliamentary democracy in 1914.

ACTIVITY

Sources I–K (pages 63–4) give different interpretations about the source of power in Germany in 1914. Read them and then answer the following questions:

1 In what way do Sources I and J disagree?
2 To what extent do Sources J and K agree?
3 Using the material from the sources and your own knowledge, consider to what extent had the *Reichstag* increased its power in Germany by 1914.

Source I From *Questions on German History*, published by the German Bundestag, Press and Information Centre, 1984, p. 233.

In the East the expropriation law passed in 1908 made it possible to confiscate Polish property as part of the Prussian policy of Germanisation. Germans were then housed on this property ... In Alsace-Lorraine the conflicts reached a peak with the Zabern incident of 1913. Prussian troops broke up a public meeting there and arrested 28 demonstrators. The commander responsible for the troops, in ordering his troops to make the arrests, had taken the law into his own hands. However, a military court pronounced him to be innocent of all charges. The *Reichstag* tried in vain to intervene. It became clear during these crises and the ensuing parliamentary debates before the war that the *Reichstag* was in no position to challenge the authority of the traditional powers in the *Kaiser's* court, in agriculture, industry, the bureaucracy and the armed forces.

Source J From *From Bismarck to Hitler: Germany 1890–1933* by Geoff Layton, (Hodder & Stoughton), 1995, p. 40.

Consequently, although the balance of power still rested with the forces of conservatism in 1914, it is also clear that their right to govern was under threat and their ability to govern as they would have liked was already being curtailed by the forces of change. The irreconcilable nature of these two sets of forces was the source of great political tension and frustration. By 1914 Imperial Germany was not yet ungovernable, partly because its economic well-being allayed discontent and also because there was still general respect for the monarchy, but it had reached a situation of political stalemate which made for weak and confused government. The *Kaiserreich* was thus a very complex socio-political organism – just as complex as its sovereign's own eccentric personality.

KEY DATES: CHANCELLOR BETHMANN-HOLLWEG

1909 Appointment of Bethmann-Hollweg as Chancellor.

1912 The SPD became the largest party in the *Reichstag*.

1913 The Zabern affair underlined the authority of the German army.

1914 The start of the First World War.

Source K From *A History of Modern Germany 1800–2000* by Martin Kitchen, (Blackwell), 2006, p. 202.

Domestic politics on the eve of the war were thus approaching stalemate. A conservative reforming chancellor could not distance himself from the court, Prussia, the military, or the conservatives. The middle parties were reluctant to seize the opportunity to strengthen their position. They could not risk refusing to pass the budget for fear of hurting their constituents, and were not yet prepared to approach the Social Democrats. The Conservatives were gradually pushed aside and resorted to drumming up support from the extra-parliamentary opposition, amongst whom there were calls for a counterrevolution. They were endorsed by the Crown Prince [August Wilhelm, the *Kaiser*'s eldest son], who had to be called to order by his father. Others felt that a war might solve Germany's problems, however great the risks involved. Germany stood at the crossroads, and the reaction to events outside its borders was to determine the road ahead.

WORKING TOGETHER

Set up a class debate to assess Wilhelm II's importance as a 'key individual'. Use the following motion:

'Wilhelm II ruled Germany essentially as an absolute monarch from 1888 to 1914.'

One group should claim that Wilhelm was indeed an absolute monarch – a kind of dictator – who personified the newly united German *Reich*. The other group should argue that he was essentially a figurehead, who acted the part of absolute monarch but did relatively little.

Which group argued the better case and why?

Chapter summary

- Wilhelm II, determined to rule as well as reign, exerted far more control than William I, and German chancellors after 1890 were less powerful than Bismarck.
- The *Reichstag* grew in importance but various interest groups, especially the Pan-German League, also influenced public opinion.
- Structionalist and anti-structionalist historians continue to debate the extent to which the elites (rather than the personality of the *Kaiser*) determined the political situation in the *Kaiserreich*.
- The German economy boomed in the period 1890–1914 and the standard of living of most Germans rose.
- There was a culture of militarism in Germany.
- German society was generally dynamic, peaceful and disciplined.
- German culture was diverse.
- Right-wing Germans were increasingly nationalist, racist and anti-Semitic.
- Chancellor Caprivi embarked on a 'new course' in 1890. Hohenlohe, who replaced Caprivi in 1894, was a figurehead. Bülow, Chancellor from 1900 to 1909, managed the *Reichstag* and Wilhelm for several years but was dismissed largely as a result of the *Daily Telegraph* affair.
- Bethmann-Hollweg, Chancellor from 1909 to 1917, had difficulty getting measures through the *Reichstag,* particularly after 1912 when the SPD became the largest party.

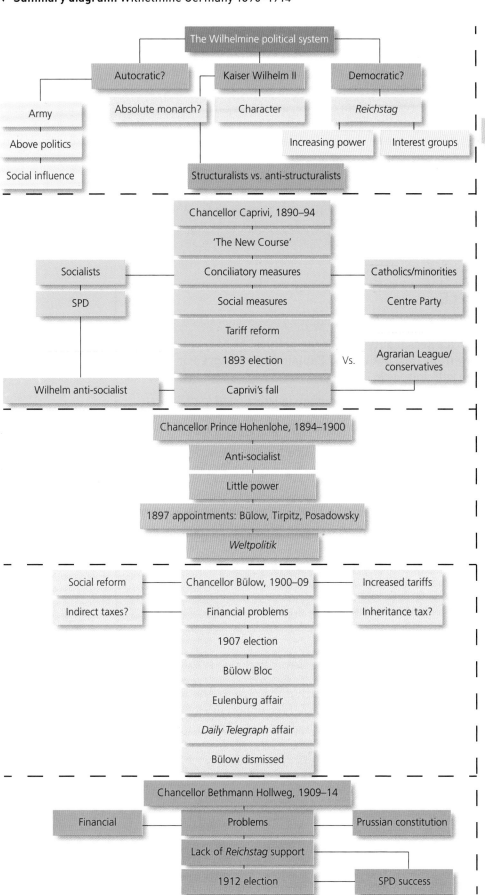

German economic success

Old industries | New industries

Reasons

Growing population
Raw materials
Transport system
Education system
Scientific research
Banking
Cartels

Social trends

People living longer
Urbanisation
Rural backwardness
Rising standard of living
Organised working class
Growing middle class
Role of women
Disciplined society

German culture

Avant-garde movement
High culture
Mass culture
Cultural diversity
Anti-modernism

Intellectual trends

Growth of nationalism
Social Darwinism
Rise of anti-Semitism

Working on essay technique: analysis

Analysis is a term that covers a variety of high-level skills including explanation and evaluation. In essence, analysis means breaking down something complex into smaller parts. This means that a clear structure which breaks down a complex question into a series of paragraphs is the first step towards writing an analytical essay.

Explanation

The purpose of explanation is to account for why something happened, or why something is true or false. An explanatory statement requires two parts: a claim and a justification.

EXAMPLE

Imagine you are answering the following AS-level practice question:

'Wilhelm II's personality shaped the political history of imperial Germany from 1890 until 1914.' Explain why you agree or disagree with this view. (25 marks)

You might want to argue that Wilhelm II determined to play a far more active role as *Kaiser* than his grandfather William I. Once you have made this point, and supported it with relevant detail, you can then explain how this answers the question.

For example, you could conclude your paragraph like this:

Claim ——— The fact that Wilhelm II was determined to rule as well as reign was
Relationship ——— important because the 1871 Constitution gave him extensive powers, especially in foreign policy. He was also able to appoint the German ——— Justification
chancellor.

The first part of this sentence is the claim, while the second part – and the second sentence – justifies the claim. 'Because' is a very important word to use when writing an explanation, as it shows the relationship between the claim and the justification.

Evaluation

The purpose of evaluation is to weigh up and reach a judgement. Evaluation, therefore, needs to consider the importance of two or more different factors, weigh them against each other, and then reach a judgement. Evaluation is a good skill to use at the end of an essay because the conclusion should reach a judgement which answers the question.

EXAMPLE

Consider the AS-level practice question on page 66.

If you were answering this question you might want to weigh up the extent to which Wilhelm II did shape the history of Imperial Germany.

For example, your conclusion might read:

Clearly it is possible to argue that Wilhelm II was a weak ruler who, despite his blustering, exerted little control over events in Germany and Europe after 1890. However, this would be mistaken. He was far more than a mere figurehead. 'There is only one ruler in the Reich and I am he', he said. His angry views of the world, his autocratic methods as ruler, and his ambitious naval and world power policies had a huge impact on Germany and Europe. In the conduct of personnel, military, foreign and armaments policy, he was very much the determining voice until the decision to go to war in 1914 – a decision in which he took a leading part. Therefore, there seems little doubt that Wilhelm's – flawed – personality was of crucial importance – for both Germany and Europe – in the years after 1890.

In this example the evaluation is helped by a series of words (highlighted) that help to weigh up the importance of the factors/arguments. This is just one example, but the same is true of answers to other essay questions. 'However' and 'nonetheless' are useful words as they can help contrast the importance of the different factors or arguments.

ACTIVITY

Again, consider the practice question in the example on page 66 and, using your notes from this chapter, write a paragraph about the powers that Wilhelm II possessed. Make sure the paragraph:

- begins with a clear point that clearly focuses on the question
- develops the point with at least three pieces of accurate detail
- concludes with explanation: a claim and a justification.

A-LEVEL PRACTICE QUESTION

'Wilhelm II held less power in 1914 than he had done in 1890.' Assess the validity of this view.   (25 marks)

Use the above question to practise all of the essay techniques that you have learned so far.

As well as studying the facts of an event in history, historians also use these facts in order to reach conclusions on, for example, why something happened. In other words, they have to interpret the facts in order to reach their conclusions. Often the evidence does not just point in one direction. There is scope for historians reaching different conclusions and producing different interpretations.

Section A of the examination requires you to read and evaluate different interpretations – that is, looking at how historians do not always agree in the judgements they reach. In Chapters 1, 3, 5, 6 and 7, there are contrasting interpretations for you to study and activities for you to practise your skills – that is, your skills in using evidence to see how far you agree with each interpretation.

In this chapter, as well as Chapters 4, 6 and 8, there is one longer interpretation to read, followed by some questions that are designed to help you build up your skills as well as helping you to consolidate your knowledge of each chapter.

Working on interpretation skills: extended reading

How militaristic was Wilhelmine society?

Victoria Harris discusses the extent to which Wilhelmine society was a militaristic society.

In 1931 the German playwright Carl Zuckmayer staged the satirical 'Captain of Köpernick,' which was based on actual events from 1906, during the glory days of Wilhelmine Germany. Wilhelm Voight, a shoemaker with a lengthy criminal record, is released from prison determined to live as an honest man. Germany's strict social rules make this impossible – without a 5 military record he cannot be legally registered and without this registration he cannot get work. Desperate, Voight takes matters into his own hands. He gets hold of a Prussian army uniform and, now an army captain, holds a town mayor for ransom and seizes the town's treasury, all in the *Kaiser's* name. Because of their obsessive admiration for men in uniform, the 10 townspeople follow Voight unquestioningly.

Historians have tended to follow Zuckmayer's line on Wilhelmine's militarism. Historian Otto Büsch famously argued that this militarism started in the 18th century, with the introduction of military conscription. As a result, the army began to command an unusual level of social prestige. 15 Germans' so-called militarised patriotism only strengthened after victories against Napoleon in 1813–14 and the military successes against Denmark, Austria and France which led to Germany's unification in 1871.

By the beginning of the Wilhelmine period, then, Germany met all the criteria of a militaristic society: there was a large, professional army, and the army 20 and its behaviours were glorified, with army officers taking leading roles in government. Because army officers were also civil administrators, the needs of the German army were often confused with the needs of German society as a whole. Because army officers mainly came from the land-owning aristocracy while enlisted men came from the lower classes, army 25 hierarchies extended into German society, with lower class men taught to defer to the commands of the upper classes.

This militarism has led historians including Hans Ulrich Wehler to argue that Wilhelmine society was fundamentally backwards looking, clinging to old-fashioned values while other European countries embraced democracy, 30 capitalism, and modernity. This conservative-militarism has also been used to explain Germany's decision to go to war in 1914 and the rise of Nazism in the 1920s. However, while this view of Wilhelmine society might be useful in explaining events that would occur in the 20th century, recently historians have begun to question whether it is as useful in explaining Wilhelmine society itself. 35

The army played a significant role in Wilhelmine Germany, but it is less clear how pervasive that role was. Yes, the Naval Arms race and Imperial expansion in the decade preceding the First World War clearly served the interests of the army. However, during this same period Germany was envied as the most modern European country, boasting prolific industrialisation, urbanisation, and cultural output. In fact some Germans were so concerned that the Army did not have *enough* influence that in 1912 they formed the German Army League, dedicated to revitalising the German's 'patriotic and military spirit'. The army may have played a leading role in government but so too did the Social Democratic Party, whose popularity grew exponentially over the period. The democratically elected parliament in which it participated may have had limited powers, but it was still able to effect important change. Indeed, it was the Social Democrats' support in that parliament which enabled Germany to go to war in August 1914.

This has led some historians to suggest that it was not militarism which dominated Wilhelmine society but the working classes. Wilhelmine Germany was a highly stratified society and this led to social conflict. The working classes organised labour unions and political parties like the Social Democrats to try to change their situation, while the upper classes used state and private organisations to improve conditions for the working classes because they feared revolt from below.

This class stratification also led to the development of distinct identities amongst the different classes. So while for the upper classes the army, patriotism and social honour were hugely important, they were far less so to working-class Germans, whose numbers increased dramatically over the period. When the First World War began only certain segments of German society supported it – mainly those from the upper classes. And while wartime society was essentially controlled by the military, growing frustration with the war and the social deprivation that came along with it led working class Germans to join a revolt against the army and government in its last days. Wilhelmine society was certainly not militaristic enough in its last days to save itself.

**Dr Victoria Harris is a research fellow
at Birkbeck College, London.**

ACTIVITY

Having read the essay, answer the following questions.

Comprehension

1 What does the author mean by the following phrases?
- 'Wilhelmine's militarism' (line 12)
- 'conservative-militarism' (line 31)
- 'Naval Arms race' (line 37)

Evidence

2 Using paragraphs 1 to 4, list the ways in which the author provides evidence suggesting that Wilhelmine society was militaristic.

Interpretation

3 Using your knowledge (and the essay), list evidence to suggest that Wilhelmine society was not necessarily militaristic.

War, revolution and democracy, 1914–23

The years 1914–23 were crucial years for Germany's political development. Germany entered the war as a semi-autocracy. Four years later the *Kaiserreich* gave way to a democracy – the Weimar Republic. This chapter will examine these developments by focusing on the following areas:

● The political, economic and social impact of the First World War
● The German Revolution, 1918–19
● The establishment of the Weimar Republic
● German economic, financial and political problems, 1919–23

When you have worked through the chapter and the related activities, you should have a detailed knowledge of all the areas listed above. You should be able to relate this knowledge to the following breadth issues defined as part of your study:

● How was Germany governed and how did political authority change and develop?
● How effective was opposition?
● How important were ideas and ideology in Germany's development?

For the period covered in this chapter, the main focus can be phrased as the following question:

To what extent was German unity threatened by right- and left-wing division in the period 1914–23?

CHAPTER OVERVIEW

From 1914 to 1918 Germany fought an exhausting war against Britain, France, Russia (until 1917) and the USA (from 1917). In November 1918 sailors mutinied, sparking a workers' revolt in many cities. Wilhelm II abdicated, a moderate socialist government, led by Ebert, took power, and an armistice was proclaimed. Several weeks of revolutionary activity followed. Ebert's government defeated the Spartacist revolt and in 1919 a National Assembly met and established the Weimar Republic.

The fact that the new democratic Weimar government had to sign the Treaty of Versailles meant that it was associated from the start with defeat and humiliation. The Republic was also weakened by economic and financial problems. Unable to rely on the loyalty of the army, Weimar governments were threatened by extreme left- and right-wing forces who, for very different reasons, rejected the Republic. A French–Belgian occupation of the Ruhr in 1923 led to hyperinflation. Despite the Republic's problems, Communist and Nazi attempts to seize power in the autumn of 1923 failed.

1 Germany at war

This section deals with Germany and the First World War. The outbreak of war in 1914 was greeted with enthusiasm in Germany. Virtually all Germans thought the war would be short and victorious. Instead, the conflict degenerated into a terrible war of attrition. Over the next four years millions of Germans were killed or badly wounded. And Germany eventually lost. The impact of the war on Germany is the focus of this chapter.

The war, 1914–16

What problems did Germany face in the period 1914–16?

In 1914 all the political parties in Germany promised their support for the war. SPD leaders, who tended towards pacifism, could not ignore the fact that most of their supporters wanted to defend the Fatherland against perceived Allied aggression and the fear of Russia – regarded as a despotic bastion of reaction and the arch-enemy of all progressive forces. On 4 August 1914 Wilhelm, addressing the *Reichstag*, insisted that Germany had done all it could to avoid war and now drew its sword with a clear conscience. 'I know no parties any more, only Germans', he declared. All the party leaders agreed to a political truce for the duration of the war. The *Reichstag* passed war credits and then adjourned, leaving the conduct of the war to the government.

Source A Wilhelm II's Proclamation of 6 August 1914.

To the German People

Ever since the foundation of our empire it has been the greatest endeavour for me and for my forefathers over the last 43 years to preserve peace in the world and to continue our powerful development in peace. But our enemies envy the success of our work. All the open and secret hostility from east and west and from beyond the sea we have endured conscious of our responsibility and power. But now these enemies want to humiliate us. They wish us to look on with folded arms as they prepare a malicious attack: they do not tolerate our standing side by side in determined loyalty with our allies who fight for their reputations as empire and with their humiliation we will lose our power and honour as well. Therefore the sword must now decide. In the midst of peace the enemy attacks us. Forward. To arms. Every moment of wavering, every hesitation is treason against the Fatherland. The existence or destruction of our re-created empire is now at stake, the very existence of German power and customs. We will resist to the last breath of air of man and horse. And we will win this fight even against a world of enemies. Germany has never lost when it has been united. Forward with God who will be with us as He was with our fathers.

Allied and Central Power strength

Germany's failure to achieve a quick victory in 1914 resulted in a war of attrition for which the country was militarily and economically unprepared and strategically ill-suited. This did not mean that defeat was inevitable. Germany had Europe's finest army and the world's second largest navy. The Central Powers – initially just Germany and Austria – had the advantage of interior lines of communication. Using their railway systems, they could move men from one front to another. Although the Allies (France, Russia and Britain) had more men, Russian forces were poorly equipped and led. Economically, Germany was Europe's strongest industrial power, producing two-thirds of the

NOTE-MAKING

This chapter covers a great deal both in terms of content and analysis and a good understanding is essential. It looks at the way the war affected Germany – politically, economically and socially. Your notes should focus on these three areas. So make notes under Political impact, Economic impact and Social impact. In which area did the war have its greatest impact – political, economic or social?

War credits – These were financial bills which were passed by the *Reichstag*. Without these measures, the German government could not have funded the war.

How did Wilhelm justify the war (Source A)?

continent's steel and half its coal in 1914. As a result of the German advance in 1914, France lost its main industrial area. In October 1914 the Ottoman Empire joined the war on the Central Powers' side. Bulgaria did so in 1915.

However, on balance, the Allies were stronger. The Russian army was the largest in Europe, while Britain possessed the world's strongest navy. Britain and France could call on their large empires for support. The Allied naval blockade, begun in 1914, ensured that Germany was unable to acquire a range of goods it desperately needed. The Allies, meanwhile, were able to continue to trade worldwide. German overseas possessions, with the exception of East Africa, were quickly gobbled up. In 1915, Italy joined the war on the Allied side.

The domestic impact of the war

Despite the failure to secure a quick victory, dissident views were few in 1914–15. Germans remained united against the perceived threat posed by 'barbaric' Russia. Lulled into a false sense of security by official propaganda, most Germans remained confident of victory. Until mid-1916 Bethmann-Hollweg faced little opposition from the public or the *Reichstag*. He did his best to keep the SPD loyal. This meant keeping secret his expansionist war aims: he knew that the SPD opposed 'wars of conquest'.

Military rule

As the war progressed, Germany's military leaders were able to interfere in political and economic affairs, with only a limited degree of accountability. Army leaders justified intervention on the grounds of military necessity. Wilhelm II exerted little control over political and military affairs. His self-confidence seemed to desert him with the onset of war. Despite being supreme warlord he was kept in the dark about military developments and his advice was rarely sought. He thus became little more than a figurehead.

Mobilisation

The German government tried to ensure that all its citizens contributed to the war effort. The War Ministry decided which men should be conscripted and which exempted. In total, some 13 million men were called up to serve in the armed forces – 20 per cent of the population. Substitute workers, particularly young women, helped Germany cope with its labour shortage in agriculture and industry.

The economic front

Faced with the consequences of the British blockade, the German government tried to organise its economic production. Although economically strong, Germany was far from self-sufficient. It lacked cotton, rubber, nitrates, petroleum, copper, nickel and tin. It was also dependent on imported fertilisers, fats and oils – all essential if Germany's population was to be adequately fed. As early as August 1914 Germany established a War Raw Materials Department. This soon exercised vast power – directing labour, controlling the railways, introducing rationing and price controls, and allocating resources to industries competing for scarce raw materials. Scientists tried to produce substitute materials for goods of which Germany was short.

In the short term the measures taken to regulate Germany's war economy were reasonably successful. However, two crucial economic weaknesses threatened to erode Germany's capacity to continue the war:

- Germany had a huge financial deficit pre-1914 and once war started it soared. Bethmann-Hollweg's government, rather than raise taxes, simply printed money. This fuelled inflation.

72

Inflation – Inflation means that prices of goods and services go up. This usually results from governments issuing too much paper money. Inflation results in a decline in the purchasing power of money. This is bad news for consumers and for people who have or depend on savings. It can be good news for those in debt.

- The blockade, a series of poor harvests, problems of transportation, shortage of chemicals for fertilisers, and mass conscription led to a serious decline in grain production. In January 1915 bread rationing started, to be followed by the rationing of virtually every foodstuff.

Hindenburg and Ludendorff

Bethmann-Hollweg, keen to shore up his own position by winning popular support, decided to ditch General Falkenhayn, Chief of the Army Supreme Command. In August 1916 Field Marshal Paul Hindenburg and General Erich Ludendorff, two officers who had won important victories against the Russians on the Eastern Front, were appointed joint Chiefs of the Army Supreme Command. Far from strengthening his position, Bethmann-Hollweg soon found that his and Wilhelm's authority had been decisively weakened, since neither of them enjoyed the popular backing of Hindenburg and Ludendorff. By the simple expedient of threatening resignation, the two generals exerted a powerful influence over events – political, economic and military. Their 'rule' is often described as 'the silent dictatorship'.

Hindenburg and Ludendorff tried to mobilise German resources more thoroughly than before.

- The Hindenburg Programme tried to increase arms production by placing contracts directly with heavy industry.
- Ludendorff ordered a systematic economic exploitation of the enemy areas occupied by German troops.
- The Auxiliary Service Act (December 1916) enabled the government to control the labour of all males aged between 17 and 60.
- A Supreme War Office was set up and given wide powers over industry and labour.

KEY DATES: THE WAR, 1914–16

1914

August The start of the First World War

August Germany set up a War Raw Materials Department

1916

August Establishment of the 'silent dictatorship' of Hindenburg and Ludendorff.

December The Auxiliary Service Act enabled the government to control male labour.

▲ Wilhelm (centre) studying maps alongside Hindenburg (left) and Ludendorff (right) in 1917. Why do you think this photograph was taken?

These measures resulted in a huge increase in munitions production. Nevertheless, Germany suffered serious shortages of coal and transport over the winter of 1916–17. Ironically, autocratic Germany failed to achieve the same degree of mobilisation as democratic Britain. The war did not result in a state-controlled German economy: industries were not nationalised and the property rights of landowners were left relatively untouched.

Germany defeated, 1917–18

What problems did Germany face in 1917–18?

By 1917 Hindenburg and Ludendorff, fearing that Germany was likely to be defeated, believed that they had no option but to take greater risks. It could be that this risk-taking actually brought about the defeat that Germany's 'silent dictators' were trying to avert. The introduction of unrestricted submarine warfare, for example, brought the USA into the war against Germany in April 1917. Meanwhile, as events deteriorated militarily, the domestic situation worsened.

German civilian morale

On the domestic front the impact of war slowly but remorselessly affected the lives of ordinary Germans, weakening morale. A disastrous food and fuel crisis over the winter of 1917–18 made life, for most, truly miserable. Civilian deaths from starvation and hypothermia increased from 121,000 in 1916 to 293,000 in 1918. Many workers resented being forced to work even longer hours as a result of the Auxiliary Service Act. The result was that social discontent grew markedly. Considerable anger was harboured against industrialists who were making vast profits from the war. In 1917 the 'left' organised an increasing number of strikes. The 'right' blamed Jews and socialists for all Germany's problems.

The July 1917 crisis

As popular disillusionment with the conduct of the war increased, so did dissent in the *Reichstag*. Socialists, with National Liberal support, succeeded in establishing a *Reichstag* committee to consider constitutional reform. Bethmann-Hollweg, hoping to maintain unity, persuaded Wilhelm to promise reform of the Prussian franchise system, to the consternation of conservatives.

Another issue dividing Germans on the left and right was the issue of war aims. Parties on the right sought territorial acquisitions, ensuring German dominance over Europe, and hoped to extract large reparation payments from the defeated enemy in the event of German victory. Parties on the left, however, believed that Germany was fighting a purely defensive war, not one of conquest. The SPD maintained that any peace settlement should be based upon reconciliation with no annexations of territory.

Bethmann-Hollweg, anxious to preserve unity, did his best to avoid debate on the issue of Germany's war aims. However, by 1917 it was impossible to overlook the widening gulf between those who sought a 'peace without victory' and those who believed that only a 'victorious peace' would legitimate the sacrifices already made. In June 1917 left-wing parties made it clear that they would vote against war credits if Bethmann-Hollweg did not support 'peace without victory'. He refused, thus losing the support of the *Reichstag*.

Ludendorff refused to work any longer with a man who supported political change and who had lost control of the *Reichstag*. Bethmann-Hollweg was thus forced to resign in July. His resignation was not a victory for the *Reichstag*. *Reichstag* deputies did not appoint his successor or use the crisis to force negotiations for peace. The July crisis simply gave the Supreme Command an opportunity to assert its superiority. George Michaelis, an insignificant Prussian administrator who had impressed Ludendorff during a brief interview, became the new chancellor.

On 19 July the *Reichstag* passed a peace resolution by 212 votes to 126.

'The Reichstag *strives for a peace of understanding and permanent reconciliation of peoples. Forced territorial acquisition and political, economic and financial oppressions are irreconcilable with such a peace.'*

The resolution, supported by the SPD and Centre Party deputies, had no influence on Germany's military leaders who remained committed to winning a victorious peace.

Michaelis and Hertling

On 1 November 1917 Michaelis was dismissed for his inept handling of a small naval mutiny. Significantly, the *Reichstag* played a key role in his dismissal but not in his replacement. Wilhelm, without consulting Hindenburg and Ludendorff, chose Count Hertling, an elderly Bavarian aristocrat, as Michaelis's successor. Hertling disliked parliamentary government, but appreciated the need for consulting the parties. He promised to support the peace resolution and to reform the Prussian franchise. Ludendorff, busy with preparations for the 1918 offensive, hoped that Hertling's conciliatory measures could keep the home front quiet long enough for Germany to win the war.

The right

Radical nationalists, alarmed by the peace resolution, founded the Fatherland Party in September 1917. Led by Tirpitz, and heavily subsidised by industrialists, the party demanded annexations east and west, and supported military rule. It soon claimed it had over one million members. (It probably had fewer than 500,000.)

The left

By 1917 German socialists were seriously divided. Most SPD deputies, unwilling to damage the war effort, were prepared to work with the other parties. However, a number of radical socialists opposed collaboration with the capitalist German state. In April 1917, 42 SPD deputies formed a new party, the Independent Social Democratic Party (USPD). The USPD was committed to a speedy end to the war and a peace without annexations. The remaining 68 SPD deputies reconstituted themselves as the Majority Socialist Party with Friedrich Ebert as chairman.

The USPD was loosely associated with two other groups, the Spartacus League and the Revolutionary Shop Stewards. The League, founded by a small group of socialist intellectuals and led by Karl Liebknecht and Rosa Luxemburg, had no mass following. The Revolutionary Shop Stewards, by contrast, had considerable grass roots influence. The League and the Shop Stewards believed that working people must use the war to destroy capitalism and inaugurate world revolution.

Revolutionary Shop Stewards – These were working-class activists who tried to organise mass action in the factories to end the war.

Strike action

In January 1918, 400,000 Berlin workers went on strike. The strike spread quickly to other cities. The strikers' demands, influenced by the Revolutionary Shop Stewards, were political as well as economic; they included democratic government and 'peace without victory'. The authorities acted firmly, placing large plants under military control, prohibiting public meetings and arresting a number of socialist leaders. Significantly, Majority Socialists and most official trade union leaders opposed the strike. The Shop Stewards quickly backed down and called off the strike.

The situation in Germany in 1918

By mid-1918 German agricultural production was 40–60 per cent below pre-war levels. Official food rations reflected the fall in output. Germans were allowed only about 20 per cent of their pre-war consumption of meat, 13 per cent of eggs, 21 per cent of butter, 41 per cent of vegetable fats and about 47 per cent of flour. There were dramatic price rises in virtually every commodity. Germans were also having to work longer. More than 60 per cent of large and medium-sized factories in the Berlin armaments industry, whose workers worked nine hours a day before the war, now worked 10–12 hours a day. In more than half the factories the workers had to work regularly on Sundays as well. In these circumstances, it is not surprising that discontent was growing. There were increasing numbers of strikes. The Russian revolutions of 1917 provided some Germans with a socialist model, helping to focus discontent on a level higher than concern for mere material things.

The German 1918 spring offensive

Germany's main advantage in early 1918 was that it no longer had to fight a two-front war. Russia's acceptance of the Treaty of Brest-Litovsk (March 1918) meant that Germany could now concentrate its military might on the Western Front. But Germany's allies were a source of concern and huge US forces would soon help the Allies. The German High Command therefore launched a great offensive in March 1918, its troops smashing through Allied lines. Further German offensives followed and by June German forces were within 60 kilometres of Paris. However, the German army did not possess sufficient manpower to exploit the breakthrough and the advance ground to a halt. In late July, the Allies successfully counter-attacked. On 8 August British forces broke through the German lines at Amiens. Morale in the German army began to crumble and there were large numbers of desertions. The Allied advance continued through early September, ensuring that Germany lost all the gains made in the spring.

The collapse of Germany's allies

On 30 September 1918 Bulgaria surrendered. Turkey agreed to an armistice on 30 October. In October 1918 the Italians smashed the Austrians at Vittorio Veneto. Later that month Czech leaders took over Prague, Serb and Croat leaders proclaimed the establishment of a Yugoslav state, and Hungary asserted its independence. The Austrian government signed an armistice on 3 November.

Germany defeated

By the autumn of 1918 Germany's situation was desperate. German troops were being pushed back towards the Rhine while 300,000 US troops a month were arriving in Europe. On 29 September Ludendorff informed Wilhelm and Hertling that the war was lost. Consequently Hertling should approach US President Wilson and ask for an armistice and a peace based on the Fourteen Points.

On 30 September, Wilhelm accepted Hertling's resignation and issued a proclamation establishing parliamentary government. Hindenburg and Ludendorff thus abdicated their power, leaving the *Reichstag* in control. In this way, they hoped that Germany might obtain better peace terms. The Allies, they believed, were more likely to be sympathetic to a democratic regime. Moreover, the new government (and not the army leaders) would be blamed for Germany's defeat.

Fourteen Points – These were US President Woodrow Wilson's main war aims. Wilson hoped to prevent future wars by eliminating secret alliances and frustrated nationalism, and by establishing a League of Nations. The League of Nations was set up, on Woodrow Wilson's insistence, to try and preserve peace in the future. Germany was to be excluded from the organisation.

KEY DATES: GERMANY DEFEATED 1917–18

1917

April The USA declared war on Germany.

April Split in the SPD: formation of the Independent Social Democratic Party and the Majority Socialist Party.

July A peace resolution was passed by the *Reichstag*. This led to the resignation of Bethmann-Hollweg; Michaelis became Chancellor.

November Hertling replaced Michaelis as Chancellor.

1918

March Ludendorff launched a German offensive in the West.

July The German advance ended: the Allies now went on the attack.

September Hindenburg and Ludendorff abdicated their power.

September Wilhelm II issued a proclamation establishing parliamentary government.

September Wilhelm accepted Hertling's resignation.

October Turkey agreed to an armistice.

November The Austrian government signed an armistice.

WORKING TOGETHER

Split into groups. Your task is to explain what problems Germany faced on the domestic front during the First World War. Work out five main problems, listing them in order of priority. Your spokesperson should then explain your list – and the reasons for your ranking – to the other groups.

2 Revolution, 1918–19

Four years of total war, culminating in defeat, brought the *Kaiserreich* to its knees. The war massively dislocated the economy, wrecked the already parlous government finances, caused serious social tensions, and exacerbated the polarisation of politics. This section will examine the situation in Germany from October 1918 to April 1919. Is it correct to describe the events of this period as a 'German Revolution'? Or were there, in reality, several different revolutions, each with its own aims and agenda? And did the changes that occurred really amount to a revolution?

Total war – A war which is not restricted to the warfront and where the economy and lives of citizens are bound up in prosecuting the war.

Soviet – Soviets were councils of workers, peasants and soldiers. Such councils had been created in Russia in 1917, eventually allowing the Bolsheviks to come to power.

NOTE-MAKING

Your notes should focus on the causes of the German Revolution of 1918–19 and the reasons for the defeat of left-wing efforts to establish a system akin to that in Russia – where the Bolsheviks had seized power. The following framework is suggested:

The Causes of Revolution
- German defeat in the First World War
- Constitutional reform (October 1918)
- Mutiny of the High Seas Fleet
- The establishment of **soviets**
- The abdication of Wilhelm II
- Left-wing activity in November and December, 1918

The Spartacist rising
Reasons for defeat
- Divisions among the socialists
- Ebert's goals
- The Ebert–Groener pact
- The Stinnes–Legien agreement
- The *Freikorps*

German parliamentary democracy established

To what extent was German parliamentary democracy in 1918 imposed from above?

On 1 October Wilhelm II asked Prince Max von Baden, a moderate conservative, to form a government. Prince Max's government, which included representatives from the Majority Socialists and the Left Liberals, was stunned when told the seriousness of Germany's position. When Prince Max raised objections to an immediate request for an armistice, Wilhelm told him:

'You have not been brought here to make things difficult for the Supreme Command.'

Thus, Prince Max (on 3 October) wrote formally to President Wilson asking for an armistice and a peace based on the Fourteen Points. Several weeks of secret negotiation followed. The main obstacle to peace was the *Kaiser*, whose removal from power Wilson insisted on as a precondition for an armistice.

Constitutional reform

Prince Max's government introduced a series of constitutional reforms that turned Germany into a parliamentary monarchy: the three-class franchise was abolished in Prussia, the *Kaiser*'s powers over the army and navy were curtailed and the Chancellor and the government were made accountable to the *Reichstag*.

At this point, Ludendorff recovered his nerve. Morale among front-line soldiers had not collapsed and the Allied advance seemed to have run out of steam. He thus issued an order (without consulting Prince Max) to army commanders calling on all ranks to resist a humiliating surrender. Prince Max was appalled. He told Wilhelm that he must choose between Ludendorff and the cabinet. On 26 October, Ludendorff resigned and fled to Sweden. The next day Prince Max reiterated Germany's wish for an armistice, emphasising that the military authorities were at last subject to the civilian government.

In a three-week period, power had been transferred peaceably from the *Kaiser* to the *Reichstag*. The changes were essentially a 'revolution from above'. Nevertheless, much of what occurred resulted from the influence of the *Reichstag*. The day Ludendorff recommended an armistice, an inter-party *Reichstag* committee called for amendments to the constitution to permit the creation of a government responsible to the *Reichstag*. Thus while Germany's first parliamentary government came into being largely by order of the Supreme Command, it is also clear that mounting pressure from the *Reichstag* for political change could not have been resisted for much longer.

Most Germans paid little heed to the hugely important (but ill-publicised) reforms. After all, Wilhelm remained *Kaiser*, a prince was still chancellor, and the war continued. Nor did the *Reichstag* behave as if the changes represented a turning point in German history. It adjourned on 5 October and did not meet until 22 October, when it again adjourned until 9 November. These were hardly the actions of an institution that wished to shape events.

The revolutionary situation

However, by late October a revolutionary situation existed in Germany. Four years of privation had eroded the old relationship between ruler and subject. The shock of looming military defeat, after years of optimistic propaganda, radicalised popular attitudes. Germans were only too ready to blame Wilhelm for their country's misfortunes. Once the public became aware that US President Wilson regarded Wilhelm as an obstacle to peace, pressure for his abdication grew rapidly. Many south Germans blamed Prussia for Germany's misfortunes. Some Bavarians pressed for independence.

The Kiel mutiny and revolution

On 29 October rumours that the German High Seas Fleet was going to be sent out on a last do-or-die mission against the Royal Navy led to a mutiny among the sailors at Wilhelmshaven. The mutiny rapidly spread to Kiel and other ports. On 4 November dockworkers and soldiers in Kiel joined the mutinous sailors and set up workers' and soldiers' councils, on the 1917 Russian soviet model. Although Independent Socialists were in close touch with some mutineers, this was more a spontaneous protest movement than a politically-led mutiny. The sailors' councils were not disloyal to the government. On the contrary, they asked for representatives to come and listen to their grievances. The government sent a Majority Socialist who promised better conditions and reassured the sailors that there would be no 'suicide offensive'.

However, news of the Kiel mutiny fanned the flames of discontent across Germany. By 8 November workers' and soldiers' councils had been established in most major cities. The councils demanded peace and assumed control of local food supplies and services. In Bavaria the Wittelsbach dynasty was deposed and an independent socialist republic was proclaimed by Kurt Eisner. There was little resistance.

Divisions among the revolutionaries

The left-wing revolutionary wave which swept Germany in November 1918 was not a united force. Socialist forces were bitterly divided. Majority Socialists upheld democracy and wanted moderate reforms. They totally rejected Bolshevik-style communism. By contrast, Spartacists and shop stewards (see page 83), intoxicated by events in Russia, believed that Germany should follow a similar road. They campaigned for a socialist republic, based on the workers' and soldiers' councils, which would smash the institutions of imperial Germany. The USPD was between the two extremes. It demanded radical social and economic change to complement political reform. Its influence was curtailed by internal factional squabbles.

Extreme left-wing socialists tried to drive forward the workers' revolution by organising strikes and demonstrations by workers. The situation appeared menacing to many Germans, alarmed by what they perceived as 'Russian solutions' being put forward for German problems. However, many of the councils were controlled by moderate socialists who were anxious to maintain law and order and ensure the functioning of local services at a time of crisis. In most cases the councils co-existed uneasily with pre-revolutionary bodies.

Wilhelm II's abdication

On 7 November, Majority Socialist leaders threatened to withdraw support from the government unless Wilhelm abdicated and socialists were given greater representation in the cabinet. When Prince Max failed to persuade Wilhelm to abdicate, the Majority Socialist ministers Philipp Scheidemann and Gustav Bauer resigned and the Party agreed to call a general strike. Majority Socialist leaders took this step reluctantly. Their hand was forced by the Revolutionary Shop Stewards who had already called a strike for 9 November in protest against the arrest of some of their leaders.

Thus on 9 November most workers went on strike. A deputation of socialists, headed by Ebert and Scheidemann, called on Prince Max. They informed him that the local garrison in Berlin was on their side and that a new democratic government must be formed at once. Prince Max hesitated no longer. At noon he announced Wilhelm's abdication. By now even Hindenburg and General Groener, Ludendorff's successor, realised that the *Kaiser* must go. Abandoned by his generals, Wilhelm accepted the reality of the situation and fled to the Netherlands. Later on 9 November, Prince Max resigned and announced the formation of a new government, to be led by Ebert.

The German Republic

Ebert issued his first proclamation on 9 November, signing himself 'Imperial Chancellor', a title chosen to emphasise continuity between his government and that of Prince Max. This device conferred some semblance of legitimacy on the new government and helped to rally the officer corps and the civil service behind it. So did the fact that Ebert's government confirmed the old officials in power. Ebert declared that the goal of the government was to bring peace. He hoped to stabilise the political situation sufficiently to enable elections to take place as soon as possible for a National Assembly. This body would then draw up a new constitution. His main worry was that the extreme left would gain the upper hand. He was determined to prevent the descent into civil strife.

Ebert was under no illusions about his government's weak position. Its authority did not extend with certainty beyond Berlin, and it was not even accepted in all parts of the capital. Furthermore he knew that the Revolutionary Shop Stewards were planning to set up a provisional government, based on the workers' and soldiers' councils. To forestall this, Ebert decided to offer the USPD seats in the government.

The USPD was deeply divided. While moderates favoured acceptance, the left opposed collaboration with Ebert and demanded that the workers' and soldiers' councils should assume full power. By 21 votes to 19 the Independents finally decided to accept Ebert's offer. As a sop to their left wing they insisted on a number of concessions: only socialists must be included in the government; the government must declare that all power resided in the councils; and elections to the National Assembly must be delayed until the revolution was consolidated.

Reluctantly Ebert accepted the conditions. Therefore, on 10 November, a new government, the Council of Peoples' Commissars was formed. It consisted of three SPD members and three USPD members: Ebert and Hugo Haase acted as co-chairmen.

The workers' and soldiers' councils

On 10 November elections to form workers' and soldiers' councils were held in all the factories and garrisons in Berlin. At a mass meeting of the councils, the delegates approved the new government by a huge majority. An executive committee was elected to manage the affairs of the Berlin councils. This committee, which consisted of seven Majority Socialists, seven Independents and fourteen soldiers (many of whom were not socialists), began negotiations with the government to define the precise relationship between the two bodies.

The armistice

The change in government did not change the Allied attitude to Germany. In November 1918 German troops still controlled most of Belgium and huge swathes of eastern Europe. Allied leaders feared that Germany intended to use the armistice as a breathing space before resuming the war. The armistice terms were therefore designed to remove Germany's ability to fight:

- German troops had to withdraw beyond the Rhine.
- Germany had to surrender its U-boats, much of its surface fleet and its air force.
- Germany had to repudiate the Treaty of Brest-Litovsk.
- The blockade of Germany would continue until a final peace treaty had been signed.

The armistice terms were hugely resented in Germany. Nevertheless, the political situation made continuation of the war impossible. On 11 November the socialist government agreed to the terms and the First World War ended.

Germany had suffered 6,193,058 military casualties in the war, 2,044,900 of whom had died. A further 624,000 civilian deaths could be attributed to the war. Few families escaped the trauma of a death or a casualty.

Revolution and counter-revolution

How successful was Ebert in 1918–19?

In November 1918 it seemed that Germany might follow Russia down the path of communist revolution. Socialists controlled the *Reichstag* and socialist-controlled soviets assumed power in many of Germany's main towns. However, German socialists were bitterly divided and events in 1918–19 proved that most Germans were fiercely opposed to Russian-style communism.

The situation in November 1918

Relations between the Majority Socialists and Independents remained tense. A key issue was the authority of the workers' and soldiers' councils. Ebert viewed the councils with suspicion as a possible rival to parliamentary government. He therefore did his utmost to speed up the calling of the National Assembly.

The Independents were not opposed to this: most believed in parliamentary democracy. But whereas the Majority Socialists maintained that the revolution was over, the Independents believed that the gains of the revolution must be consolidated before the assembly met. They believed that the councils, the embodiment of the revolutionary will of the people, should supervise the implementation of a crash programme of socialism – the nationalisation of key industries, the breaking-up of the great landed estates and the democratisation of the army, the civil service and the judiciary.

As the weeks passed Ebert's position grew stronger. Permanent officials co-operated willingly enough with him, regarding him as Prince Max's legitimate successor. They would not work with the executive committee of the councils.

The Ebert–Groener pact

On 10 November General Groener telephoned Ebert. Groener agreed that the army would support the government in return for Ebert's promise to resist Bolshevism and to preserve the officers' authority against the councils. Ebert's critics, both at the time and since, have claimed that this 'pact' was proof that he betrayed the revolution. However, Ebert never made any secret of his distaste of Bolshevik revolution. His understanding with Groener was a reasonable precaution to protect his government against violence from the extreme left.

The Stinnes–Legien agreement

On 15 November the Stinnes–Legien agreement strengthened Ebert's position. (Hugo Stinnes was an industrialist and Carl Legien a trade union leader.) The trade unions agreed not to interfere with private ownership. In return, employers guaranteed full legal recognition to trade unions, agreed to workers' councils (which were to be introduced into all large factories) which would help to regulate wages and working conditions, and accepted an eight-hour working day. This agreement, quickly endorsed by the government, did much to satisfy workers' grievances.

The all-German Congress of Workers' and Soldiers' Councils

The Congress met in Berlin from 16 to 21 December. Over 300 of the 500 delegates supported the Majority Socialists and only 90 the Independent Socialists. Delegates passed resolutions demanding the nationalisation of key industries and the democratisation of the army.

Nevertheless, most delegates wanted Germany to be a parliamentary democracy. On 19 December Congress approved by a huge majority the government decision to hold elections to the National Assembly on 19 January. In the meantime, it agreed that power should be vested in Ebert's government.

The resignation of the Independent Socialists

On 23 December a force of sailors, which had come from Kiel to defend the government, was ordered to evacuate its quarters in the former royal palace. The disgruntled sailors barricaded themselves in the palace. Faced with a direct challenge to its authority, the government ordered a regular army division to attack the palace. Failing to dislodge the sailors, the troops withdrew. Violence quickly spread to other parts of Berlin. Fortunately for Ebert the sailors agreed to leave the building once the question of their back pay – the real cause of the action – was settled.

The Independents were incensed by Ebert's action, undertaken without their knowledge. On 29 December the three Independent ministers resigned. While Ebert now had a freer hand in the government, he also faced growing opposition from the streets.

Source B The Programme of the Majority Socialists – 29 December 1918.

To the German people!

Workers! Soldiers! Citizens! Citizenesses!

The Independents have left the government. The remaining members of the Cabinet vacated their posts so that the Central Council could have a wholly free hand. The latter unanimously re-instated them. The crippling disunity is at an end. The Reich government is reconstructed and united. It professes but one principle: the well-being, the survival, the indivisibility of the German Republic above all party interest ... And now for our programme.

At home:

To prepare for the National Assembly, urgently attend to feeding the people, initiate socialisation ... deal severely with war profiteering, to create jobs and support the unemployed, improve dependants' relief, to develop the people's army with all means and to disarm unauthorised personnel.

Abroad:

To achieve peace as quickly and as favourably as possible and to re-staff the foreign representations of the German Republic with men imbued with the new spirit. That is the broad outline of our programme prior to the National Assembly.

How, according to Source B, did the SPD hope to win the support of the electorate in the forthcoming elections to the National Assembly?

The Spartacist rising

On 1 January 1919, the Spartacists broke with the Independent Socialists and founded the German Communist Party. Led by Karl Liebknecht and Rosa Luxemburg, the communists declared that the National Assembly would be an organ of counter-revolution and called instead for government by workers' and soldiers' councils. On 6 January a revolutionary committee of 53 communists and shop stewards was set up. It issued a proclamation deposing Ebert and announcing the establishment of a revolutionary government. At the same time armed communists occupied newspaper offices and various public buildings in Berlin. The Spartacists hoped for a revolution on similar lines to that in Russia.

Faced with this challenge, Ebert's government first tried to negotiate with the Spartacist leaders, to no effect. It thus had little option but to turn to the army. Groener, in addition to using regular units, recruited hundreds of right-wing ex-soldiers, organised into *Freikorps* units. The *Freikorps* were only too willing to suppress the communist activity. By 15 January the Spartacist revolt was crushed after savage street fighting. Liebknecht and Luxemburg were shot while in police custody.

The events of January 1919, especially the murder of Liebknecht and Luxemburg, ensured the implacable hostility of the Marxist left towards the Majority Socialists (who now again called themselves the SPD) and the new parliamentary republic. In March 1919 the Independent Socialists came out in favour of government by workers' councils. Many Independents agreed with the Communists that Ebert had sold his soul to the conservative forces of imperial Germany.

Freikorps

The *Freikorps* or Free Corps were armed groups, formed mainly of nationalist and anti-communist ex-soldiers, which came into existence after the dissolution of the Imperial army. Many initially fought in the east in efforts to defend Germany's borders from communists, Poles and other national groups. They were also used by the army against communist risings in Germany. The *Freikorps* were formally disbanded in 1920 but some units continued to exist in secret. Many *Freikorps* members joined right-wing paramilitary organisations.

▲ Photograph of barricades in Berlin during the Spartacist rising. Are the men likely to be Spartacists or *Freikorps*? Explain your answer.

Further bloodshed

In February 1919 widespread strikes were organised by communists and in some towns there was sporadic street fighting. In March, the communists called for a general strike. Again Berlin became the scene of fighting; again the *Freikorps* were sent in. By mid-March 1919 order had been restored at the cost of over one thousand dead.

Bavaria

The elections to the Bavarian parliament in mid-January 1919 resulted in an overwhelming defeat for Eisner's Independents: they won only three seats. On the way to opening the first session of the new parliament in February, Eisner was murdered by a right-wing fanatic. Disorder broke out and the new coalition government, led by Majority Socialists, fled from Munich, leaving the city in the hands of Independents and Communists. On 9 April, the Communists, brushing aside the Independents, set up a soviet republic in Bavaria. The coalition government called on a local *Freikorps* unit for help. The army and *Freikorps* restored order in Munich after days of savage fighting. Hundreds of communists were shot.

Was there really a German revolution in 1918–19?

By the spring of 1919 a degree of stability had returned to Germany. The German revolution had run its course and the Weimar Republic had been established (see below). Serious doubts remain about the nature and extent of the supposedly revolutionary changes. Indeed, it is possible to argue that there was no real revolution at all.

Undoubtedly there existed the potential for revolutionary upheaval in November 1918. The effects of war and the shock of defeat shook the faith of large numbers of Germans in the old order. The *Kaiserreich* did not survive Germany's defeat. The *Kaiser* and the other German princes were deposed and parliamentary democracy was introduced. These were important changes. However, in the event, the revolution did not go much further than the October 1918 reforms. Society was left almost untouched by events. The civil service, judiciary and army all remained essentially intact. While improved working conditions were implemented, there was no major change in the structure of big business and land ownership.

Divisions on the left played into the hands of the forces of conservatism. It may be that the threat from the extreme left was over-exaggerated by contemporaries. While the Spartacists were vocal in propagandising their revolutionary creed, their actual base of support was minimal. They were thus easily defeated by a small number of soldiers and *Freikorps*. Indeed, the increasing dependence of the moderate left on the elites of imperial Germany in early 1919 strongly suggests that the forces of counter-revolution were already beginning to assert a dominant influence.

WORKING TOGETHER

Each of you should use your notes to construct a chronological table for the period 1914–19. Divide a sheet of paper into three columns with the following headings:

● Domestic social developments
● Domestic economic developments
● Domestic political events

List no more than ten main events/developments in each column. When you have finished, compare your table with those of your partner/group. What have you both/all included? What have you included that is different? Construct a joint table of what you both/all agree are the ten crucial events/developments. (You may have to reach some kind of compromise to complete the task.) In your opinion, is the joint list better or worse than your own original list?

KEY DATES: REVOLUTION AND COUNTER-REVOLUTION

1918

October The appointment of Prince Max von Baden as Chancellor led to the introduction of constitutional reform.

3 November German sailors mutinied at Kiel, sparking revolution across Germany.

9 November Wilhelm II abdicated. A provisional government under Ebert was formed.

10 November Ebert and General Groener agreed a pact.

11 November Germany signed an armistice with the Allies.

15 November The Stinnes–Legien agreement did much to satisfy workers' grievances.

1919

January The Spartacist uprising in Berlin was defeated by *Freikorps*.

January Election of the National Assembly which met at Weimar.

April A soviet republic in Bavaria was put down by *Freikorps*.

3 The establishment of the Weimar Republic

This section will examine the problems faced by the Weimar Republic in 1919. There could surely not have been a worse time for the establishment of a new democratic government. The war, and its immediate aftermath, had dislocated the economy, helped to initiate run-away inflation, and polarised divisions between right and left. Massive recriminations about where responsibility for Germany's defeat should lie served only to deepen political bitterness.

NOTE-MAKING

This section focuses on the establishment of the Weimar Republic and on the Versailles Peace Settlement. Both are crucial in terms of understanding what happened in Germany in the next two decades. For this reason ensure that your notes provide you with an understanding of how the Weimar Republic operated and its strengths and weaknesses. Your notes must also explain why Germans loathed the Treaty of Versailles. Finally, you should list the main problems facing the new government in 1919.

The 1919 constitution

What were the strengths and weaknesses of the Weimar constitution?

Having survived the threat from the left in 1918–19, Ebert's government was able to push ahead with plans to establish a new constitution. It was hoped that this constitution would establish full parliamentary democracy in Germany.

The 1919 elections

The elections for the National Assembly took place on 19 January 1919. Most political parties took the opportunity to re-form themselves. New names did not hide the fact that there was considerable continuity in the structure of the party system. The Nationalist Party (DNVP) was essentially an amalgamation of the old Conservative parties. The liberals remained divided between left (the Democrats) and right (the People's Party).

Friedrich Ebert (1871–1925)

Ebert was the son of a tailor. He became a saddler and entered politics through his trade union activities. In 1905 he was elected secretary to the SPD's central committee. His hard work behind the scenes was partly responsible for the SPD's success in the 1912 elections. Ebert himself was elected to the *Reichstag* in 1912. On the death of August Bebel in 1913, he was elected joint leader of the SPD alongside the more radical Haase. During the war, he worked with other left-wing parties, hoping to push the *Kaiser*'s administration towards an acceptance of parliamentary democracy. As well as a democrat, Ebert was a patriotic German who lost two sons during the war. By 1918–19 he was effectively leader of Germany.

Ebert was not a great orator or charismatic leader. His skills lay in other directions. He was a calm, patient and subtle negotiator – more concerned with improving the lot of the working class by evolutionary rather than revolutionary change.

Radical critics at the time and since have accused Ebert of betraying the interests of workers and of ensuring the failure of the revolution by allying with the forces of conservatism. In the eyes of the left, the new Germany looked remarkably like the old. The *Kaiser* was gone but the imperial institutions, run by men with imperial mentalities remained. The structure of German society was hardly affected by the revolution. The old elites – industrial barons, great landowners, civil servants and army officers – retained their power. In truth, however, radical socialism had limited support and little to offer Germany in 1918–19. Nationalisation of industry or massive land redistribution would have led to economic chaos. Any attempt to extend the power of the workers' councils might well have resulted in civil war.

Ebert had no wish to preside over chaos. Like most SPD leaders, he was suspicious of the extreme left. Given the left-wing threat, he had little option but to rely on the forces of reaction. In the context of 1918–19, Ebert had a sensible set of goals – to end the war, to maintain law and order and (most importantly) to establish parliamentary democracy. In the event, he achieved most of his goals – at least in the short term.

The results were a success for the forces of parliamentary democracy. Over 80 per cent of the electorate (including women) turned out to vote. The SPD won 165 seats (38 per cent of the vote) and the USPD 22. The Centre won 91 seats, the Democrats 75, the Nationalists 44 and the People's Party 19.

On 6 February 1919 the National Assembly met at the small town of Weimar: Berlin was considered unsafe given the unsettled conditions in the capital. On 10 February Ebert was elected first president of the Republic by 277 votes to 51. Given that no party had a clear majority, he asked the SPD to form a government. The SPD found allies in the Centre and Democrat parties – the so-called 'Weimar Coalition'. Over 75 per cent of the electorate had voted for these three parties, all of which were committed to the new republic. The election, a clear repudiation of the extreme right and left, seemed a promising start to a new chapter in German history. The new government was headed by Scheidemann and consisted of six Social Democrats, three Centrists and three Democrats.

Party	Percentage of votes	Number of seats
SPD	38	165
Centre	19.7	91
DDP	18.5	75
DNVP	10.3	44
USPD	7.6	22
DVP	4.4	19

▲ **Figure 1** The results of the first National Assembly.

Party name	Leaders	Political stance
Social Democratic Party SPD	Friedrich Ebert, Philipp Scheidermann, Hermann Müller	Largest socialist party, pro-Weimar
Centre Party	Matthias Erzberger, Heinrich Brüning	Catholic, pro-Weimar
German Democratic Party DDP	Walther Rathenau	Pro-Weimar, left-wing liberal
German Nationalist People's Party DNVP	Karl Helfferich, Alfred Hugenberg	Conservative, monarchist, anti-Weimar, racist
Independent Social Democratic Party USPD	Hugo Hasse	More left-wing than the SPD
German People's Party DVP	Gustav Stresemann	Became pro-Weimar under Stresemann, right-wing liberal
German Communist Party KPD	Ernst Thälmann	Communist party, founded 1919, anti-Weimar
National Socialist Party NSDAP	Adolf Hitler	Extreme right-wing, racist, anti-Weimar

▲ **Figure 2** The main German parties and their political stance 1912–29.

The Weimar constitution

The Assembly's main task was to draw up a new constitution. Largely the work of Hugo Preuss (a legal expert, scholar and liberal), the Weimar constitution attempted a careful balance of political forces, building on the traditions of German politics.

● Germany was to be a republic, its sovereignty based on the people.
● It remained a federal rather than a unitary state. The *Reich* was to comprise eighteen states (or *Länder*).
● The central government would control direct taxation, foreign affairs, the armed forces and communications.
● The states retained their powers over education, police and the churches.

Land (plural, *Länder*) – A state of the Federal Republic of Germany.

Proportional representation – This system of voting ensures that a party receives the same percentage of seats as votes received.

At national level Germany was to be governed by a president, a *Reichstag* and a *Reichsrat*. *Reichstag* deputies were to be elected every four years by all men and women over the age of twenty. A system of **proportional representation** was introduced, ensuring that all German views would be represented in the *Reichstag*. The chancellor and his ministers had to possess the *Reichstag's* confidence and were obliged to resign when they forfeited it. The *Reichstag* was to initiate and approve legislation.

The *Reichsrat* was to be composed of delegates from the German states. Each state was represented according to its population, except that no state was allowed to have more than two-fifths of the seats: this was designed to prevent Prussian preponderance. The *Reichsrat* could veto *Reichstag* legislation: its veto, in turn, could be over-ridden by a two-thirds vote of the *Reichstag*.

The president, directly elected by the people for seven years, was supreme commander of the armed forces, convened and dissolved the *Reichstag*, could block new laws by calling a referendum, and appointed the chancellor and the *Reich* government.

The Weimar constitution passed a bill of rights which guaranteed German people personal liberty, equality before the law, freedom of movement, expression and conscience, and freedom to belong to a trade union.

On 31 July 1919 the new constitution was passed by 262 votes to 75. Only the USPD and the right were in opposition. The adoption of the black, red and gold revolutionary flag of 1848 enraged right-wing nationalists.

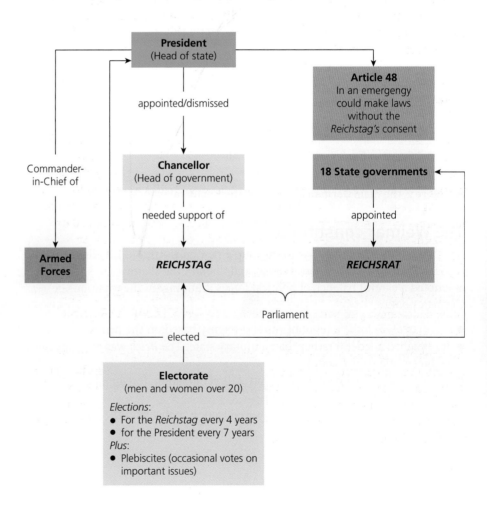

Figure 3 How the Weimar Republic ▶ was governed.

The weaknesses of the constitution

For historians looking for structural reasons to explain the Republic's eventual collapse, it is easy to claim that the 1919 constitution was a major source of weakness. The introduction of proportional representation is often seen as a major problem for the fledgling Republic. This system of voting encouraged the formation of new parties, usually representing particular interests. The fact that there were so many parties ensured no political party was ever likely to win an overall majority in the *Reichstag*. This led to coalition governments, which came and went with spectacular frequency. Such instability meant there was weak government.

The creation of a presidency, intended to act as a political counter-balance to the *Reichstag*, created a somewhat ambiguous system. Was the ultimate source of authority in the Republic vested in the *Reichstag* or the presidency? The situation was further exacerbated by the powers conferred on the president by Article 48. This provided the president with the authority to suspend civil rights and to take whatever action was required to restore law and order by the issue of presidential decrees. Although the intention was to create the means by which government could continue to function in a temporary crisis, Article 48 gave the president considerable potential power.

The strengths of the constitution

Arguably there was nothing structurally wrong with the 1919 constitution. It reflected both a broad spectrum of political opinion and successful constitutional practice at the time. It was thoroughly democratic and guaranteed a wide range of civil liberties. It also tried to build on Germany's traditional practices. In recognising an element of regional authority (for example, over the police) and regional influence, such as representation of the *Länder* in the *Reichsrat*, the constitution reflected pre-1914 practice.

Although there had been no proportional representation system before 1919, there had been a spate of political parties. Parties in pre-1914 Germany had usually represented sectional – usually class – interests. None of those parties ever won overall majorities in the *Reichstag*. Parties were used to forming coalitions. This was the way German politics operated. Proportional representation ensured that a wide variety of interests were represented in the *Reichstag*. The abundance of small parties did not necessarily mean weak government. The fundamental problem was the main parties' difficulty in creating coalitions and agreeing policies.

Presidential powers were strictly limited. Article 48 allowed the government sufficient flexibility to overcome the serious problems facing the Republic between 1919 and 1923.

Arguably, by providing an essentially liberal democratic framework, the 1919 constitution represented a major improvement upon the far more authoritarian 1871 constitution. Unfortunately, the Weimar Constitution could not control the conditions and circumstances in which it had to operate. No constitution could have provided for all the possible consequences arising from the immense problems Germany faced following its defeat in 1918.

The Versailles Peace settlement

What was the impact of the Treaty of Versailles on the Weimar Republic?

In January 1919 Allied leaders assembled in Paris to make peace with the defeated Central Powers. The main decisions were taken by the 'Big Three': Woodrow Wilson (the US president), David Lloyd George (the British prime minister) and Georges Clemenceau (the French premier). The peacemakers faced huge problems. The map of Europe as it had existed in 1914 had been swept away. There was political and economic chaos across much of central and eastern Europe and the possibility that Bolshevism might spread westwards from Russia.

To make matters worse, the Big Three held different views about how to ensure a durable peace settlement. Clemenceau wanted Germany punished and its power permanently reduced. Wilson was primarily concerned with establishing a just and lasting system of international relations. Lloyd George, not wanting to leave an embittered Germany, was inclined to leniency. Germany was not allowed to participate in the peace negotiations. On 7 May 1919 German delegates were handed a document consisting of 440 articles. They were told that they had three weeks to consider it and to formulate counter-proposals.

The Terms of the Treaty

Scheidemann's government lodged its objections at considerable length to the terms – to little effect. On 19 June the German cabinet rejected the Treaty and Scheidemann resigned. The new government, led by Bauer, knew that rejection of the Treaty was not really an option. Germany was in no state to fight a new war, a war which might result in Germany being dismembered. Accordingly the *Reichstag* sanctioned the signing of the Treaty (see Figure 4). This took place on 28 June 1919 in the Hall of Mirrors at Versailles – the same place in which the German Empire had been proclaimed in 1871.

The territorial terms

- Germany lost Alsace-Lorraine to France, Memel to Lithuania, Eupen and Malmédy to Belgium, and West Prussia and Posen to Poland.
- Danzig was to be a free port under League of Nations control.
- Germany lost North Schleswig to Denmark after a **plebiscite** in 1920.
- Germany lost parts of Upper Silesia to Poland after a plebiscite in 1922.
- The Rhineland was to become a demilitarised zone to act as a buffer between France and Germany. It was to be occupied by the Allies for fifteen years.
- The Saar was placed under League of Nations control. Its coalfields were to be controlled by France.
- Union with Austria was forbidden.
- Germany lost all its colonies.

The military terms

Germany was to have no tanks or military aircraft and its army was limited to 100,000 men. It was to have no large battleships and no submarines. Most of its fleet was to be surrendered to the Allies. (The German crews, in a last act of defiance, scuttled their ships at Scapa Flow in the Orkneys in June 1919.)

Plebiscite – A vote on a single issue on which the whole electorate is asked a yes / no question; an old-fashioned term for a referendum.

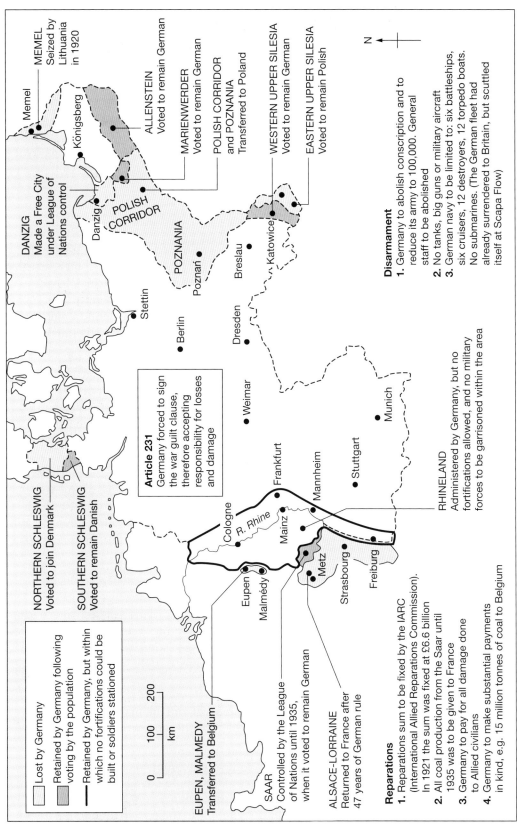

Memel
MEMEL Seized by Lithuania in 1920

Königsberg

ALLENSTEIN Voted to remain German

MARIENWERDER Voted to remain German

POLISH CORRIDOR and POZNANIA Transferred to Poland

WESTERN UPPER SILESIA Voted to remain German

EASTERN UPPER SILESIA Voted to remain Polish

DANZIG Made a Free City under League of Nations control

Danzig

POLISH CORRIDOR

POZNANIA

Poznań

Breslau

Katowice

Stettin

Berlin

Dresden

Weimar

Munich

N

Disarmament
1. Germany to abolish conscription and to reduce its army to 100,000. General staff to be abolished
2. No tanks, big guns or military aircraft
3. German navy to be limited to: six battleships, six cruisers, 12 destroyers, 12 torpedo boats. No submarines. (The German fleet had already surrendered to Britain, but scuttled itself at Scapa Flow)

Article 231
Germany forced to sign the war guilt clause, therefore accepting responsibility for losses and damage

Frankfurt

Mannheim

Stuttgart

RHINELAND
Administered by Germany, but no fortifications allowed, and no military forces to be garrisoned within the area

Cologne

R. Rhine

Mainz

Metz

Freiburg

Strasbourg

Eupen
Malmédy

NORTHERN SCHLESWIG Voted to join Denmark

SOUTHERN SCHLESWIG Voted to remain Danish

EUPEN, MALMEDY Transferred to Belgium

SAAR Controlled by the League of Nations until 1935, when it voted to remain German

ALSACE-LORRAINE Returned to France after 47 years of German rule

Lost by Germany

Retained by Germany following voting by the population

Retained by Germany, but within which no fortifications could be built or soldiers stationed

0   100   200
km

Reparations
1. Reparations sum to be fixed by the IARC (International Allied Reparations Commission). In 1921 the sum was fixed at £6.6 billion
2. All coal production from the Saar until 1935 was to be given to France
3. Germany to pay for all damage done to Allied civilians
4. Germany to make substantial payments in kind, e.g. 15 million tonnes of coal to Belgium

▲ **Figure 4** The Treaty of Versailles.

Reparations and War Guilt

By Article 231 Germany and its allies had to accept full responsibility for causing the war. This War Guilt clause provided a moral base for the Allied demands for Germany to pay reparations. The main difficulty was deciding how much Germany could and should pay, and how this money should be divided among the Allies. No single issue caused more acrimony. Wilson wanted a reparations settlement based on Germany's ability to pay. However, the British and French publics wanted to extract huge payments which would help the Allied countries to meet the cost of war and also weaken Germany financially for years to come. A Reparations Commission was eventually set up to determine the amount Germany should pay.

German opposition to Versailles

Germans were united in their condemnation of the Versailles Treaty. It was seen as a humiliating diktat – at variance with the Fourteen Points. If self-determination was the guiding principle, Germans found it incomprehensible that Germans in Austria, Danzig, Posen and West Prussia, Memel, Upper Silesia, the Sudetenland and the Saar were all placed under foreign rule. Germans, convinced they had fought a war of self-defence, found it impossible to accept the War Guilt clause and regarded reparations as totally unfair.

Given the different aims of the Big Three, the Treaty of Versailles was inevitably a compromise. It was not the Wilsonian peace envisaged by many Germans. But nor was it as severe as many Britons and Frenchmen had demanded. Arguably the Treaty was the worst of all worlds – too harsh to be permanently acceptable to most Germans, and too lenient to constrain Germany. After 1919 every German government would do its best to overthrow the Treaty. Accordingly, the peace settlement would last only as long as the victorious powers were in a position to enforce it on resentful Germans. However, in fairness to the peacemakers, it is hard to conceive of any peace treaty acceptable to the Allied powers and to their electorates in 1919 which the Germans would not have found humiliating. In the circumstances it may be that Versailles was a rational attempt at marrying principle and pragmatism in a dramatically altered world.

The vast majority of Germans did not see matters this way. They thought the Treaty unfair and in the years after 1919 saw it as the cause of most of Germany's problems. The fact that Republican politicians had been forced to accept the Treaty was unfortunate. From the start the Weimar Republic was associated with defeat and humiliation. The association of the Republic and Versailles was a means whereby the anti-republican right was able to attack the entire Weimar system.

> **Diktat** – A dictated settlement allowing for no negotiations.
>
> **Self-determination** – The right of people to decide their own form of government.

1 According to Source C, what was wrong with the Treaty of Versailles?

2 What did Hugo Preuss mean when he wrote that Versailles had turned Germany 'into the pariah among European nations by malevolently draining its national life-blood'?

3 Was Preuss's criticism of Versailles fair?

Source C Hugo Preuss, a German democrat and the man largely responsible for drawing up the Weimar constitution, writing in 1923.

.... everyone still expected a peace settlement in accordance with Wilson's 14 Points which all the belligerent countries had bindingly accepted as the basis for the peace. This would have left the new Germany with the political and economic chance to survive and gradually pull itself up again, instead of turning it into the pariah among European nations by malevolently draining its national life-blood. The criminal madness of the Versailles Diktat was a shameless blow in the face to such hopes based on international law and political common sense. The Reich constitution was born with this curse upon it. That it did not collapse immediately under the strain is striking proof of the intrinsic vitality of its basic principles; but its implementation and evolution were inevitably fatefully restricted and lamed thereby.

The Weimar Republic in 1919

What problems did the Weimar Republic face in 1919?

Having to sign the Treaty of Versailles was by no means the only problem the Weimar Republic had to deal with in 1919. The new government faced severe economic and financial difficulties. It also had to meet threats from Germans on the left and right who were totally opposed to the democratic Weimar system.

Economic and financial problems

The Weimar government was burdened with a terrible financial and economic legacy. Between 1913 and 1919 Germany's national debt had risen from 5,000 million marks to 144,000 million marks. Rather than increase taxation, the German government had financed the war through short-term loans and by printing money. Between 1914 and 1919 the value of the mark against the dollar had fallen from 4.20 marks to 14.00 marks and the price of basic goods had increased three- to four-fold. The situation only grew worse with the coming of peace. By early 1920 a dollar was worth 100 marks. Narrowing the massive gap between government income and expenditure, thereby bringing about the control of inflation, could only be achieved by increasing taxation and/or by cutting expenditure. Neither of these options was politically attractive.

Germany also faced severe economic problems. As a result of the First World War, Germany lost most of its merchant shipping, much of its fishing fleet and all its property in Allied territories. The Allied blockade, which did not end until the signing of the Versailles Treaty, had worsened an already dire food supply situation. By the terms of Versailles, Germany lost:

- nearly 15 per cent of its arable land
- 75 per cent of its iron ore
- 68 per cent of its zinc ore
- a quarter of its coal production.

Not surprisingly German manufacturing output was 30 per cent lower in 1919 than in 1914. The country moreover had a large trade deficit and faced the difficulties of re-adjusting a war economy to the requirements of peace. Its economic and financial problems would not be helped by the enormous reparation payments demanded by the Allies in 1921 (see pages 90–2).

The threat from the left

After the revolution of 1918–19 socialist politics remained in a state of confusion. The SPD was committed to parliamentary democracy. The KPD, by contrast, took its lead from Bolshevik Russia and pressed for proletarian revolution. The USPD, caught in the middle, pressed for the creation of a socialist society but within a democratic framework. In December 1920 the USPD came to an end. Its members either joined the KPD or the SPD. By 1920 the KPD was thus a mass party with some 400,000 members. It wanted to overthrow the Weimar Republic, establish a one-party socialist state which would then restructure Germany's social and economic fabric. The threat from the KPD, which frightened many Germans, was probably exaggerated. Unable to win the mass support of the working classes, the Communists proved incapable of mounting a unified attack on the Republic. The repression they had endured at the hands of the *Freikorps* in 1919

The 'stab in the back' myth

In November 1919 Hindenburg gave evidence to a committee of the *Reichstag* studying Versailles. According to Hindenburg, the shameful Treaty was signed because of the anti-patriotic sentiments of a group of left-wing politicians, the so-called 'November Criminals' who had founded the Republic – men like Ebert and Matthias Erzberger. They were the same men responsible for the 'stab in the back' of the armed forces that led to military collapse in 1918.

The war, Hindenburg and nationalists argued, had been lost not because of military defeat but as a result of the betrayal of unpatriotic forces within Germany – pacifists, socialists, democrats and Jews. This distorted interpretation of the events of 1918–19 was universally accepted by right-wing parties. It absolved military leaders from responsibility for their own failings in 1918 and it played on popular resentment of the humiliating Treaty of Versailles. It acted as a powerful stick with which to beat the new leaders of Germany.

Volkisch **groups** – These groups had their roots in the *Kaiserreich*. Their members were nationalist, racist and anti-Semitic. They demanded strong, authoritarian government.

removed some of their ablest and most dedicated supporters. There was little hope of reconciliation between the KPD and the SPD. The suppression of the Spartacists by Ebert's government in 1919 was neither forgotten nor forgiven by the extreme left.

The threat from the right

Ebert's willingness to compromise with the old order in 1919 did not endear him to those who regretted its passing. Right-wing political forces totally rejected the Weimar system and its democratic principles. They demanded strong government, vied with each other to attack the Versailles settlement, and had considerable success in propagating the notion that the German army had been 'stabbed in the back' in 1918 by the 'November Criminals'.

The right was divided between conservatives and radicals. Conservatives, many of whom wished to restore the monarchy, tended to join the Nationalist Party (DNVP). This was a coalition of nationalist forces which included the old imperial conservative parties but also embraced such groups as the Fatherland Party (see page 75) and the Pan-German League (see page 36). It remained the party of landowners and employers but it also had the support of many middle-class Germans. Conservatives continued to exert influence in a number of key institutions – the army, civil service, the judiciary and the education system, all of which were preserved in much their old form. Large numbers of army officers, bureaucrats, judges and professors were lukewarm or indeed actively hostile to the new Republic.

After 1918 there were numerous radical right-wing – or *volkisch* – groups, which had little sympathy with the conservatives. These groups, nationalistic, anti-democratic, anti-socialist and anti-Jewish, wanted to smash the Republic. Ex-soldiers, many of whom had belonged to *Freikorps* units, were particularly attracted to the radical right. Extreme right-wing groups were particularly active in Bavaria (see page 84). In September 1919 an obscure corporal joined one such right-wing group, the German Workers' Party, in Munich. The obscure corporal was Adolf Hitler.

WORKING TOGETHER

Work in pairs. One of you should defend the new Weimar Republic. What were its strengths? Why was it better than what had gone before? The other should attack it. What were its weaknesses? What form of government did Germany require instead?

Now decide whether it is easier to attack or defend the Weimar Republic. Then, between you devise a poster praising or criticising the new government. This should be done in graphic form. Use no more than twenty words. Explain your poster to other members of the class.

4 Troubled years, 1919–23

The creation of a broadly based democratic coalition did not result in a period of stability and consolidation for the new Republic. The years between 1919 and 1923 were years of almost continuous crisis. This section will examine the nature of the problems faced by Weimar politicians.

The threat from the right and left in 1920

Why did the Kapp Putsch fail?

The new constitution came into effect on 14 August 1919. One week later the National Assembly left Weimar and returned to Berlin which was now regarded as safe. The most pressing task of the new *Reichstag* was to try to resolve Germany's awesome financial problems. The Minister of Finance, Matthias Erzberger, set about trying to cut government expenses by reducing the army and increasing taxation, particularly on the wealthy classes. His measures were attacked by the right-wing press. Erzberger, hated by the right for signing the armistice in 1918, was seriously wounded in an assassination attempt in January 1920. Assassination was just one of the methods used by the extreme right in its battle with the Weimar government.

The Kapp Putsch

The need to reduce the size of the army created great unease within the ranks of the army and the *Freikorps*. Dr Wolfgang Kapp, a former Prussian civil servant and a founder member of the Fatherland Party (see page 75) and Captain Waldemar Pabst, who had ordered the murder of Rosa Luxemburg and Karl Liebknecht, plotted to overthrow the government. They had the support of General von Luttwitz, who commanded troops in Berlin and who was considered to be 'the father of the *Freikorps*'. When the government ordered the disbanding of Captain Ehrhardt's Marine Brigade, Kapp and Luttwitz determined to exploit the situation. Ehrhardt's 5,000 *Freikorps* troops marched into Berlin in March 1920.

President Ebert and Gustav Bauer's cabinet prudently moved to Stuttgart. Kapp installed himself in the vacant chancellery and declared that the Weimar government was overthrown. Despite requests from Ebert and Bauer to put down the putsch, the regular army did nothing to support Germany's legitimate government. But nor did it support Kapp. General von Seeckt, the senior officer in the Defence Ministry, declared:

'Troops do not fire on troops … When Reichswehr fires on Reichswehr then all comradeship within the officers corps will have vanished.'

Despite the army's neutral stance, the putsch quickly collapsed. It is usually claimed that this resulted from a general strike, called by the SPD and supported by the Communists. However, President Ebert opposed a general strike, fearing that it would plunge Germany into civil war and the Communists initially refused to support the SPD-initiated strike. The strike only really got going when the putsch was on its last legs.

In reality, the putsch collapsed because *Reichswehr* leaders, placing unity of the army above everything else, did not back Kapp and the vast majority of the government bureaucrats refused to acknowledge the legitimacy of Kapp's government or obey his orders. After four days, when it was clear that they exerted no real authority, Kapp and Luttwitz fled the country and Ehrhardt's troops left Berlin. In some respects, the quick collapse of the Kapp Putsch was a major success for the Republic. But the fact that it had occurred at all highlighted the threat from the right.

NOTE-MAKING

This section examines the years of crisis from 1919 to 1923. Your notes should ensure that that you are aware of the main threats to the Weimar Republic in this period. The headings and sub-headings in the text should help your note-making. As you make your notes, try to decide whether the problems facing Weimar's politicians were essentially economic. What other factors threatened the Republic's stability?

Threat from right

Reichswehr – The name for the German army after 1919.

3 War, revolution and democracy, 1914–23

95

The influence of the *Reichswehr*

The army leadership had revealed its dubious loyalty to the Republic in March 1920. Yet amazingly Seeckt, who had not lifted a finger against Kapp, was appointed Chief of the Army Command at the end of the month. Seeckt accepted the need to co-operate with the Republic: he feared civil war and wanted stability. But from 1920 to 1926, under Seeckt's influence, the army was turned, according to Scheidemann, into a 'state within a state'. It appeared to have a privileged position which placed it in effect beyond direct democratic accountability. The army was supposedly non-political. But this was not the case. Most of its officers were conservative reactionaries. Given the small size of the German army after 1919, officers were able to pick recruits for military service. Many were men who had served in the *Freikorps*. The result was that the *Reichswehr* would act to crush communist revolt. But there was no guarantee that it would put down a right-wing putsch.

The situation in Bavaria

While Kapp was in Berlin, and the government paralysed, there was unrest in Munich. The local army commander General von Mohl demanded that he be given full emergency powers. Johannes Hoffman, Bavaria's SPD minister-president resigned in protest. He was replaced by conservative Gustav von Kahr. Kahr's government provided a safe haven in Bavaria for right-wing extremists.

Adolf Hitler (1889–1945)

Hitler was born in Austria in 1889. From 1908 to 1913 he lived as something of a down-and-out in Vienna, making a living selling posters and postcards. In 1913 he moved to Germany. Enlisting in the German army in 1914, he quickly found his vocation, fighting in many of the major battles on the Western Front. There are two remarkable facts about his army career: first he survived; and second he only rose to become corporal. His superiors thought he had no leadership qualities. He was a good soldier, winning the Iron Cross for bravery.

For Hitler the war was a crucial experience. He enjoyed the comradeship of the trenches and the fact that his life had a purpose. He was horrified when, recovering in hospital from a gas attack, he heard news of Germany's surrender. He wrote later:

So it had all been in vain. In vain all the sacrifices. In vain the hours in which, with mortal fear clutching at our hearts we did our duty. In vain the death of two million. Had they died for this, so that a gang of wretched criminals could lay hands on the fatherland?

On leaving hospital, Hitler returned to Munich. Impressing army authorities with his speaking talents and his nationalist views, he was given two jobs: lecturing troops in (right-wing) political education; and keeping an eye on extremist groups. In September 1919 he was sent to investigate the German Workers' Party – founded in January 1919 by Anton Drexler. Drexler's intention was to win working-class support for nationalist ideas. His 'party' (it only had 55 members) was one of many such groups springing up in Munich. Hitler accepted Drexler's invitation to join the party. He was soon its leading member. Indeed by 1923 he was the leading right-wing politician in Bavaria.

Hitler can be seen as a cynical opportunist who simply wanted power for power's sake. However, most historians now see him as a genuine idealist who held very strong principles to which he clung until his death. He certainly could be pragmatic, seizing the main chance when it presented itself, even if this meant putting his long-term plans on ice. But belief in principles and skill at tactical manoeuvring are not mutually exclusive.

While Hitler's ideology was described as 'a vast system of bestial, Nordic nonsense' by historian Hugh Trevor-Roper, his views – which were by no means new – had a certain (brutal) logic. He saw life as a struggle (his book *Mein Kampf* translates as 'My Struggle') in which only the strongest nations, races and individuals triumphed. He believed that Germany was – or should be – the world's greatest nation and that the Germans were – or should be – the master race. For Hitler, the opposite of the German was the Jew. He blamed Jews for all Germany's ills and saw them plotting to take over the world. Hitler did not believe in equality or democracy. He believed that, just as some nations and races were superior, so some individuals were superior. He believed that Germany needed a strong, heroic leader who would express the popular will, and that that leader should work to ensure that Germany dominated Europe. This meant expanding eastwards, acquiring land from the inferior Slav races and destroying the evils of Communism in Russia. The fact that this might lead to war did not worry Hitler. In his view, war was the highest form of struggle.

The Nazi Party

Adolf Hitler, who joined the German Workers' Party in September 1919, ensured that the Party was more successful than other right-wing groups in Bavaria. Resigning from the army, he threw himself into politics, soon proving himself a brilliant speaker in the Munich beer halls. In February 1920 he announced a 25 Point Programme, a mix of nationalism and socialism, to a 2,000-strong audience at the Hofbrauhaus beer cellar. The German Workers' Party now adopted a new name – the National Socialist German Workers' Party (NSDAP). In 1921 Hitler became Party leader. By 1922 the Party, helped by Bavarian army officers who provided recruits and money, was the biggest and best organised right-wing group in Bavaria, with its own newspaper – the *Volkischer Beobachter* (*Volkisch Observer*). Attracting support from all types of people, especially ex-soldiers and young idealists, it seemed to be a party of action. In 1921 Hitler created the SA (*Sturm-Abteilung* or storm troopers) – a paramilitary organisation which defended Nazi speakers and attacked left-wing groups. By mid-1923 the Party had some 55,000 members.

Source D Some of the 25 Points of National Socialism, 24 February 1920.

1 We demand the union of all Germans, on the basis of the right of the self-determination of peoples, to form a Greater Germany.

2 We demand equality of rights for the German People in its dealings with other nations and abolition of the peace Treaties of Versailles and Saint-Germain.

3 We demand land and colonies to feed our people and to settle our surplus population.

4 Only those of German blood ... may be members of the nation. No Jew may be a member of the nation.

8 All further non-German immigration must be prevented.

10 It must be the first duty of each citizen of the State to work with his mind or with his body. The activities of the individual may not clash with the interests of the whole, but must proceed within the frame of the community and be for the general good.

11 We demand the abolition of incomes unearned by work.

14 We demand profit-sharing in large industrial enterprises.

16 We demand ... the immediate communalising of big department stores.

Unrest in the Ruhr

In the Ruhr industrial area, the Communists, making use of the general strike, tried to seize power in March 1920. Some 50,000 people formed a Red Army and took control of the Ruhr. After attempts at negotiation failed, the government sent military units to crush the revolt. Over a thousand workers lost their lives in the bloodshed that followed. The brutal suppression of the Ruhr workers in April had a sobering effect on the labour movement. There were no more general strikes during the whole period of the Weimar Republic.

Unequal justice

Those responsible for the Ruhr uprising were severely punished. However, those who supported the Kapp Putsch were let off virtually scot-free. In August 1920 there was a general amnesty for *Freikorps* officers who were then welcomed into the armed forces. Kapp returned to Germany in 1922 to face trial but died before proceedings began. Luttwitz was granted early retirement. The judiciary, like the army, remained a conservative force, which doubted the legitimacy and principles of the new republic.

The 25 Point Programme – The NSDAP party programme, announced by Hitler on 24 February 1920 to a packed audience of about 2,000 people in the function room of the Hofbräuhaus, Munich's most famous and prestigious beer hall.

1 Which of the points in Source D are 'nationalist'?
2 Which of the points are 'socialist'?
3 Why might Hitler's programme appeal to Germans in 1920 and thereafter?

KEY DATES: THE THREAT FROM THE RIGHT AND LEFT IN 1920

February The 25 Points of National Socialism proclaimed by Hitler.

March The Kapp Putsch took place in Berlin; it soon failed.

April A Communist rising in the Ruhr was crushed by the army.

Political and financial instability 1920–22

What were the main political and financial problems facing Germany between 1920 and 1922?

Having survived the Kapp Putsch, the Republic faced serious financial and political difficulties. Coalition governments proved unable or unwilling to tackle Germany's deep-seated financial problems

The 1920 elections

The Weimar coalition fell apart in the wake of the unrest in 1920. In elections in June 1920, the SPD share of the vote fell by 43 per cent. The DDP dropped by 55 per cent. The KPD fielded candidates for the first time but obtained only 1.7 per cent of the votes. The USPD, however, more than doubled its share so that it was only three points behind the SPD. On the right, votes for the DVP trebled and the DNVP improved its showing by almost 50 per cent.

Before the election, the main Weimar coalition parties – SPD, Centre and DDP – had commanded 78 per cent of the seats in the National Assembly. Now those parties had only 45 per cent of the *Reichstag* seats. Centre Party politician Konstantin Fehrenbach eventually agreed to form a minority government that included the Centre, the DDP and the DVP – but not the SPD. Fehrenbach proved unequal to the weighty problems that faced Germany.

8 different governments between 1918–1923

Chancellor	Date	Partners
Friedrich Ebert (SPD)	November 1918–February 1919	Coalition of socialists
Philipp Scheidemann (SPD)	February 1919–June 1919	SPD, Centre, DDP
Gustav Bauer (SPD)	June 1919–March 1920	SPD, Centre, DDP (from October)
Hermann Müller (SPD)	March 1920–June 1920	SPD, Centre, DDP
Konstantin Fehrenbach (Centre)	June 1920–May 1921	DDP, Centre, DVP
Joseph Wirth (Centre)	May 1921–October 1921	SPD, DDP, Centre
Joseph Wirth (Centre)	October 1921–November 1922	SPD, DDP, Centre
Wilhelm Cuno (non-aligned)	November 1922–August 1923	DDP, Centre, DVP

▲ **Figure 5** The chancellors and the coalitions of the Weimar Republic from 1919 to 1923.

The problem of reparations

In May 1921 the Allies set reparations at 138 billion gold marks. They declared that unless the German government made a back payment of 12 billion gold marks in reparations, the Ruhr industrial area would be occupied. One billion was to be paid by the end of the month. Finding it impossible to meet these terms, Fehrenbach resigned in May. He was replaced by a minority government led by Joseph Wirth, also from the Centre Party. Despite bitter opposition from nationalists, Wirth agreed to accept the demands for reparations under the policy that became known as fulfilment. By seeking to fulfil the reparation terms, Wirth and his Minister of Reconstruction Walther Rathenau sought to demonstrate that the Treaty obligations were impossible. They hoped that this would lead to a revision of the Allied demands. Opposed to reparation payments, the right mounted a massive hate campaign against the Wirth government and its fulfilment policy.

The problem of inflation

German finances, according to historian V. Berghahn (1973) remained in 'an unholy mess'. Rather than reducing government spending and increasing taxation – both of which would have been highly unpopular – Weimar governments continued to print more money, believing that this would enable Germany to overcome the problems of demobilisation while also reducing the real value of its internal debt. The result was that the inflationary trend continued – with a vengeance.

Not all historians are convinced that the inflationary policy was a mistake. Economic historian Holtfrerich, for example, has claimed that in the years from 1919 to 1922, Weimar's inflationary economic policy amounted to a 'rational strategy' which was in Germany's national interest. By printing money, the Republic was able to maintain economic growth and increase production. The mark's devaluation against all other currencies meant that German goods were cheap abroad while foreign goods were expensive in Germany. The result was that Germany recovered some of its lost markets overseas. The high demand for German goods also meant that there was little unemployment. Indeed, the German economy compared very favourably with other European countries between 1919 and 1922. Britain, for example, had an unemployment rate of nearly 17 per cent in 1921. In the same year Germany had only 1.8 per cent unemployed and rising wage levels. This industrial activity acted as a major stimulus for investment and large sums of money, especially from the USA, poured into Germany. Holtfrerich argued that the inflationary policy was not only economically beneficial but was politically unavoidable for the survival of the Republic. Any kind of retrenchment policy in the first years of the Republic would have had dire economic and social consequences which would have decisively destabilised the new democracy.

But Holtfrerich's claims are not totally convincing. Arguably, the so-called 'good inflation' up to 1923 simply led to the 'bad inflation' of 1923 (see pages 101–2) with all its accompanying problems. Thus, Germany was living on borrowed time. The Allied demands for reparations added to Germany's financial problems. The Weimar governments found it more convenient to print even more money than to raise taxes or cut spending.

The problem of Upper Silesia

Events in Upper Silesia in the spring of 1921 increased the sense of crisis. The Polish government refused to accept the result of a plebiscite in March 1921, in which 60 per cent of the population voted for Germany. Instead, the Polish government supported Polish insurgents who laid claim to the bulk of the province. The German government responded by arming paramilitary units, determined to ensure that the vote be respected and Upper Silesia be returned to Germany.

The Allies managed to put an end to the fighting and accepted a report by the League of Nations which suggested that four-fifths of Upper Silesia should be given to Poland, including certain industrial areas that had voted overwhelmingly for Germany.

Political extremism

In March 1921 the army and police suppressed a Communist revolt in Saxony. Right-wing groups were also prepared to use violence, assassinating men they considered traitors. (Erzberger, for example, was assassinated in August 1921.) Many of the assassinations were committed by ex-*Freikorps* members who formed murder squads to carry on the fight against the left. Judges usually condoned their crimes. Between 1919 and 1922 there were 376 political assassinations – 22 by the left and 354 by the right. Ten left-wingers were sentenced to death. Not a single right-wing assassin received the death sentence. Of the 354 right-wing murders, 326 went unpunished.

Political instability

Wirth felt obliged to resign in October 1921 when the *Reichstag* majority insisted that the government should step down in protest at the flagrant disregard of the right of self-determination in Upper Silesia. It was a futile gesture since no government could be formed without the Centre Party and Wirth soon returned to office.

The outstanding figure in the second Wirth cabinet was the new foreign secretary Walther Rathenau, an enthusiastic advocate of the policy of fulfilment. In 1922 he signed the Treaty of Rapallo with the Bolshevik government in Russia. The Treaty restored diplomatic relations between the two countries – the two 'outcast' nations in Europe. The Treaty satisfied the need of the Bolshevik state for foreign aid and capital investment. Germany was able to use Russia, which was inaccessible to the Allied Control Commission, to secretly develop new military weapons and techniques.

Growing anti-Semitism

Six weeks after signing the Treaty of Rapallo, Rathenau, a Jew, was gunned down by a right-wing extremist. Rathenau's murder was the most alarming sign of the mounting tide of anti-Semitism. The fact that a number of leading figures on the left were Jewish was taken as clear evidence among right-wing Germans that the Jews were responsible for Germany's defeat in 1918. The right blamed the Jews for subverting loyal German workers with their Judeo-Marxist ideology (Marx was Jewish) and for accepting the humiliating peace. Right-wing politicians and newspaper editors claimed that many Jews had avoided service in the war, fattening themselves with war profits. They were also blamed for inflation, the black market and fulfilment politics.

Some 100,000 orthodox Jewish immigrants from the east, escaping persecution in Poland and Russia, did not help matters. With their strange dress and alien habits, and speaking only Hebrew and Yiddish, they were seen as foreign invaders and a threat to the German race, culture and identity.

The financial crisis, 1922–23

In July 1922 the German government asked for permission to suspend reparation payments. The Allies refused. By December Germany's national debt had reached 469,000 million marks. Meanwhile inflation increased at a frightening pace, providing fresh ammunition for right- and left-wing extremists. Tension between capital and labour mounted when industrialist Hugo Stinnes suggested that German workers should work an extra two hours per day without additional pay for at least ten years in order to overcome the present problems. His suggestion was anathema to most Germans. Instead the government tried to cut back expenditure to balance the budget.

The SPD, which had united with the rump of the USPD (the remainder of the USPD had joined the KPD), now refused to support Wirth's government. Wirth resigned in November 1922 and was replaced by Wilhelm Cuno. Cuno's government crucially lacked the support of the SPD.

KEY DATES: POLITICAL AND FINANCIAL INSTABILITY 1920–22

1920 After the June elections, the SPD, Centre and DDP parties were no longer strong enough to control the *Reichstag*.

1921

March A Communist rising in Saxony was crushed.

May The Allies set reparations at 138 billion gold marks.

1922 Germany signed the Treaty of Rapallo with Russia.

The crisis of 1923

Why did the Weimar Republic survive the crisis of 1923?

In 1923 the Republic's economic, financial and political crisis came to a head. So serious was the crisis that by the autumn of 1923 the Republic's survival seemed improbable. The fact that it survived, according to historian D. Peukert (1991), demonstrates that 'there are no entirely hopeless situations in history'.

The occupation of the Ruhr

When Germany failed to deliver reparation payments to the Allies in January 1923, French premier Poincare determined to act. French and Belgian troops numbering 60,000 occupied the Ruhr valley, the industrial heart of Germany. Too weak to take military action, Cuno's government ordered the suspension of reparations and supported a policy of 'passive resistance'. It urged workers in the Ruhr to go on strike and to refuse to co-operate with the French–Belgian invaders, in return for the continued payment of their wages by the German government.

The French–Belgian invasion initially helped to unite Germans in a common cause. Even the Communists joined in the struggle against the invaders. In retaliation, the French seized the Ruhr coalmines and railways and began the confiscation of German assets. As the crisis deepened, there were a number of attacks on the invaders. The French responded by executing Germans held responsible for the attacks.

The cost of passive resistance to Germany was huge – possibly more than twice the annual charge of reparations which it declared itself unable to pay. Prepared to pay out millions of marks to those who lost revenue as a result of the policy, the government was also unable to collect taxes from the Ruhr. Moreover, the French prevented the delivery of coal to the rest of Germany, thus forcing its import. In this situation German finances fell into total disarray. The government simply issued vast quantities of paper banknotes – with the result that the mark collapsed to meaningless levels. In December 1922 the exchange rate had stood at 8,000 marks to the dollar. By November 1923 it had reached 4.2 billion. Some 200 factories worked full time to produce bank notes. By the autumn of 1923 it cost more to print a note than the note was worth. The German currency in effect became worthless. Workers were paid by the day. In cafes a cup of coffee increased in price as people drank it. In 1919 a loaf of bread had cost one mark; by late 1923 a loaf cost 100 billion marks.

The effects of hyperinflation

Some Germans lost but others benefited from the effects of hyperinflation. There were winners and losers in every social class. Levels of indebtedness and savings were crucial to a person's fortune or misfortune.

The real winners from inflation were those Germans who were able to pay off their debts, mortgages and loans with inflated and worthless money. This worked to the advantage of such groups as landowners, businessmen and homeowners (including many members of the middle class). Those who recognised the situation for what it was, made massive gains by buying more real estate from the naïve and desperate. This was particularly true of big business which exploited the cheap credit to create large business conglomerations. Hugo Stinnes, for example, controlled a fifth of German industry by the end of 1923. In some respects the German state was the biggest financial beneficiary: the hyperinflation relieved it of the crippling burden of debt.

BREAD PRICES IN GERMANY (IN MARKS)
1908
0.63
January 1923
250
September 1923
1,500,000,000
November 1923
201,000,000,000

Hyperinflation

Hyperinflation occurs when the amount of money in an economy increases massively. This simply pushes prices up and the spiral of printing money spins out of control.

The losers as a results of Germany's hyperinflation were the savers, particularly those who had purchased war bonds which became worthless. Those living on fixed incomes or welfare support – not least the retired and sick – also suffered. Most grants and pensions lost value in real terms since the increases generally did not keep pace with inflation.

The mass of the population was probably between the extremes of profit and loss. German farmers coped reasonably well since food remained in demand and farmers were less dependent on the money economy for the provision of the necessities of life. The wages and salaries of employees are the most difficult to interpret. While workers' real wages had probably increased between 1918 and 1922, in 1923 trade unions were unable to negotiate wage settlements which kept pace with the rate of inflation. Thus there was probably a decline in living standards. However, given the amount of money in circulation there was relatively little unemployment.

Traditionally the hyperinflation has been portrayed as an economic catastrophe with damaging social consequences which paved the way later on for the collapse of the Republic and the rise of Hitler. This may be going too far. But many Germans undoubtedly suffered in 1923. The Republic was totally discredited in the eyes of millions who had patriotically brought war bonds and who now felt betrayed. The republicans it seemed had first stabbed the country in the back and then robbed the little man of his savings. Moreover, when another economic crisis developed after 1929 many Germans had little confidence in Weimar's ability to deal with the situation.

Gustav Stresemann

By August 1923 Cuno's government was replaced by a new government led by Gustav Stresemann, the leader of the People's Party (DVP). It was clear to Stresemann that Germany teetered on the verge of complete collapse. It was equally clear that inflation had to be brought back under control, the German currency stabilised and the occupation of the Ruhr ended. Consequently, in September Stresemann called off passive resistance in the Ruhr, promised to resume reparation payments, and set in motion plans to introduce a new currency. However, Germany's economic woes could not be rectified overnight. Worse still, from the government's point of view, economic suffering resulted in political action.

Bavaria vs Berlin

When Stresemann's government ordered an end to passive resistance, the Bavarian government, led by Kahr (see page 96), declared a state of emergency. Berlin then invoked paragraph 48 to give *Reichswehr* minister Otto Gessler full executive powers. A struggle for power now developed between the government in Munich and the government in Berlin. When Gessler demanded that the local army commander General von Lossow be dismissed, Kahr increased the stakes by appointing him commander-in-chief of an independent Bavarian contingent. Kahr now contemplated setting up a national dictatorship.

Communist action

As the economic crisis deepened, Communist support increased. In October Heinrich Brandler, the KPD leader, acting on orders from Moscow, planned to organise a general strike in Saxony and Thuringia that would spark a German revolution. Ebert acted firmly and the Communist insurgency was suppressed almost before it began. Nevertheless, there were three days of bloody fighting in Hamburg before the army and police crushed a workers' revolt.

The Munich Putsch

In November 1923 Hitler attempted to seize power. Within the NSDAP he had built up excitement to such a degree that he had to do something to maintain his credibility. What he did made sense. In September 1923 he was instrumental in forming a Battle League of right-wing groups. War hero General Ludendorff gave his support. The Battle League's plan was to win control of Bavaria and then to march on Berlin, much as Italian Fascist Benito Mussolini had seized power by marching on Rome in 1922. Preparations were reasonably thorough and Kahr had indicated that he might support a putsch. When, at the last minute, he backed down, Hitler decided to go ahead anyway.

On 8 November Kahr was addressing a large meeting at the Burgerbraukellar in Munich. Some 600 SA men surrounded the beer cellar and Hitler burst in, brandishing a revolver. Announcing that the National Revolution had begun, he 'persuaded' Kahr, Lossow and the police chief Hans von Seisser to support him. The people in the beer cellar roared their approval. But the putsch soon began to go wrong. Kahr, Lussow and Seisser, set free at Ludendorff's insistence, promptly informed the Berlin government of the situation. The Weimar government immediately ordered the Bavarian authorities to crush the putsch.

On 9 November Hitler led some 3,000 men into Munich, hoping for a show of mass support. Instead, as the Nazi column neared the town centre, armed police opened fire and sixteen marchers died. Hitler, lucky to survive, escaped the scene. Refusing to flee to Austria, he was quickly arrested.

In early 1924 Hitler and Ludendorff were tried for treason. The trial made Hitler a national figure. Claiming that he had only acted as a patriotic German, Hitler turned the trial into a propaganda victory. The sympathy of the judges ensured that sentences were light. Ludendorff was acquitted. Hitler, who was found guilty, was sentenced to five years imprisonment. He served less than a year of his sentence in relative comfort in Landsberg prison where he whiled away the time writing the first volume of *Mein Kampf*. The light sentences given to Hitler and Ludendorff were very much in line with the way right-wing terrorists were treated by the German courts.

Kahr remained in office as *Reich* Commissar for Bavaria, and Lossow remained in command of local *Reichswehr* units. Neither was ever punished for their violations of the constitution. However, both men quietly resigned in February 1924.

Why did the Republic survive the crisis of 1923?

In the autumn of 1923 it had seemed likely that the Weimar Republic would be overthrown by right- or left-wing forces. Historian Kolb claims that Weimar's survival in 1923 should be viewed as 'almost a miracle'. But it survived – in marked contrast to its collapse ten years later. Why?

After August 1923 Stresemann's government took decisive political action to confront the crisis. Calling off 'passive resistance' and promising to resume the payment of reparations were the first, crucial, steps. However, Stresemann's financial reforms did not come into effect until 1924 while the ending of passive resistance was bitterly opposed by right-wing groups across Germany.

Other factors played a part in ensuring Weimar's survival. Arguably, popular German resentment was channelled more towards the French than towards Weimar itself. Arguably, despite the effects of inflation, workers did not suffer to the same extent as they did when there was long-term mass unemployment (see page 43). Arguably, although there was distress and disillusionment in 1923, disaffection with Weimar had not yet reached critical proportions.

Benito Mussolini

In October 1922 Benito Mussolini, leader of the right-wing Fascist Party in Italy, had threatened to lead his black-shirted followers in a 'March on Rome'. Rather than ordering the Italian army to crush the fascists, Italian King Victor Emmanuel accepted that Mussolini should become Italian premier. The 'March' actually occurred after Mussolini had been appointed Prime Minister.

KEY DATES: THE CRISIS OF 1923

January French and Belgian forces occupied the Ruhr.

August Stresemann was appointed Chancellor.

September Stresemann ended passive resistance in the Ruhr.

November The Munich Putsch failed.

Importantly, in 1923 there was no clear political alternative to the Republic. The extreme left had not recovered from its divisions in the years after 1918 and the Communists did not have enough support to overthrow the Republic. The extreme right was similarly divided and also lacked mass support.

The fact that the Republic survived the major storm of 1923 suggests that it was not merely 'a fair weather system'. Its survival was a sign of political strength and credibility. Moreover, having successfully met the threats from the radical left and the radical right, Stresemann's government was now in a position to set about improving Germany's financial situation.

WORKING TOGETHER

A lot of ground is covered in this chapter both in terms of content and analysis. A good understanding is essential. A knowledge of the main political developments in the period is vital for an understanding of the later history of Weimar and the rise of the Nazis to power.

Work in pairs. First consider the following issues:

- Why did the extreme left wing not gain power in 1918–19?
- What were the strengths and weaknesses of the Weimar Republic?
- Why did the Versailles Treaty have a detrimental effect on the Weimar Republic?
- How dangerous to the Republic was the economic crisis in Germany from 1919 to 1923?
- How serious was the political situation in 1919–23?

Compare the notes you have made on the chapter. Take each question above. One of you should try to answer the first question from his/her notes. The other should indicate where there might be gaps in the argument. Note down the gaps in facts and analysis. The other person should now do the same for the second question with the first person critically commenting on gaps. Keep going, taking each question in turn.

After you have finished, discuss your findings. To complete the process, write a summary of no more than five sentences, answering each of the above questions. Share your summaries with other members of the group. How do they differ? How can yours be improved?

Chapter summary

- The First World War began in August 1914. After the failure of the Schlieffen Plan, the war on the Western Front became a war of attrition.
- In 1917, the 'silent dictators', Hindenburg and Ludendorff re-commenced unrestricted submarine warfare which brought the USA into the war.
- As a result of the British blockade, Germany suffered severe food and fuel crises over the winter of 1917–18 and there were an increasing number of strikes.
- After the failure of the German 1918 offensive, Hindenburg and Ludendorff stepped down allowing a new government, led by Prince Max, to negotiate peace.
- In November mutinous sailors and workers established soviets, Wilhelm II abdicated and a new government, led by the moderate socialist Ebert, accepted the Allies' armistice terms.
- Ebert's government, aided by *Freikorps* units, put down Communist risings in Berlin and Bavaria in 1919.

- The new democratic government, the Weimar Republic, had to accept the Treaty of Versailles in June 1919.
- The Republic faced huge economic and financial problems and political challenges from the extreme right and left. The 1920 Kapp Putsch failed.
- Allied reparation demands in 1921 increased Germany's financial problems. In January 1923 French and Belgian forces occupied the Ruhr because Germany was not adhering to the reparation terms; hyperinflation followed.
- A new government, led by Stresemann, ended passive resistance and defeated Communist efforts to spark revolution in Saxony and Thuringia and the Munich Putsch.

▼ **Summary diagram:** The German revolution, 1918–19

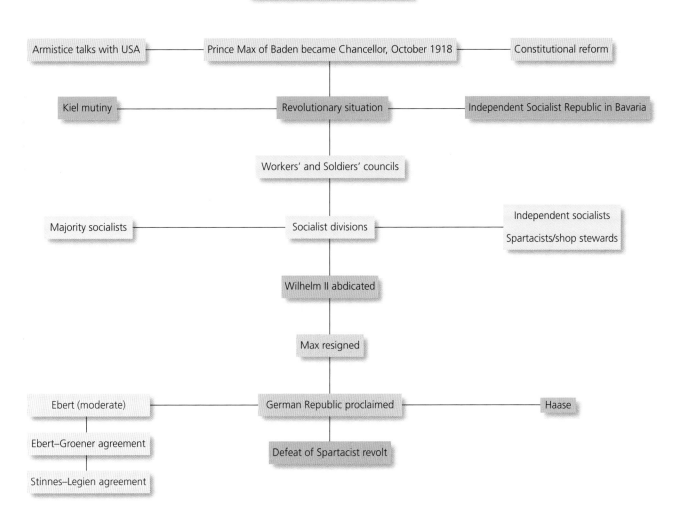

▼ **Summary diagram:** The establishment of the Weimar Republic

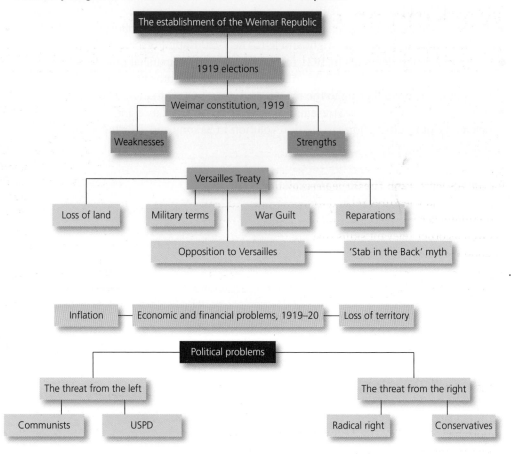

▼ **Summary diagram:** Troubled years, 1919–23

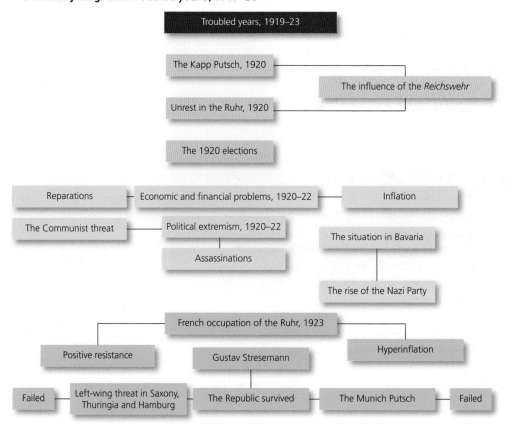

Working on essay technique: argument, counter-argument and resolution

Essays that develop a good argument are more likely to reach the higher levels. This is because essays with an argument are much more likely to develop sustained analysis. As you know, your essays are judged on the extent to which they analyse. The mark scheme opposite is for the full A-level. It is virtually the same for the AS-level. Both stress the need to analyse and evaluate the key features related to the periods studied. It distinguishes between five different levels of analysis (as well as other relevant skills that are the ingredients of good essays).

The key feature of an outstanding answer is sustained analysis: analysis that unites the whole of the essay.

You can set up an argument in your introduction, but you should develop it throughout the essay. One way of doing this is to adopt an argument, counter-argument structure. A counter-argument is an argument that disagrees with the main argument of the essay. Setting up an argument and then challenging it with a counter-argument is one way of weighing up, or evaluating the importance of the different factors that you discuss. Essays of this type will develop an argument in one paragraph and then set out an opposing argument in another paragraph. This approach will be very relevant on certain topics and questions where there are different opinions. We will first look at techniques for developing sustained analysis and argument before looking at the counter-argument technique.

Argument and sustained analysis

Good essays will analyse the keys issues discussed in the essay. They will probably have a clear piece of analysis at the end of each paragraph. This will offer a judgement on the question and is likely to consist of little or no narrative.

Outstanding answers are more likely to be analytical throughout. As well as the analysis of each factor discussed above, there will be probably be an overall analysis. This will run throughout the essay and can be achieved through developing a clear, relevant and coherent argument.

High-level arguments

Typically, essays examine a series of factors. A good way of achieving sustained analysis is to consider which factor is most important as in the example on page 108.

Level 5	Answers will display a very good understanding of the full demands of the question. They will be well organised and effectively delivered. The supporting information will be well selected, specific and precise. It will show a very good understanding of key features, issues and concepts. The answer will be fully analytical with a balanced argument and well substantiated judgement. *21–25 marks*
Level 4	Answers will display a good understanding of the demands of the question. They will be well organised and effectively communicated. There will be a range of clear and specific supporting information showing a good understanding of key features and issues, together with some conceptual awareness. The answer will be analytical in style with a range of direct comments relating to the question. The answer will be well balanced with some judgement, which may, however, be only partially substantiated. *16–20 marks*
Level 3	Answers will show an understanding of the question and will supply a range of largely accurate information, which will show an awareness of some of the key issues and features, but may, however, be unspecific or lack precision of detail. The answer will be effectively organised and show adequate communication skills. There will be a good deal of comment in relation to the question and the answer will display some balance, but a number of statements may be inadequately supported and generalist. *11–15 marks*
Level 2	The answer is descriptive or partial, showing some awareness of the question but a failure to grasp its full demands. There will be some attempt to convey material in an organised way, although communication skills may be limited. There will be some appropriate information showing understanding of some key features and/or issues, but the answer may be very limited in scope and/or contain inaccuracy and irrelevance. There will be some, but limited, comment in relation to the question and statements will, for the most part, be unsupported and generalist. *6–10 marks*
Level 1	The question has not been properly understood and the response shows limited organisational and communication skills. The information conveyed is irrelevant or extremely limited. There may be some unsupported, vague or generalist comment. *1–5 marks*

EXAMPLE

Consider the following A-level practice question:

To what extent was German unity threatened by right- and left-wing division in the period 1890–23? (25 marks)

Introduction 1 addresses the question but does not develop an argument:

Introduction 1

In the years between 1890 and 1923 German unity was threatened by right- and left-wing division. For most of his reign, Kaiser Wilhelm II, whose political views were militantly right wing, feared the growing strength of German socialism and made efforts to repress the movement. Nevertheless, for most of the First World War, most Germans united behind the German war effort. But after four years of terrible suffering, and ultimate defeat, German unity collapsed. Kaiser Wilhelm II was forced to flee to Holland. The new German government – the Weimar Republic – which was established in 1919 – faced serious challenges from both the Communists on the left and Nationalists on the right, culminating in the Munich Putsch in November 1923. Somehow the Weimar Republic survived.

Clear focus on the question

Recognises that can't just cover named factor

Wide range of factors

This introduction could be improved by the introduction of an argument. An argument is a type of explanation. It makes a claim about the question and supports it with a reason.

A good way of beginning to develop an argument is to think about the meaning of the words in the question. With the question above, you could think about the words 'to what extent'.

Here is an example of an introduction that begins an argument:

Introduction 2

On the surface, Germany was bitterly divided between 1890 and 1923. Extreme right- and left-wing Germans hated each other. Many on the left hated the autocratic regime of the Kaiserreich pre-1914. After 1918 Communists and Nationalists hated the Weimar Republic. However, the right-left divisions in Germany pre-1914 can be exaggerated. Germans remained united for most of the First World War. Left-wing revolution in 1918 was more a symptom than a cause of German defeat in November 1918, whatever the view of the German right. The extreme left challenge to democracy was defeated in 1919 with relative ease. While the moderate politicians of the Weimar Republic continued to face serious challenges, particularly from the right after 1919 (for example the Kapp Putsch), it survived. Despite political instability and huge financial and economic problems, most Germans voted for moderate parties in German elections until 1930. In that sense, Germany was united. However, there is no doubt that right-left divisions did – at times – seriously threaten German unity.

The introduction begins with a claim

Introduction continues with another claim

Concludes with outline of argument

This introduction focuses on the question and sets out the main factors that the essay will develop. It also sets out an argument that can then be developed throughout each paragraph, and then rounded off with an overall judgement in the conclusion. Having made a case that right–left-wing divisions can be exaggerated, it then ends by asserting that, nevertheless, those divisions did pose problems for Germany. This means that Introduction 2 would start the essay at a higher level than Introduction 1.

Counter-argument

You can set up an argument in your introduction as we have seen above, but you should develop your argument throughout the essay. One way of doing this is to adopt an argument, counter-argument structure. A counter-argument is an argument that disagrees with the main argument of the essay. Setting up an argument and then challenging it with a counter-argument is one way of weighing up, or evaluating (see page 66) the importance of the different factors that you discuss. Essays of this type will develop an argument in one paragraph and then set out an opposing argument in another paragraph.

ACTIVITY

Imagine you are answering the following A-level practice question:

To what extent did the extreme left pose a problem for the German governments in the period 1890–23? (25 marks)

Using your notes from this and the previous chapter, one way to tackle this question would be to:

1 Divide your page as follows:

A serious left-wing threat	A not very serious left-wing threat

2 Consider the following points and place them either in the left- or right-hand column:
- The Social Democratic threat, perceived by Wilhelm II in the 1890s
- The Social Democratic threat to Wilhelm II from 1912 to 1914
- The threat to Germany from the left in the First World War
- Left-wing activity in November 1918

- Spartacist activity over the winter of 1918–19
- Events in Bavaria in 1919
- The merger of the Independent Socialists and the Communists in 1922
- Communist risings in 1923

3 Now write a short argument that addresses the question of how serious the left-wing threat was. Remember, your argument must contain a statement and a reason.

4 Begin with the side of the argument that you agree with (either that the left-wing threat was serious or it was not serious). Write two sentences that explain this side of the argument.

5 Now write two sentences for the side of the argument that you don't agree with. This is your counter-argument. Remember that it has to consist of a claim and a reason.

6 Use your original argument and counter-argument as the basis for writing two paragraphs in answer to the question.

Remember, this is a useful approach to apply when facing this type of question.

Resolution

The best written essays are those that contain sustained analysis. We have seen that one way of achieving this is to write an essay that develops a clear argument (see page 107) and counter-argument (see above).

Next you should resolve the tension between the argument and the counter-argument. One way of concluding an essay is to resolve this debate that you have established between the argument and the counter-argument as in the example on page 110.

EXAMPLE

Imagine you are answering the following practice question:

'Nationalism posed a far greater threat to Germany than Communism in the period 1890–1923.' Assess the validity of this view. (25 marks)

A possible way to tackle this question would be to write several clear paragraphs arguing that nationalism (and Nationalists) did indeed pose a greater threat to Germany than communism (and Communists). Then write a couple of paragraphs arguing against this. In an essay of this type you could then resolve the tension by weighing up the argument and counter-argument in the conclusion. In so doing, you can reach a supported overall judgement. For example, a possible conclusion could look like this:

In conclusion, nationalism posed a greater threat to Germany both before and indeed after the First World War. Although nationalist parties did not have much support in the Reichstag in 1914, German nationalism was undoubtedly a major factor in bringing about the First World War – the greatest disaster to befall Germany in this period. However, this was not the way nationalists viewed the situation. They regarded the left – both moderate and extreme – as a threat in 1914, the cause of German defeat in 1918 and a threat thereafter. But support for the left was not as strong as nationalists feared. This was shown in the 1919 elections, when even the SPD did not do as well as expected. While extreme right-wing parties also fared badly in the 1919 elections, nationalists posed a far greater threat to the Weimar Republic than the Communists Party in the years 1919–23. Although the Kapp Putsch (1920) and the Munich Putsch (1923) failed, the nationalists posed a threat to Germany's democratic government because there was always the possibility they might win the support of the German army – a body which would never support the Communists. The fact that many Germans accepted the myth of the 'stab in the back', and virtually all hated the Treaty of Versailles, meant that nationalists had emotive issues which could arouse considerable support.

Begins with main argument
Counter-argument contrast
Limitations of counter-argument
Resolves tension

This conclusion evaluates the argument and counter-argument. It resolves the tension by identifying a problem with the counter-argument, and reaching an overall concluding judgement in relation to the question.

The process of evaluating the argument and the counter-argument is helped by the use of words such as 'however' and 'nonetheless', indicating that the paragraph is weighing up contrasting arguments.

ACTIVITY

Imagine you are dealing with this practice question:

'Despite the divisions between right and left, most Germans were remarkably united in the period 1890 to 1923.' Assess the validity of this view. (25 marks)

Use the ideas on page 109 and look at the work you did on this question in order to complete the following activities.

1 Answer the following questions:
   – Which is stronger, the argument or the counter-argument? Why is it stronger?
   – What are the flaws in the weaker argument?
   – What strengths does the weaker argument have?
2 Having answered these questions, write a conclusion that weighs up the argument and the counter-argument in order to reach an overall judgement.

Use the words 'however', 'nonetheless' and 'therefore' to structure the paragraph.

Working on interpretation skills

The advice given here builds on the help given at the end of Chapter 1 (see pages 29–30).

For the AQA A-level exam, Section A gives you three extracts, followed by a single question. The wording of the question will be something like this:

'Using your understanding of the historical context, assess how convincing the arguments in these three extracts are in relation to …'   **(30 marks)**

The A-level mark scheme is very similar to the AS one on page 29.

Level 5	Shows a very good understanding of the interpretations put forward in all three extracts and combines this with a strong awareness of the historical context to analyse and evaluate the interpretations given in the extracts. Evaluation of the arguments will be well supported and convincing. The response demonstrates a very good understanding of context. *25–30 marks*
Level 4	Shows a good understanding of the interpretations given in all three extracts and combines this with knowledge of the historical context to analyse and evaluate the interpretations given in the extracts. The evaluation of the arguments will be mostly well-supported, and convincing, but may have minor limitations of depth and breadth. The response demonstrates a good understanding of context. *19–24 marks*
Level 3	Provides some supported comment on the interpretations given in all three extracts and comments on the strength of these arguments in relation to their historic context. There is some analysis and evaluation but there may be an imbalance in the degree and depth of comments offered on the strength of the arguments. The response demonstrates an understanding of context. *13–18 marks*
Level 2	Provides some accurate comment on the interpretations given in at least two of the extracts, with reference to the historical context. The answer may contain some analysis, but there is little, if any, evaluation. Some of the comments on the strength of the arguments may contain some generalisation, inaccuracy or irrelevance. The response demonstrates some understanding of context. *7–12 marks*
Level 1	Either shows an accurate understanding of the interpretation given in one extract only or addresses two/three extracts, but in a generalist way, showing limited accurate understanding of the arguments they contain, although there may be some general awareness of the historical context. Any comments on the strength of the arguments are likely to be generalist and contain some inaccuracy and/or irrelevance. The response demonstrates limited understanding of context. *1–6 marks*

Notice that there is no reference in the mark scheme to *comparing* the extracts or reaching a judgement about which of the extracts is the most convincing.

On page 112 is an A-level practice question. Guidance on how to answer it is on pages 113–114.

Using your understanding of the historical context, assess how convincing the arguments in these three extracts are in explaining the impact of the political changes that occurred in Germany during the period 1890–1923.

Extract A

The transition from the 'Bismarckian' era, dominated by the consequences of political unification and the need to consolidate a national state, to the 'Wilhelmine' era, where the political agenda was shaped by the rise of a new kind of popular politics and the desire to secure Germany's place as a world power, represented a significant *caesura* [division] in the lives of most subjects of the Kaiserreich. The changes in the political landscape from the late 1880s obviously reflected the rapid transformation of Germany's economy and society, as well as a shifting cultural climate under the impact of new intellectual currents (or the popularization of older ones) and ideological challenges. Many of these changes were not unique to Germany but had a wider European resonance. Yet for contemporaries the departure of the conservative 'founder of the Reich' in 1890 and the advent of the brashly self-assertive young Kaiser, Wilhelm II, appeared to symbolize the changed mood. From 1890 German politics reflected not only the fears and insecurities which accompanied unprecedented social change, but also the inflated expectations, overweening self-confidence and optimism about the future which were engendered by a growing consciousness of Germany's military and economic dynamism.

From 'Wilhelmine Germany' by Katherine A. Lerman in *German History Since 1800* Mary Fulbrook, ed. (Arnold), 1997.

Extract B

There is a natural desire to believe that large and terrible events have deep-rooted origins. It is therefore important not to underestimate the importance of the short-term, particularly at moments when history seems to have speeded up, as it did between the outbreak of the First World War and Hitler's appointment as German Chancellor less than nineteen years later. The war marked a watershed in German history. In countless ways, the years 1914–18 spawned new elements in German political life ... Then after the war, came a period of revolution and counter-revolution that further helped to poison the politics of the 1920s. And yet, even burdened with these and many other encumbrances, the Weimar Republic was not doomed. Its most brilliant recent historian [D. Peukert] has rightly reminded us that the Republic did not just have a beginning and an end; its difficulties and its ultimate failure deserve to be treated in their own right, not passed over briefly as a prelude to National Socialism – or a postscript to Imperial Germany. Only with the perfect vision of hindsight do we know that it was to be a democratic interlude ... Imperial Germany before the guns of August [1914] was no golden age but the complex tendencies at work in it pointed towards different potential futures: towards reform as well as authoritarianism, social emancipation as well as repression, cultural diversity as well as culture driven into exile.

From *History of Germany 1780–1918: The Long Nineteenth Century* by David Blackbourn, (Blackwell), 2003.

Extract C

Many historians try to explain Weimar's endemic political instability by pointing to the legacy of Germany's imperial past, when relatively powerless political parties struck largely negative ideological postures, a habit they found hard to overcome when they were given real political responsibility. More cogently, one might argue that, once the smoke-and-mirrors illusions of the empire had vanished, Germans were left with nothing but the spectacle of competing special interests, which the Republic's threadbare symbolism poorly concealed. This view was current at the time, among such right-wing constitutional theorists as Carl Schmitt, who wished to reassert the primacy of state over mere society. Other scholars focus on the demagogic populism of such extra-parliamentary nationalist associations as the Navy League or the Pan-German League of the Wilhelmine period as a harbinger of extreme fascist potential, although these seem fuddy-duddy affairs compared with the more plebeian, intemperate and violent National Socialists. Members of the Navy League did not physically attack socialists or Jews. Some vital moral threshold was crossed during the war, transforming the conduct of German politics.

From *The Third Reich: A New History* by Michael Burleigh, (Macmillan), 2000.

Possible answer

First, make sure that you have the focus of the question clear – in this case, the nature of political change in Germany during the period from 1890 to 1923.

Then you can investigate the three extracts to see how convincing they are.

You need to analyse each of the three extracts in turn. A suggestion is to start with a large page divided into nine blocks.

Extract's main arguments	Knowledge to corroborate	Knowledge to contradict or modify
A		
B		
C		

- In the first column list the main arguments each uses.
- In the second column list what you know that can corroborate the arguments.
- In the third column list what might contradict or modify the arguments. ('Modify' – you might find that you partly agree, but with reservations.)
- You may find, of course, that some of your knowledge is relevant more than once.

Planning your answer – one approach

Decide how you could best set out a detailed plan for your answer. You could, for example:

- Briefly refer to the focus of the question.
- For each extract in turn set out the arguments, and the corroborating and contradictory evidence.
- Do this by treating each argument (or group of arguments) in turn.
- Make comparisons between the extracts if this is helpful. The mark scheme does not explicitly give credit for doing this, but a successful comparison may well show the extent of your understanding of each extract.
- An overall judgement is not required, but it may be helpful to make a brief summary, or just reinforce what has been said already by emphasising which extract was the most convincing.

Remember that in the examination you are allowed an hour for this question. It is the planning stage that is vital in order to write a good answer. You should allow sufficient time to read the extracts and plan an answer. If you start writing too soon, it is likely that you will waste time trying to summarise the *content* of each source. Do this in your planning stage – and then think how you will *use* the content to answer the question.

Then the actual writing!

- Think how you can write an answer, dealing with each extract in turn, but making cross-references or comparisons, if this is helpful, to reinforce a point.
- In addition, make sure your answer:
  - shows very good understanding of the extracts
  - uses knowledge to argue in support or to disagree
  - provides a clear argument that leads to a conclusion about each extract, and which may reach a conclusion about the extracts as a whole.

Extracts that have an argument and counter-argument

Sometimes an extract will give opposing views within a paragraph – that is, an attempt at providing balance. The extract may reach a conclusion on which argument is stronger, or it may leave an open verdict. Look at Extract D.

Extract D

Wilhelm was not a dictator. He was always obliged to come to accommodation with the incumbent Reich Chancellor and minister-president of Prussia, the Prussian Ministers of State, the Reich secretaries, the Reichstag and the Prussian parliaments, as well as the allied governments of the other German kingdoms, grand duchies and free cities in the federation. Increasingly too, public opinion, as expressed through political parties, churches, trade unions, special interest groups, pamphlets, press criticism and popular demonstrations, acted as something of a brake on his personal influence. But at the centre of power, and above all in the conduct of personnel, military, foreign and armaments policy, Kaiser Wilhelm's was very much the determining voice until the decision to go to war in 1914 – a decision in which he took a leading part. It is true that during the First World War his role was quickly overshadowed by that of the generals, but even then he retained the last word on all matters of importance.

From *Kaiser Wilhelm II* by J. C. G. Rohl, (Cambridge University Press), 2014.

This extract presents an argument in:

- the first half suggesting that Wilhelm's power was limited
- the second half suggesting that Wilhelm's power was huge.

If this extract were being studied, your plan could highlight the balance within the extract, and could seek to find evidence to support and refute both sides.

This would have to be reflected in your answer in relation to how convincing the arguments are. An extract that includes counter-argument as well as argument *could* be more convincing, but not necessarily so. It will depend on the context – and your own knowledge which you are using in order to reach a judgement.

Part 1 Empire to Democracy, 1871–1929

114

Recovery and stability, 1924–29

This chapter covers the years from 1924 to 1929. These years are usually regarded as the high point of the Republic – 'the golden twenties' – a short-lived interlude between the early years of crisis and eventual decline and collapse after 1929. Undoubtedly, the Republic did achieve some economic success and political stability in the mid- and late-1920s. However, historians, fully aware that the Republic was soon to disintegrate, have increasingly come to question the extent of Weimar's success and stability. This chapter will examine the period by focusing on the following areas:

- Economic and political recovery 1924–25
- The economic situation 1925–29
- German society and culture
- The political situation 1925–29

When you have worked through the chapter and the related activities, you should have a detailed knowledge of all the areas listed above. You should be able to relate this knowledge to the following breadth issues defined as part of your study:

- How was Germany governed and how did political authority change and develop?
- How effective was opposition?
- How and why did the economy develop and change?
- What was the extent of social and cultural change?

For the period covered in this chapter, the main focus can be phrased as the following question:

How successful was the Weimar Republic in the period 1924–29?

CHAPTER OVERVIEW

The Weimar Republic made a remarkable recovery after 1923. Three important achievements marked the years from 1924 to 1929. The first was the stabilisation of the currency. The second was the Dawes Agreement (1924) which regulated Germany's reparations payments, and the third was the Locarno Treaty (1925). Moderate parties had success in the 1924 and 1928 elections. In the late 1920s Weimar Germany was fertile ground for experimentation in all aspects of culture and arts.

However, the extent of the Republic's success in this period can be questioned. The economy, heavily dependent on foreign loans, was not as strong as it appeared and by 1929 unemployment was rising. Many Germans opposed the cultural experimentation. Weimar governments continued to be unstable. In 1929 the Nazi Party, winning support from discontented farmers, began to have success in local elections. Hitler's role in the opposition to the Young Plan in 1929 gave him considerable publicity. The Weimar Republic had survived the 1923 crisis. Despite the 'golden years' (1924–29), it was not in the best of shapes to survive another crisis.

1 German recovery, 1924–25

This section deals with Germany's recovery after the 1923 crisis. The economic recovery was quite remarkable, given the situation in 1923. Nevertheless, Weimar's economic health and political stability were not necessarily based on very strong foundations.

Economic recovery, 1924–25

Why did Germany's economy recover in the years 1924–25?

By November 1923 the German mark was no longer worth the paper it was printed on. Serious political unrest looked set to continue unless something was done to stabilise the currency.

The stabilisation of the currency

Largely as a result of the prompting of Food and then Finance Minister Hans Luther, Stresemann's short-lived government in November 1923 accepted a new currency – the *Rentenmark* – to be based on Germany's agricultural property and industrial resources. The currency was to be supervised by a specially constituted authority, the *Rentenbank*, which issued a loan to the Reichsbank. The *Reichsbank* could then issue *Rentenmarks* to the value of its loan holding. *Rentenmarks* were valued at one gold mark each. Twelve noughts were struck off the mark so that one dollar was now equal to 4.2 *Rentenmarks*.

The agrarian backing for the new currency was largely fictitious because land is not convertible in the same way as gold. Nevertheless, since Germany lacked enough gold to launch a new bullion-backed currency, the psychological effect of the *Rentenmark*'s mortgage helped to maintain its value. The restricted amount of the new currency available to the *Reichsbank* also prevented a slide towards inflation. The government could no longer draw on unlimited currency credits from the *Reichsbank* but had to try to balance expenditure against income.

The *Rentenmark* scheme's success was largely due to the firmness and energy of Luther, and to the financial skill of Currency Commissioner Hjalmar Schacht, who dealt with a host of problems arising from the new mark's introduction. As a result of the government's careful housekeeping and responsible fiscal policy, the new currency quickly stabilised and the *Rentenmark* was converted back into *Reichsmarks* in August 1924. The stabilisation programme meant that economic life revived throughout Germany, although dearer money initially caused a high level of unemployment.

The Dawes Plan

The establishment of a stable currency and Stresemann's promise to resume the payment of reparations provided a basis for international negotiations on Germany's economic plight. The fact that a new French government, led by Edouard Herriot, replaced Poincare's government, was also important. Herriot, facing financial problems of his own as a result of French occupation of the Ruhr, was more interested in conciliation than extortion.

NOTE-MAKING

Your notes should explain why and how Germany managed to recover economic and political stability in 1924–25. To what extent does Stresemann deserve praise for Germany's recovery? How great were his efforts on the international stage?

Early in 1924 an inter-Allied Committee, chaired by two Americans, Charles Dawes and Owen D. Young, was set up to examine the problem of German financial stability. Its major concern was to establish a scale of reparations payments which would not prevent Germany from stabilising its currency and balancing its budget. In April 1924 the committee submitted its recommendations.

The Dawes Plan, while not reducing the overall reparations bill, proposed that it should be paid over a longer period. Germany was to make annual payments of 1,000 million marks (£50 million) in the first five years, after which time the payments were to rise to 2,500 million marks (£125 million). To ensure that Germany would make regular annual payments, the creditor nations were to be given a degree of control over Germany's central banking system and also over the German railway system. Henceforward, these would be supervised by committees consisting of German and Allied representatives. While this was somewhat humiliating, the bitter pill was to be sweetened with a loan of 800 million marks (£40 million), which would help Germany start its payments. The promise that French forces would quit the Ruhr once Germany accepted the terms was also an implicit part of the Dawes Plan.

Source A Charles Dawes, speaking on the German economy in 1924. From *Weimar and the Rise of Hitler* by A. J. Nicholls, (Macmillan), 1979, pp. 84–85.

The task would be hopeless if the present situation of Germany accurately reflected her potential capacity; the proceeds from Germany's national production could not in that case enable her to meet the national needs and to ensure the payment of her foreign debts.

But Germany's growing and industrious population; her great technical skill; the wealth of her material resources; the development of her agriculture along progressive lines; her eminence in industrial science; all these factors enable us to be hopeful with regard to her future production …

Germany is therefore well equipped with resources; she possesses the means of exploiting them on a large scale; when the present credit shortage has been overcome, she will be able to resume a favoured position in the activity of a world where normal conditions of exchange are restored.

Many right-wing Germans were critical of the Dawes scheme simply because they opposed the notion of reparation payments. Others hated submitting to Allied controls over the central banking system and the railways. This was seen as a monstrous invasion of German sovereignty. The Nationalist Party (DNVP) campaigned against the Plan as a 'second Versailles'. But influential industrialists and members of the business community within the Party saw that the Plan would bring Germany great material advantages. In a crucial vote in the *Reichstag* in August 1924, the Nationalists split on the issue: 52 DNVP members voted in favour of the Dawes Plan and 48 against, ensuring that it was carried into effect.

The success of the Dawes scheme required a prosperous Germany. In 1924 there seemed some cause for optimism on this score. Germany undoubtedly had the physical capacity to increase production. Moreover, the prospect of further investments, particularly from the USA, had an immediate stimulating effect on the economy.

> According to Source A, why was Charles Dawes confident about Germany's economic prospects?

KEY DATES: ECONOMIC RECOVERY, 1924–25

1923 Introduction of the *Rentenmark*.

1924 The Dawes Plan was accepted by Germany.

The political situation, 1924–25

Why did the political situation remain unstable in the years 1924–25?

German politics continued to be unstable in 1924–25. The fact that the SPD, the largest party in the *Reichstag*, objected to joining a coalition with bourgeois parties – for example, the DDP, Centre and DVP – meant it was virtually impossible to construct a government with a majority.

The situation in 1923–24

The SPD was outraged by the unequal treatment meted out to Bavaria and Saxony in the autumn of 1923. In Saxony an elected socialist government had been suppressed by the German army. Meanwhile, right-wing politicians in Bavaria had been left in power after the Munich Putsch, in which Kahr and others had been implicated (see page 102). SPD demands that Bavaria should be given the same treatment as Saxony were rejected by the bourgeois parties, who feared this would tear Germany apart.

When Stresemann lost a vote of confidence, President Ebert called upon Centre Party leader Wilhelm Marx to form a new government. Marx, a dull speaker who lacked popular appeal, was a capable administrator, an open-minded pragmatist, and a man with the courage to take tough decisions. He was to be the Republic's longest-serving chancellor. His government was a coalition of the Centre, BVP, DVP and DDP.

Marx's minority government, reliant on the support of the SPD, had to take some unpopular decisions. Many of the middle class had lost all their savings in the hyperinflation but the government could not afford any compensation. In an effort to cut back government expenditure, pay in the civil service was reduced to below pre-1914 levels.

▲ Gustav Stresemann

Gustav Stresemann (1878–1929)

Stresemann is generally considered to be the most influential cabinet minister in the Weimar Republic period. Born into a lower middle-class family, he nevertheless had an excellent education, eventually achieving a doctorate. At university, he involved himself in politics. His student views, which combined liberalism with strident nationalism, did not change much during the course of the rest of his life. Joining the National Liberal Party, he was elected to the *Reichstag* in 1907. By 1917 he was National Liberal leader. He briefly joined the German Democratic Party after the war but was expelled for his right-wing views. He then gathered the main body of the old National Liberal Party into the German People's Party (DVP) with himself as chairman. Most of the Party's supporters were middle- and upper-class Protestants. The DVP supported Christian family values, secular education and lower tariffs, and was hostile to socialism in all its forms.

By the early 1920s Stresemann was prepared to co-operate with the parties of the left and centre, while remaining a monarchist at heart. In August 1923 he became chancellor of a coalition government. The following month he courageously called off resistance against French occupation of the Ruhr (see page 101). He also supported the introduction of the *Rentenmark* in an attempt to end hyperinflation.

Losing the support of the SPD, his coalition government collapsed in November 1923. Although he was no longer chancellor, he remained foreign minister for the rest of his life, serving in eight successive governments ranging from centre-right to centre-left. As foreign minister, his greatest achievement was probably the Locarno Treaty with the Western powers in 1925 – for which he received the Nobel Peace Prize in 1926.

Stresemann's politics defy easy categorisation. He was undoubtedly a liberal, who favoured democracy. But he was also a German nationalist who wished to overthrow the Versailles Treaty. He believed the best way to achieve this was to win the friendship and co-operation of Britain and France.

The 1924 elections

The radical right and left made significant gains in the May 1924 elections. The parties in the centre lost voters to the DNVP, whose electoral campaign was based on a repudiation of the Dawes Plan. The DNVP, with 20 per cent of the vote, became the second largest party in the *Reichstag*. Even the Nazis, whose leader, Hitler, was in prison, won 6.5 per cent of the vote. On the left, the SPD lost ground and a large numbers of workers turned to the Communist Party (KPD) which won 12.6 per cent of the vote. The KPD was henceforward a dangerous magnet for working-class militants, especially the young.

Marx's minority government had great difficulty in gaining a majority on any proposal (for example, the ratification of the Dawes Plan). After a series of defeats in the *Reichstag*, Marx called for fresh elections in December 1924. By then the economy was showing signs of recovery. Unemployment was falling and wages were rising. In these circumstances, the SPD made significant gains at the KPD's expense. On the right the Nazis lost more than half their support. However, the DNVP managed to improve its showing.

After lengthy negotiations, a government was formed in mid-January 1925 under Hans Luther. He was without a party affiliation and had gained a reputation as an effective minister of finance. The new coalition included members of the DNVP for the first time – a major achievement because the Party had previously adopted a policy of outright opposition to the Republic. The DNVP soon found itself in the embarrassing situation of supporting policies it had denounced during the election campaign.

Below are the results of the elections in May and December 1924 and May 1928.

Election date		Party							
		DNVP	**DVP**	**Centre**	**BVP**	**DDP**	**SPD**	**KPD**	**NSDAP**
May 1924	**Votes (millions)**	5.6	2.7	3.9	0.9	1.7	6.0	3.6	1.9
	%	19.5	9.2	13.4	3.2	5.7	20.5	12.6	6.5
	No. of seats	95	45	65	16	28	100	62	32
Dec 1924	**Votes (millions)**	6.2	3.0	4.1	1.1	1.9	7.9	2.7	0.9
	%	20.5	10.1	13.6	3.7	6.3	26	9.0	3.0
	No. of seats	103	51	69	19	32	131	45	14
May 1928	**Votes (millions)**	4.4	2.7	3.7	0.9	1.5	9.2	3.2	0.8
	%	14.2	8.7	12.1	3.1	4.9	29.8	10.6	(2.6)
	No. of seats	73	45	62	16	25	153	54	12

▲ **Figure 1** Results of elections to the *Reichstag*, 1924.

Chancellor	Date	Partners
Gustav Stresemann (DVP)	August 1923–October 1923	SPD, DDP, Centre, DVP
Gustav Stresemann (DVP)	October 1923–November 1923	DDP, Centre, DVP
Wilhelm Marx (Centre)	November 1923–June 1924	DDP, Centre, BVP, DVP
Wilhelm Marx (Centre)	June 1924–January 1925	DDP, Centre, DVP
Hans Luther (Non-party)	January 1925–December 1925	DVP, DNVP, BVP
Hans Luther (Non-party)	January 1926–May 1926	DDP, DVP, BVP
Wilhelm Marx (Centre)	May 1926–December 1926	DDP, Centre, DVP, BVP
Wilhelm Marx (Centre)	January 1927–June 1928	DVP, DNVP, BVP
Hermann Müller (SPD)	June 1928–March 1930	SPD, DDP, Centre, BVP, DVP

▲ **Figure 2** German Chancellors and coalition partners: 1923–30.

The *Reichsbanner Schwarz-Rot-Gold*

The turbulent events of 1923 provoked an active response among those who wished to protect German democracy. In 1924 a new Republican paramilitary organisation – the *Reichsbanner Schwarz-Rot-Gold* – was formed. Within a year it could claim over a million members, becoming the strongest paramilitary formation in Germany. SPD supporters formed the basis for its growth. Its demonstrations and propaganda encouraged Germans to celebrate the foundation of the new Republic, and honour its flag and its constitution. The *Reichsbanner* proved that Republicans could don uniforms, march and fight for their beliefs with as much enthusiasm as their nationalist rivals.

1 Explain why the SPD did so much better in December than in May 1924.
2 Why were there two elections in 1924?

10 governments in 7 years

The SPD, the largest party was not part of 8 of these governments

The 1925 presidential election

In February 1925 President Ebert died. A new presidential election followed. In the first round of voting none of the politicians managed to win an overall majority. Accordingly, the SPD and the Democrats decided to unite their forces behind the Centre Party candidate, Wilhelm Marx. The right-wing parties rallied around Field Marshall Paul von Hindenburg, the hero of the First World War. In the second round of voting, Hindenburg (with 48.3 per cent of the vote) defeated Marx (with 45.3 per cent). Had the Communists not run their own candidate Ernst Thalmann, who won 2 million votes, Marx might have won – assuming Thalmann's supporters had voted for him rather than for Hindenburg.

Hindenburg's election was in many ways a vote against the Republic. Hindenburg, who never identified himself whole-heartedly with Weimar, still felt bound by ties of loyalty to Wilhelm II and had many anti-Republican figures among his friends. Nevertheless, Hindenburg's status gave the Republic added authority. Moreover, he accepted the Weimar constitution and did not set out to betray it. Indeed, he proved a great disappointment to those on the right who hoped he might support a monarchist restoration.

Improved international relations

How successful was Stresemann in diplomatic terms?

After French forces left the Ruhr, Foreign Minister Stresemann managed to improve Germany's relations with Britain and France. Like the vast majority of Germans, Stresemann hoped to revise the Versailles settlement, especially in the east. But he was a pragmatist. Unlike many nationalists, he recognised that Germany lacked the power to challenge Poland, never mind Britain and France. If offensive action was out of the question, Stresemann's only recourse was diplomacy. He appreciated it would be no easy matter achieving his aims when, as he himself once remarked, he was backed up only by the power of German culture and the German economy. In essence, Stresemann's general strategy was in the tradition of Wirth's fulfilment policy (see page 98). In the long term, he wanted Germany to be the leading power in Europe once again. To that end co-operation with the Western powers seemed to be in Germany's best short-term interests.

The Locarno Treaties

After months of negotiations, the Locarno Treaties were signed in December 1925. By the Treaty of Mutual Guarantee, Germany, France and Belgium agreed to respect their existing frontiers. Britain and Italy assumed the role of guarantors. By the Treaties of Arbitration, Germany, Poland and Czechoslovakia agreed to settle future disputes peacefully. However, unlike in the West, Germany did not accept the finality of its frontiers in the east. Indeed, Stresemann made it perfectly clear that he hoped to revise Germany's frontiers with Poland at some stage in the future.

The Locarno Treaties were undoubtedly a success for Stresemann. No longer diplomatically isolated, Germany was again treated as an equal partner. In confirming the status quo in the West, Stresemann had curtailed France's freedom of action. The occupation of the Ruhr or annexation of the Rhineland were no longer legitimate French options.

The Locarno Treaties indicated that a new era of peaceful co-operation had begun. In 1926 Germany was admitted to the League of Nations. While Stresemann regarded the League with no more enthusiasm than most Germans, he realised that Germany would be better able to defend its interests from within the League than if it stayed outside. Relations between Germany and the Western powers continued to improve.

How successful was Stresemann?

Given Germany's weak position, Stresemann had achieved a great deal in a short space of time, particularly considering the situation in 1923 and the internal and external forces stacked against him. Able to use only conciliatory methods, his policies resulted in Germany regaining diplomatic influence and the ability to influence the Allies.

However, it may be that Stresemann's achievements have been exaggerated. There is no doubt that circumstances, especially Britain and France's willingness to co-operate, worked strongly in his favour. Moreover, it can be claimed that he failed to achieve his aims. There was no early restoration of German sovereignty over the Saar and the Rhineland as he had hoped. Indeed, Stresemann became increasingly disappointed by the slow pace of revision of the Versailles Treaty. His right-wing opponents in Germany were even more scathing of his failure on this score. Unsurprisingly, Stresemann was rated more highly abroad than he was in Germany.

> **KEY DATES: IMPROVED INTERNATIONAL RELATIONS**
>
> **1925** The Locarno Treaties were signed.
>
> **1926** Germany joined the League of Nations.

Source B Part of the obituary to Stresemann in the socialist newspaper *Vorwarts* in October 1929.

Stresemann's achievement was in line with the ideas of the international socialist movement. He saw that you can only serve your people by understanding other peoples. To serve collapsed Germany he set out on the path of understanding. He refused to try to get back land which had gone forever. He offered our former enemies friendship. Being a practical man he saw that any other path would have left Germany without any hope of recovery. He covered the long distance from being a nationalistic politician of conquest to being a champion of world peace. He fought with great personal courage for the ideals in which he believed.

- Why does Source B praise Stresemann?
- How might a right-wing German have regarded Stresemann's achievements?

2 Stability and prosperity, 1925–29?

This section will examine the years from 1925 to 1929 – a period when Germany enjoyed internal peace and seeming prosperity. Republican politicians were no longer under a constant threat of assassination. The number of right-wing paramilitary formations dwindled. The army began to show itself more amenable to civilian control. Even the DNVP compromised its monarchist principles in the quest for political power. It seemed that the Weimar Republic might be able to establish itself on a firmer foundation than had been possible in the difficult years after 1918.

The economic situation, 1925–29

To what extent was Germany's seeming economic success from 1925 to 1929 a false prosperity?

For contemporaries looking back from the standpoint of the early 1930s, it seemed as if Germany had enjoyed remarkable economic success in the period 1925–29. However, many historians now believe that the actual condition of the German economy was unsound and that there was something of a false prosperity.

Economic progress

Between 1924 and 1929 there was monetary stability and (thanks to the Dawes Plan) a significant influx of foreign capital – around 25.5 billion marks. Foreign investors, especially Americans, were attracted to Germany because of its relatively high interest rates.

German industry, despite its loss of resources arising from Versailles, did well. By 1928 production levels generally exceeded those of 1913. This was the result of more efficient production techniques, particularly in coal mining and steel manufacture. German industry also achieved economies of scale by the growing number of cartels. Between 1925 and 1929 German exports rose by 40 per cent. The chemicals giant I. G. Farben became the largest manufacturing enterprise in Europe.

This economic progress was reflected in social terms. A state arbitration scheme was introduced in 1924 to try to prevent strikes. Workers, through their trade unions, were able to argue their case for more pay or less hours before neutral judges who were often sympathetic to the workers' claims. Hourly wages rose in real terms every year from 1924 to 1929. As a result, national income was 12 per cent higher in 1928 than in 1913. There were also improvements in the provision of social welfare:

- There were generous pension and sickness benefits.
- In 1927 a compulsory unemployment insurance covered 17 million workers – the largest of its kind in the world.
- Better health insurance meant that there was better medical provision.
- Public spending on housing grew rapidly throughout the 1920s. By 1929 the state was spending 33 times more on housing than it was spending in 1913. The result was to considerably improve the quality of homes.
- State subsidies were provided for the construction of local amenities – parks, schools and sports facilities.

These developments, alongside the more overt signs of affluence, such as the increasing number of cars and the growth of the cinema, suggested that the economy was booming.

NOTE-MAKING

The key word in this section – indeed in the entire chapter – is 'stability'. Your notes must be geared towards you trying to get clear in your own mind the extent of the stability achieved during this period, especially in economic and political matters.

Read the sections on the economic situation in Germany from 1925 to 1929. You should realise that historians are divided about Weimar's economic health. To what extent was the economy improving? To what extent was it weak? Now re-read the sections. Have a column headed 'Economic and financial strengths' and another headed 'Economic and financial weaknesses'. Note down the information and arguments which support each side of the debate. As you make your notes try to reach your own conclusion about Weimar's economic state.

Do just the same for the cultural, social and political sections.

Source C Gilbert Parker, the American financier and the Agent for Reparations Payments, reporting to the Reparations Commission in December 1928.

German business conditions generally appear to have righted themselves on a relatively high level of activity. A year ago, it will be recalled, German business was in the midst of a process of expansion which threatened to result in over-production in certain of the principal industries ... As the year 1928 comes to a close, it appears that this very over-expansion has been checked before it reached dangerous proportions, and that a condition of relative stability has now been attained ... Since 1924, when stabilisation was achieved ... Germany's reconstruction has at least kept pace with the reconstruction of Europe as a whole, and it has played an essential part in the process of European reconstruction.

> Why, according to Source C, did Germany have good cause to be optimistic about its economic future?

Economic weakness

In many respects, Germany's economic recovery was deceptive. There was economic growth but it was far from even. Germany's trade figures always showed imports exceeding exports. Unemployment never fell below 1.3 million in the period and by 1929 had reached nearly 3 million – 14.5 per cent of the workforce. The fall in world prices from the mid-1920s placed a great strain on farmers who made up one-third of Germany's population. By the late 1920s per capita income in agriculture was 44 per cent below the national average. Subsidies and protective tariffs only partially alleviated the problem. The marked decline in the income of such a sizeable section of the population contributed to a contraction in demand within the economy as a whole.

German economic historian Kurt Borchardt (1982) claimed the years 1924–29 were years of slow growth and 'relative stagnation'. Germany, Borchardt argued, was living well beyond its means. Not only were public finances out of control but wage levels were rising excessively without taking sufficient account of productivity. Borchardt claimed that this was the result of government intervention in the labour market which generally exhibited too much sympathy towards organised labour. For example, the introduction of compulsory wage arbitration and the higher employer contributions for social insurance both increased production costs, which led to lower investment and sluggish economic growth. Borchardt maintained that the Weimar economy was 'a sick economy which could not possibly have gone on in the same way, even if the world depression had not occurred'.

Rural problems

A third of the German population still lived and worked on the land. Rural Germany had long been anxious about long-term flight from the land and the competition of cheaper foreign foodstuffs. While farmers had benefited from a doubling of prices during the war, they had been obliged to put up with stringent government controls. From the outset, most had been bitterly antagonistic towards the Weimar Republic, which they saw as serving the selfish interests of the industrial proletariat and urban consumers.

Hyperinflation had offered farmers temporary relief from the burden of debt. However, after 1923 they faced heavy taxes on landed property. These were obviously resented by farmers who saw them as being used to subsidise the unemployed and a growing army of bureaucrats. Forced to purchase fertiliser, machines, seed and stock, most farmers were soon back in debt. The fact that that they were dependent on expensive short-term loans did not help. Nor did a series of natural disasters – floods, hail and outbreaks of foot-and-mouth disease. If this was not bad enough, farmers faced a crisis in the late 1920s as world food prices collapsed. Farmers grew increasingly angry. They regarded themselves as vital to the economy and society. But successive Weimar governments appeared to disregard their interests, preferring to support policies which ensured that urban workers were fed cheaply. By the late 1920s there were rural protests across Germany as desperate farmers, large and small landowners alike, turned more militant.

Financial problems

In an effort to prevent a repetition of hyperinflation, the *Reichsbank* was prevented by the Dawes legislation from allowing its interest rate to drop below five per cent. High interest rates proved attractive to overseas investors who could achieve better returns on capital lent on a short-term basis to Germany, than they could from longer-term investments in their own countries. But Germans, who had lost a great deal of money in the post-war inflation, were less inclined to save or invest. Starved of investment capital from within Germany, the economy increasingly relied on investors from abroad. As a result Germany's economic well-being became dependent on, and vulnerable to, the investment whims of foreign capital.

Government finances remained a cause for concern. While the government succeeded in balancing the budget in 1924, from 1925 it continually ran deficits while at the same time continuing to expand its financial commitments. It was thus increasingly forced to rely on international loans. Indeed, the reparation payments made by Germany in this period were really being financed by foreign loans.

Source D A police report of a mass demonstration by farmers in the city of Oldenburg in north-west Germany in January 1928.

In meetings of the rural population which were held in many places in the state of Oldenburg during the past weeks, the majority of those participating demanded again and again that an open-air protest meeting should be held in the state capital of Oldenburg, in order to give weight to the demands of the rural population, outlined below, which emerged in the meetings and were in the meantime formulated by a committee. It would also open the eyes of the state government to the masses of discontented who stand behind these demands ... According to fairly accurate estimates approximately 20,000 country people had assembled in the Horsefair by 12 noon ...

The general secretary of the Oldenburg Farmers' Association ... announced the following demands ...

- An **embargo** on all superfluous foreign imports.

- Protection of agriculture through tariffs equivalent to those already applied to industry ...

- Tax remission for farmers, craftsmen, and shopkeepers who are in distress.

- Speedy radical reduction of government activity and expenditure ...

- Reduction of social insurance contributions to a level which business can stand ...

- Availability of long-term cheap credit for the improvement of the debt situation with the aim of wiping out debts ...

The reading out of the demands drew loud and prolonged applause from the majority of the participants.

Embargo – A ban or prohibition on trade with a particular nation.

124

1 According to Source D, what were the main grievances of north-west German farmers?

2 Why were most German farmers discontented by 1928?

German society and culture

How progressive was German society and culture in the 1920s?

It is often claimed that the cultural climate of the Weimar Republic was astonishingly rich and fertile. Arguably Berlin, rather than Paris, became the cultural and artistic capital of Europe in the 1920s. Did these developments reflect a progressive society?

German society

German society in the 1920s was not dissimilar to that in the years before 1914. Given that most Germans lived in cities rather than working on the land, German society was more diverse – and advanced – than most societies in Europe.

The elite

Five per cent of the population (of some 64 million by 1929) were in the economic elite – rich industrialists, successful entrepreneurs, wealthy financiers or great landowners. Thanks to their material assets, most had weathered the storm of inflation. They remained the objects of envy, denounced on the left as capitalist exploiters. Accordingly, most felt threatened by the organised working class. Many looked for an authoritarian solution to the pressing social, economic and political problems that beset the Republic.

The middle classes

The middle class made up at least a third of the population, ranging from doctors, lawyers and professors at the top to the growing number of people in the lower ranks of the civil service and in service industries and white-collar occupations at the bottom end. The middle classes found themselves uncomfortably trapped between big business and organised labour. Most longed for stability, an end to the increasingly virulent class antagonisms and a renewed sense of community.

The working classes

The working classes comprised over 50 per cent of the population. Whatever Communists liked to think, the working class was far from united. There were a great number of working classes. Wages varied from industry to industry. Some workers were skilled, others unskilled. There were important regional and religious differences. Farm labourers, who earned a pittance, had little in common with industrial workers. Nevertheless, the proletariat did have some sense of comradeship. The call for socialist policies – whether Marxist or of a more moderate nature – was a source of concern to many non-proletarian Germans.

German women

The role of women and the debate about their status was an important feature of Weimar society. The media propagated the idea of the Weimar 'new woman'. Illustrated magazines displayed images of cigarette-smoking, silk-stockinged, short-skirted, lip-sticked young women out in the streets, in bars or on the sports field. The 'new woman' image had some social reality.

- Women had gained formally equal rights under the Weimar constitution.
- There was a growing number of women in new areas of employment, especially in public services (for example, the civil service, teaching or social work), in shops and on assembly lines.
- More women (particularly those who were young and single) spent their leisure time at sports clubs, dance halls and in cinemas.
- Women had more sexual independence.

Women thus constituted a more visible presence in the public sphere and in the economy than they had done before 1918.

Nevertheless, the 'new woman' wasn't entirely a reality.

- The proportion of women who worked outside the home during the 1920s remained roughly the same as before 1914 – as did their type of work.
- Despite the large numbers of women who worked during the war in so-called 'men's jobs', for example, heavy industry, these better-paid jobs were taken back by men after 1918.
- Social attitudes to women's role in society remained conservative. Hitler's view – that women's role was in the kitchen, at church and producing children – was the view of many Germans – male and female. Married women were not expected to work outside the home. Those who did – the so-called *Doppelverdiener* – became a source of considerable controversy.

Doppelverdiener – This translates as second wage earner. It was a term of abuse aimed at married women who went out to work.

Type of employment	Percentage of the workforce that was female	
	1907	1925
Domestic servants	16	11.4
Farm workers	14.5	9.2
Industrial workers	18.3	23
White collar and public employment	6.5	12.6
Percentage of women in employment	31.2	35.6

▲ **Figure 3** Women in employment in Germany: a comparison between 1907 and 1925.

The changing urban landscape

In the 1920s local governments attempted to improve the urban environment. Effort was particularly focused on the construction of new public parks, libraries, transport and housing schemes. Such reforms, often supported and implemented by Social Democrats, were fuelled by an optimistic vision of the hygienic management of cities and their populations. The public authorities in Berlin, for example, promoted the city as one which had an efficient infrastructure, combating social evils through appropriate welfare intervention and encouraging a democratic culture based on a rational lifestyle balancing work, domesticity and healthy leisure pursuits. Modern architects associated with the Bauhaus (see page 128) believed such a culture would be fostered by functionally designed mass housing projects. From the mid-1920s they gained major contracts in the capital. Building societies and the electrical engineering company Siemens commissioned housing projects and under Martin Wagner, director of the municipal central building administration from 1927, police stations and public swimming baths came to be designed in the new style. Even if these projects comprised only a fraction of new buildings, they were striking symbols of the 'New Berlin'. It should be said that at the same time department stores and advertising hoardings were shaping cities in a different way as sites of consumerism.

Anti-urbanisation

Some Germans – right and left – disliked the growing urbanisation of Germany.

- Anti-urbanism was particularly associated with right-wing volkisch groups who saw a return to working and living on the land as the route to Germany's national rebirth.

- Some on the extreme left denounced modern cities as steeped in the evils of capitalism and saw rural communes as the road to a classless and peaceful society.

Education

The German education system, with its emphasis on obedience and authority, had long been a target of Social Democrats and liberal critics of the old order. Once that order collapsed they hoped to be able to do something to alter the education system. In particular, reformers aimed to:

- break down the old religious barriers which kept Catholic and Protestant children apart
- end the virtual monopoly by the middle classes of secondary-grammar and higher education
- develop a more democratic consciousness among teachers which would be passed on to their pupils.

The reformers had limited success.

- While more secular and inter-denominational schools were established, the majority of schools remained denominational. The Catholic Centre Party was at odds with the SPD on this issue.
- The lack of an adequate scholarship system still prevented most gifted working-class children from getting secondary education. In 1930 only about 7 per cent of secondary-school pupils were from working-class families.
- Old monarchical-conservative ideas persisted, particularly among secondary-school teachers. Many ignored appeals from politicians for the teaching of loyalty to the Republic's democratic ideals. Most university professors were also nationalist-inclined – as were the majority of their students who sometimes hounded those lecturers who were known to have socialist or pacifist views.

Education experimentation

A few new schools were established in Germany, using experimental methods of learning. The most famous were those influenced by the ideas of Austrian philosopher Rudolf Steiner whose first Waldorf school was set up in Stuttgart in 1919. Steiner's methods stressed the role of imagination in learning and favoured integrating intellectual, practical and artistic activities across the curriculum rather than learning through particular academic disciplines.

How diverse was German society?

German society was diverse. Its structure did not change greatly in the 1920s. It may be that people's perception of the nature of German society changed. Class antagonisms existed in pre-war Germany but they were partly disguised by the trappings of monarchy, regional loyalties and ingrained deference. Much of this disappeared after 1918. There was a growing sense of class division. Nevertheless, class solidarity was not as strong as socialists hoped. Many Germans – of all classes – wished to see an end to class antagonism.

Weimar culture

Artistic conventions and established assumptions about the function of art had been widely challenged in Wilhelmine Germany (see pages 47–9). However, aesthetic experiment flourished in the Weimar Republic as never before. In the 1920s there was experimentation in all forms of culture – literature, art, architecture, music, dance, drama and the cinema. The republican state itself fostered artistic pluralism.

- The Weimar constitution declared, albeit with some qualifications, that censorship 'does not take place' and proclaimed the freedom of the arts and scholarship.
- The newly democratised municipal and regional governments became a source of patronage, sometimes favouring the performance or display of avant-garde works as a badge of their progressiveness. Despite the problems of public finances in the early 1920s, politicians at local level continued to channel substantial public funding into the arts.

To many foreign observers and visitors, Weimar Germany seemed outstanding for its diverse, cosmopolitan and innovative cultural climate.

But Germans were bitterly divided about the cultural changes that were taking place. While some applauded the various manifestations of cultural modernity, others were hostile to phenomena as diverse as jazz, anti-war paintings, cinema and pulp fiction. In the eyes of their enemies these types of cultural output became the scapegoat for Germany's problems. Cultural conservatives accused them of undermining social stability, moral values and cultural standards. Right-wing attacks on modernism and mass culture became attacks on the Republic itself, which because it provided a framework for cultural innovation became identified with it. Through such attacks, cultural debates in Weimar Germany became polarised to an extreme and politically destabilising degree.

The Bauhaus movement

During the 1920s Germany became a leading centre of creative effort, particularly in architecture. The Bauhaus in Dessau, a new school of architecture and design set up by Walter Gropius in 1919, became famous for breaking down the barriers between art and science and bringing into design the techniques of engineering. As well as stressing the relationship between art and technology, the Bauhaus movement emphasised functionality of design and freedom from the past. Its basic idea was to discard conventional ornamental styles for functional ones of steel, glass and concrete. The new designs were meant to give people a greater insight into reality, and make life easier – especially for women.

The Bauhaus style – austere and rectangular – spread rapidly across the whole of Germany, impacting on both domestic and public architecture. In 1928

Photograph of the exterior of the ▶
Bauhaus factory at Dessau, designed
by the architect Walter Gropius.

in Stuttgart, a city not usually noted for being progressive, an architectural exhibition was held for which members of the Bauhaus including Gropius, Mies van der Rohe, Mendelsohn and Le Corbusier designed 'the new house'. The city government then provided the money for the plans to be transformed into bricks and mortar. Bauhaus's architectural style brought with it similarly revolutionary designs in furniture and interior decoration.

Literature and drama

In literature Weimar provided the climate in which experimentation could occur. The modernistic style and content offered by new German writers in the novels of the 1920s stood for frankness, especially in sexual matters, and for (often bitter) social comment. Perhaps the most successful Weimar novel was Eric Maria Remarque's *All Quiet on the Western Front* – a book highly critical of the First World War. First serialised in a Berlin newspaper, it quickly became a worldwide bestseller in 1929. Remarque, like the brothers Heinrich and Thomas Mann, and the writer Alfred Döblin, presented a bleak look at the world and the failure of politics and society.

In the 1920s Berlin became a mecca for theatre-goers. The works of dramatists such as Peter Lampel concentrated on a range of social issues. *The Threepenny Opera*, produced by Erwin Piscator in 1928, was deliberately Marxist in bias. The aim of agitprop theatre, associated with Bertolt Brecht, was to add elements of public protest (agitation) and persuasive politics (propaganda) to the theatre in the hope of creating a more involved and activist audience. (Agitprop is a combination of the words 'agitation' and 'propaganda'.) Brecht's theatre in Berlin was regarded as one of the most progressive in Europe.

Visual art

German visual art was strongly influenced by German Expressionism in 1918. However, in the early 1920s, the *Neue Sachlichkeit* movement emerged – in part a reaction against the romanticism, fantasy, subjectivity, raw emotion and impulse of Expressionism. Most of those who painted in its style focused on precision and depicting the factual. Most were left-leaning: their paintings show the horrors of war, social hypocrisy and the plight of the poor. Artists linked to *Neue Sachlichkeit* included Otto Dix, George Grosz, Max Beckmann and Käthe Kollwitz. Dix and Grosz referred to their own movement as *Verism* – a reference to the Roman classical approach called *verus* meaning 'truth'. In their art, they were striving to portray both a sense of realism and a criticism of life in Weimar Germany.

Neue Sachlichkeit – This translates as matter-of-factness or objectivity. *Neue Sachlichkeit* became a major undercurrent in all of the arts during the Weimar Republic.

The importance of Berlin

Berlin was generally seen as the centre of revolutionary art and cultural experiment. Much of the artistic avant-garde gravitated to Berlin where they found institutional support and receptive audiences. Thus the musician Schoenberg began teaching classes in composition at the Prussian Academy of Arts in 1925 and new musical works were premiered in the city's main concert halls. Berlin art galleries promoted the work of contemporary German painters.

In the 1920s, foreign writers and artists travelled to the German capital, attracted by the city's dynamic culture. The German capital had a reputation for its exotic – not to say erotic – nightlife. The cabaret scene in Berlin was described by British author Christopher Isherwood in his novel *Goodbye to Berlin*, on which the musical *Cabaret* was based. There were hundreds of nightclubs. Such venues provided outlets for experimental performers. They were also places where a sub-culture such as that of Berlin's gay community could thrive.

At the same time, Berlin was developing as a centre of mass cultural production – in journalism, film and fashion – and as a showcase for the latest cultural imports from abroad, especially the USA. While American cultural influence on Germany was by no means restricted to Berlin, cultural imports from the USA found particularly enthusiastic audiences in the German capital in the 1920s. Jazz was one of the most popular cultural imports from the USA. Jazz-playing dance bands could be found all over Berlin in hotels, cafes and bars. American films seemed to be better received in Berlin than elsewhere in Germany. In its embracing of American culture, Berlin seemed to some observers more American than America.

Source E William Shirer, an American journalist, writing about his first impressions of Germany in the 1920s.

I was stationed in Paris and occasionally in London at that time, and fascinating though those capitals were ... they paled a little when one came to Berlin and Munich. A wonderful ferment was working in Germany. Life seemed more free, more modern, more exciting than in any place I had ever seen. Nowhere else did the arts or the intellectual life seem so lively. In contemporary writing, painting, architecture, in music and drama, there were new currents and fine talents. And everywhere there was an accent on youth ... They were a healthy, carefree, sun-worshipping lot, and they were filled with an enormous zest for living life to the full and in complete freedom. The old oppressive Prussian spirit seemed to be dead and buried. Most Germans one met – politicians, writers, editors, artists, professors, students, businessmen, labour leaders – struck you as being democratic, liberal, even pacifist.

1 To what extent is Source E a reliable source of evidence for German cultural life in the 1920s?
2 Why did the author of Source E approve of German cultural life in the 1920s?

The impact of the avant-garde

The various competing styles and versions of modernism, though flourishing spectacularly in the Weimar years, never actually dominated German cultural output in quantitative terms or in terms of public performances, exhibitions or bestseller lists. Modernist works were received differently in different parts of Germany. If Berlin was the avant-garde pace-setter, some provincial areas dragged their heels with regard to modernism.

Nevertheless, there were important centres of avant-garde creativity outside Berlin. The Bauhaus, for example, set up in Weimar and moved to Dessau in 1925. The *Neue Sachlichkeit* visual arts movement flourished in a number of cities – notably Dresden, Karlsruhe, Munich, Hanover, Cologne and Dusseldorf. Artistic modernism was promoted by some (but by no means all) provincial city politicians who sought to 'catch up' with Berlin not only in the quality of their town's cultural facilities but in the content of its publicly subsidised arts programme. In the Ruhr, for example, the city councils of Bochum and Essen backed the conductor Rudolf Schulz-Dornburg in his efforts to convert local audiences to the works of musicians like Schoenberg and Stravinsky.

But on the whole theatre directors and conductors in provincial towns tempered their enthusiasm for new work with consideration for the preferences of their paying audiences. Concert and theatre audiences were still predominantly middle class and tended to be middle-of-the-road in taste. Theatre schedules and concert programmes including more advanced contemporary works tended to be cushioned by more familiar fare to keep audiences happy. The need for caution was underlined by cases where the scheduling of avant-garde work provoked outright hostility – as did Bartók's world premiere of *The Miraculous Mandarin*, performed in the Cologne Opera House in 1926. The performance ended with the audience yelling and booing.

Public reaction to the works of modernists was predictably diverse, ranging from enthusiasm through respectful curiosity to suspicion, bewilderment or downright hostility.

Mass culture

The impact of the avant-garde was felt most in the world of 'high' culture – a sphere dominated by an educated, essentially middle-class public. Changes in the cultural sphere which had a greater impact on the mass of the population were those resulting from the development of radio and cinema.

The impact of radio

The first public radio programme began broadcasting in 1923 from Berlin. Soon other regional stations started up. The number of registered radio listeners increased steadily and by 1932 there were 4.2 million registered radio sets. However, there were significant disparities across Germany in the distribution of listeners. For most of the 1920s, regional transmitters emitted such weak signals that to pick them up outside a certain radius would-be listeners needed an expensive radio set, which few Germans could afford. In 1927 less than a third of Germans lived in areas within which cheaper 'detector' sets could be used.

The difficulties with reception and the resulting costs of buying radio sets, together with the often highbrow programmes offered, made radio a medium which was used disproportionately by the middle classes. Moreover, given the difficulties with reception, it was a medium of urban-dwellers. In 1932, in villages of fewer than 2,500 inhabitants only 10 per cent of households had a radio. The sluggish take-up of radio in rural areas was in spite of the efforts of 'radio vans' equipped with demonstration sets which travelled round the countryside trying to drum up interest in the medium. It confounded the hopes of radio companies and politicians that radio was the medium with the potential to bring the wider world to rural Germany and perhaps even counteract the flight from the land by making rural life less monotonous.

The cinema

Cheap entertainment outside the home could be found at variety theatres, new sports stadia, dance halls but above all at the cinema. By 1930 there were more than 5,000 cinemas in Germany; in 1928 around 353 million cinema tickets were sold – to people of all classes. By comparison, attendance figures for the performances staged by municipal theatres in 87 towns and cities in 1926–27 were just under 12 million.

Cinema for most of the Weimar period meant silent films; 'talkies' only appeared in the final years of the Republic. Much of the German film production after 1918 was concerned, like much of production elsewhere, with escapist themes – comedies, adventures in far-off places, detective stories, fantasies and musicals. But more serious themes were dealt with too.

Serious film directors were often concerned with the same issues as serious writers. Unlike the writers, they had the problem of financing their projects. The UFA organisation (Universum Film AG – a German motion-picture production company, founded in 1917) possessed a dominant position both in the production and distribution of films. From 1927 this company was controlled by Alfred Hugenberg, a right-wing businessmen who controlled a great media empire (see page 134). Hugenberg had no enthusiasm for critical or controversial themes. Nevertheless the UFA did fund *Metropolis* (1927), a film directed and written by Fritz Lang. The film, a pioneering work of science fiction genre, cost 5 million *Reichsmarks* to make – the most expensive film released up to that point. Set in the future, it follows the attempt of Freder, the rich son of the city's ruler, and Maria, a poor worker, to overcome the vast gulf separating the classes of Metropolis. Some critics praised the film's social metaphors. Others dismissed it as unconvincing and overlong.

People of all classes attended the cinema, often viewing the same films – which were far more likely to be costume dramas than futuristic, expressionist or serious films. However, it seems unlikely that there was any sense of class unity arising from a common experience of the same entertainment – which was quite likely to be American-produced.

Access to the cinema varied greatly depending on the region and the size of the locality. Some rural areas were miles from the nearest cinema. In such places, leisure continued to revolve around pubs and clubs, with men constituting the majority of regular pub-goers and club members. (Once women got married, they generally stayed in while their husbands went out in the evenings.)

The reaction against modernism

Partial though it was, the impact of artistic modernism and mass culture in the Weimar period was sufficient to spark a powerful backlash. Middle-class Germans were accustomed to the idea of Germany as an outstanding 'cultural nation' with a heritage meriting protection. To many Germans, developments in Berlin (in particular) embodied important shifts in culture and society which were affecting Germany generally. Accepted norms governing the form and content of 'high culture' were being challenged by the avant-garde. 'Mass culture' was becoming more pervasive. The rise of the cinema and the radio appeared to be loosening people's ties to the traditional cultural milieu.

Right-wing opposition

The harshest attacks on modernism and the greatest anxieties about the impact of modernisation on cultural life came from bourgeois organisations and from the right.

- Many conservatives believed that Weimar's cultural life was irredeemably debased by foreign and Jewish influence and 'shallow materialism'. The Nazis and other groups on the far right believed that the avant-garde had to be destroyed and that a new order was needed to ensure the victory of German *Kultur* over 'Americanisation'.
- Many Church organisations campaigned against 'immorality' in modern life, whether this took the form of atheism, nudity, pornography, prostitution, homosexuality, birth control or abortion.
- Others simply railed against the 'tides of filth' engulfing Germany and called for tougher censorship as a matter of cultural hygiene. One step in this direction was the passing by the *Reichstag* of a bill to 'protect youth from pulp fiction and pornography' in 1926. On the basis of this law, a list was set up of publications which were not to be sold to young people under 18: 'true-crime' publications, erotic magazines and sex education books were among the 103 publications on the index by 1930.
- Various groups were founded to protect authentic German culture, threatened from Berlin and other cities. Many groups celebrated regional folk traditions as a bulwark against what were seen as the homogenising and centralising influences of modern urban culture.

Left-wing opposition

A sense of alienation from – and alarm about – the new cultural forces was not restricted solely to the middle classes nor politically to the parties of the right. While left-wing intellectuals were often committed advocates of artistic modernism, many Social Democrats were more inclined to approve traditional culture than the works of the avant-garde. Communist cultural organisations, meanwhile, pursued their own goals of creating a proletarian counter-culture. The left generally was also dubious about many aspects of commercial mass culture. Social Democrats were as concerned as bourgeois organisations about

WORKING TOGETHER

Work in groups. Each person should choose one of the people mentioned in this cultural section and carry out their own online research on them. For each you should find out why they were important and what cultural impact they had on Germany in the 1920s. Share your findings with the group.

the impact of pulp fiction on youthful minds. Both the SPD and Communist Party regarded the rise of cinema with concern, fearing that the labour movement would never be able to offer a socialist alternative to match the sophisticated products of the international film industry.

Nevertheless, on the whole, there was more curiosity on the political left than on the right regarding both avant-garde art and the new forms of mass communication.

Conclusion

The 1920s were thus years of cultural division, reflecting the divisions within Weimar politics and society. The matter-of-factness *of Neue Sachlichkeit* contrasted with the nostalgia, romanticism and escapism of much popular literature, the modernity of Bauhaus with the traditional taste of the majority of the population. Arguably, the cultural developments – and cultural divisions – of the period helped to destabilise the Republic. It had very few defenders of note among the cultural and intellectual elite, many of whom quickly became disenchanted with Weimar and the values which underpinned it. Some left-wing writers, artists and intellectuals looked to the Communist Party as the source of a class-conscious proletarian counter-culture and to the Soviet Union as an alternative model of modernity to Western capitalism. They often attacked the new republican establishment with work which was either satirical or deliberately shocking.

So, while Weimar became identified with cultural experimentation and liberation, these forces did not act as a foundation for stability. And those who felt alienated by the artistic and cultural changes blamed the Republic for, what they saw as, decadence.

German politics, 1925–29

To what extent was Germany politically stable by 1929?

German politics remained unstable in the late 1920s. Nevertheless, most Germans in 1928 voted for parties which supported the Republic. The likelihood of the Communists on the left or the Nazis on the right ever winning power seemed remote.

The political situation, 1925–28

The Locarno Treaty was opposed by the Nationalists who saw it as a craven appeasement of the Western powers and they withdrew their support for Hans Luther's government. The Treaty was only ratified with the backing of the SPD. But the SPD refused to join Luther's minority coalition. The Luther government fell a few weeks later over the question of whether German embassies should be allowed to fly the black, white and red flag (flown by German merchant ships) in place of the black, red and gold flag symbolic of republicanism.

A new minority government was formed in May 1926 under Wilhelm Marx but the SPD continued to stand aloof. In December 1926 Philipp Scheidemann made a sensational speech in the *Reichstag* in which he exposed the illegal financing of armaments and the close links between the *Reichswehr* and right-wing paramilitary groups which were designed to circumvent the restriction of the army to 100,000 men. He also stated that the KPD was well aware that armaments, forbidden by the Treaty of Versailles, were being imported from the USSR. The Marx cabinet fell as a result of these revelations. But there was no alternative to yet another minority government under Marx in which the DNVP played a prominent role. The appointment of Walter von Keudell, an avowed anti-Semite and a leading figure in the Kapp Putsch (see page 95) as Minister of the Interior was an indication of a sharp right turn.

NOTE-MAKING

The key issue remains stability. How stable was Germany politically in these years? Try to structure your notes so that you list the strengths and weaknesses of the Weimar's political system in this period. Your notes should then provide the basis for you to decide whether the Republic was politically weak or strong.

The *Reichswehr*

The *Reichswehr* showed a greater willingness to collaborate with Republican politicians after Von Seeckt's resignation in 1926. His successor General Wilhelm Heye made genuine efforts to improve relations with the government. The government, in turn, provided the army with more money than it should have done under the terms of the Versailles Treaty. Fundamentally the army had changed very little since 1919. The officer corps was overwhelmingly anti-Republican. Recruitment was restricted largely to men of nationalist or apolitical backgrounds, mainly from rural areas.

The fourth Marx cabinet was responsible for the most important piece of social legislation in the Republic's history – the unemployment insurance bill of July 1927. Financed by both employers and employees, it provided comprehensive coverage for all employees. The state was obliged to grant a bridging loan if the unemployment insurance fund fell into the red. The new system was admirably suited to deal with the problems of moderate unemployment as existed in 1927. However, it was certain to be an embarrassment if unemployment rapidly increased.

Marx's government fell over a failure to reach a compromise, this time over the financing of confessional schools.

The 1928 elections

The election campaign of 1928 was dominated by the issue of whether the proposed building of the pocket-battleship Battle Cruiser 'A' should go ahead. The SPD and Communists demanded that the money designated for the ship should be spent on free school meals for the needy.

> **Pocket-battleship** – A small battleship, built to the specifications laid down by the Treaty of Versailles.

The May 1928 elections produced a clear victory for those parties which accepted the Weimar constitution. Extremists on the right and left gained less than 30 per cent of the votes cast. (This figure includes the supporters of the DNVP which had participated in Republican cabinets.) The DNVP lost 30 seats in 1928. The Nazis won only 2.6 per cent of the vote, gaining twelve *Reichstag* seats. The SPD gained 22 seats and the KPD (with 10.6 per cent of the vote) increased their seats by nine. There was also a rise in the vote of splinter parties. The *Bauernbund*, for example, which represented farmers' interests, won 4.5 per cent of the vote.

Chancellor Hermann Müller

After the 1928 elections, SPD ministers entered the cabinet for the first time since 1923 and an SPD member, Hermann Müller, became chancellor. Müller's ministry included members of the SPD, DDP, DVP, Centre and BVP. President Hindenburg seemed quite willing to work with the SPD. Indeed, he came to have a high opinion of Müller, comparing him favourably with other chancellors. Unfortunately, Müller lacked the qualities to inspire his followers or to make a great impact as a national leader. The Müller government was immediately faced with a crisis when the cabinet decided to go ahead with the building of Battle Cruiser 'A', even though the SPD had fought the election campaign in fierce opposition to the proposal. When the bill was debated in the *Reichstag*, the SPD, with the exception of only Müller and the three SPD cabinet ministers, voted against it. The bill was nevertheless approved.

Changes in the Nationalist Party

The DNVP's sharp fall in support – down from 20.5 per cent in 1924 to 14.2 per cent in 1928 – led to demands for change within the Party. Some members, willing to co-operate with other parties in order to influence the conduct of the government, wanted the DNVP to renounce the desire for the return of the monarchy and accept the permanence of the Republic. But many DNVP supporters opposed such action. They rallied around Alfred Hugenberg, Germany's most influential newspaper and film company owner. Offering the cash-stripped Party financial aid and the propaganda machine of his media empire, Hugenberg was elected leader of the DNVP in October 1928. The policy of the DNVP now became one of strident and unrestrained opposition to the Republic.

The Nazi Party, 1924–28

In May 1924 the Nazis, in alliance with other parties of the extreme right, had won 1.9 million votes (6.5 per cent) in elections to the *Reichstag*. By December 1924 the figure had fallen to 907,000 votes – 3 per cent. Nevertheless, Hitler was convinced that the Nazis must win power by democratic means.

It seemed highly unlikely that Hitler would ever win power democratically. If he was to win mass support, he needed discontent and Germans were less discontented as the economic situation improved. Moreover, the NSDAP had fallen apart during his year in prison and he was banned from speaking publicly in most German states.

In 1925 Hitler re-established control over the NSDAP in Bavaria. Throughout 1925 the Party was reorganised. In May 1926 a new centralised structure was introduced which stressed complete obedience to Hitler – the all-powerful *Führer* (leader). He saw off the challenge from north German Nazis, led by Gregor Strasser, who wanted to make the Nazi programme more socialist. In the late 1920s Hitler reorganised his Party. A host of new departments – for example, for youth, students and women – were set up. Elaborate Nazi ritual was established and the Party's first Nuremberg rally was held in 1927. Hitler developed a new image for himself. No longer a revolutionary fanatic, he appeared instead a calm, reasonable man awaiting the call of history – which must surely come. That call did not come in 1928. Although his Party had some 100,000 members by 1928 (partly because it had succeeded in absorbing many of the other *volkisch* groups), in the May elections the Nazis won only 2.6 per cent of the vote.

Failing to win much support from industrial workers, the Nazis turned their attention to the distressed farmers in north Germany (see page 123–4). The Nazis promised to guarantee prices and markets for German agricultural products. They also emphasised the importance of farmers – Germany's lifeblood according to Nazi propaganda. From the outset many farmers had been bitterly antagonistic towards the Weimar Republic, which they saw as serving the selfish interests of the industrial proletariat and urban consumers. As food prices fell, discontented farmers began to flock to the Nazi Party in late 1928.

The Young Plan

In February 1929 a committee of experts met to discuss a final plan for reparations. It was headed by Owen Young, an American who had been vice-chairman of the Dawes Committee. For the first time the timescale for reparation payments was set. Germany was to pay 2,000 million marks a year (rather than the 2,500 million marks as laid down by the Dawes Plan) for the next 59 years. The German government was made responsible for the payment. Allied controls over Germany's railways and banking system were to be dropped so that Germany regained its economic sovereignty. Moreover, if Germany agreed to the plan, the French promised to evacuate the Rhineland by mid-1930, five years ahead of schedule. The Young Plan was signed in June 1929.

Opposition to the Young Plan

Although the effect of the Young Plan was to reduce Germany's reparation payments, Nationalists, rejecting the whole concept of reparations, furiously opposed the scheme. In July 1929, DNVP leader Hugenberg formed the

Source F Hitler, writing from prison, in 1924.

When I pursue active work, it will be necessary to pursue a new policy. Instead of working to achieve power by an armed coup, we will have to hold our noses and enter the Reichstag against Catholic and Marxist members. If outvoting them takes longer than outshooting them, at least the result will be guaranteed by their own Constitution. Sooner or later we shall have a majority, and after that – Germany.

1 What evidence in Source F suggests that Hitler intended to use democratic means to destroy democracy?
2 Was there any cause for Hitler's optimism in 1924 about winning power at the ballot box?

The _Stahlhelm_ – This translates as 'steel helmet'. This was a right-wing organisation – strongly nationalist, monarchist and anti-Communist. Most of its members were ex-soldiers.

Reich Committee for a Referendum to oppose the Young Plan. (Article 73 of the Constitution allowed political parties to petition for a referendum.) This committee included representatives from the DNVP, the _Stahlhelm_, the Pan-German League and the Nazi Party. The Nazis – rabble rousers, radicals, socialists as well as nationalists – were an unusual ally of what was otherwise a socially conservative movement. But Hugenberg believed that Hitler's dynamic oratory would assist the Nationalist cause.

The campaign against the Young Plan culminated with a plebiscite in December 1929. Only 5.8 million Germans voted against the Young Plan, far less than the 21 million votes needed. In March 1930 the _Reichstag_ accepted the Young Plan. In June 1930 French forces evacuated the Rhineland.

The campaign against the Young Plan – albeit a failure – proved a godsend for Hitler. By associating with the Nationalists, he and his Party gained an aura of respectability they had previously lacked. Hitler came into contact with men of wealth and influence who could be of great material help to his Party. Even more important was the publicity Hitler received from Hugenberg's media empire.

Hitler, rather than trying to win the working class away from the Marxist parties, now began to focus his attention on the disaffected middle classes. Many Germans were attracted by Hitler's promises that National Socialism would supersede all conflicts of class and interest and create a harmonious 'racial community'. Money began to flow into the Party's coffers. A Nazi surge had begun in late 1928 as the Party's focus on northern farmers began to pay dividends. By 1929 the Nazis were winning 10–20 per cent of the vote in state and local elections across northern Germany.

How successful was the Weimar Republic politically in the period 1925–29?

On the surface, the Republic seemed to have done reasonably well politically between 1925 and 1929. There was no putsch from left or right. Law and order was restored and the activities of the various paramilitary groups was severely curtailed. In the election of 1928, the extremist parties of both left and right (including the DNVP) polled less than a third of the votes cast. By contrast, the parties sympathetic to the Republic generally maintained their share of the vote.

But the results of the 1928 election should not be allowed to disguise the continuing fundamental weaknesses of the parliamentary and party system. The main democratic parties, representing very different interests, had failed to recognise the necessity of working together in a spirit of compromise. There was thus no political stability. Of the seven governments between 1924 and 1930 only two had majorities and the longest survived 21 months. In fact, the only reason governments lasted as long as they did was because of the inability or the unwillingness of the opposition to unite. More often than not it was the ever-changing shifts of power within the parties of government which actually led to collapse. Not surprisingly many Germans became cynical of party politics and the wheeler-dealing associated with the creation of coalitions.

WORKING TOGETHER

Split into groups. In order to gain a fuller understanding of the mind-set of Germans in this period, itemise their concerns and grievances by 1928–29, carrying out more research if you need to. Write each one on a sticky note. Each group should then attach these to the wall or whiteboard. Compare the points raised by each group. Discuss what seem to be the main problems/issues. Also discuss whether Germans might have felt a sense of optimism in 1928–29. Why and to what extent might some Germans have praised the Weimar Republic?

Interpretations: How successful was the Weimar Republic in the period 1924–29?

Historians remain divided about the political and economic well-being of the Weimar Republic in the period 1924 to 1929. Some think that it was generally successful and, but for the crisis following the Wall Street Crash in October 1929 (see page 149–150), might have survived and prospered. Others think the Republic's foundations were far from firm. They point out that the Nazi Party's fortunes were on the rise in the months before October 1929.

Source G Adapted from *A History of Modern Germany 1800–2000* by M. Kitchen, (Blackwell), 2006.

The unemployment insurance bill of 1927 was admirably suited to deal with the problems of moderate unemployment as existed at the time, but was soon to be stretched to the limit when the depression began to be felt in the following year. The depression had already had a devastating effect on the economy by the spring of 1929, and it was obvious that Germany would not be able to meet the increased payments demanded by the Dawes Plan that year. With three million unemployed by February 1929 it was unlikely that the unemployment insurance fund would be able to meet the demands made upon it. A new reparations commission was formed and the resulting Young Plan reduced the annual payments.

The right-wing parties mounted a massive campaign against the Young Commission. Hitler and the NSDAP joined the campaign and Hitler's tactics paid handsome dividends. He was now in respectable company and he began to focus his attention on the disaffected middle classes. The response was immediate; money began to flow into the party's coffers and spectacular gains were made in state elections in Thuringia and Baden. All this seemed to have escaped the notice of the politicians in Berlin.

Source H Adapted from *Nazi Germany: A New History* by K. Fischer, (Constable), 1995.

The middle years of the Weimar Republic, sometimes referred to as the Roaring or Golden Twenties, saw a temporary return of domestic prosperity. Many western loans were made to Germany creating an impressive boom that persuaded many that the crisis of 1923 had been resolved. Germany used the borrowed capital in two profitable ways: financing a programme of public works and investing in the modernisation of industry. In 1923 German industrial output had fallen to 47 per cent of 1913 levels, but by 1929 it surpassed 1913 levels by 4 per cent.

The economic recovery brought with it a corresponding improvement in international relations, partly because the Western powers recognised that the economic well-being in an increasingly interconnected economic order rested on cooperation rather than on conflict. This also lowered the political temperature in Germany. In 1925, the Weimar Republic gained new respectability with the election as president of the venerable Paul Von Hindenburg who would painstakingly observe his oath to the Republic despite his monarchist convictions.

ACTIVITY

Sources G–I (pages 137–8) give different interpretations of the Weimar Republic's political and economic stability by the late 1920s. Read each one in turn, listing the main points made and the evidence used to support those points. Then answer the following questions:

1 In what way do the sources agree and disagree?
2 Using your understanding of the historical context, assess how convincing the arguments in these three sources are in relation to the economic and political success of the Weimar Republic before 1929.

Source I Adapted from *A History of Germany, 1815–1985*, by William Carr, (Hodder Arnold), 1987.

It is sometimes said that Weimar Germany experienced boom conditions between 1924 and 1929. Certainly iron and steel, coal, chemicals and electrical products recovered quickly after the war. Recent research suggests, however, that the extent of the 'boom' has been greatly exaggerated. In the late 1920s growth rates were unsteady; capital investment was already falling by 1929; unemployment was never less than 1.3 million and reached 3 million by February 1929.

The relative affluence of these years was reflected politically in a sharp decline of support for parties on the extreme right and left. Middle-of-the-road parties were making steady progress. When the Republic celebrated its tenth anniversary in 1929, there seemed reasonable grounds for optimism. A closer look at political life in the late 1920s quickly destroys these illusions. From the start the existence of a multi-party system made the task of creating a viable democracy difficult. Proportional representation accentuated the difficulty. It proved immensely difficult to form coalitions with majority support in the Reichstag.

Chapter summary

- The *Rentenmark* and the Dawes Plan improved Germany's financial situation in 1924.
- Parties supporting the Weimar Republic won *Reichstag* elections in May and December 1924 but the SPD refused to join any coalition until 1928.
- President Ebert died in 1925. Hindenburg's election as president was seen as a swing to the right but his prestige gave the Republic some respectability.
- Stresemann improved Germany's relations with Britain and France. In 1925 Germany signed the Locarno Treaties and in 1926 joined the League of Nations.
- *Reichstag* elections in 1928 were a success for the SPD. SPD leader Müller became German Chancellor.
- German right-wing parties opposed the Young Plan (1929) which reduced Germany's reparation payments.
- The Nazi Party, benefiting from the support of discontented farmers and Hitler's publicity arising from his opposition to the Young Plan, began to have election success in state elections in 1928–29.
- Unemployment in Germany was increasing before the Wall Street Crash.
- German society, although diverse, remained divided, mainly by class.
- The Weimar Republic saw a great deal of experimentation in all aspects of art and culture. The experimentation was approved by some and loathed by others.

▼ **Summary diagram:** Recovery and stability, 1923–29

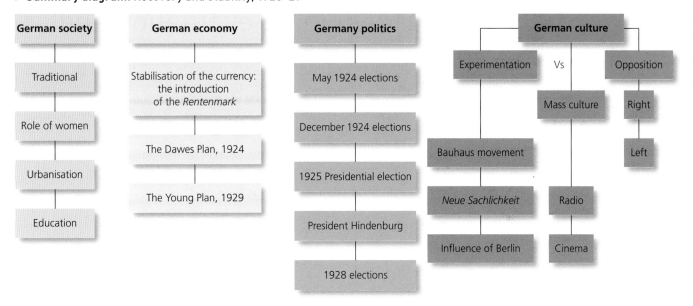

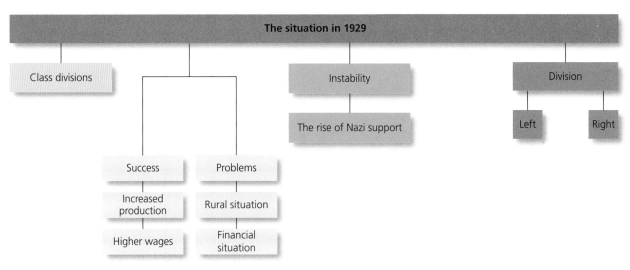

Working on essay technique: evaluation and relative significance

Reaching a supported overall judgement is an important part of writing good essays. One very important way to do this is by evaluating the relative significance of different factors, in the light of valid criteria. 'Relative significance' means how important one factor is compared to another. This section examines how to evaluate and how to establish valid criteria.

The purpose of evaluation is to weigh up and reach a judgement. This means that you need to consider the importance of two or more different factors, weigh them against each other, and then reach a judgement. Evaluation is a good skill to use at the end of an essay, because it helps support your overall judgement.

Clearly, the arguments in the example on page 141 about the nature of the right- and left-wing threat to Germany can be based on new evidence and new interpretations. The best essays will always make a judgement about which was most important based on valid criteria.

It is up to you to come up with valid criteria. Criteria can be very simple – and will depend on the topic and the exact question.

The following criteria are often useful:

- **Duration**: which factor was important for the longest amount of time?
- **Scope**: which factor affected the largest number of people?
- **Effectiveness**: which factor achieved most?
- **Impact**: which factor led to the most fundamental change?

For example, for this essay, you could compare the factors in terms of their duration and their impact.

The conclusion on page 141 provides an example of what could be high level work (if written in full with appropriate details) because it reaches an overall judgement and supports through evaluating the relative significance of different factors in the light of valid criteria.

ACTIVITY

Now use the technique on page 141 to address the following practice A-level question:

To what extent was the political situation in Germany in the years 1890 to 1929 affected by economic and financial developments? **(25 marks)**

Think about the following when planning your answer to this question. The same points can be taken into consideration for other questions of this type:

- How will you define 'to what extent'?
- Identify two key areas in which the *Kaiserreich*, German governments in the First World War and the Weimar Republic were affected by economic and financial developments.
- Decide on the criteria with which you will judge the 'extent' to which the political situation was affected.
- Write an argument in a sentence that summarises how far the Weimar Republic was affected by economic and financial developments.
- Support this by writing four more sentences specific to the areas you have chosen.
- Use words such as 'however' and 'nonetheless' to weigh contrasting points.

EXAMPLE

Look again at the following A-level practice question from Chapter 3 (page 110):

'Nationalism posed a far greater threat to Germany than Communism in the period 1890–1923.' Assess the validity of this view. (25 marks)

Look back at the sample concluding paragraph on page 110. It would be possible to improve it by adding references to precise information so that the arguments are supported and not just statements.

For example, your conclusion might read:

Begins with main argument →

Limitations of counter-argument →

← Counter-argument contrast

← Precise information supporting the arguments

In conclusion, nationalism posed a greater threat to Germany than Communism. It is true that support for socialist parties had been considerable before 1914 and remained strong after 1918. Nevertheless, support for the extreme (as opposed to the moderate) left was limited. The Spartacist revolt failed in 1919 and the Communists thereafter failed to win more than 10 per cent of the vote. Although right-wing parties did not have much election success prior to 1930, they posed a serious threat to the Weimar Republic. It was possible that in a crisis situation they would have the support of the Reichswehr. The fact that many Germans accepted the 'stab in the back' myth and virtually all hated the Treaty of Versailles meant that German nationalists had emotive issues which continued to arouse considerable support throughout the 1920s.

In this example the evaluation is helped by adding detail that helps to stress the nature of the nationalist threat – the total rejection of the Weimar system, the demand for strong government and the fact that there was a radical as well as a conservative right. 'Clearly', 'however', 'in reality' and 'nevertheless' are useful words as they can help contrast the importance of different factors and different views.

This conclusion could be improved upon by explicitly weighing the relative significance of the factors in the light of valid criteria.

Working on interpretation skills: extended reading

How did developments in German culture impact on political development in Weimar Germany?

Jochen Hung considers the conflict between modernist and traditionalist notions of culture during the Weimar Republic.

In the Weimar Republic, culture and politics were very closely intertwined. The binding agent and catalyst of this often explosive mixture was the contemporary debate about modernity.

Weimar Germany is often remembered as a hotbed for artistic experimentation and an era when some of the most influential works of   5
modern art and culture were created, such as Fritz Lang's futuristic film *Metropolis*, the designs of the Bauhaus, Bertolt Brecht's *Threepenny Opera*, Alfred Döblin's montage novel *Berlin Alexanderplatz*, or Otto Dix's anti-war painting *Der Krieg*. However, while these works certainly left their marks in art history, they were hardly representative of wider popular tastes   10
and cultural production in Germany at the time. In film and literature, for example, nostalgic visions of a by-gone imperial past and romanticised portrayals of rural life enjoyed great popularity, while only a minority were interested in innovative works like *Metropolis*. Still, modernist culture played an important role in the public debate about the political future of   15
Germany after 1918. For many Germans, modern art, film and literature was not only an attack on traditional tastes, but also part of a general 'modernisation' of society that threatened their accustomed way of life. Thus, to reject modernist culture became not just a question of personal taste, but was also seen as an outcry against complex developments such   20
as the establishment of a democratic order, the introduction of progressive social legislation and the increased rationalisation of the economy, all of which had been introduced in Germany after the war.

This emotional reaction against modern culture as a symbol for a social and political upheaval had its roots in Germany's traditional self-image   25
as a *Kulturnation* (nation of culture): as a 'belatedly' unified state, art and literature had acquired an important role as symbols and substitutes for an elusive national unity. Thus, writers like Goethe, Schiller and Kant were elevated as the representatives of a virtual 'nation of poets and thinkers'. Even after the formal unification of Germany in 1871, art and culture   30
remained an important factor of national distinction: many Germans saw a difference between their organic *Kultur*, with a deeply-rooted spiritual and moral character, and the supposedly superficial 'civilisation' of Western nations like France and the United Kingdom. One of the most prominent advocates of this view was Thomas Mann, arguably the most famous   35
German novelist of his time. In his book *Reflections of a Nonpolitical Man*, written during the First World War, Mann argued that 'Western' ideas like democracy and even politics in general were alien to German nature.

However, after the Revolution of 1918–19, this view was challenged by many people in Germany, who believed that artists could no longer live as the nation's neutral pillar saints (ignoring the events going on in the real world), but had to join the political fray that raged on the country's streets. The Communist playwright Friedrich Wolf expressed this feeling in his pamphlet *Art is a Weapon!*, published in 1928, in which he called on German artists to actively involve themselves in society and to 'forge ahead into hard, wild, crusty, unadorned life, of which art *today* is a part!' This call was echoed, albeit in a very different tune, by Nazi ideologue Alfred Rosenberg, who in the same year founded the 'Militant League for German Culture', aiming to defend 'Germanic values' against 'the pacifism, cowardice and corruption' supposedly reflected in modern culture and the new political order. And even Thomas Mann, shocked by the increasingly violent political climate in his country, had by then climbed down from the spheres of high culture into the murky depths of politics, throwing his weight behind the democratic order in his speech *On the German Republic* (1922).

By the onset of the Great Depression at the end of the 1920s, art and culture had become a battleground in the highly politicized – and increasingly bloody – struggle about the future of the German state. More and more Germans blamed the economic collapse, unemployment and political instability on a cultural and spiritual 'degeneration' of their nation, with modernist art and culture as its most vivid expression. The National Socialist vision of Germany's future, which combined a supposed return to traditional *Kultur* with the promise of access to the technological advancements of modernity, offered an attractive solution and soon drowned out all other voices. In the event, many representatives of modern German culture, like Brecht, Döblin and Mann, had to flee the country and found a new home in the USA and other parts of the world.

Dr Jochen Hung, Teaching Fellow in German and European History, University College London.

ACTIVITY

Having read the essay, answer the following questions.

Comprehension

1 What does the author mean by the following phrases?
   a) 'general "modernisation" of society' (line 17)
   b) '*Kulturnation*' (line 26)

Evidence

2 What evidence does the author use to suggest that Weimar Germany was a hotbed of experimentation and modernism?

Interpretation

3 Using the essay and your own knowledge, why did many Germans reject the modernisation of society?

Key questions: Germany 1871–1929

The specification on The Quest for Political Stability: Germany 1871–1991 states that it requires the study in breadth of issues of change, continuity, cause and consequence in the period through six key questions. These have been either featured or mentioned at various points in the four chapters you have studied. The questions set in the examination (both the interpretation question and the essays) will reflect one or more of these key questions. Even though in the examination the questions may focus mostly on one specific period (for example, the *Kaiserreich*), rather than the period as a whole, it is very useful to pause to consider developments across the wider time period you have studied so far, as this will help you to see and analyse change and continuity with a sense of perspective.

KEY QUESTION 1
How was Germany governed and how did political authority change and develop?

Who held political authority in Germany at different periods (for example, 1871, 1890–1914, 1916–18, 1919–29)?

What powers did German governments in this period possess? In particular, what powers did they possess over the thirty-odd states that made up Germany?

Suggests extending or increasing. Can you relate this to the Bismarckian period, the personal rule of Wilhelm II or the Weimar Republic?

Questions to consider

- How extensive were Bismarck's powers in Germany from 1871 to 1890? To what extent was he dependent on the *Kaiser*? To what extent was he dependent on the *Reichstag*?
- Who held political power in Germany from 1890 to 1914? Was it Wilhelm II? Or was he merely a figurehead?
- How was Germany governed after 1919? What were the problems with the Weimar Republic's constitution? Was Germany too democratic?

Working in groups

Considering the period as a whole:
1 Discuss the way that Germany was governed in the *Kaiserreich* (from 1870 to 1914).
2 Discuss the view that Germany was essentially a modern, democratic state for most of the period 1871–1929.
3 Discuss how political authority changed and developed during the period 1871–1929.

KEY QUESTION 2
How effective was opposition?

How can you judge success? Was it merely success in *Reichstag* elections?

What exactly was the 'opposition'? What happened when 'opposition' parties won power?

Questions to consider

- Who were the main opponents of Bismarck? To what extent did the opposition change? How successful were Bismarck's opponents?
- Who were the main opponents of Wilhelm II? What success had they had by 1914?
- To what extent did Germans oppose the First World War? Who led the opposition? Why was there considerable opposition to the government by 1918? How successful was the opposition in 1918–19?
- Which groups opposed the Weimar Republic and why? How successful were the Republic's opponents prior to 1929?

Working in groups

Considering the period as a whole, discuss the following:
- The effectiveness of opposition to Bismarck
- The effectiveness of opposition to Wilhelm II
- The rise of opposition to the government and the First World War and the result of that growing opposition
- The different challenges to the Weimar Republic from its opponents on the right and left

KEY QUESTION 3
How and with what results did the economy develop and change?

Does this include the financial situation as well as the economic situation?

To what extent did the German economy develop? Was change always for the best?

Questions to consider

- What were the main economic developments in Germany in the late nineteenth century? Why did they occur and what were their social and political effects?
- What were the main economic developments between 1890 and 1914? Why did Germany have so much success on the industrial front prior to 1914?
- What impact did the First World War have on Germany's economy and on Germany's finances?
- What impact did Germany's defeat in 1918 have on Germany's economic development post-1919? What effect did Germany's financial policies have on Germany's economic development between 1919 and 1929?

Working in groups

Considering the period as a whole, discuss the following:

- The reasons for Germany's economic success prior to the First World War
- The effect of the First World War on the German economy
- The state of the Germany economy in the 1920s
- The extent to which the economic situation affected German financial development and vice versa

KEY QUESTION 4
What was the extent of social and cultural change?

Be clear about the meaning of 'extent'.

Think about the way that the lives of different groups – or classes – of Germans changed over the course of the period.

What exactly is 'culture'? To what extent is it related to society? Do different classes of society have different cultures?

Questions to consider

- How had German society changed between 1870 and 1929?
- Which class was the dominant class after 1919?
- Was German society neatly divided into classes?
- Why were many Germans suspicious of modern 'Weimar culture'?

Working in groups

Considering the period as a whole, discuss the following:

- The factors that encouraged change in German society
- The factors that encouraged tradition and stability in society
- Why cultural trends in the 1920s divided Germans

How important were ideas and ideology?

How do you measure importance? At the time? In retrospect?

Ideology means the ideas which support a political theory or system.

Questions to consider

- Think of the ways in which German intellectual thought, particularly that of the right, was developing in the late nineteenth and early twentieth century.
- To what extent was German left-wing ideology affected by developments in Russia?
- To what extent did different ideologies affect the development of political parties in Germany?

Working in groups

Considering the period as a whole, discuss the following:
- The changes in nationalist ideology in the late nineteenth century: how did this affect Germany?
- The impact of the rise of anti-Semitism in Germany
- Why left-wing German ideology was so much at odds with right-wing ideology

- -

KEY QUESTION 5

How important was the role of key individuals and groups and how were they affected by developments?

How do you measure importance? At the time? In retrospect?

Which individuals will you consider and why?

Which groups will you consider and why?

'developments' refers to economic, political and social changes.

Questions to consider

- Think of the key individuals, such as Bismarck, William I, Wilhelm II, Hindenburg, Ludendorff, Ebert, Stresemann. Summarise their contributions to the government of Germany and/or to changes that took place in the period.
- Think of key groups, such as army leaders, political parties, the Spartacists, the *Freikorps*. How important was their contribution?
- How were key individuals affected by developments over which they had little control?
- Which individuals seemed more in control of events?
- To what extent did groups determine events? To what extent did they react to events?

Working in groups

Considering the period as a whole, discuss the following:
- The contributions of William I and Wilhelm II. Who made the more important contribution and why?
- What you understand by 'groups' that influenced the situation in Germany. Which group had the greatest influence and why?
- Which politician had the greatest influence and why?

The Nazi experiment, 1929–45

5

The first section of this chapter explores the reasons for the death of Weimar democracy and its replacement by a Nazi dictatorship. Subsequent sections explore the nature of government and society in the Third *Reich*, and the development of the economy, up to Germany's defeat in 1945. The following areas are covered:

- The changing nature of political authority in the years 1929–45, from the collapse of Weimar democracy to the establishment of the one-party authoritarian Nazi state, with a particular focus on the roles of Hindenburg and Hitler
- Nazism as an ideology and the nature of political control and opposition in the Nazi state
- Economic developments in peace and war
- The nature of German society to 1945

All the key breadth questions are touched on in this chapter. However, the connecting thread running throughout the narrative is the idea that ideological objectives underpinned everything the Nazis did. In short, the Third *Reich* was an ideologically driven state. The following question therefore lies at the heart of the chapter:

How significant were ideas and ideology in determining social, political and economic developments in Germany in the years 1929–45?

147

CHAPTER OVERVIEW

Hitler always referred to the events that led to the establishment of the Nazi regime as the 'seizure of power'. This, as with so much of Nazi propaganda, was a myth. Hitler was levered into power by Germany's social and political elites to do their dirty work: the dismantling of the hated Weimar democracy. Once this was achieved, they thought he could be discarded. However, the puppet was soon pulling the strings. What emerged in the years 1933–45 was not simply the dismantling of democracy, but the dismantling of the whole German state in catastrophic and bloody defeat. Hitler had created the ideological basis for a new party that would amalgamate various strands of Nationalism and Socialism in a toxic mix with extreme racism. From the National Socialist point of view, it was inevitable that the Aryan race would have to fight against the Jewish, Bolshevik, and Slavic 'sub-humans' for living space – *Lebensraum* – in the East. Hitler embarked Germany on a life-or-death struggle. The year this book was written, 2015, fell on the 70th anniversary of the liberation of Auschwitz. Nowhere else on Earth provides greater testimony to the evil perpetrated in Germany's name. This chapter provides the merest overview of those events between 1929 and 1945 about which more has been written than any other period in ancient or modern history.

1 From democracy to dictatorship, 1929–34

No single problem 'caused' the downfall of the Weimar Republic. Neither was it inevitable that it would be replaced by a Nazi dictatorship. There was no irresistible wave of popular enthusiasm for the NSDAP. Indeed, by late 1932 the Party was in deep trouble:

- Its votes had fallen in the November 1932 election.
- It was in debt as contributions from the rich and powerful had fallen.
- The Party's membership was falling.
- Party in-fighting threatened to split the remaining membership.

However, what is clear is that the collapse of Weimar democracy and the rise of the one-party authoritarian Nazi state were two overlapping, inter-related historical processes. The extent to which the rise of the Nazis was a cause, or a consequence, of the failure of the Weimar Republic is a matter of interpretation, and each student of the period needs to reach their own judgement about this inter-relationship.

The collapse of Weimar democracy

What factors brought about the collapse of Weimar democracy?

The main long-term causes contributing to the failure of the Weimar Republic are set out below:

- Too few Germans believed in the Republic. The political culture of the Republic was shaped not by a belief in democracy but by the authoritarian heritage of Wilhelmine Germany. According to the historian E. J. Feuchtwanger (*From Weimar to Hitler*) 'the most pervasive cause of Weimar's failure was that too many Germans did not regard it as a "legitimate regime"'.
- Weimar's inheritance was incredibly damaging. It was founded in the aftermath of a catastrophic defeat, attacked by left- and right-wing insurgents, saddled with a vindictive peace settlement and invaded again by the French in 1922 with grave economic consequences.
- The Republic was unable to throw off the myths and lies propagated by its powerful right-wing enemies, notably the 'stab in the back' and the accusation that the Kaiser and the army had been betrayed by a bunch of 'November Criminals'.
- The Republic generated too few leaders of great authority and ability. Its most effective statesman was Gustav Stresemann, yet even he was a luke-warm Republican, as much a nationalist as a democrat, more concerned about restoring Germany's international reputation and recovering her lost territories than establishing a secure democracy.
- The Weimar constitution itself, one of the most democratic in the world, contained loopholes that its enemies could exploit. The most obvious was the power given to the President under Article 48; another was the lack of restriction on minor parties entering the *Reichstag*, which contributed to political fragmentation.
- It has been suggested that the system of voting by proportional representation was a weakness, producing short-lived coalition governments rather than stable single party majority government. However, this is a somewhat flawed

NOTE-MAKING

This is a complex section of study, requiring an understanding of the long- and short-term factors which brought down the Weimar Republic. You need both a broad sense of the main developments and an understanding of the roles of key individuals.

First of all, put together a mind map, with Hitler at the centre, and three main explanatory lines leading from the centre: 'political', 'economic' and 'social'. Develop 'long-term' and 'short-term' strands from each of your main lines. Use the heading: 'Factors leading to Hitler's appointment'.

Secondly, make notes on the roles of key individuals and their relative importance for Hitler coming to power:

- Heinrich Brüning
- Kurt von Schleicher
- Franz von Papen

The Working Together activity on p. 149 is designed to build on your own notes. The roles of the two key players in this drama, Hitler and Hindenburg, are covered in the next part of this section.

argument: the problem under the Weimar system rather lay with the lack of safeguards built into the constitution to prevent the election of extremist, anti-democratic parties unwilling to support the 'system'.

- Deep-rooted economic difficulties undermined the Republic. It was unable to generate its own 'economic miracle' that sustained West German democracy in the 1950s (see Chapter 8, page 227); the territorial losses, war debts and reparations constituted a mountain that the Republic could never climb. It became commonplace to criticise the Republic for not being able to return Germany to its pre-war levels of prosperity, leading to the simplistic, but powerful, assertion among many Germans that 'under the Kaiser everything was better'.

Such long-term factors hindered the Republic's chances of survival. However, by the beginning of 1929 it seemed as if it was recovering from its difficult birth. Two further short-term factors, however, combined to bring about the collapse of Weimar democracy. One was external, a world economic crisis, and totally unanticipated; the other was internal, a cynical act of political betrayal, and completely calculated.

- The economic crisis was the onset of the Great Depression, which sounded the death knell for the Republic, and provided its opponents with the opportunity to destroy the last vestiges of support for democracy.
- The act of political betrayal was conducted by Germany's social, political and economic elites, who had retained a great deal of their pre-1918 authority and therefore dominated the army, the judiciary and the civil service, as well as big business.

Different interpretations of the reasons for the collapse of the Republic have been put forward by historians. Weimar's authoritarian political culture and the extent of its economic problems are often ranked higher than other causes of failure. Others argue that the burdens placed on Germany by the peace settlement in 1919 were a legacy it could never overcome. And some argue that it was the combined weight of the problems faced by the Republic that brought it down. This is the view of the historian Knut Borchardt (in *Perspectives on Modern German Economic History and Policy*):

'We should ask whether the problem did not lie in the accumulation of causal factors, each of which may not on its own have proved decisive, but which when put together proved disruptive'

The historian Richard Bessel is a 'pessimist', arguing that Weimar politicians never created a wide enough base of popular support for the Republic. On the other hand, historian Edgar Feuchtwanger represents the 'optimistic' view, arguing that the Republic was enormously resilient and that it was only the exceptional problems associated with the Great Depression that brought it down.

The impact of the Great Depression on Germany

Given the weight attached to the economic causes of the Weimar Republic's collapse, it is worth reiterating briefly the psychological, as well as material, impact of economic problems on the German people in the 1920s, before we consider the impact of the Depression itself.

The cost of defeat in the First World War was enormous: the war debt, reparations, the burden of widows' pensions, the loss to the economy of the dead and crippled can all be quantified in monetary terms. However, it is less easy to quantify the psychological cost, the trauma of defeat and the

WORKING TOGETHER

Divide into groups. Consider each of the long- and short-term reasons given for the collapse of Weimar democracy and put them into rank order of importance, allocating each reason a mark out of ten, one being the lowest and ten being the highest. Share your scores and identify areas of similarity and difference. Each group should explain its reasoning behind the rank order chosen.

Discuss as a whole class whether you think that the failure of the Weimar Republic was inevitable.

As a follow-up you could write your own response, supporting either the 'pessimistic' or the 'optimistic' view.

insecurities this created. In a culture where orderliness and stability were paramount, the fear of indebtedness and the loss of status and autonomy were immense. The 1923 hyperinflation added enormously to this fear. The savings of the middle classes were wiped out and their pensions made worthless. Economic insecurity did much to alienate these people from the Republic; the erosion of income differentials between themselves and blue-collar workers further angered them. Even before the Great Depression, therefore, the Republic had experienced a decade of blame and criticism over its economic record.

The Great Depression, triggered by the Wall Street Crash in October 1929, hit Germany harder than any other major industrial country. By 1929 Germany had become a major exporting nation, but world trade collapsed by one-third and a great deal of American investment was withdrawn. The German economy was, therefore, hit with a double whammy: the loss of sales and the loss of investment. The crisis worsened inexorably:

● By February 1932 there were 6 million officially unemployed, though the real figure was nearer 8 million, and the output of the German economy was only 58 per cent of its best period in the 1920s.
● By autumn 1932 those unemployed and those on short time totalled more than those in full-time work.
● The majority of the unemployed were under 25.
● Those still in work were having to accept wage cuts; real wages fell on average by one-third in 1932.
● The German social security system was totally overwhelmed.

All of this contributed to the psychological despair many Germans had felt since the end of the First World War. There was a sense that the Depression might go on forever; apathy and despair predominated; rates of juvenile suicide increased greatly amidst an increasing sense of disorientation. Not only did the Great Depression blow apart the shaky foundations of the German economy, it accelerated the disintegration of normal democratic, parliamentary procedures and ushered in a period of political wheeling and dealing.

The politics of intrigue

The problems of enacting legislation in a *Reichstag* in which inter-party disputes predominated had been apparent throughout the chancellorship of Hermann Müller (26 June 1928–27 March 1930). His Grand Coalition, a 'cabinet of personalities' formed from the SPD, DDP, DVP, BVP and ZP, had been plagued by internal divisions. The constant bargaining and negotiating needed to agree ways of tackling the economic crisis contributed significantly to the weakening of belief in parliamentary institutions. Müller resigned on 27 March 1930 when Hindenburg made it clear that he would not back his government with emergency powers. Müller had found it impossible to find an agreed basis on which to tackle the economic crisis.

Müller's resignation was a turning point; the *Reichstag* was now increasingly marginalised, with power largely in the hands of President Hindenburg and his advisers, manipulating a series of minority governments. The period from Müller's resignation to the appointment of Hitler as chancellor on 30 January 1933 is one of the grubbiest periods in modern German history, as Germany's anti-democratic elites consciously manoeuvred and counter-manoeuvred to replace democratic institutions with right-wing authoritarian government.

The state of the political parties in 1930

Increasingly, party polarisation and factionalism was undermining the credibility of parliamentary politics. The credit of party politics, or *Das System* (the system) as many had started to call it, was at rock bottom. This fragmentation added significantly to the unstable nature of German politics.

- There was a growing drift to extremism at each end of the political spectrum: both the KPD, stuck in an ideological straitjacket and slavishly following the Moscow line, and the NSDAP, worked to undermine and destroy the 'system'.
- From 1928, the Communists totally opposed co-operation with the SPD and welcomed National Socialism as the final and unavoidable stage of capitalism.
- The SPD, well meaning but increasingly out of touch and unimaginatively led, was fragmenting between its left- and right-wing factions.
- The assorted 'liberal' parties had failed to generate any kind of moderate dynamic to sustain the Republic and were a fading force.
- The Centre Party, which had been the backbone of the Republic, playing a part in 19 out of 21 cabinets, was becoming increasingly divided on social and economic policy.
- From 1928, the Nationalists fell under the leadership of Alfred Hugenberg, a man deeply hostile to the Republic and all it stood for; any voice of moderation was overwhelmed by the voices of reaction.

These conditions led to the unedifying spectacle of under-the-counter deals being struck. It is not surprising that many, particularly middle-class, voters began to flock to the Nazis in the crisis years of 1930–33. Of all the parties, the Nazis increasingly seemed the only ones who could extricate Germany from a bankrupt political system.

Source A 'Hitler: Who voted for him?' by David Welch, *History Review*, September 1995.

As the economic crisis deepened and class tension increased, the various sections of the *'Mittelstand'* [German middle classes] came together within the Nazi movement. The *'Hitlerbewegung'* (the 'Hitler movement') was the 'mobilisation of disaffection' and as such far more successful than the traditional political parties which had become discredited through their association with the Republic and its failure to redress genuine or imagined grievances. There can be little doubt that under Goebbels' direction the NSDAP exploited these grievances for the purposes of propaganda, exploiting the growing sense of crisis to appeal to both the interests and ideals of the *'Mittelstand'*.

> According to Welch (Source A), why were the Nazis successful in attracting middle-class support?

Heinrich Brüning, 29 March 1930–30 May 1932

Müller's successor, Heinrich Brüning, leader of the Centre Party, headed a minority government containing representatives of the parties of the Grand Coalition except the SPD.

Brüning's actions further undermined democratic procedures. He was pre-disposed towards an authoritarian solution to Germany's problems by forming a majority right-wing government. However, his hopes of achieving this goal died with the results of the September elections. Gains for the KPD and the electoral breakthrough of the Nazis, winning 107 seats, showed a panic flight to the extremes. Brüning was stuck leading a minority government. He continued in office but was increasingly reliant on the use of Article 48 to govern by emergency decree. Between 1930 and 1932 the *Reichstag* passed 29 relatively minor bills, as opposed to 109 emergency decrees ratified by the President. Parliamentary government was effectively dead.

Real political authority was increasingly being wielded by the army under the direction and control of Kurt von Schleicher. He had the President's ear and indeed had been instrumental in appointing Brüning. However, by spring 1932 von Schleicher had lost confidence in Brüning and used his influence with Hindenburg to dismiss him. Brüning resigned on 30 May, replaced as chancellor by Franz von Papen.

Presidential government –
Government dependent on the President using his powers under Article 48 of the Weimar constitution to pass legislation through the *Reichstag*; government coalitions reliant on the President, not on parliamentary majorities. Presidential government became the norm from the fall of Müller's government in 1929.

Von Schleicher and the Nazis

By the middle of 1931 Schleicher was already considering how he might use the Nazis to further his own ambition. He had no great admiration for Hitler but saw the Nazi's strength in the *Reichstag* as a means of securing a majority for a new right-wing presidential government as a step towards creating an authoritarian dictatorship. He was of the view that the Nazis could be 'tamed' by being brought into government. He had already been in regular contact with Ernst Röhm, head of the SA (see page 157).

He confided in Röhm that he saw the SA developing closer links with the army and he ensured that the SA had access to weapons. For Schleicher, the greater the mayhem perpetrated by the SA on the streets, the less support there would be for democratic institutions clearly unable to maintain law and order. When Brüning began to show too much independence and, under pressure from several German *Land* governments, banned the SA on 13 April 1932, Schleicher's intrigues went into overdrive:

- He engineered the resignation of Groener who opposed Schleicher's intention to integrate the SA into the army.
- He met in secret with Hitler on several occasions in May to get a 'gentleman's agreement' that he would support a new Presidential government if Brüning were to fall.
- He persuaded Hindenburg that Brüning was unable to prevent a drift to civil war and to accept von Papen as his replacement.

Source B Adapted from a letter written by General Groener to a friend, 22 May 1932. Groener had initially been Schleicher's friend and 'mentor', and had been instrumental in getting Schleicher appointed as Head of the *Ministeramt* in 1928.

Schleicher is undoubtedly the army's guiding spirit. Since I did not stick with him over the Nazi question, I spoilt his finely calculated game. It is not the Nazis, whom he wants to help into power, but himself … But the old man has become difficult … The old man dropped me without shame and will do the same to Brüning, if he can only find a chancellor to attempt to tame Schicklgruber [Hitler]. Schleicher trusts in his skill to lead the Nazis by the nose. He takes a lot upon himself, but dares to do so because he has Hindenburg in his pocket. Schleicher has long had the idea of ruling with the help of the *Reichswehr* and without the *Reichstag*.

What does Groener reveal in this extract (Source B) about Schleicher's ambitions and character?

Franz von Papen, 1 June–17 November 1932

The degree of intrigue influencing Weimar politics was expanding as that of the *Reichstag* was diminishing. Von Papen was Schleicher's nominee. Indeed, he hand-picked Papen's cabinet. He felt that he could control him; Papen was a relatively obscure Centre Party politician without a power base of his own. On 4 June Papen called new elections in which Schleicher expected the Nazis to do well, providing the *Reichstag* votes for Papen to govern without continual recourse to the use of emergency decrees, which Hindenburg was demanding. As part of the deal with Hitler to support Papen's government, the ban on the SA was lifted. The timeline (Figure 1) charts the key developments in this complex period of intrigue and counter-intrigue.

20 June 1932

Von Papen lifted the ban that had been placed on the SA and SS in April.

20 July

Papen removed the Prussian SPD government. He assumed control himself as Reich Commissioner of Prussia. His justification was the need to bring to an end the uncontrolled street fighting perpetrated by the SA and the Communists. In reality, the intention was to remove one of the last strongholds of democracy.

31 July

Federal elections. The NSDAP saw the greatest gains, securing 37 per cent of the vote and making it the largest party in the *Reichstag* for the first time. The combined seats of both anti-Republican parties (the NSDAP and KPD) totalled more than 50 per cent of the Reichstag, effectively blocking the creation of any majority government which did not include them.

13 August

Hitler's demand to be made chancellor was rejected by Hindenburg. Hitler refused to take any other post in Papen's cabinet, reneging on his 'gentleman's agreement' with Schleicher to support Papen's government. New elections were scheduled for November. Hitler's 'all or nothing' strategy was a huge risk, leading to rumbles of discontent in the NSDAP about his tactics.

4 November

Papen addressed an open letter to Hitler:
'It is the exclusiveness of your Movement, your demand for everything or nothing, which the Reich President could not recognise and which led to his decision of 13 August. What is at stake today is this: The question is not whether this or that party leader occupies the Chancellor's chair, whether his name is Brüning, Hitler, or von Papen, but rather that we meet on common ground so that the vital interests of the German people can be assured.'
Hitler had been demanding presidential powers, which Hindenburg refused to grant to a party leader.

6 November

Federal elections. The results saw a significant drop for the Nazi Party and increases for the Communists and the national conservative DNVP. The results were a great disappointment for the Nazis who once more emerged as the largest party with 33 per cent of the vote but not enough to form a government majority in the *Reichstag*.

17 November

Papen resigned and submitted his resignation to Hindenburg. The resignation was accepted pending the appointment of a successor. Von Papen had been trying to form a coalition government with the Nazis but deemed Hitler's demands unacceptable.

23 November

Hindenburg again rejected Hitler's demand for the chancellorship. Hindenburg reasoned that the powers Hitler insisted on would transform the chancellorship into a dictatorship.

3 December

Kurt von Schleicher was appointed Reich Chancellor by Hindenburg and formed a cabinet.

▲ **Figure 1** A timeline of events, June–December 1932

Kurt von Schleicher and the role of the army

Von Schleicher was the head of the political office, the *Ministeramt*, of the German army. The army was much more than the military arm of the state. It exercised enormous social and political power in Germany and operated almost as a state within the state. The army was fundamentally anti-democratic and in the crisis years following the onset of the Great Depression, it exerted enormous influence on political developments. Schleicher was the 'fixer-in-chief'. Together with Hindenburg's son Oskar, a major in the army, General Groener, the Minister of Defence, and Otto Meissner, the head of the President's office (a group that came to be known as the 'Camarilla'), Schleicher plotted the destruction of the democratic system by persuading Hindenburg to use his presidential powers to by-pass the *Reichstag*.

For Schleicher, the issue was simple: democracy was an impediment to military power; it was too much of

a 'lottery' and Germany needed to return to its pre-1918 authoritarian roots. Just as Hitler was to do when he took office, Schleicher was careful to undermine democracy by the appearance of acting within the law. In effect, between 1930 and 1933, he was plotting a coup d'état by 'legal' stealth. His reputation for deviousness was legend. Arrogant in the extreme, he believed he was the 'strong man' Germany needed to recover its lost honour and power.

Kurt von Schleicher, 3 December 1932–30 January 1933

Politics had now become akin to a high stakes poker game. Hindenburg was increasingly tired of Schleicher's intrigues but gave in to his demands to be appointed chancellor. Schleicher was taking a huge gamble by emerging from the background; his arrogance convinced him that now was 'his time'. He believed that Hitler needed him more than he needed Hitler, and that Hitler's 'all or nothing' strategy was unsustainable at a time when the Nazis were losing seats and were in financial difficulties. To bring further pressure on Hitler, Schleicher began secret negotiations with Gregor Strasser, Hitler's loudest critic in the Nazi Party, in a covert attempt to split the NSDAP.

However, Schleicher's control was diminishing:

- Hitler forced Strasser to resign on 8 December, preventing any possible split.
- Schleicher had offended Hindenburg's son Oskar with an off-the-cuff social remark; the President began to listen to Papen more than he did to Schleicher.
- The influential *Junker* Agrarian League were lobbying Hindenburg against Schleicher because of the latter's refusal to protect their interests by raising tariffs on food imports.
- Papen, obsessed by getting his revenge on Schleicher for being forced out of the chancellorship, was meeting with Hindenburg and Hitler in secret, proposing a Hitler-led government with Papen as vice-chancellor; Papen promised Hindenburg that Hitler could be controlled. His biggest lever with Hindenburg was his assertion that unless Hitler be 'used', the army would have to step in and rule by martial law, a step that Hindenburg abhorred.

In the end the entourage around Hindenburg persuaded him that he had no choice. Hitler promised that he would be able to get a majority in the elections and Hindenburg hoped that he could at last take a back seat. Hitler's gamble had paid off; Schleicher's had not. Hitler was appointed chancellor on 30 January 1933. The bringing of the Nazis into government, supposedly on von Papen's terms, was seen as a last ditch way out of the governmental crisis. For

Hitler's appointment as Chancellor was the opportunity he had shrewdly held out for; it had taken a mixture of luck, intrigue and political miscalculation to put him at the head of government. The Nazis did not know where they were going, but they knew they had arrived. Hitler immediately called for fresh elections to be held in March, determined to use his new authority to win the overall majority his pursuit of 'legal' power necessitated.

The establishment of the Nazi dictatorship, January 1933–August 1934

How did Hitler create a one-party authoritarian state?

Initially, Hitler's position seemed weak. Only three out of a cabinet of twelve were Nazis and Hindenburg retained his power as President. However, it took Hitler just eight weeks to achieve total control, and by August 1934 most major German institutions had been either 'co-ordinated' or neutralised. This was achieved by a combination of means: a 'legal revolution', terror and a process of co-operation and compromise with key institutions. Hitler's consolidation of power in this period is often referred to as *Gleichschaltung* (literally: co-ordination).

Hitler's strengths

Papen convinced Hindenburg that Hitler would be 'framed' within the Cabinet by Conservatives who would control policies. Papen boasted: 'Don't worry, we've hired him'. However, Papen did not understand how Hitler might exploit his position:

- Hitler was Chancellor, superior to other members of the cabinet in constitutional terms; this was well understood by Hitler and was the basis of his 'all or nothing' strategy.
- The two other Nazi cabinet members had important posts. Goering, as Prussian Minister of the Interior, had direct control over Berlin; he was ruthless in purging the Prussian government and police of all potential opponents, appointing Nazi sympathisers in their place. Frick, as Minister of the Interior, had a key role in drawing up plans for the March elections.
- Hitler was able to employ his paramilitary forces, the SA and SS, to intimidate and crush opponents.
- Von Blomberg, the Defence Minister, was sympathetic to the Nazis and ensured that the army did not attempt to stop Nazi terror attacks.
- The propaganda campaigns orchestrated by Goebbels were successful in complementing the campaign of terror, portraying the government's actions as necessary to deal with a national emergency.
- The influential right-wing elites threw in their lot with the Nazis, as outlined in Source C.

Source C Adapted from *Hitler, a Study in Tyranny* by Alan Bullock, (Penguin), 1962.

What the German Right wanted was to regain its old position in Germany as the ruling class; to destroy the hated Republic and restore the monarchy; to put the working classes in their places; to rebuild the military power of Germany; to reverse the decision of 1918 and to restore Germany to a dominant position in Europe. Blinded by interest and prejudice, the Right made the gross mistake of supposing that in Hitler they had found a man who would enable them to achieve their ends.

NOTE-MAKING

Though it took only approximately eight weeks for Hitler to obtain dictatorial powers, it was not until August 1934 that the 'consolidation' phase was completed when he assumed Presidential powers on the death of Hindenburg.

Firstly, divide your notes into three sections under the heading: 'Hitler's consolidation of power' and use the following sub-headings:

- The use of legal power
- The use of terror
- The use of compromise

Follow this up by writing summary notes on the roles of Hitler and Hindenburg in bringing about the death of Weimar democracy.

Schutzstaffel (SS) – The SS was set up in April 1925 as a section of the SA, and acted as Hitler's personal bodyguard. Fanatically loyal to Hitler and his ideas, by 1934 the SS, under the leadership of Heinrich Himmler, had expanded to become the main agency of terror in Nazi Germany.

According to Bullock (Source C), how important was the Right in Hitler's rise to power?

The *Reichstag* fire

On 27 February 1933 a fire broke out in the *Reichstag* building, probably started by a Dutch Communist, Marinus van der Lubbe, acting alone, though numerous conspiracy theories have attributed the fire to the Nazis themselves fabricating a reason to take action against their greatest political opponents, the KPD. Whatever the truth of the cause of the fire, it was seized on by Hitler as proof that it was the start of a Communist revolution, thereby confirming the dire warnings the Nazis had been proclaiming for years. Hitler used the opportunity presented by the fire to persuade a reluctant President Hindenburg to grant him emergency powers with which to deal with this existential threat to the German nation.

The Enabling Act

The Nazis secured 44 per cent of the vote in the elections held on 5 March 1933. This was their best ever result but not enough to give Hitler the decisive two-thirds majority he required in the *Reichstag* to amend the constitution. What followed was political calculation and corruption masquerading as legitimacy. Hitler won backing for a proposal to suspend rule by majority in parliament, and to replace it with rule by chancellor decree. The DNVP readily gave Hitler their support and, shamefully, so did the Centre Party in return for an assurance that the Nazis would allow the Catholic Church absolute independence in Germany – the Concordat, struck with the Pope in July 1933. Having banned the KPD and already imprisoned 26 SDP deputies, only the remaining SPD members voted against the Bill, which was passed by 441 votes to 94.

The 'legal revolution'

Hitler's abortive putsch in Munich in 1923 (see page 103) taught him a vital lesson: power in Germany could not be obtained through a coup, but through the democratic and constitutional processes of the Republic. Hitler would use democracy to destroy democracy by undermining it from within. His route to total power, therefore, had to give the appearance, at least, of legitimacy. And if it meant that he would have to 'hold his nose', as he put it, in the company of Weimar democrats in the *Reichstag*, this was the price he would pay for 'legal' power.

The legal basis of the Nazi consolidation of power was established by two pieces of legislation:

- The first was the Decree for the Protection of the People and the State (sometimes referred to as the *Reichstag* Fire Decree), passed on 28 February 1933, which suspended constitutional civil rights. It also gave the federal government greater powers of arrest, allowing it to hold 'political opponents' in prison indefinitely in so-called 'protective custody'. The Decree, which remained in force for the duration of the Third *Reich*, was used by the Nazis to ban the KPD and to arrest thousands of Communists; it gave the Nazis the legal power to arrest whoever they wanted without giving any reason, and to imprison them for as long as they wanted without any judicial interference. In effect, it was the basic law of the Third *Reich*, abolishing all civil liberties.
- The second piece of legislation was the Enabling Act, passed on 24 March. This gave Hitler the right to rule by decree for four years, allowing the government to pass laws without consulting the *Reichstag*. It was never repealed. The Act removed all democratic accountability and was the foundation stone of one-party rule, which was formally established on 14 July by the Law against the Formation of New Parties. On 30 January 1934 the Law for the Reconstruction of the State dissolved all state assemblies, replacing them by Nazi-appointed *Reich* Governors.

If Hitler's dictatorship was effectively achieved within his first eight weeks in power, and formally established by the first anniversary of his appointment, he did not yet hold all political authority in his hands. While President Hindenburg lived, Hitler could still be dismissed, particularly if he alienated the army, which remained loyal to the President. The army was the one institution which Hitler feared might act against him. His relationship with the army was threatened by the SA. By May 1934, the army was making its position very clear to Hitler: either he take action against the SA or Hindenburg would declare martial law and the army would remove him. Hitler moved quickly to purge the SA in an action which became known as the Night of the Long Knives (see page 157). Hitler's purge not only removed an internal threat to his authority, but it also ensured the loyalty of the army. On 2 August 1934, following President Hindenburg's death, the army swore an oath of allegiance to Hitler as commander-in-chief of the armed forces and head of state; Hitler had essentially combined the posts of chancellor and President.

The use of 'terror'

The democratic Weimar constitution, basic civil liberties, freedom of the press, pluralism and federalism were all abolished by 'legal' process. Parallel with this process was the use of terror. Following the *Reichstag* Decree, SA and SS men were appointed as auxiliary policemen, given firearms and free rein. Nazi political opponents were attacked in the streets, in the public eye, spreading 'paralysing fear'. Those elites who had brought Hitler into power failed to foresee the extent of the violence that would accompany the establishment of one-party Nazi rule.

Nazi terror targeted not just their Communist and socialist political opponents, but also critical journalists, writers and artists. Jews were indiscriminately attacked and threatened in the streets. The Enabling Act itself was passed in an atmosphere of intimidating terror, SA and SS men filling the Kroll Opera House where the vote was taken. According to historian Ludolf Heist:

'When the SA persisted in threatening a "Second Revolution", and continued its uncontrolled violence and intimidation on the streets, Hitler turned terror on the terrorists, unleashing the SS in the purge of the SA in the Night of the Long Knives. Legitimacy was undeniably important to Hitler in his consolidation of power, but its legal power was achieved on the back of terror.'

(Quoted in 'Topography of Terror', a collection of documents published by *Stiftung Topographie des Terrors*, Documentation Centre, Berlin, 2010.)

The use of compromise

Hitler's purge of the SA in the Night of the Long Knives was a key example of his political pragmatism, by putting his own political interests ahead of personal friendship and principle. He knew the importance of ensuring the army remained loyal to the Nazi state, sacrificing both Röhm and the SA, and the more socialistic aspects of the Party's 25 Point Programme in order to accommodate the army's demands. Hitler did the same with big business interests by promising to ignore the anti-capitalist elements of the Party's programme. Similarly, anxious not to alienate the Catholic Church, in July 1933 Hitler completed the Concordat with the Pope, which had been part of the deal with the Centre Party in eliciting its support for the Enabling Act. All three of these actions indicate Hitler's willingness to compromise with powerful elements in the state and society in order to consolidate his position in power.

The role of Hindenburg

The vital events of the years 1929–34 were shaped by a small group of people who had access to Hindenburg. His role was crucial in a number of ways:

- His constitutional powers were central: Article 23 allowed him to dissolve the *Reichstag*; Article 48 gave him the authority to issue emergency decrees, by-passing normal *Reichstag* procedures; under Article 53 he had the power to appoint the chancellor. 'Presidential' government effectively replaced parliamentary government from the fall of Müller's cabinet in 1930.
- Hindenburg's military career had made him a national hero; as commander-in-chief, the army's oath of loyalty to his person was inviolable. Germany was a country in which the army took precedence over every other institution; in effect, whoever had the army's loyalty controlled Germany.
- His social position placed him at the apex of German society; he was regarded by many Germans as the emperor the Republic never had; in this respect Hindenburg was a national icon and living myth, transcending political fault lines.

Hindenburg, however, was keen to stick to the rules of the constitution. He believed in duty but was a conservative who had little sympathy with democracy. He was also in his 80s and tired of the extra responsibility he had had to bear since 1930; increasing senility made him open to suggestion. He wanted nothing more than to retire to his estate in Prussia. Neither had he any love for the Nazis. He called Hitler 'that Austrian corporal'. He thought he was mediocre but at least he was a nationalist. He liked the Nazis even less after

The Night of the Long Knives

On the night of 30 June 1934, Hitler ordered the SS, with tacit army support, to arrest and murder Ernst Röhm and other prominent SA leaders. The SA had become a political embarrassment, a threat to Hitler's relationship with the conservative elites and, particularly, with the army; the SA had refused to rein in its intimidation and violent actions on the streets, continued to demand a 'Second Revolution' against Germany's privileged elites and lobbied for control of the army. Hitler increasingly regarded Röhm as a personal threat to his leadership. The purge of the SA delivered significant benefits to Hitler: it removed a threat within the Party, won over powerful conservative critics and guaranteed that the army would swear an oath of personal allegiance to Hitler as leader on Hindenburg's death. Hitler's purge continued until 2 July, using the SA action as an opportunity to settle some old scores: von Schleicher, Gregor Strasser and von Kahn, who had suppressed Hitler's putsch in Munich in 1923, were all murdered.

The Day of Potsdam, 21 March 1933

Following the success of the Nazis and their conservative supporters in the *Reichstag* elections, a 'day of national unity' was held in the city of Potsdam, long associated with Germany's royal past. The event was a stage-managed piece of pure propaganda. Hindenburg was presented in front of huge, adoring crowds, in the company of the fawning Hitler, to send out a symbolic message of fascist and conservative unity, designed to further legitimise Nazi rule.

Machiavellian – Machiavelli (1469–1527) was an Italian diplomat, political theorist and writer. His book, *The Prince*, is renowned for its portrayal of an amoral, opportunistic and deceitful political leader. 'Machiavellian' suggests cynical and unscrupulous political behaviour and strategy.

they had attacked him during the 1932 Presidential campaign. Both Schleicher and Papen unashamedly used their access to Hindenburg to pursue their own anti-Republican agenda.

Further evidence of Hindenburg's crucial role in the establishment of Hitler's dictatorship is provided by Hitler's all-too-easy manipulation of Hindenburg following the arson attack on the *Reichstag*. He was persuaded, on trumped-up evidence, that the fire was the prelude to a Communist revolution, acceding to Hitler's demand for emergency powers, which effectively put Hitler beyond the law. Hindenburg allowed himself to be flattered by Hitler by events such as the Day of Potsdam and by Hitler's constant, grovelling public pronouncements about the high esteem in which Hindenburg was held and the public debt owed to him by the nation. Though it did not entirely disappear, his distrust of Hitler was replaced by a grudging thankfulness that the responsibilities of state no longer weighed so heavily on him. This is also evident by Hindenburg's reaction to the Night of the Long Knives:

'*Through your decisive intervention and your courageous personal commitment you have nipped all the treasonable intrigues in the bud. You have saved the German nation from serious danger and for this I express to you my deeply felt gratitude and my sincere appreciation.*'

Hindenburg died on 2 August 1934, a revered national treasure, yet he had largely been blind to the **Machiavellian** way in which he was manipulated. Perhaps there can be a degree of sympathy for an old man increasingly tired and incapable of the duties required of him, yet duty aside, his social and political orientation, his values and mindset, predisposed him against democratic institutions and in favour of authoritarianism. There is certainly an argument to be had that without Hindenburg, a Nazi dictatorship would not so easily have occurred.

▲ Hitler greeting Hindenburg at the Day of Potsdam, 21 March 1933. What is your interpretation of Hitler's manner in greeting Hindenburg?

The role of Hitler

The 'role of the individual' is a tricky concept to quantify. Hitler is perhaps the supreme example in the debate about the historical role of the 'great' individual. More words have been written about Hitler than any other modern or ancient political leader. Certainly, Hitler's general strategy was extraordinarily effective. He avoided the details of policy, feeling that it was more important to generate an image of the Nazi movement: dynamic, radical, visionary, full of energy and sacrifice. He was sufficiently empathetic to understand that the Germans wanted to be rescued; he simplified complicated issues and invented scapegoats: Jews, Communists, the Allies. Hitler knew the importance of capitalising on despair, appealing to envy, fear and resentment: find out what people want to hear and then tell them that in the new Germany they will get what they want.

Hitler was charismatic, a dreamer, but he also had an opportunist's eye; he was a shrewd political realist who had learned from his mistakes. He knew that it was no good taking on the state, and neither was he prepared to accept non-jobs such as the vice-chancellorship. This was one area where he was not prepared to compromise: the top job was the key. Above all, he had an unshakeable belief in his own destiny.

The significance of Hitler's role in the establishment of the Nazi state is undeniable, but not everything that happened can be attributed to Hitler, before or after 1933. He was in part the product of his times. His ideology was a hotchpotch of existing beliefs; luck played into his hands; and he could not have reached the top of politics' 'slippery pole' without the support and co-operation of many German people. Whether he was a product or a creator of his times is a question that encompasses many shades of grey. The following are some points to consider about Hitler's role and significance:

- Economic difficulties and the desire of the middle classes for order and stability played into Hitler's hands.
- His denunciation of the Versailles Treaty was popular.
- Hitler claimed to be the protector of Europe against Communism, and this gained him much support from German capitalists.
- Hitler was able, amidst the chaos of the Depression, to create a sense of purpose, especially among the unemployed enrolled in the SA.
- His preaching of German superiority over other peoples on account of their pure Aryan race (a totally fallacious argument) was a revival of attitudes which had existed during the Second *Reich* and appealed to many Germans.
- Many army leaders saw in Hitler the means of re-establishing German military strength.
- Germany was not freed in 1919 from the militaristic elites who had supported the Kaiser. These groups threw in their lot with Hitler. It was Hindenburg himself who handed over power to Hitler.
- The leftist forces in Germany were unable to unite against Hitler.
- Hitler's hysterical oratory exercised a powerful influence over his audiences. It aroused extremes of emotion, expressing the frustrations felt by so many Germans after 1919.
- He convinced millions of Germans that every opponent of the Nazis was responsible for the sufferings of Germany after 1919.

In the end, he became chancellor, and later dictator, because the political forces of the left and the centre were respectively too divided and too weak, and because the conservative right wing was prepared to accept him as a partner in government in the mistaken belief that he could be tamed. But the puppet quickly began to pull the strings. In trying to reach a judgement about the significance of Hitler's role, it is perhaps worth asking the question: would Nazism have existed without Hitler?

German Chancellors, 1930–33

Hermann Müller	26 June 1928–27 March 1930
Heinrich Brüning	29 March 1930–30 May 1932
Franz von Papen	1 June 1932–17 November 1932
Kurt von Schleicher	3 December 1932–30 January 1933
Adolf Hitler	30 January 1933–

KEY DATES: 1933–34

1933

27 February The *Reichstag* fire.

28 February The Decree for the Protection of the People and the State.

5 March *Reichstag* elections.

24 March The Enabling Law.

1934

30 June The Night of the Long Knives.

2 August Hindenburg's death.

2 Government and opposition, 1933–45

The Third Reich was a one-party terroristic dictatorship. Although opposition was relatively limited, and opponents had very few outlets to express their views, the Nazis remained acutely conscious of the importance of maintaining favourable popular opinion.

The nature of political authority and leadership in Nazi Germany

How was Germany governed during the Third *Reich*?

Political authority in the Third *Reich* was based on the concept of charismatic leadership centred on the *Führerprinzip*. This belief, that Hitler was the supreme leader of a 'new' Germany, was closely linked to the Hitler Myth.

The Hitler Myth

The Hitler Myth was the creation of Joseph Goebbels. He recognised that a key part of ensuring support for the regime was in encouraging people to believe in Hitler as Germany's saviour. Many in Germany remained very sceptical of Hitler at the time that he took power. With a system in which so much power was concentrated in Hitler's hands, at least in theory, and an ideology which emphasised obedience and unity, it was vital that the German people had absolute trust in Hitler. Goebbels created a cult of personality, portraying Hitler as both an ordinary man, yet also a superhuman and heroic figure, utterly and solely devoted to the service of his country. Hitler's uncompromising iron will lay at the root of his political genius. It was his sacred, personal duty and mission to solve all of Germany's problems.

However, the Hitler Myth was much more than a simple propaganda tool; it provided crucial justification for the legitimacy and stability of Nazi government. Not only did the Myth build on Hitler's great popular appeal, it also allowed Nazi propaganda to contrast Hitler's selflessness with self-serving, corrupt Weimar politicians, and promised unity and stability as opposed to the divisions and instability of Weimar democracy.

In this way, it served two crucial functions: firstly, it satisfied people's emotional need for strong government and, secondly, it allowed the Nazis to claim that Hitler's personal legitimacy as the Leader rested not only in the office of chancellor but, importantly, also on the will of the people. The Myth, therefore, gave real credibility to the principle of authoritarian leadership by identifying Hitler as the sole protector of the German nation. This explains how, for example, he could offer a pseudo-legal justification for his actions on the Night of the Long Knives by asserting that, at a time of national crisis, he had been the 'Supreme Judge of the German People'.

Hitler's personal standing was perhaps at its highest in 1940, following the conquest of Norway, the Low Countries and France, and seemingly only weeks away from forcing Britain to surrender. It was not until 1942–43 that the power of the Hitler Myth began to wane as the tide of the war began to turn with defeats in North Africa and at Stalingrad. Yet even after this, many Germans clung to their faith in Hitler, believing that he was working on a 'miracle weapon' which would turn defeat into victory.

Führerprinzip – Literally, the '*Führer* principle', the *Führerprinzip* was the operating principle for the Nazi state when Hitler was in power; the belief that Hitler possessed all power and authority within the Nazi Party; sometimes referred to as the 'leadership principle'. (*Führer* translates as 'leader'.)

NOTE-MAKING

This section examines both the ideological basis of Hitler's political authority and the actuality of day-to-day government in the Third *Reich*. It is important that you have a clear understanding of Hitler's position as *Führer* (leader) above and beyond Party and state. To help you with this, focus your notes in two parts:

1 The theoretical basis of Hitler's authority
2 Hitler's style of leadership – day-to-day government in the Third *Reich*

Political authority was sustained both by 'ideology' and 'terror'. Make notes under both headings, identifying the main elements of Nazi ideology and the main 'arms' of the Nazi terror apparatus.

National Socialist ideology

The concept or ideal that lay at the heart of Nazi ideology and the Nazi state was that of the *Volksgemeinschaft*: the nation and people as a community or national community, which put common good before personal advancement; a community in which the individual was de-personalised; one which was based on race not class. It was a community, therefore, into which you could only be born and where everyone had a shared genetic inheritance. By definition, it could not be inclusive – a 'foreigner' could not become a 'national' – and nor could it be multi-cultural, nor multi-faith. It was a vision of a society which would operate as a racial meritocracy, where the best, synonymous with the most loyal, would rise to lead this community of one people. At the apex of this national community was the *Führer*, whose leadership was validated not by any democratic process but by an emotional bond. It was: '*Ein Reich, Ein Volk, Ein Führer*' – 'one nation, one people, one leader'. Nazi ideology required that the people, the *Volk*, give unquestioning obedience to the Leader according to the *Führerprinzip*.

Hitler's ideological world view rested on his Social Darwinist outlook, which recognised a natural struggle for existence between peoples and races. He was convinced of the superiority of the Aryan race. Nazi ideology also drew on the science of eugenics, advocating action against those considered genetically unfit, the mentally and physically disabled who were a threat to the aim of breeding a pure and healthy 'master race'. This view also extended to cover those whose personal practices the Nazis considered unnatural, such as homosexuals.

Another way of understanding Nazi ideology is to identify what it opposed. It was anti-modern, anti-capitalist, anti-democratic and anti-Communist. In this respect, Nazi ideology was backward looking, designed to appeal to 'traditional' German values of family, faith and nation. Such an outlook is represented by concepts such as Blood and Soil and the Cult of Motherhood. Nazism was presented as a movement, not as a party in the traditional sense.

In many respects, Nazi ideology was a rather vague catch-all set of beliefs, designed to appeal to a broad mass of patriotic Germans who longed for national unity and revival and an end to the humiliation, economic weakness and political divisions associated with Weimar democracy. There was little that was radically new in Nazi ideology but its strength was its all-embracing big picture, which offered solutions and scapegoats for Germany's problems. To the workers, Nazism promised an end to economic and social privilege, yet Hitler courted big business and the social elites by promising to block the advance of Communism. Often contradictory and incoherent, Nazi ideology consisted of a mass of positive and negative stereotypes, ranging from idealised versions of German peasant families and biologically pure, blond-haired and blue-eyed Aryan men and women, to the ugly parasitic Jew, the grasping capitalist and the self-seeking liberal democrat.

In practice, the economic objectives of autarky (economic self-sufficiency) and rearmament always took precedence over ideological objectives like Blood and Soil. Ideology which idolised farmers as the life spring of the nation were routinely sacrificed to prepare for a war only a modern industrial society could manage. The Nazi glorification of the Aryan peasant as the key to the nation's racial health and the finest upholder of traditional moral values proved little more than empty rhetoric. Nevertheless, ideology infiltrated every aspect of German society and state under the Nazis, permeating the lives and activities of every German; every individual had to put nation before self. Being a *Volksgenosse* (national comrade) was everything. Nazism was more than a political or economic revolution, it was an ideological revolution, a struggle to the death between Aryans and their racial enemies, especially the Jews. Struggle, force, violence: these were the eternal values of Nazism.

Meritocracy – A system of promotion or advancement based on individual ability or merit rather than birth or privilege.

Eugenics – A branch of science which, in simple terms, justifies the view that the purity of races can be preserved through selective breeding. Eugenics had a strong body of scientific support not only in Hitler's Germany, but throughout Western Europe and the United States.

Blood and Soil (*Blut und Boden*) – A part of Nazi ideology which promoted an intimate and mystical relationship between the blood of the German people and the soil of the German Fatherland.

Cult of Motherhood – The belief that a woman's main role in life was as wife and mother; the Honour Cross of German Motherhood was awarded to women for giving birth to four or more children. Motherhood was elevated to the highest national status to which a woman could aspire.

Hitler's style of government

Contrary to what one might imagine about a modern totalitarian dictatorship, the Nazi state was far from a smooth-functioning, rationally organised regime; there was no coherent system of government in the Third *Reich*. Historians instead are fascinated by the relative chaos of Nazi institutions and the rampant competition within its power structures, as individuals and groups fought to establish their own domination within the state. Indeed, this situation gradually worsened as Party bureaucracies expanded, often operating in parallel with existing state ministries. The lines of power and authority between state and Party, and between social and economic institutions, blurred amidst this struggle for influence and scarce resources. It is hardly surprising that students of this period find it difficult to discern the lines of decision-making in a state whose only reason for being seemed to be the imposition of its own ideological world view on others.

The key Nazi leaders were indefatigable in creating their own power bases and in defending them by whatever means they could:

● Goering created his own military-industrial complex around his roles as head of the air force and as Plenipotentiary of the Four-Year Plan (see page 170), forging close links with Germany's industrial giants such as the chemical firm I. G. Farben, and enriching himself immensely in the process.
● Himmler's power bloc comprised the whole security apparatus and the Race and Settlement Office, giving him the power and authority to re-shape German society and the occupied territories along racial–ideological lines.
● Goebbels dominated the media and access to information through the Ministry of Public Enlightenment and Propaganda; next to Hitler, he was the voice of the regime.
● Martin Bormann had his power base as head of the Party Chancellery and as Hitler's personal secretary. Perhaps of all the leading Nazis, Bormann was the least visible but arguably by the end of 1942 the most powerful. He was a master of intrigue and in-fighting; his control of the Party bureaucracy, his power over appointments and promotions and, perhaps more important than anything else, his position as the recipient of Hitler's total trust, made him virtually second in the Party to Hitler. Known as the 'Brown eminence' for his almost invisible control of Party affairs, Bormann increasingly decided who Hitler saw, managing his appointments and his schedule.

Hitler was at the centre of this web of competing individuals and power blocs, untouchable, standing above the fray. Hitler was the integrative force that held the state together, his massive popularity undeniable; it is not surprising that Goebbels always insisted that the Hitler Myth was his greatest creation, elevating Hitler to messianic proportions. Inevitably, access to Hitler was the key to power and influence in the Third *Reich*, and, when this was not possible, actions could always be taken by the ubiquitous justification of 'working towards the *Führer*'. The historical debate over whether Hitler was a weak dictator, allowing subordinates to direct policy, or a strong dictator, responsible for all major decision-making, seems rather redundant when put into the context of the chaotic power structures within the Third *Reich*. The weight given to his habits of work – the late nights watching films, long morning lie-ins, and his frequent absences from Berlin – also seems unconvincing as evidence of weak leadership. In the end, all political authority emanated from Hitler, whether by direct order, or whether it was justified by being in line with the *Führer*'s pronouncements.

Hitler was extremely careful to avoid public association with unpopular policies, just as he was to avoid marriage, until the day before his suicide, lest the adoration of German women diminish by losing his claim to be married to the nation. It was only in defeat that Hitler's 'untouchability' disappeared as he came to be primarily blamed for the policies which led to war. In the ruins and devastation of defeat, most Germans could no longer stomach Hitler's 'survival of the fittest' dictum; his thousand-year *Reich* had lasted merely twelve years, and Nazi boasts of racial superiority lay in tatters.

The terror state

The Nazi state was a terroristic state. The 'legal' destruction of the rule of law went hand-in-hand with the National Socialist takeover of the police, purging it of political opponents and recasting it as an instrument of the regime. The so-called 'terror complex' grew inexorably.

The *Gestapo*

The Prussian Secret State Police (*Gestapo*) was created on 26 April 1933 under the leadership of Rudolf Diels. In April 1934 it was absorbed into the SS under the overall control of Heinrich Himmler. Given almost complete autonomy above the law, the *Gestapo* was able to target the regime's ideological opponents with impunity. The *Gestapo* was rightly feared as an instrument of terror but it also had widespread support from the general population, relying on denunciations from ordinary citizens for many of its arrests. The popular view of a *Gestapo* officer on every street corner was a myth; the Prussian *Gestapo*, for example, had less than 4,000 members in 1935.

The SS

Himmler was appointed *Reich* Leader of the SS in 1929. The SS had originally played a minor role in the state as Hitler's elite bodyguard within the broader SA movement. However, the SS became an independent Party organisation following its prominent role in the purge of the SA in the Night of the Long Knives. Himmler was assiduous in developing his SS 'empire' and in 1936 he was appointed Chief of the German Police, assuming total control of all elements of the police system. The SS now fully symbolised National Socialist repression.

Alongside the General SS, there were also special Death's Head units which guarded the concentration camps, and, fighting alongside the regular army (the *Wehrmacht*) during the war, the *Waffen* SS, whose members viewed themselves as 'political soldiers' and a military elite. Himmler regarded the SS as a State Protection Corps whose primary goal was to pursue the ideological and racial objectives of the Nazi state. For example, special mobile units (*Einsatzgruppen*) of the SS, SD and police carried out killing expeditions in the eastern occupied territories, murdering tens of thousands of Jews, Slavs and Communists. SS training demanded unquestioning obedience, contempt for the inferior and arrogance towards those who did not belong to the SS.

The SD

The SD was the security service of the SS under the leadership of Reinhard Heydrich from 1931 until his assassination in Czechoslovakia in 1943. He was replaced by Ernst Kaltenbrunner. The SD was tasked with gathering intelligence on and surveillance of the ideological opponents of National Socialism.

The *Reich* Security Main Office (RSHD)

In 1939 the *Gestapo*, SD and the Criminal Investigation Police (CRIPO) were combined within the RSHD under the direction of Heydrich. By 1944 its staff numbered more than 50,000: 31,374 in the *Gestapo*, 12,792 in the CRIPO, and 6,482 in the SD. During the war, it controlled Nazi extermination policy, organising the deportation of Jews from all over Europe to the SS-controlled extermination camps in the East. It was tasked with maintaining the racial purity of the *Volk* (the people).

The concentration camp system

The early camps set up in 1933 were known as 'wild camps' and used as overflow prisons for the thousands arrested in the early months of the Nazi terror. Many of these early camps were disbanded by the middle of 1934 and gradually replaced by a network of 25 purpose-built camps with about 1,200 sub-camps. These new camps were modelled on the first of the concentration camps set up at Dachau, near Munich, in 1933. Dachau was unique as the only camp which existed throughout the twelve years of the Third *Reich*.

Protective custody

Protective custody was one of the Nazi state's most notorious means of repression. The *Gestapo* could issue a protective custody order to detain anyone it considered an enemy of the state. Protective custody was enforced in concentration camps. From May 1943, the *Gestapo* could send prisoners directly to concentration camps without issuing an order.

Conclusion

The terror complex was not bound by any norms or legal restrictions because it claimed to exercise the '*Führer*'s will'. Nazi terror was unrestrained and unlimited. Himmler made this clear in a statement in 1937:

'The National Socialist police derives its powers not from specific laws, but from the reality of the National Socialist Führer State and the tasks set by the leadership. Its powers must, therefore, not be hampered by formal barriers.'

Opposition and resistance in Nazi Germany

Why was there relatively little overt opposition to the Nazi state?

A difficulty in any study into opposition and resistance is: how do you identify opposition within a totalitarian state, and how do you find out what people thought in a terroristic regime? The numbers involved in active resistance in Nazi Germany were very limited, but equally there were many examples of small-scale non-conformity. One of the enduring fascinations with the Third *Reich* is why so few Germans actively resisted the regime.

Repression

The most simplistic answer to this question is that the consequences of resistance were either imprisonment or death. For example, of 300,000 KPD members in 1933, over one half had been imprisoned and 40,000 murdered by 1945. Individuals did not have the protection of the law. The normal judicial processes did not exist; there were no basic civil rights or liberties. People could be arrested not just for what they had done, but for who they were. There was no support from any independent organisations that might offer protection from the Nazis – they were either dissolved or co-ordinated. It is significant that the two main areas from which the Nazis experienced most opposition – the Church and the army – were the two that maintained a semblance of independent organisation. The official instruments of state terror were in evidence from the beginning of the regime. It is not surprising, therefore, that many Germans retreated into private life, preferring to keep their head down, particularly as time went by and more and more types that the Nazis considered to be asocial began to be herded into the concentration and labour camp system. However, repression was not the only reason why the state faced so little overt opposition.

Surveillance and spying

The Nazis were obsessed by knowing public opinion. There was a universal system of surveillance and spying, but not based on large numbers of secret police. Instead it was usually ordinary Germans who denounced fellow Germans:

- Block leaders in flats
- Stewards on the shop floor of factories
- Hitler Youth in families

Many of these informers were not denouncing others for ideological reasons, but probably for personal or private reasons. Large numbers of people, therefore, were implicated in the terror system who were not necessarily committed Nazis.

Consensus

Many German groups agreed or acquiesced with many Nazi policies.

The military

There was general agreement between the military and the Nazis on:

- rearmament, and removing the restrictions of the Treaty of Versailles
- defeating Communism
- getting rid of the Weimar state.

But there was not a complete uniformity of opinion: some believed Hitler's foreign policy ambitions were dangerous or would lead to disaster; some, a few, rejected Nazi barbarism; some, again only a few, rejected Hitler socially. The most well-known army opposition actions centred on General Beck in the 1930s and the Stauffenberg bomb plot of July 1944.

The Church

There was a similar range of attitudes in the Church as there was in the military. The Protestant Church had a long tradition of support for political authoritarianism, was strongly anti-Communist and agreed with the Nazis on traditional family values and the role of women. A few, such as the 'German Christians', even agreed with the racist aspects of Nazism. A few, however, most notably Dietrich Bonhoeffer, opposed the Nazis on principled and moral grounds. Most Christians refused to relinquish their faith; congregations never deserted the Church.

The Catholic Church shared many of the Protestant's pro-Nazi values but, more than the Protestant Church, disliked Nazi interference; this was often seen at a local rather than a national level.

> **German Christians** – The German Faith Movement was set up in 1932. Led by Ludwig Müller, they called themselves German Christians. They were fanatical in their desire to Nazify the Protestant Church, however the movement failed in its aim to co-ordinate the Protestant Church.

The middle classes

The *Mittelstand* (middle classes) liked the pursuit of national greatness and the restoration of national pride; this was hugely popular. There was also much general support for anti-socialist and anti-Communist policies. Similarly, the clampdown on asocials had widespread backing; many of the traditional middle classes were anti-gay, anti-Gypsy, anti-juveniles and anti-outsiders. However, their response to anti-Jewish policies was much more ambivalent. The Nazis were generally successful when playing on traditional desires and prejudices, but less successful when they tried to change people's long-held attitudes and forms of behaviour.

Limitations

There were limitations to the appeal of the Nazis. They were never able to generate any support for their ideals in the German working class. The most common reaction here was a kind of 'sullen apathy'. However, it would be an error to think that *all* workers did not see any benefit in the Nazis. For example, the KdF (see page 175) was largely popular. There was also a division between younger and older generations. The young tended to be more amenable to Nazi propaganda; the young, fit, skilled Aryan German could do quite well in a state that idolised youth as the Nazi leaders of tomorrow. However, it is important to be aware that not all young people were pro-regime. The Swing

Youth movement was an example of how the Nazis could not just brainwash youth into change. There were also youth gangs like the Edelweiss Pirates who remained unintegrated.

Conclusions

The idea of an undivided, totally loyal population is largely fictitious, an invention of the Nazi propaganda machine. Some Germans may have accepted some aspects of the Nazi 'package' but not others; some may have held Hitler in very high esteem, but denigrated lower Nazis who might be regarded as self seeking. Attitudes varied over time and place. Clearly, many people did collaborate with the regime, but equally there were many examples of minor acts of non-conformity. For example, the German historian Martin Broszat has argued that civil disobedience, such as refusing to give the Hitler salute or to hang out swastika flags, or making anti-Hitler jokes, were relatively common; a tendency that increased as morale dipped in war time.

Papal Encyclical – In its most basic meaning, an encyclical is a letter written by the Pope on matters of significant concern to the Catholic Church. The Papal Encyclical written by Pope Pius XI, entitled *Mit brennender Sorge* (With burning concern), was smuggled into Germany and read from the pulpit on Palm Sunday, 21 March 1937 in all Catholic churches in Germany. It condemned Nazi breaches of the 1933 Concordat, accusing the Nazis of breaking their promises.

The main opposition up to 1939

- Underground networks of resistance were formed by the Communists, such as the Red Orchestra and socialists in exile communicated anti-Nazi material through their organisation SOPADE, but both were very small and barely any threat to the regime.
- There was some opposition from the Protestant Church. Led by Martin Niemöller and Dietrich Bonhoeffer, a group of Protestant pastors set up the Confessional Church in opposition to attempts to Nazify the main Protestant Church. However, this involved only about 3,000 pastors, one-sixth of the total in the Church, and their breakaway was motivated largely over Church autonomy not on broader moral or political grounds. Niemöller was imprisoned in Dachau from 1937 to 1945 but survived the war; Bonhoeffer was hanged in Flossenburg concentration camp in April 1945, two weeks before the war's end.
- The main opposition from the Catholic Church prior to the war was a **Papal Encyclical** read out from church pulpits in 1937 condemning state interference in the Church. As with the Protestant Church, the Catholic Church as an institution did not speak out about the regime's anti-Jewish policies or its racial ideology.
- By the end of the 1930s small numbers of disaffected young people set up their own groups in opposition to the Hitler Youth: the mainly working-class Edelweiss Pirates set up their own gangs with their own distinctive dress code, often fighting with the Hitler Youth. The middle-class Swing Youth were also non-conformist in their dress and their musical tastes, preferring to listen to banned American swing and jazz music.
- A group around General Beck opposed Hitler in 1938. Beck was Chief of Staff of the German army from 1935 to 1938; increasingly disillusioned with Hitler's aggressive foreign policy, Beck tried but failed to persuade the German General Staff to resign en masse; he himself resigned in August 1938. He was executed in 1944 for his part in the 1944 bomb plot.

Opposition during wartime

Most people in Germany still did not actively challenge the Nazis during wartime, but the strains of fighting the war produced an increase in opposition, particularly from 1943:

- The Catholic Church continued to protect its own interests and independence. In 1941 its protests against the removal of crucifixes from Bavarian schools caused this order to be reversed; Bishop Galen led protests against the Aktion T4 euthanasia programme (see page 179), which was publically halted, though continued in secret.
- Bonhoeffer continued to speak out against the Nazis and played a role in the 1944 bomb plot. However, individuals such as Bonhoeffer within the Church were relatively rare.
- Some of the Edelweiss Pirates became more active during the war, working with the Communist underground, helping to smuggle escaped prisoners out of Germany. Thirteen of the leaders of the Pirates in Cologne were publicly hanged in 1944.
- The White Rose student movement, formed in Munich in 1942, urged Germans to reject Nazism on moral and ethical grounds through the distribution of anti-Nazi pamphlets. Six students, including brother and sister Hans and Sophie Scholl, and Professor Huber, a supporter of the White Rose, were executed in 1943.
- The invasion of Russia in 1941 led to a resurgence of Communist resistance, but this was short lived; most of the underground groups had been discovered and broken up by 1943.
- Conservative and military opposition was the greatest threat to the Nazis during the war: the Kreisau Circle was a conservative group, led by Helmuth Graf von Moltke. It had contacts with left-wing and military opponents of the regime but it did little more than talk and plan – its diverse membership, fear of discovery and disagreements on goals limited its effectiveness. Army officers led by Claus von Stauffenberg carried out the 1944 bomb plot.

Why there was so little opposition to the Nazis when the war was obviously lost seems, on the surface, quite a paradox. A lack of popular support was an obvious factor; opposition groups had very few members – most Germans were largely preoccupied with simple survival amidst the chaos and destruction caused by Hitler's decision to fight to the end on German soil. Moreover, terror and repression intensified during the war; resistors faced enormous risks. Even in the final months of the war fanatical SS units carried out arbitrary executions of Germans even suspected of 'defeatism', desertion or collaboration with the enemy. Fundamentally, key groups such as the elites and elements of the armed forces acted too late, only starting to resist the regime when their own power was secure. Of course, there were still those who retained belief in Hitler's capacity to find a 'miracle weapon', or clung to their faith in Hitler and Nazism. Unlike in 1918, there was no repeat of a revolution against the state, whether from above or below. For most, surviving another day was their best hope.

The July 1944 bomb plot

The conspirators of the July bomb plot of 1944 had mixed reasons for attempting a coup. Many believed that Hitler was leading Germany to utter destruction and the likelihood of a Communist takeover led by the Soviet Union. Others were motivated by ethical considerations, anxious to put a stop to the exterminations occurring in the East; others had more pragmatic reasons, believing that there was a greater likelihood of a more favourable negotiated peace with the Allies with Hitler dead. Many had never had full faith in Hitler and now saw a leader losing touch with reality. The assassination attempt failed, and in the following months about one thousand actual or suspected conspirators were executed or committed suicide.

KEY DATES: OPPOSITION AND RESISTANCE

11 September 1933 The foundation of the Pastors' Emergency League, the forerunner of the Confessional Church.

21 March 1937 The Papal Encyclical: 'With burning concern'.

22 February 1943 The execution of Hans and Sophie Scholl, the founders of the White Rose.

20 July 1944 The Stauffenberg bomb plot.

3 Economy and society, 1933–45

The constant refrain of the Nazis in the years leading up to Hitler's accession to power was that the German economy and society were 'broken'. The Party would stand or fall on its ability to 'fix' the economy and to restore hope, pride and purpose to the German people.

NOTE-MAKING

There are a number of ways you might process this material on economic developments. Either follow the headings in the text for your own summary notes or consider a slightly different format:

- Aims
- Successes
- Failures

The sections on 'successes' and 'failures' could be sub-divided into two chronological parts: 1933–39: The peace-time economy and 1939–45: The wartime economy. As you make your notes, focus as much on analysis – the extent and causes of success or failure – as on description.

Deficit spending – The spending of public funds raised by borrowing rather than by taxation.

Living space – Living space, or *Lebensraum*, was one of Hitler's key ideological goals: territory in the East was needed not only for economic exploitation, but primarily for settlement; 'superior' Germans needed room to expand, evicting their 'inferior' Slav neighbours.

Economic developments

How successful were the Nazis in reviving the German economy and preparing the economy for war?

The Nazis were very late in developing a coherent economic programme. Hitler had little interest in economics; for him, economics was simply about providing the material resources to achieve his racial and political goals. The economic points outlined in the party's 25 Point Programme written in 1920 largely consisted of a few, largely disparate goals aimed at winning the votes of discontented workers and the lower middle classes. By 1932, however, when the prospects of achieving power seemed imminent, a much more cogent programme of economic recovery and development was needed to tackle the persistent problems of the Depression and to attract the support of industrialists and big business. By 1933 a number of broad policy goals, or aims, had been established.

Economic aims

- The immediate priority was to begin a major expansion of public work-creation schemes, directed by the state and paid for by a policy of **deficit spending**, to solve the unemployment problem and to revive the economy by boosting domestic demand.
- Two longer-term priorities focused on the attainment of autarky and the acquisition of **living space**.
- A further goal focused on the concept of a *Wehrwirtschaf* (defence economy). One of the conclusions reached about Germany's defeat in the First World War was that it had failed to organise the economy effectively enough to fight a total war. This concept became the main goal of Nazi economic policy prior to the outbreak of war. Indeed, economic policy between 1933 and 1939 was dominated by the conflicting priorities of preparing for war and at the same time ensuring a reasonable standard of living for the German people. This conflict of goals is often referred to as 'guns or butter'.

The peace-time economy

As already outlined (see page 149, Section 1) the condition of the economy was grim. By the time of Hitler's appointment the number out of work had reached about 8.5 million and those in work had seen their earnings decline and the average working day cut from about 7.5 hours to 6 hours. Hitler typically believed that the solution to Germany's economic problems was, as with all things, a matter of will. Germans would have to pull together as a national community, abandoning their class differences and become one people dedicated to the needs of the state; the *Volk* would be expected to work hard and to make personal sacrifices for the greater good of the nation. Hitler had promised time and time again to put people back to work; he knew that his regime would stand or fall on this issue. The task of reviving the German economy was made easier by the general recovery of world trade from about 1932, however the NSDAP was almost devoid of economic specialists. Hitler, therefore, gave the responsibility for economic recovery to Hjalmar Schacht, a Nazi sympathiser though not a member of the Party. He was made President of the German central bank, the *Reichsbank*, in March 1933.

The Battle for Work

This was one of several propaganda schemes in the first years of the regime, aimed at restoring confidence and creating the impression of something being done. The Law to Reduce Unemployment in June 1933 set in motion perhaps the most effective assault on unemployment in the industrialised world. Money was poured into public works schemes. The most trumpeted of these is the construction of the *autobahns* (motorways), but there was investment in a wide range of projects such as house building, railroads and forest planting, all of which absorbed hundreds of thousands of the jobless. Unemployment was further reduced by the creation of the *Reich* Labour Service (RAD) and, in 1935, by the introduction of conscription, plus a great expansion in the state bureaucracy. Between 1932 and 1938 government spending rose from 5 billion to 30 billion marks and by 1936 the number out of work had fallen to 1 million and by 1938 there was a labour shortage of about 0.4 million. These figures have been challenged: women were not included in the statistics, and neither were Jews after 1935. The so-called 'work shy' – a mix of vagrants, the persistent unemployed and petty criminals – found themselves shipped off to concentration camps for 're-education'. Nevertheless, the decline in unemployment was real and won much admiration at home and from abroad. For example, the former British Prime Minister David Lloyd George, who visited Germany in 1936, reported:

> **The *Reich* Labour Service (RAD) –** From June 1935 all men aged 18–25 had to do six months' labour, mostly in agriculture or on public works schemes. This was extended to women in 1939.

'*Whatever one may think of Hitler's methods, and they are certainly not those of a parliamentary country, there can be no doubt that he has achieved a marvellous transformation in the spirit of the people, in their attitude to each other and in their social and economic outlook. This great people will work better, sacrifice more, and, if necessary, fight with greater resolution because Hitler asks them to do so. Those who do not comprehend this central fact cannot judge the present possibilities of modern Germany.*'

> How does Lloyd George qualify his admiration for Hitler's achievements?

The New Plan

By 1934 Germany was facing two related economic crises: a debt crisis caused by the demands of spending on both rearmament and public works, much of which necessitated raw materials bought from abroad, draining Germany's foreign currency reserves; and a balance of payments deficit caused by a fall in exports and a rise in imports. Schacht's solution was his New Plan:

- This set up a more tightly regulated system of controlling imports, and a series of trade agreements with countries in south-eastern Europe prepared to allow Germany to pay for raw materials with *Reichsmarks*, which would have a dual benefit: a saving on foreign currency reserves and reducing dependence on overseas imports in the event of a war.

The New Plan worked as a short-term measure only. By 1935–36 another crisis point was reached; three linked, general trends were working to undermine Schacht's strategy and Germany's economic situation:

- Export prices were declining and import prices increasing, worsening Germany's balance of payments deficit.
- The work-creation and rearmament programmes were causing an enormous increase in the demand for imports.
- Once again, Germany lacked the foreign currency to maintain both the import of foodstuffs to feed the population, particularly fats and meat, and the raw materials needed to meet the army's requirements for rearmament.

The Four-Year Plan

Schacht fell out of favour with Hitler in 1935–36 by arguing against Hitler's priorities: he criticised the prioritisation of spending on rearmament, recommended the abandonment of autarky and advocated less state control of the economy. For the first time Hitler intervened directly in economic affairs, writing a long, detailed memorandum, announcing his new Four-Year Plan in August 1936. Hermann Goering was put in overall charge of economic development and given the bombastic title of Plenipotentiary of the Four-Year Plan; he was awarded exceptional powers in the economic domain despite his ignorance of economics. The plan entailed:

- a strict control of imports, prices and wages
- an absolute priority given to the manufacture of essential war materials, particularly 'ersatz' products such as synthetic rubber and oil, as well as a focus on extracting more of Germany's raw materials, particularly coal and iron, even when this was more expensive than importing from abroad
- restrictions on workers' freedom, giving the state the powers to force people to work where the economy most needed them
- an absolute focus on autarky and self-sufficiency.

Hitler finished his memorandum with the following two demands:

- The German armed forces must be operational within four years.
- The German economy must be fit for war within four years.

The Four-Year Plan was a watershed in German economic policy, initiated because Schacht's New Plan could not solve the problem of providing the raw materials needed for rearmament or sustain the levels of food imports to avoid the possible need to ration key foodstuffs, both politically unacceptable to Hitler. Schacht had to go.

The economy by 1939

The Four-Year Plan failed to meet a number of key targets, particularly in the production of synthetic oil, which increased by 130 per cent in the years 1936–39 but covered only 18 per cent of the demand. By the outbreak of war Germany still imported one-third of her raw material needs. The fundamental problem was that it was trying to square the circle: it could not rearm as fast as possible, feed its population and put enormous sums of money into prestigious, awe-inspiring construction projects, such as the Nuremberg rally grounds, all at the same time. By 1939 the economy had managed to sustain tolerable levels of food production, and had provided a clear improvement in people's material circumstances but the goal of achieving a defence economy had not been achieved. The country may have been better prepared for war in 1939 than it had been in 1914 but the cracks were beginning to show, particularly in the inadequacies in planning and co-ordination.

The wartime economy

German economic and armaments planning was characterised by the existence of a great number of competing authorities – a situation that on the one hand offered some flexibility, but on the other also created planning chaos and led to rivalries that created weakness all around. In 1940, economic and armaments planning was undertaken by all of the following: Göring's Office of the Four-Year Plan, the Defence Economy and Armament Office under General Georg Thomas, the Ministry for Armaments and Munitions under Fritz Todt, and the Economics Ministry under Walther Funk. The following extract from the memoirs of Hans Kehrl, written in 1973, provides some insight into the fragmented and inefficient management of the economy by autumn 1940. At

Ersatz – An artificial or synthetic substitute for something natural or genuine; usually of inferior quality.

the time, Kehrl was General Consultant for Special Affairs in the Economics Ministry, where he was responsible for obtaining raw materials from the occupied territories. He later became Chief of Planning in the Armaments Ministry under Albert Speer.

Source D From the memoirs of Hans Kehrl, 1973 (at the German History in Documents and Images website: http://germanhistorydocs.ghi-dc.org/).

The attempt to get any kind of sense of direction or guidelines for my future work from within the Ministry of Economics proved fruitless. State Secretary Dr. Landfried had only a modest conceptual ability as far as economic matters were concerned and certainly lacked the imagination to develop new ideas. Essentially, he restricted his activities to making sure that whatever occurred was done according to the book and to carrying out instructions from the Four-Year Plan whenever there were any. A conversation with Walter Funk revealed that he had no contact whatsoever with Hitler since, following the outbreak of war, the latter had been entirely preoccupied with military–political considerations. No directives had been issued by the Four-Year Plan and none were expected. As Commander-in-Chief of the Air Force, Göring had been concentrating his attention on the military actions in Poland, Norway and the western campaign. All his energy and thoughts were focused on military events. As a result the Four-Year Plan, which had been conceived as a control centre for the whole economy, was almost completely inactive. I could not expect even the most limited guidance or any suggestions from them. Only ongoing matters were being dealt with. Funk was concentrating mainly on his role as President of the Reichsbank because he was primarily an expert in financial and currency matters.

The invasion of the Soviet Union in June 1941 and the ensuing protracted war in the East required Germany to focus the entire resources of the economy to war production. By 1941, 55 per cent of the workforce was involved in war-related projects. However, war productivity remained lower than that of the Allies; greater efficiency was needed.

Albert Speer

Speer was appointed Minister for Armaments in February 1942 to improve productivity. He took a number of measures to put Germany on a greater total war footing:

- A Central Planning Board was established to co-ordinate economic organisation.
- Speer encouraged the employment of women, which Hitler had long resisted, put greater numbers of concentration camp prisoners to work as forced labour, and prevented the conscription of skilled workers in armaments industries.
- An Armaments Commission was established to facilitate the standardisation of production, which the planning chaos implicit in the Four-Year Plan had failed to bring about.

Speer's measures were broadly successful. Between 1942 and 1944 German war production trebled and productivity per worker increased by 60 per cent in munitions. However, a number of factors limited productivity in comparison with the Allies:

- Labour shortages were key: women were not fully mobilised until after Goebbels' 'total war' speech in February 1943; the increasing reliance on forced labour as German war casualties mounted proved inefficient: undernourished and badly treated, it was calculated that their productivity was 60–80 per cent lower than that of German workers.

According to Kehrl (Source D), why was German economic planning unable to function effectively?

Goebbels' 'total war' speech

The defeat at Stalingrad in January 1943 led to a turning point in Nazi propaganda, and was linked to changes in economic policy begun by Speer in the course of 1942. Goebbels' 'total war' speech at the Sportpalast in Berlin in February 1943 was carefully orchestrated. He called on the German people to support total war, demanding absolute self-sacrifice. His aim was to gain public support to mobilise the whole population and economy to fight a war to save German civilisation from total annihilation, hoping to create 'strength through fear'.

The mass bombing campaign

The British had bombed industrial and military targets in Germany from 1940, but by 1943 they had extended their targets to include civilian areas in day-and-night bombing in tandem with the American air force. While air raids did not deliver a knock-out blow to German industrial capabilities and morale, they did hinder the German war effort. In total, Allied bombing killed 305,000 people, injured 780,000 and destroyed 2 million homes. The most destructive attacks were on Hamburg in 1943 and Dresden in 1945, killing tens of thousands of civilians in firestorms which engulfed both cities.

- Shortages of raw materials, despite the exploitation of the occupied territories, could not be overcome; ersatz materials could not overcome this shortfall.
- The Allied mass bombing campaign disrupted production and transport facilities, and diverted important resources towards civilian needs.
- Speer could not entirely solve the problem of competing agencies; the SS in particular often protected its own 'business' interests in exploiting forced labour.

The longer the war continued, the greater the economic collapse. The success of the Allied invasions in Italy and France, and the Russian advances in the East put intolerable strains on the economy. Transport infrastructure and utilities ceased to function effectively, working conditions deteriorated and civilians focused on day-to-day survival; winning the war largely ceased to be a realistic function of existence.

Social developments and tensions

To what extent did life improve under the Nazis?

The Nazis had promised the German people 'a better deal'. The extent to which the quality of life improved in Nazi Germany is an extraordinarily contentious subject. On the one hand, life for many Germans of all social classes, in material terms, did get better, with hopelessness giving way to greater confidence and self-assurance. The *Volksgemeinschaft* was more than just mere rhetoric and the achievements of the Nazi 'economic miracle', if less than claimed by the regime, were much more than mere propaganda. Had Hitler died in 1937 or 1938 he would undoubtedly have been regarded as one of the greatest Germans ever. However, all of this must be balanced, and the question – at what cost? – must be answered. Ultimately, Germany under the Nazis was a terroristic regime, based on power, domination and a megalomaniacal world view. For those Germans who fell short of the Nazi ideal, all those who did not fit the 'picture': the political, social, racial and religious outsiders who were excluded from the national community, and even for many who were not, this was a regime which inexorably, step by step, stripped away civil and social liberties, discriminating against and gradually dehumanising great swathes of society.

KEY DATES: ECONOMIC DEVELOPMENTS

August 1934 Hjalmar Schacht becomes Minister of Economics.

September 1934 Schacht's New Plan.

August 1936 Goering's Four-Year Plan.

1 September 1939 Germany invades Poland.

22 June 1941 Germany invades the Soviet Union.

2 February 1942 Albert Speer becomes Minister for Armaments.

2 February 1943 The German surrender at Stalingrad.

18 February 1943 Goebbels' 'total war' speech.

▲ Volkswagen automobiles parked outside a new car factory in Fallersleben. Hitler, wearing a dark coat, stands behind the cars, preparing to dedicate the new factory.

Standards of living

The difficulty for the historian in deciding whether the German people got their 'better deal' is typified by the debate over living standards. The extent to which day-to-day life improved is an especially contentious matter and open to much interpretation.

The 'positive' interpretation

On face of it, the evidence for a 'positive' interpretation looks very strong. For many Germans, wages and working conditions generally did improve steadily from 1933. So too did living conditions: rents remained stable, and there was a relative decline in the costs of heating and lighting. Prices actually declined for some consumer goods, such as electrical appliances, clocks and watches, as well as for some foods. According to Niall Ferguson, 'consumer prices rose at an average annual rate of just 1.2 per cent between 1933 and 1938. This meant that German workers were better off in real terms: between 1933 and 1938, weekly net earnings (after tax) rose by 22 per cent, while the cost of living rose by just seven per cent'. Even after the outbreak of war in September 1939, workers' income continued to rise. By 1943 average hourly earnings of German workers had risen by 25 per cent, and weekly earnings by 41 per cent.

The normal working day for most Germans was eight hours, and pay for overtime work was generous. In addition to higher wages, benefits for industrial workers included markedly improved working conditions, such as canteens with subsidised hot meals, sports fields, parks, subsidised theatre performances and concerts, exhibitions, sports and hiking groups, dances, adult education courses and subsidised tourism, most of which was provided through the German Labour Front. The launch of the People's Car, the *Volkswagen*, proved very popular. An already extensive network of social welfare programmes, including old age insurance and a national health care programme, was expanded.

> ### The People's Car (the *Volkswagen*)
>
> In his speech at the opening ceremony to mark the launch of this scheme in 1938, Hitler promised to solve the problem of transport for ordinary working people: 'The car will serve as a symbol of the Nazi *Volk* community.' Money from a savings scheme for those wishing to save up for a car paid for the factory. However, all production went to the armed forces as the Second World War broke out before any cars were produced.

> ### The German Labour Front (DAF: *Deutsche Arbeitsfront*)
>
> The working class was the social grouping least likely to favour the Nazis. Workers traditionally favoured left-wing parties and employers expected the Nazis to limit strikes and control wages. This was a major dilemma for the Nazis: they had alienated workers by removing their political representation in creating a one-party state and had abolished independent trade unions in May 1933, but needed to win the workers over to achieve their ambitions of autarky and rearmament.
>
> The DAF was set up on 6 May 1933 under the leadership of Robert Ley to represent all workers, and included employers. The key aim of the DAF was to reconcile the workers to the Nazi Party, and to act as a kind of 'honest broker' between employers and workers, promoting the concept of *Volksgemeinschaft*. It grew to become the biggest organisation in the Third *Reich*, with a membership of 22 million by 1939. The DAF set up two subsidiary organisations in November 1933 to promote this aim: Strength through Joy (*Kraft durch Freude*, or KdF) and Beauty of Labour (*Schönheit der Arbeit*, or SdA). The KdF was created to organise workers' leisure time, and the SdA was set up to improve working conditions in factories and to provide a greater range of amenities such as sports grounds.

To what extent was Hitler's statement mere propaganda or genuine intention?

Social mobility

Hitler insisted, particularly in the early years of the regime, that it was his aim to promote social mobility. In an interview with an American journalist in early 1934, Hitler said:

'*Germans must have the highest possible standard of living, In my opinion, the Americans are right in not wanting to make everyone the same but rather in upholding the principle of the ladder. However, every single person must be granted the opportunity to climb up the ladder.*'

There is some evidence to suggest that some progress was made towards achieving this goal. The Nazis encouraged the acquisition of new skills in the workforce, greatly expanded vocational training programmes, and offered generous incentives for further advancement of 'efficient' workers. Both National Socialist ideology and Hitler's basic outlook inclined the regime to favour breaking down class differences. Hitler was fully conscious that the working class had traditional left-wing leanings. He could not afford to risk alienating this group, hence the substantive fringe benefits for workers provided by the DAF. In his critical biography of Hitler, even historian Joachim Fest (in *Hitler*) acknowledged that some social levelling was achieved:

'*The regime insisted that it was not the rule of one social class above all others, and by granting everyone opportunities to rise, it in fact demonstrated class neutrality. These measures did indeed break through the old, petrified social structures. They tangibly improved the material condition of much of the population.*'

Agriculture

German agriculture in 1933 was in a depressed state. The 29 per cent of Germans engaged in agriculture in 1933 experienced immediate gains from Nazi policies. The *Reich* Food Estate was set up in September 1933 under the direction of Richard Walther Darré to regulate agriculture, control prices and wages and set about launching a Battle for Production. The impact on wages was significant: farmers' incomes increased by 41 per cent between 1933 and 1936. Farmers also received a number of financial benefits such as: a reduction of interest on mortgage payments; a reduction in National Insurance payments; generous grants for improvements; and a state-allocated 650,000 *Reichsmarks* to clear farmers' debts.

Other indicators

A number of other indicators support the view that the overall quality of life was improving. Between 1932, the last year of the pre-Hitler era, and 1938, the last full year before the outbreak of war, food consumption increased by one-sixth, while clothing and textile turnover increased by more than a quarter, and furniture and household goods by 50 per cent, suggesting that even 'average' households were experiencing material improvements. During the Third *Reich*'s peacetime years, wine consumption rose by 50 per cent, and champagne consumption increased five-fold. Between 1932 and 1938, the volume of tourism more than doubled, while car ownership during the 1930s tripled and vehicle production doubled between 1932 and 1937. Air passenger traffic in Germany more than tripled from 1933 to 1937. German business revived and prospered. During the regime's first four years, net profits of large corporations quadrupled. Between 1933 and 1938, Germany's gross domestic product grew, on average, by 11 per cent a year, with no significant increase in the rate of inflation. All of this suggests that the great majority of Germans were reconciled with a regime which satisfied many of their basic needs and represented many of their basic values. This interpretation is summed up by J. Noakes and G. Pridham (see Source E).

Source E *Nazism 1919–1945, volume 2* by J. Noakes and G. Pridham, (University of Exeter Press), p. 379.

The regime aimed to depoliticize its people by turning them into passive consumers who listened to undemanding radio programmes, watched entertaining films, interspersed with the occasional patriotic but not usually overtly Nazi one, followed the fashions, and aspired to purchase the ultimate consumer durable, the new Volkswagen.

The 'negative' interpretation

However, a number of qualifications are needed to balance this positive view of improving working and living standards. The Nazis undoubtedly doctored unemployment statistics, and the most current research suggests a more nuanced view is needed. Skilled factory workers seemed to have benefitted from Nazi policies more than others. Many road-building workers had pay levels lower than welfare payments, lived in barracks and were subjected to harsh work discipline. Of course, many people gained by being in work, but many worked much longer than the 'normal', and often 60 hours or more per week. Increases in real wages were often the result of large amounts of overtime earnings. Hitler imposed strict price and wage controls to combat inflation and by 1939 wages had risen on average by only one per cent. The rearmament boom produced fierce competition for scarce, skilled labour, and workers here did much better than those employed in consumer-based industries. Putting 'guns before butter' led to a fall in consumer consumption to levels well below those in Britain and the USA, irrespective of the number of radios or cars produced by the regime.

The fringe benefits for workers associated with schemes operated by the DAF are also not quite what they seemed. The Strength through Joy (KdF) movement appears to have been relatively popular, particularly the 'luxury' tourism. Holiday entitlement did increase and, though expensive cruises remained beyond the means of most, many people took advantage of the benefits they offered. The Beauty of Work (SdA) movement was given much less credit and was regarded as too paternalist. There were lots of complaints that bosses provided facilities only by making workers pay for them. Many young Germans saw the RAD as little more than slave labour.

Early measures to help peasants and farmers proved very limited. After an initial recovery from 1933, farmers' incomes had stagnated by 1937 and labour costs had risen. The strict wage controls meant the gap between urban and rural wages widened, accelerating a rural migration: between 1933 and 1939, 1.5 million agricultural labourers had moved to the towns and cities.

Social conformity

The image of German society conveyed by Nazi propaganda was one of great enthusiasm and loyalty. Social tension was absent. The 'national community' existed. Loyal Germans were 'protected' by a regime that had identified the 'asocials' and 'outsiders' and hived them off into concentration camps. The Party rallies held in Nuremberg every September were the physical manifestation of this community, where the Party faithful met in self-congratulation in an annual process of renewal, and as an expression of strength and unity. Here the manipulative rituals of the Nazi Party found their full force; Hitler, the High Priest of the movement preached to his congregation, the sacred *Volk*, at a solemn event of messianic proportions captured on film in Leni Riefenstahl's propaganda masterpiece, *Triumph of the Will*.

However, there are major problems in identifying what ordinary Germans really thought. There were no opinion polls, the media was rigidly controlled,

Sudetenland

The Sudetenland was the western area of Czechoslovakia bordering Germany and Austria. In the 1930s it was inhabited by about 3 million ethnic Germans. The Sudeten crisis in September 1938 was provoked by Hitler's demand that the Czech government transfer this territory to Germany or face invasion. In order to prevent war, the leaders of Britain, France and Italy met Hitler in Munich on 29 September and gave in to his demands.

What does Source F reveal about the public mood in Nazi Germany at this time?

elections and plebiscites were manipulated. There was no independent public opinion. Most people outside the Party cadres quickly realised that the best way of surviving the regime was to keep one's head below the parapet and to refrain from public criticism. Nevertheless, social tensions clearly did exist. Industrial workers took what was on offer but most saw organisations like Strength through Joy for what they were: poor substitutes for the freedom to speak out, accepted not only because the regime's system of terror enforced conformity, but also because at least full employment offset to some extent the more negative features of the regime. Farmers too saw the regime's empty promises for what they were, as did small businesses and shop keepers, who were still neglected in favour of major industrial enterprises feeding Hitler's rearmament drive. Hints of nonconformity could be glimpsed among the youth and church goers but this was minimal, certainly up to 1939.

The balance between social conformity and social tension is clearly a difficult one to identify. The Nazi state demanded fanatical adherence but by 1939, as war clouded the horizon, it seems to have been satisfied with social docility. The paradox between relative economic well-being and peoples' concern about the future is illustrated by a report of the Military Economic Inspectorate on 9 September 1938 (Source F), when war over the Sudetenland seemed a possibility.

Source F A report of the Military Economic Inspectorate, 9 September 1938, quoted in *Nazism 1919–1945 volume 2* by J. Noakes and G. Pridham, (University of Exeter Press), p. 597.

There is full employment right down the line and, what is more, rising wages which are welcome on social grounds but economically dubious. The theatres are fully booked, the cinemas full, and the cafes are overflowing into the early hours with music and dancing; there are record numbers of outings on Sundays. And yet despite all these signs of a favourable economic situation the mood among large numbers of people is not one appropriate to a boom. It is in many cases depressed about the future. There is serious concern among the broadest sections of the nation that a war will sooner or later put an end to the economic revival and have terrible consequences for Germany.

Gender and family

Nazi social policies were profoundly interlinked, particularly in relation to gender, and family. The role of women in the state was central to the aim to build a national community based on common blood and common values.

Women

The Nazis were profoundly anti-feminist; they believed women should be confined to their 'natural' roles as wives and mothers. A major decline in the German birth rate led to fears that their racial inferiors may 'out-birth' them. A whole raft of policies was introduced to try to counter this trend:

- The prohibition of abortion
- Restrictions on contraception
- Financial incentives for larger families
- Marriage loans
- The opening of Mother Schools to provide improved facilities for pregnant women.

Women, therefore, had their own battle: they had to see their role as providing future 'national comrades' to improve the racial stock. Fundamentally, gender, population, race and family were a coherent whole for the Nazis: marriage and family was a duty for race production.

Youth

Policies towards youth were similarly linked to the state's ideological goals. Hans Schemm, leader of the Nazi Teachers' League put the relationship succinctly: 'those who have youth on their side control the future'. The regime's aim was to secure the total loyalty of the younger generation, primarily through indoctrination in school and in the various youth groups.

In 1933, the Hitler Youth (HJ) represented only one per cent of all organised youth; by 1938, 77 per cent of all Germans between the ages of ten and eighteen were in the movement and in 1939 membership was made compulsory. Girls had their own equivalent: the League of German Maidens (BDM). The impact on youth was mixed. Over-rapid expansion brought in poor leaders and by 1939 the incessant indoctrination, militaristic regimentation, endless physical demands and sometimes brutal discipline began to alienate significant numbers of young people, some of whom found their way into alternative anti-establishment 'gangs' such as the Edelweiss Pirates and Swing Youth. Though the success in indoctrinating youth through the HJ was limited, there are numerous testimonies from contemporaries who were fully committed to the values of the Nazi state, many of whom fought courageously right through to the end of the war.

Education

Education too was a significant conduit for indoctrination. The curriculum underwent radical alteration to produce tough, fit, obedient, unquestioning, conformist young people:

- More curriculum time – 15 per cent – was allocated to physical education.
- Key subjects such as German, biology and history were given special priority, and had to reflect Nazi racial and national perspectives.
- The intention was to phase out religious education; by 1939 all denominational schools had been abolished.
- From 1935 all textbooks had to be officially approved and their content Nazified.
- Girls received an education appropriate to their gender roles: needlework, cooking, music and home crafts.

A number of specialist schools were set up to train the Nazi elite and universities too saw some re-modelling of their curriculum to reflect the state's ideological goals. However, higher education was not a priority for the Nazis, who regarded academic learning as inferior to practical vocational and physical education.

The impact of war on daily life

Despite evidence that many Germans were not wholly in favour of the decision to go to war in 1939, early successes helped to bolster morale and the war initially had a limited impact. It was not until reverses in the East in 1942–43 that the pressures of total war significantly worsened the lives of the civilian population.

Workers

In order to try to maximise the productivity of German workers, wages were reduced and bonuses and extra overtime payments banned at the start of the war. This strategy backfired, however, as there was then a higher level of absenteeism. Consequently, by October 1939, wage levels were restored. As part of the policy of total war, the regime tried to mobilise labour more efficiently by forcibly moving people from 'non-essential' to 'essential' work. As the war

WORKING TOGETHER

Using the information in this section and your own knowledge, split into two groups to debate the motion: 'This house believes that the Nazis fulfilled their promise to give the German people "a better deal"'.

Writing a response to the following question would be a useful consolidation task:

'The historian Helmut Krausnick has described the mood of the German nation on the eve of war as one of "reluctant loyalty".' Assess the validity of this view.

Reserved status – Reserved occupations were jobs considered essential to the war effort; men employed in these jobs were exempt from conscription.

dragged on into 1944, the impact of the war grew more severe. Holidays were banned and working hours were extended to a minimum of 60 hours per week. Workers could be fined for absenteeism or have their reserved status removed.

Women

Nazi ideology emphasised the role of women as mothers and home-makers, providing the regime with a dilemma at the beginning of the war. At this stage, Hitler refused to authorise the mass conscription of women into the workforce. The National Socialist Women's League (NSF) played a prominent role in advising women in such matters as economising in wartime, and organised women to help with the war effort through helping with evacuees, organising food and clothing parcels for the troops, and bringing in the harvest. The families of conscripted men received enhanced welfare benefits to cover the absence of the husband. The numbers of women employed in industry actually decreased between 1939 and 1941. However, from January 1943, all women aged between 17 and 45 were required to register for work, although there were exceptions for pregnant women, those with two or more children and farmer's wives. By 1945, 60 per cent of workers were women and the upper age limit for compulsory work had been extended to 50; by the end of the war nearly half a million women were working for the military in auxiliary roles.

Youth

While membership of the Hitler Youth and the League of German Maidens was made compulsory in December 1939, the Nazi regime did not conscript the young in the early period of the war. However, the emphasis on military training increased. The demands of total war saw young people caught up more directly in the war effort. Two million young people were organised to help with the harvest in 1942, while the age of conscription for young men was reduced to seventeen in 1943 and to sixteen in 1945. By the end of the war, boys as young as twelve were deployed in the front line using anti-tank weapons in direct combat with Soviet forces.

The racial state

How were minorities treated in Nazi Germany?

The attempted genocide of the Jews is the most well known and horrific of the racial actions of the Nazi state. However, though the largest victim group, the Jews were only one of a number of minorities considered to be 'alien to the community', and who were defined in biological terms. The members of the German 'national community' were expected to conform to clear norms: genetically healthy (*erbgesund*), socially efficient (*leistungsfähig*), and politically and ideologically reliable. Those who were not healthy, such as anyone suffering from hereditary defects or mental or physical disabilities, or those who were inefficient, such as tramps and the work-shy, or whose behaviour offended, such as homosexuals, were unacceptable to the Nazis on eugenic grounds.

Eugenics

The science of eugenics was gaining credibility in Europe and the United States towards the end of the nineteenth century; improvements in medical science had led to increasing numbers of those with hereditary illnesses and disabilities surviving beyond their early years. Eugenicists argued that this would lead to a deterioration of the race. In addition, social scientists had begun to attribute social 'ills', such as habitual criminality, alcoholism, homosexuality and prostitution, to heredity.

NOTE-MAKING

Race and culture were two sides of the same coin: racial principles lay at the heart of the Nazi world view, and all cultural forms had to reflect and transmit that view. The material below is structured under a series of headings, which can serve as a template for your own notes to provide an overview of racial policies and cultural developments.

Sterilisation

By the 1920s in Germany, sterilisation had come to be seen as the preferred option for halting the alleged deterioration of the race. On 14 July 1933 the Nazis issued a Sterilisation Law legalising the compulsory sterilisation of all those suffering from illnesses alleged to be hereditary. Hereditary courts were established to pass judgement on individual cases, but decisions were largely subjective, based on social and political prejudice rather than scientific 'fact'. For example, having a reputation for being work shy, or of strong left-wing views might be used to support a decision to sterilise. Between 1934 and 1945, about 350,000 German men and women were sterilised under this law.

Euthanasia

However, notions of 'racial hygiene' went much further than sterilisation. A body of opinion was growing that those suffering from physical and mental disabilities were becoming 'burdens on the community' (*Ballastexistenzen*). This led to the 'euthanasia programme', a euphemism for the mass murder of the mentally sick and handicapped, which began in secret in the early summer of 1939 for children, and was extended in August 1939 to adults on Hitler's order. Initially, children were murdered either by lethal injection or deliberate malnutrition, but as the policy was extended to adults, murder by gassing was initiated. Gas chambers were constructed in six mental hospitals throughout Germany. By the time the programme, officially known as Aktion T4, was officially stopped in August 1941 after public protests led by the Roman Catholic Archbishop von Galen, over 70,000 people had been murdered. Despite being officially halted, the process continued unabated in the concentration camps, with 30–50,000 murdered over the next two years.

Many of those experienced in working on the T4 programme transferred to Poland to work in the death camps to murder the non-Aryans, predominantly the Jews, but also the Gypsies, who had long been regarded by the Nazis as asocial, work shy or habitually criminal. Gypsies were often subject to intensive scientific experiment by Nazi 'racial experts' who were fascinated by the way that they had sustained their own strong sense of race identity, albeit of an inferior nature, and because of their propensity to give birth to twins. A special Gypsy camp was set up at Auschwitz, mainly to facilitate the experiments of the notorious 'Angel of Death', Dr Josef Mengele.

'Asocials' were subject to regular round-ups and harassment. It is thought that at least 10,000 tramps and beggars were imprisoned in concentration camps; few of them survived. This policy had the approval of many Germans. Even juvenile delinquents were targeted and a special Youth Concentration Camp was set up near Hanover. The Third *Reich*'s policy towards racial and social minorities is a warning to history, but one that the modern world has yet fully to embrace.

The Jews

German Jews formed less than one per cent of the German population, about 500,000 in total in 1933. Most were assimilated into the life of the community. For the rank-and-file Nazi, the Jew was a sub-human creature responsible for all of Germany's troubles. Anti-Semitism was at the heart of Hitler's ideological world view; however, once in power he had to 'manage' the outbursts of anti-Semitic violence that greeted his appointment as German chancellor, if only initially in the interests of protecting the Party's image as the protector of law and order. The Party's anti-Jewish policies advanced in a series of stages, each more extreme than the last, in a process termed 'cumulative radicalisation'.

- **March 1933:** a boycott of Jewish shops, intended originally to last longer than one day but restricted to 24 hours because of public apathy and the need to avoid adverse foreign reaction.
- **April 1933:** Jewish civil servants were dismissed, though Hitler had to yield to Hindenburg's demands that Jews who had fought in the First World War were exempted.
- **September 1935:** the Law for the Protection of German Blood was introduced, forbidding sexual relations between Jews and Gentiles, and Jews also lost their rights of citizenship. These were the so-called Nuremburg Laws.
- **1937–38:** Jewish businesses were expropriated as the regime aimed to Aryanise the economy, removing all Jews from economic activity; many professions were also closed to Jews.
- **November 1938:** an attack on Jewish synagogues and property, known as the Night of Broken Glass (or Crystal Night), resulted in the deaths of 91 Jews and the deportation of between 20,000 and 30,000 Jews to the concentration camps.

As early as 1934 attempts were made to encourage Jewish emigration from Germany but this was not particularly successful. Only 120,000 of the 503,000 Jews living in Germany in 1933 had left the country by 1937. This process accelerated in 1939: a further 78,000 left following the atrocities on Crystal Night.

The outbreak of the war saw an enormous radicalisation of actions against the Jews. The invasion of Poland in 1939 brought a further 3 million Polish Jews under German jurisdiction. Many were arbitrarily persecuted and killed alongside tens of thousands of Poles; by 1941 most Eastern Jews had been herded into ghettos, sealed off and isolated from the Aryan parts of towns and cities. The German invasion of Russia in June 1941 sealed the fate of the Jews, escalating the war to a racial war of conquest and extermination. On 20 January 1942, fifteen representatives of the Nazi state met, under the chairmanship of Heydrich, in the Berlin suburb of Wannsee, to discuss and set in motion the Holocaust of the European Jews. A decision had been reached by Hitler, in the late summer or autumn of 1941 – no written order has ever been found – to proceed with the 'Final Solution' of the Jewish problem: the extermination of Europe's 11 million Jews. Six 'death camps' were identified in Poland as sites for the mass industrialised killing of the Jews. By the end of the war, about 6 million Jews had been murdered. The Holocaust remains as perhaps the greatest crime in human history and is proof, if it is needed, not only of the evil and the irrationality of the Nazi movement, but also of what happens when common humanity is blinded by intolerance and prejudice.

The legacy of Nazism

This is an issue which you will return to in the following chapters. However, it is important, at the end of this section, to begin to reflect on the legacy of a state that attempted to define the world according to its own version of reality; a state that set out with fanatical ruthlessness to impose its own interpretation of normality on the German nation and on the rest of Europe. It is a legacy that all those Germans who survived the war had to bear; and it is a burden that is still carried by the German nation to this day.

With Hitler's suicide, the German nation ceased to exist. Just as defeat on the battlefield in 1918 destroyed Imperial Germany, defeat in 1945 destroyed the Third *Reich*. One legacy of defeat in 1918 was the loss of large tracts of territory, so too in 1945 Germany lost forever its pre-war provinces of Silesia, eastern Brandenburg, Pomerania and East Prussia. In 1918 the nation experienced embarrassment and humiliation in defeat; in 1945 it suffered worldwide opprobrium for the actions of a criminal regime supposedly committed in the name of the German nation. The last months of the war witnessed the death throes of a once proud nation torn apart and eventually abandoned by a regime which had little regard for the norms of human civilisation: death marches, the reckless mass sacrifice of boys and older men thrown into the battle lines as cannon fodder, lynchings on the streets as SS fanatics took out their frustrations of failure on any suspected 'shirker' or 'defeatist', youth gangs living in anarchy in the rubble of destroyed towns and cities, women hiding in cellars in dread of rape and repeated rape.

Eventually, the physical scars would disappear, as subsequent chapters will show, but the psychological scars would be a legacy all but permanently imprinted on the psyche of future generations of Germans. The complicity of German Christianity, especially of Protestantism, with the regime would cause many Germans to abandon their faith, unable to remove the stain of the Holocaust from its soul; collective guilt would, in the 1950s, transpose into collective amnesia as people tried to forget what could not and should not be forgotten. Hitler's immediate legacy, therefore, was a rudderless people, whose only means of coping with the shame and the guilt was denial, and, in the West, a manic spasm of material reconstruction and material enrichment and, in the East, the search for a utopia of socialistic reconstruction. Hitler bequeathed a future that was no longer in German hands; his ideologically driven war to the death had placed Germany's fate in the hands of the Allies, a poisoned chalice that would result in division, perhaps the most visible and lasting legacy of all.

> **Death marches** – As Russian troops advanced westwards, the extermination camps and labour camps in the East were abandoned. Those camp inmates still alive and capable of walking were evacuated by their guards, ostensibly to reach camps deeper within Germany. In the brutal winter of 1944–45, thousands died of exposure, starvation and exhaustion; many hundreds more, incapable of keeping up, were murdered by their guards. It seemed to the prisoners that the evacuations were simply another means of extermination.

KEY DATES: THE RACIAL STATE

6 May 1933 The German Labour Front (DAF) is founded.

14 July 1933 The Sterilisation Law.

13 September 1933 The *Reich* Food Estate is set up.

9–10 November 1938 The Night of Broken Glass (Crystal Night).

24 August 1941 Aktion T4 is officially stopped.

20 January 1942 The Wannsee Conference.

30 April 1945 Hitler commits suicide.

Nazi culture

How did the Nazis use culture to reflect and represent the German national community?

Just as in the political sphere, all artistic and cultural organisations were 'co-ordinated' under the direction of Goebbels' Propaganda Ministry and purged of Jews, other 'un-Germans' and anyone accused of holding the 'wrong' political, racial or artistic views, which the regime labelled as 'degenerate'. The *Reich* Culture Chamber, set up in September 1933, was the umbrella organisation designed to police the arts, comprising separate Film, Music, Press, Theatre, Literary, Fine Arts and Radio Chambers. Nothing was to be produced, written or spoken that was not prior approved. For Goebbels the aim of *Reich* culture was to 'purify' the German soul, and to 'mobilise the spirit'; the SS could be left to purify the German state but Goebbels saw himself with the greater mission: he would fuse together art, culture and state.

Art

Hitler regarded art in particular as the pure expression of the ideals of National Socialism. He condemned 'degenerate' art, by which he meant all modern, abstract and impressionist art, in favour of 'healthy' Aryan art, heroic and literal in its idealisations of the *Volk*. This was particularly true of sculpture, which was invariably designed to depict the biologically pure and athletic Aryan. Public buildings were considered incomplete without such adornment. Hitler designated Munich as his 'city of art' and in 1937 opened one of the first of Nazi Germany's monumental public buildings, the *Haus der Deutschen Kunst* (House of German Art), to exhibit great German works of art.

Hitler had very clear and unambivalent views on the role of art. He was absolutely clear that it must play a central role in building the nation. His pronouncements had the force of law. Art must represent the German soul and the German identity; it had to be national not international, eternal and comprehensible and not some passing, indecipherable, expressionist whim or fad. Above all, it had to be uncritical.

Architecture

Architecture too had a function beyond the prosaic. Public buildings were intended to represent the grand vision of a thousand-year *Reich*. Buildings were a form of propaganda in themselves, often built of granite, to last, and faced with marble, to impress. The scale of these enterprises reflected the scale of the Nazi vision; they were built for eternity. Perhaps the greatest physical representation of monumental buildings were Albert Speer's plans for the Nuremberg rally grounds, covering 11 square kilometres, though only one structure was ever finished, the Zeppelinfeld, an arena built to hold 200,000 seated spectators. Speer was Hitler's architect-in-chief, spending hour upon hour with Hitler planning their great schemes of reconstruction, including the almost total re-building of central Berlin, which would be renamed Germania.

Film and radio

Hitler was at one with Goebbels about the importance of cinema and the radio, impatient with other leading Nazis who saw entertainment as a diverting sideshow to the main business of power domination. But for Hitler, politics was the greatest art of all, and film and radio were ideal vehicles for transmitting emotion. When he spoke to the masses he aimed for the heart and soul, not the brain. He wished to engage their feelings not their powers of critical analysis. Over 50 of Hitler's speeches were broadcast on the radio in 1933 alone; it was the sole medium that could take Hitler into the living room, the workplace and the cafes. The mass transmission of the Hitler Myth was the purpose behind the most famous film to come out of Nazi Germany: *Triumph of the Will*, shot at the 1934 Nuremberg Party rally, and released in 1935. Though grandiose in its scale and conception, its real significance is the film's subtle manipulation of image and illusion, a kind of emotional remote control. In the film, Hitler is the lead. The *Volk* are the film extras; only the leaders can speak. Hitler is portrayed as wedded to the nation, the High Priest of the Nazi movement, offering spiritual guidance from the pulpit of the rally-ground podium. Ultimately, it may be argued that Hitler came to believe his own mythic propaganda, lost in his own adulation, believing that his will was omnipotent and could achieve all.

Goebbels was a vicious anti-Semite, but he waited until war had broken out before using film as a means of radicalising emotion against the Jews. The two most infamous examples of this radicalisation were released in 1940: *Der Ewige Jude* (The Eternal Jew), depicting Jews as infestations of rats, and *Jud Suess* (The Jew called Suess), portraying the Jew as subversive money-lender, rapist and torturer. An estimated 20 million people saw *Jud Suess*; it was often screened in areas where deportations of Jews were planned and shown to SS soldiers before actions against Jews. If further evidence is needed of the power of cultural forms to influence and to manipulate, the stories of ordinary Germans attacking Jews on the street after seeing this film are persuasive of the impact of culture to influence behaviour.

Literature, theatre and music

Literature, theatre and music also had to promote Nazi virtues. The book-burning ceremonies in many German cities in May 1933, where books of non-approved authors were ceremoniously thrown into the flames and their crimes read out, were intended to symbolise the beginning of a new era.

As with art, 'decadent' music was banned, particularly jazz, considered Western and negroid, in favour of patriotic, classical German composers such as Richard Strauss and Wagner. In theatre too, only ideologically sound productions were permitted, and performers had to be politically vetted, with background checks the norm.

Conclusion

Whether cultural quality decreased in the Third *Reich* is open to some debate, but not much. Most commentators in most fields of cultural activity have pointed to a decline in creativity and imagination, a stultification of expression and the intellect. The requirement to extol the virtues of National Socialism left little room for experimentation or risk. In many ways, Nazi culture spoke volumes but said very little. Neither were the Nazis truly successful in censoring the forbidden. Banned books remained in people's homes and were read; jazz still found itself on the radio, at least until the latter stages of the war, to cheer up returning troops; the Exhibition of Degenerate Art, held in Munich in 1937, had more visitors than the parallel Exhibition of German Art. Essentially, Hitler feared freedom of expression; criticism was anathema, as was individualism, because it could not be

Negroid – The word 'negroid' was used in the nineteenth century as a racial classification for people with brown / black skin who generally originated in sub-Saharan Africa; it was adopted by the Nazis as part of their 'racial classification' ideology. It is now a term considered offensive and is no longer in scientific or common usage.

ACTIVITY

The fusion of art, culture and the Nazi state is a fascinating area for research. Bjel, writing in the *Jewish Magazine* (www.jewishmag.com) in November 2011, explores 'the transmission of Nazi ideology through art and culture.' This is a useful article with which to begin your own internet research on Nazi culture.

▲ Against the un-German spirit. A book-burning ceremony in Berlin, 10 May 1933.

controlled. In the end, all Nazi culture ended as caricature, devoid of meaning beyond the 'dream machine' of Goebbels' Propaganda Ministry. Goebbels was engaged in his own version of the *Truman Show* and, as in this film, the real world could not be kept out. Perhaps the last word on Nazi culture should go to Charlie Chaplin in his satirical film condemnation of Hitler, *The Great Dictator*, released in 1940:

'To those who can hear me, I say – do not despair. The misery that is now upon us is but the passing of greed – the bitterness of men who fear the way of human progress. The hate of men will pass, and dictators die, and the power they took from the people will return to the people. And so long as men die, liberty will never perish …

Soldiers! Don't give yourselves to brutes – men who despise you – enslave you – who regiment your lives – tell you what to do – what to think and what to feel! Who drill you – diet you – treat you like cattle, use you as cannon fodder. Don't give yourselves to these unnatural men – machine men with machine minds and machine hearts! You are not machines! You are not cattle! You are men! You have the love of humanity in your hearts! You don't hate! Only the unloved hate – the unloved and the unnatural! Soldiers! Don't fight for slavery! Fight for liberty!'

KEY DATES: NAZI CULTURE

10 May 1933 The burning of books in many German university cities.

22 September 1933 The *Reich* Culture Chamber is set up.

28 March 1935 The film *Triumph of the Will* is premiered in Berlin.

18 July 1937 The House of German Art is opened in Munich.

Chapter summary

- The Great Depression was a major cause of the collapse of Weimar democracy, in psychological as well as political and economic terms.
- Democratic accountability through the *Reichstag* ended following the appointment of Heinrich Brüning in March 1930.
- Hitler came to power through a combination of political intrigue and calculation; the German elites intended to use him to finish off Weimar democracy and to establish a right-wing authoritarian government.
- Hitler consolidated one-party Nazi rule through a mix of 'legal power', terror and unprincipled compromises with key institutions and groups.
- The Hitler Myth was fundamental in propagating the concept of '*Führer* power', which underpinned Hitler's claim to absolute political authority; there was no coherent system of government in the Third *Reich*.
- The Third *Reich* was an ideological, racial state; racial ideology and the concept of *Volksgemeinschaft* were the connecting threads running through Nazi society and culture.
- Opposition to the Nazis was very limited and the numbers involved were very small.
- The Nazis all but eliminated unemployment but the Germany economy was not ready for war in 1939.
- Living conditions improved steadily for most Germans in the 1930s but at the cost of losing all civil liberties and being subjected to arbitrary and unlimited state power.
- The German defeat in 1945 was catastrophic and total; the nation forged by Bismarck in 1871 was completely torn apart.

▼ **Summary diagram:** The Nazi state: insiders and outsiders

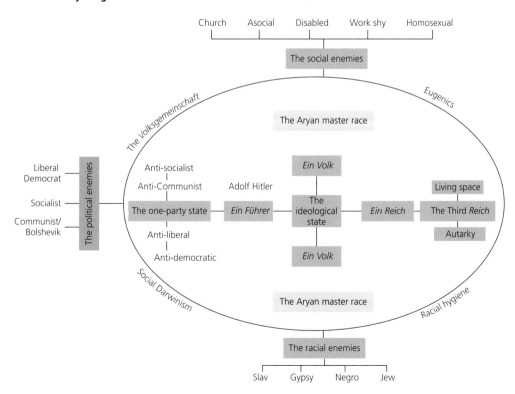

Working on essay technique

The essay writing sections in Part 2 of this textbook build on the basic skills and structures outlined in Chapters 1–4, a summary of which is given below:

- **Focus and structure:** identify the focus of the question; plan your paragraphing.
- **Introduction:** direct your opening sentences at the question focus; maintain this focus in each paragraph.
- **Detail:** use your knowledge to support the focus of your argument.
- **Analysis:** focus on explanation; avoid basic description.
- **Argument and counter-argument:** a balanced argument is essential, showing your understanding of opposing interpretations.
- **Resolution:** avoid sitting on the fence; identify arguments which in your view carry the greatest weight.
- **Judgement:** offer a judgement; consider the inter-relationship of arguments as well as their relative importance and significance.

ACTIVITY

Consider the following A-level practice question:

'The army was primarily to blame for the failure of democracy and the establishment of authoritarianism in Germany in the years 1914–39'. Assess the validity of this view.

(25 marks)

Your essays should develop both breadth and conceptual understanding. As a starting point, this requires you to clarify the breadth issue(s) at the heart of the question and the key question(s) targeted. It is important for you to develop a methodical approach to planning to build a coherent and directed argument. Consider this template:

- What is the breadth issue?
  This seems to target significance: the view offered suggests that the army was 'primarily to blame', that is, the most significant factor, in the failure of democracy and the establishment of authoritarianism.
- What key question(s) underpin(s) the essay?
  This essay focuses on the role of a particular key group – the army. It is also linked to changes in political authority.
- What aspects of the specification, between 1914 and 1939, might be applied?
  Make a list of headings, in sequence, that seem applicable.
  For example, the culture of militarism in 1914; the role of the army in the 1918 revolution and the crisis years of 1919–23; von Schleicher and the role of the army in undermining Weimar democracy; its tacit support for Hitler following his assurances about rearmament and military expansion; its role in the Night of the Long Knives; the army's acceptance of Hitler's military and racial aims enshrined in his ideology of *Lebensraum*; Hindenburg's role.
- What balancing counter-arguments can you identify?
- What is your overall argument which will anchor your opening paragraph?
  Think of your introductory paragraph as a simple equation: **C**+**A** = **I**. **C**ontext plus **A**rgument = **I**ntroduction: think about your opening paragraph, in which you put the question into its historical context and signpost the crux of your argument; practise expressing your argument concisely in one or two sentences.

Working on interpretation skills

Hitler's style of government and leadership has been interpreted in different ways. Historians have disagreed about whether Hitler was an omnipotent, or strong, leader, with his decisions implemented by his subordinates, or whether he was a weak leader, reluctant to take decisions, or simply concerned with upholding his prestige and personal authority.

Analyse and evaluate the three extracts below and attempt the A-level practice question that follows. For each extract, identify how the interpretation is developed, starting by explaining the overall argument. Use your own historical knowledge to evaluate how convincing you find each interpretation. Although Hitler only came to power in 1933, the question covers the whole of his political career from 1919 to 1945, so remember to consider his style of leadership and his decision-making throughout the full chronological span of the question.

After you have worked your way through each extract, write a final paragraph in which you reach a conclusion about the relative strengths and weaknesses of the interpretations put forward and offer your overall judgement.

Extract A

Hitler's personalised form of rule invited radical initiatives from below and offered such initiatives backing, so long as they were in line with his broadly defined goals. This promoted ferocious competition at all levels of the regime, among competing agencies, and among individuals in those agencies. In the Darwinist jungle of the Third Reich, the way to power and advancement was through anticipating the 'Führer's will', and without waiting for directives, taking initiatives to promote what were presumed to be Hitler's aims and wishes. Through 'working towards the Führer', initiatives were taken, pressures created, legislation instigated – all in ways which fell into line with what were taken to be Hitler's aims, and without the dictator necessarily having to dictate. The result was continuing radicalisation of policy ... which brought Hitler's own ... aims more plainly into view as practicable policy options. The disintegration of the formal machinery of government resulted directly from the specific form of personalised rule under Hitler.

Adapted from *Hitler 1889–1936* by Ian Kershaw, (Hubris), 1998.

Extract B

One of the keys to understanding the Nazi regime lies in Hitler's characteristics as a leader and in the nature of the Nazi movement as it had developed before 1933. While the Nazis were still trying to gain power, the main requirements were to appeal to as wide a section of the community as possible. What was needed was a dynamic and inspirational kind of leadership. But after 1933 the task was no longer to win power but to retain it and to achieve goals. It was here that the limitations of Hitler's own personality and political background and those of his movement became apparent. Hitler was essentially a propagandist – what he had always lacked was an awareness of the problems involved in translating policy into action, problems of organization and administration. Hitler hated bureaucratic structures and procedures and the mentality which went with them. He saw politics essentially as the actions of great individuals such as himself. He saw the solving of problems as a matter of determination and will-power.

Adapted from *Nazism 1919–1945 volume 2* by J. Noakes and G. Pridham, (University of Exeter Press), 1994.

Extract C

The absence of routine in Hitler's style of leadership meant that he paid little attention to detailed issues in which he was not interested. It also meant that those who had, or controlled, direct personal access to him could wield considerable influence. Access became an increasingly important key to power. Hitler's Bohemian [unconventional] lifestyle did not mean, however, that he was lazy or inactive. When the occasion demanded, he could intervene powerfully and decisively. Hitler, in other words, was erratic rather than lazy in his working habits. He wrote his own speeches, and, in areas where he did take a real interest, in art and culture, for instance, he did not hesitate to give a direct lead. Hitler took a leading role, pushing on or slowing down the implementation of anti-Semitic and other measures as he thought circumstances dictated. In areas such as these, Hitler was not merely reacting to initiatives from his subordinates, as some have suggested. It was Hitler who laid down the broad, general principles that policy had to follow.

Adapted from *The Third Reich in Power* by Richard J. Evans, (Penguin Books), 2005.

Using your understanding of the historical context, assess how convincing the arguments in these extracts are in relation to Hitler's style of leadership in the years 1925–1945. (30 marks)

6

Defeat, occupation and division, 1945–49

This chapter covers the period from Germany's defeat in 1945 and the subsequent Allied occupation, to the formal division of Germany into two separate states in 1949: the Federal Republic of Germany (West Germany) and the German Democratic Republic (East Germany). It covers a number of areas:

- The social and economic legacy of the Second World War for Germany
- The development of post-war occupation policies following the agreements reached at the Potsdam Conference
- The denazification of Germany
- Political, economic and social developments in East and West
- The Berlin crisis, 1948–49 and the subsequent division of Germany

The chapter provides both a chronological study of events and a focus on two breadth issues: how political authority changed and developed and the impact of ideas and ideology on this process. The overarching question which lies at the heart of this chapter is:

How did the broad consensus in 1945 that Germany should remain one political and economic unit reach the point where two German states had emerged by 1949?

The focus of the evaluation is on the issue of responsibility for this development, which determined the nature of political authority in Germany for the next four decades.

CHAPTER OVERVIEW

The Second World War in Europe officially ended at 11.01 p.m. on 8 May 1945. Despite Hitler's vision of a thousand-year *Reich*, it had lasted just over twelve years. Essential administration was in the hands of the occupying armies, which were having to deal with a humanitarian crisis of monumental proportions. This chapter examines how the Allies coped with the problems of destruction and dislocation, and outlines the steps by which civilian administration was restored and how the process of tackling the psychological, as well as physical, legacy of twelve years of Nazi rule was begun.

The material in the chapter charts the development of the 'German problem' within the context of the breakdown of relations between the Allied powers, and examines how the emerging Cold War between East and West determined the eventual division of Germany into two separate states, destroying the unity Bismarck had forged in 1870–71. By outlining how this situation developed, the latter part of the chapter introduces the debate about the responsibility for separation, and helps you to understand why political authority took such differing forms in the two halves of Germany.

1 Germany in 1945

Germany surrendered unconditionally on 8 May 1945. The country lay in ruins. Defeat had been total and overwhelming. No one was certain what the future would hold.

The social and economic legacy of war

What was the condition of Germany in the immediate aftermath of war?

The immediate aftermath of the Second World War was called *Stunde Null* (Zero Hour) by the Germans. For most survivors, the end of the war did not feel like either defeat or liberation, merely a continuation of suffering. The economy had collapsed, as had transport and communication links, and no central government remained to implement any policies to combat starvation and epidemics.

Many people's lasting memories of this time are of fear, scrounging for food and fuel, and of finding themselves at the total mercy of 'the enemy'. Indeed, many of the images of Zero Hour are of women, a generation of grey-skinned, hardened survivors who had learned to manage without men. Perhaps the most well-known examples are the *Trümmerfrauen*, the rubble-women, whose job was to clear Germany's 14 billion cubic feet of bricks and rubble.

NOTE-MAKING

As you read this section focus your note-making not only on the facts of defeat but, more importantly, on the legacy of Nazism in the immediate aftermath of the war. The following framework could serve as a template:

The legacy of defeat:

- Physical impact: destruction and death
- Demographic impact: expulsions and refugees
- Emotional impact: retribution and guilt
- Governmental impact: military occupation and division

▲ *Trümmerfrauen*, the rubble-women, worked six days a week to clear the debris of wartime.

Berlin: the final days

'When the war in Europe ended – when Berlin fell to the Red Army in May 1945 after taking 40,000 tons of shells in the final fourteen days – much of the German capital was reduced to smoking hillocks of rubble and twisted metal.'

(From *Postwar: A History of Europe since 1945* by Tony Judt)

Hitler's suicide precipitated the end of the Second World War in Europe.

- **20 April 1945:** Hitler's 56th birthday; the Red Army began its final assault on Berlin.
- **27 April:** Hitler was informed of the capture and murder of his Italian ally Mussolini and his mistress Clara Petacci, and of the public desecration of their bodies, hung upside-down from the gantry of a petrol station in Milan for all to witness. This was the final confirmation for Hitler that he would avoid such public humiliation in death by committing suicide and having his body subsequently cremated.
- **29 April:** Soviet troops had reached the government quarter around Potsdamer Platz in the heart of Berlin, no more than a few hundred metres from Hitler's bunker. On the same day he and his mistress Eva Braun were married.
- **30 April:** both Hitler and Eva Braun committed suicide.

Berlin was virtually cut off from the outside world. The Russian 'liberators' had already begun to take their rewards. Many of the Russian troops seemed fascinated by elements of modern life totally new to them: light bulbs, flush lavatories, cigarette lighters. They seemed particularly taken with

▲ Berlin, 1945.

gramophone records and watches. They stole all the bicycles they could find. Their biggest reward was German women and girls.

The Western Allies did not enter Berlin until July. Stalin refused all access to the city until British and American troops had pulled back to their allocated zones of occupation, which had been agreed at the Yalta conference in February 1945. Only then could the Americans, British and French occupy their sectors of Berlin. This gave the Russians two months to consolidate their position in the capital and to place their supporters strategically in every part of the new city administration. This process was spearheaded by several waves of exiled German Communists, who had spent the years of the Third *Reich* in Moscow. The first arrived on 27 April, led by Walter Ulbricht.

From this point, until the building of the Berlin Wall in 1961, Berlin would become the front line of East–West confrontation: what the world would come to know as the Cold War. A divided Berlin was to become the ultimate symbol of the Nazi legacy.

Chaos

The sheer scale of the physical destruction and death is difficult to grasp. It is estimated that at the end of the war:

- Approximately 6.5 million Germans had been killed and some 20 million were homeless.
- There were 7 million more women than men; a ratio of 170 women to every 100 men.
- Two out of every three German men born in 1918 did not survive Hitler's war.
- Over one-quarter of all houses were destroyed; in Berlin 75 per cent of the buildings were uninhabitable and in Dusseldorf nine out of every ten houses were damaged.
- In Berlin alone there were over 50,000 'lost', or orphaned, children.

Migration

Not only was German society in a state of crisis, it was also a society on the move. From the summer of 1944 hundreds of thousands of Germans had been trying to escape from the fighting on both Eastern and Western fronts. The end of the war was followed by further mass expulsions of Germans from Eastern and Central Europe. The Allies agreed to a formal transfer of Germans from Poland, Czechoslovakia and Hungary to begin in January 1946. This was intended to take place 'in an orderly and humane manner' but the reality was quite different. Estimates suggest that around half a million Germans died as a direct result of flight and expulsion. This shifting of populations was unprecedented. Overall, between 12 and 14 million ethnic Germans fled or were forcibly expelled from the Eastern territories.

There were also thousands upon thousands of 'displaced persons' in transit across Germany; these included forced labourers of many different nationalities from all over Europe and freed concentration camp prisoners. In addition, there was the problem of what to do with 1.5 million German POWs (Prisoners of War) and about a further million wounded German soldiers. The arrival of millions of expellees from Eastern Europe added to the chaos, putting even greater strain on the provision of food, housing and medical resources.

Food

Destroyed agricultural land and disrupted communications caused significant problems in feeding the survivors. The average calorie intake of Germans had fallen dramatically (see Figure 1). However, this average figure masks harsher

1941	2,445 calories
1943	2,078 calories
1945–46	1,412 calories

▲ Figure 1 The average calorie intake of German citizens, per day.

realities. For example, in June 1945 in the American zone, the official daily ration for Germans was only 860 calories. Food was available on the black market but at extortionate prices. For many Germans, therefore, any initial relief that the war was over must have quickly given way to desperation amidst the peace-time chaos.

Black market

The currency – the *Reichsmark* – quickly lost any worth and a barter economy took over, with cigarettes becoming the new alternative currency. The area of Berlin around the *Tiergarten*, for example, became a widely recognised centre of operation for the black market, where food and goods could be traded.

At the end of 1945 the verb *fringsen* (to scavenge) found its way into the German language following a New Year's Eve sermon given by Archbishop Frings of Cologne: 'there's no harm in scavenging for coal'. It seemed that even the Church recognised that desperate people had the moral right to resort to desperate, and perhaps not entirely honest, measures.

Retribution

The war may have been over but the Germans were still regarded as the enemy and there was little Allied sympathy for their situation. For many in the occupying forces, the distinction between 'German' and 'Nazi' was too fine to care about. Germans had to know their place and had to work or they did not receive rations, and many were evicted from their homes with little regard for their welfare, like the family of Gerda Schulz (see Source B on page 193), given two hours to get out of their house because it was being allocated to a British army chaplain. When Gerda's mother went back a few days later to ask for their cooker the chaplain dismissed her with the words: 'this is my house now'.

Rules forbidding fraternisation were soon found to be unenforceable. There were many liaisons between Allied troops and German women, often prompted by the desperate circumstances in which many women found themselves. Sex, as much as cigarettes, became central to survival in the immediate post-war period.

Terror

However, such indignities as eviction and bartering sexual favours for food pale into insignificance when compared with the wave of terror unleashed against ethnic Germans in the occupied Eastern territories and particularly in Poland, Czechoslovakia and the former Yugoslavia. Retribution for Nazi atrocities was immediate and brutal. German historian Klaus Dietmar-Henke described what was happening as 'a tempest of reprisal, revenge and hatred'.

Source A A German refugee, Hermann Fischer, describes a scene he witnessed in a village in eastern Germany in March 1945. Quoted in 'A Time of Retribution' by Christian Habbe, published in *Der Spiegel* online, 27 May 2011.

I saw the graves of 11 people at the bottom end of the village, including that of Paul Bisler, who was buried in front of his own house (he had been shot to death; his ... body had been found in his bed by a school boy). In another house were the graves of two women who had taken their own lives. The Wersel family were looking after the surviving child of one of the women. Gustav Anders-Horn had also been shot dead ... So there were graves everywhere. The village looked sad and desolate, with rubble everywhere, furniture, doors, windows ripped from their hinges and smashed. The wind howled through the open houses and buildings.

Tiergarten – A former royal hunting ground, the *Tiergarten* is Berlin's most popular and largest inner-city park. The *Reichstag* and the Brandenburg Gate lie at the eastern edge of the park.

Fraternisation – Associating with others, especially an enemy, in a friendly way,

Source B Gerda Schulz, a seventeen-year-old girl, describes her 'liberation' in the town of Bad Lippspringe in western Germany in April 1945.

It took me four days to come out of the cellar after we were liberated by the Americans. I was scared of the American Negroes. We had been told they were as bad as the Russians. In fact, they were the friendliest. The Americans were very generous. We had a hawthorn hedge and our house was next to the American camp. They left us bread and cans of food in the hedge even though this was forbidden because they were not supposed to fraternise with German civilians. One of them seemed sweet on my sister but he got orders he was being sent to the Far East and we never saw him again. It was not unusual for people just to 'disappear'. All the Americans left in July and were replaced by the British because our town was in their occupation zone.

Another significant act of retribution too sensitive to be widely discussed in the immediate post-war period was the mass rape of women. It is estimated that 2 million German women were raped by Soviet soldiers in the months before and following the end of the war. About 90,000 women were raped in Berlin, most in the week 2–8 May, immediately preceding the German surrender. Stalin dismissed any complaints, saying: 'the boys deserve their fun'. Between 150,000 and 200,000 'Russian babies' were born in the Soviet occupied zone of Germany in 1945–46.

Many women followed the *Führer*'s example, committing suicide rather than submitting to rape, preferring death to dishonour. *Frau komm mit* (woman come here) was a German phrase all Russian troops knew and German women dreaded. One woman who chose to take her own life was an aunt of Gerda Schulz (Source B). Other women quickly realised the benefits of acquiring a higher ranking Russian 'companion' who would act as their 'protector'.

Many of these atrocities were not reported until years later. The Western Allies at the time were reluctant to condemn such barbarities, given the information that was emerging about the Nazi death camps and the countless acts of murder carried out by the Nazis as they imposed their own racial ideology in the occupied territories. Similarly, the future West German government, anxious to avoid any discussion of Nazi crimes, also suppressed such accounts.

Guilt

An issue that immediately surfaced after the war was that of guilt. Those Germans who survived the war had to live with the reality of the murderous and genocidal policies of the Third *Reich*. In some places, such as at Bergen-Belsen near Hanover and at Buchenwald near the city of Weimar, German civilians were forced to view the horrors of the concentration camps first hand and, where this was not practicable, there were cinema viewings of film shot by the liberating Allies which many Germans were compelled to attend.

All Germans were forced, to some degree, to question their action, or lack of action during the Third *Reich*, and the denazification process itself, which is more fully discussed on pages 199–202, sought to identify the degree of guilt and participation of hundreds of thousands of Germans in the atrocities committed against the Jews, asocials, foreign nationals and other minorities.

However, most Germans proved notably reluctant to talk about their role in the Third *Reich* and mostly tried to dissociate themselves from it. There was almost a collective amnesia and denial of guilt, with many claiming that they had played no role or were simply 'following orders'. Indeed, it was not until the 1960s in West Germany that the children of the so-called

Use Source A and Source B.

How can you explain the different experiences of Hermann Fischer and Gerda Schulz?

'Auschwitz generation' demanded an open debate. Though the first West German government of Chancellor Adenauer acknowledged collective German responsibility for the crimes of the Third *Reich*, it was not until the 1990s, after reunification, that Germany fully and publically acknowledged this aspect of the Nazi legacy, notably through the highly visible Holocaust memorial sites located in the heart of a once again unified Berlin.

Allied attitudes to the German people

What were the Allied perceptions of the German people in the early months of the occupation?

The view that the Allied treatment of Germans was essentially benevolent is something of a post-war myth. The historian Giles MacDonagh, in his book, *After the Reich*, calculated that up to 3 million Germans, civilian as well as military, died unnecessarily after the official end of hostilities. Neither can the deaths be solely attributed to accident or disease or Soviet reprisals, or the forced expulsions in eastern and central Europe discussed earlier in this chapter; many thousands also died in the British and American zones, partly through neglect or simple force of circumstance. The Allies had won the war but it quickly became apparent that winning the peace might prove an even harder task.

Fraternisation

There was a general view among all of the Allies that Germans 'deserved what they got', which was entirely the rationale behind the vengeful Morgenthau Plan, outlined below, which initially had some support in London and Washington. For the British and Americans, the guiding policy was that the Germans should be shown no sympathy and that there should be no socialising, or fraternising, with the 'enemy'. Indeed, British soldiers were bluntly warned in an army guide issued to all troops fighting in Germany: 'You are going into Germany. You are about to meet a strange people in a strange enemy country'. In short, Germans were to be treated as a conquered race; it was initially forbidden to talk to them except to give orders; there should be no shaking of hands with Germans and no presents or favours given. Gerda Schulz's memory of finding food secretly left under their hawthorn hedge accurately reflects this early attitude (see Source B). In reality, the ban on fraternisation proved unenforceable and was lifted in October 1945.

The Russians had no equivalent ruling on fraternisation. Contact by soldiers with the civilian population was informally permitted. Though they were far from benevolent, the Russians stressed from the beginning that the Germans were not to be treated as the Germans had treated them. There were to be no exterminations. For the German Communists returning from exile, hearts and minds needed to be won if socialism was to triumph over capitalism. The German Communists, under the direction of their Soviet superiors, were quick to set up a new political structure in Berlin and to encourage cultural activity. This theme of winning hearts and minds is one we will return to when examining Communist rule in East Germany after 1949.

The French showed the most hostility and were determined to punish the Germans, not only in retribution for three crushing invasions of their country, in 1870, 1914 and 1940, but also as reprisal for war crimes such as that committed at Oradour. The French believed that the German race was fundamentally militaristic and that there was no hope of changing the German character. In a poll conducted in France in August 1945, 78 per cent voted in favour of dividing Germany into three separate states, each centred on a major river: the Rhine, Elbe and Danube.

Oradour-sur-Glane

On 10 June 1944, troops of the 2nd SS-Panzer Division *Das Reich* destroyed the entire French village of Oradour, murdering 642 men, women and children, apparently in retaliation for the activities of the French resistance in the area. The village has been left in its abandoned state and is now open to visitors as a memorial site.

British and American attitudes towards the Germans changed relatively quickly, partly due to humanitarian concern, as increased contact between the occupying forces and German civilians began to facilitate personal reconciliation and to weaken wartime propaganda stereotypes. However, perhaps a more significant factor was the growing realisation that economic and political reconstruction was vital to counter a new threat: the perception in the West that the Soviet Union was intent on expanding Communist control throughout the whole of Germany. By early 1946 the British and Americans had reached the conclusion that they needed West Germans as political partners. Hitler was dead and the Third *Reich* defeated, but a new era of Cold War was about to begin.

Government and administration

How was Germany to be governed in the immediate aftermath of war?

Post-conflict reconstruction after any war, let alone a war of the scale and magnitude of the Second World War, is always problematic. Regime change, as the recent Iraq and Afghanistan wars have demonstrated, does not inevitably lead to better or more stable government. Indeed, what happens after a war is won is often more important than the war itself.

Following the Allied agreements made at Yalta, Germany was divided into four zones of occupation: Britain was to occupy north-western Germany, the United States the south, France the south-west and the Soviet Union the east. Berlin, too, was divided into four occupation sectors.

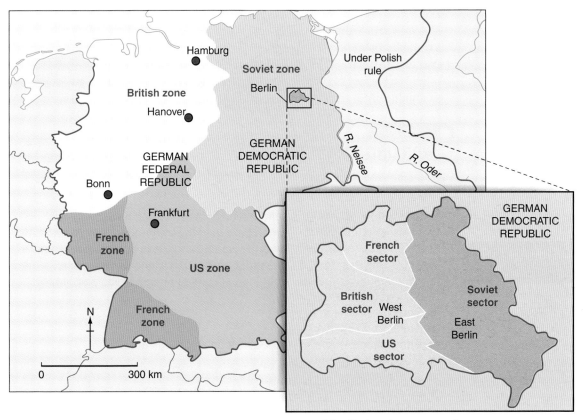

▲ **Figure 2** Germany divided into four occupation zones, and Berlin into four occupation sectors.

Allied Control Council (ACC) – The body responsible for day-to-day government in post-war Germany; it was composed of the military commanders of the four Allied occupying powers.

Germany was to be governed in the immediate post-war period by the military commanders of the four Allies acting jointly through the **Allied Control Council (ACC)** in Berlin. The original intention was to treat Germany as one economic unit, that it would remain united, and that it would be neutral and disarmed. Numerous proposals had been suggested as a blueprint for a post-Nazi German state, including one extreme plan put forward by the American Secretary of State Henry Morgenthau, which envisaged a totally de-industrialised Germany, returned to some kind of 'rural' pre-industrial condition.

However, the Allies in 1945 had no clear or agreed vision of what the new Germany should look like or how it should be governed. They were, of course, determined that Germany should never again become a threat to them, but beyond this there was only the most general of policy agreements, often referred to as the four Ds: demilitarisation, denazification, decentralisation and democratisation. However, in reality, each of the Allies ran their zone more or less independently for the first two years of the occupation.

The slide to division

This lack of clarity and of agreement about Germany's future is fundamental to an understanding of Germany's slide towards division. As the war neared its end, significant disagreements began to appear among the Allies as the Cold War gathered pace. Indeed, it could be argued that the eventual division of Germany by 1949 was not necessarily the result of a series of conscious Allied policy decisions, but, ultimately, an unintended consequence of the emerging Cold War.

Who was primarily responsible for this division is a key question of debate, and is the subsequent focus of the final section of this chapter. Undoubtedly, the so-called 'German problem' – what was to be done with Germany – was rooted in the Nazi legacy of defeat and Germany was to remain ideologically and geographically at the forefront of the Cold War from 1945 to 1990.

KEY DATES: GERMANY IN 1945

8 May German surrender.

5 June Allied Control Council established.

9 June Occupation zones established.

1–4 July Western troops enter their sectors of Berlin.

WORKING TOGETHER

Consider the statement: 'The predominant feeling of the German people at the end of the war was one of relief'.

As a group, discuss the extent to which 'relief' would have been the primary emotion of the German people in the immediate aftermath of the war. Balance this against other personal responses such as gratitude, hope, emptiness, fear, anger, sadness, despair. Consider the social, economic, political and psychological consequences of the war legacy. You could focus your discussion on:
● The physical destruction
● The human costs
● The problems of finding shelter, food and medication
● Displaced persons
● The question of guilt
● Different experiences in the East and West of Germany.

2 Occupation and division, 1945–48

Day-to-day political authority in Germany in the immediate post-war period was in the hands of the military commanders of each Allied country, co-ordinated through the ACC. The key longer-term issues of how to deal with the legacy of Nazism and how to re-build a united German state were the focus of debate at the post-war conference held at Potsdam between 17 July and 2 August 1945.

The Potsdam Conference

How significant was the Potsdam Conference?

Potsdam, which today advertises itself to tourists as the City of Palaces and Gardens, is located 15 miles south-west of the centre of Berlin. From the eighteenth century until 1918, Potsdam had been Germany's second capital, the home of the German royal family. The Conference took place in the relatively undamaged and opulent surroundings of the 176-room Cecilienhof Palace, built in the English mock-Tudor style by Kaiser Wilhelm II for his son Wilhelm and his wife Cecilie. Here, the Allied leaders – Winston Churchill (replaced by Clement Attlee on 28 July as a consequence of the Labour Party's general election victory), the new American President Harry Truman and Joseph Stalin – met in person to finalise their plans for post-war Germany. The Allied leaders never met again collectively.

Disagreements had already become apparent between the Soviet Union and the Western Allies in their previous meeting at Yalta. These differences were merely papered over at Potsdam. The Protocol of Proceedings issued at the end of the Conference was a vaguely worded compromise broadly reiterating agreement on the four Ds (see page 196), but failing to clarify specific policy proposals that could be put into practice across the four zones of occupation.

◄ Churchill, Truman and Stalin at the Potsdam Conference.

NOTE-MAKING

This is a very complex period and requires a clear knowledge of events. Focus your own notes on identifying the key developments in both East and West which contributed to the growth of division. 'Denazification' is covered in a Working Together activity at the end of this Section (see page 217). You could use the following as a template for your own notes:

A The Potsdam Conference
  ● Main concerns
  ● Outcomes
  ● Significance
B Developments in the East
  ● The role of Walter Ulbricht
  ● Events leading to the formation of the SED
  ● Economic developments
  ● Social developments
C Developments in the West
  ● Formation of the Bizone: economic and political considerations
  ● The Truman Doctrine
  ● Marshall Aid
  ● The significance of the currency reform

The Wartime Conferences

Prior to the Potsdam Conference, the Big Three – Churchill, Roosevelt and Stalin – met at Teheran (28 November–1 December 1943) and at Yalta (4–11 February 1945) to discuss post-war arrangements. At Yalta, relationships between the Big Three appeared cordial. However, several key issues remained unresolved: the amount of reparations to be demanded of Germany, the borders of a re-formed Poland, and the precise nature of a future German state.

Fait accompli – An accomplished fact.

Council of Ministers – The Council was composed of the Foreign Ministers of Great Britain, the Soviet Union, the United States, France and China. Its purpose was to agree peace treaties with the defeated European states and to settle outstanding territorial disputes. It met five times, the last of which broke up in acrimony in London in December 1947 without any agreement on a peace settlement with Germany.

Main concerns

Decision-making at Potsdam proved very problematical. The emerging divisions and suspicions among the Allies themselves, and their increasingly divergent national and ideological goals, are reflected in their disagreements over the following issues:

- East and West differed in their interpretation of democracy: the Western powers were anxious to avoid a strong centralised German government and to limit the spread of Communism by establishing Western-style democracy throughout Germany.
- Stalin, on the other hand, was determined to install Communist control in the Soviet zone; he believed that this might act as a catalyst for the eventual Communist domination of post-war Germany.
- The Soviet Union had already begun to establish a Communist-dominated administration in Berlin, thereby antagonising the Western powers.
- The areas of greatest disagreement, however, were the issues of Poland's borders and the extent of reparations to be taken from Germany.

Summary of outcomes

The following is a summary of the main points of agreement reached at the Conference:

- Poland's western frontier was fixed at the Oder and Neisse rivers, which was further west than the Americans and British had wanted but, given the Soviet occupation of Poland, they had to accept it as a virtual *fait accompli*.
- Germany's former eastern territories were incorporated into Poland and the Soviet Union.
- Reparations were to be taken separately by each power from its own zone, with the Soviet Union receiving an additional 25 per cent from the Western zones in recognition of its greater war losses; part of this was to be compensated by the Soviet Union providing additional foodstuffs from its zone to the West.
- Confirmation that Germany would be divided into four zones of occupation, with a French zone being carved out of the American and British zones. Initially the Western Allies had assumed that a French zone would be allocated from the larger Soviet zone, but Stalin refused.
- It was agreed to introduce representative and elective principles of government (democratisation) in Germany and to decentralise the German economy.
- A Council of Ministers would be established.
- The Nazi Party was to be outlawed and Germany was to be denazified.
- Confirmation that Germany would be demilitarised.

In some respects it could be argued that the Conference was of little significance given that it merely ratified much that had already been discussed and agreed at Yalta. The Protocol issued at the end of the Conference mainly confirmed the four Ds. A compromise was reached on reparations, though it did not really satisfy anyone fully, and a decision, albeit a relatively unpalatable one for the British and Americans, was agreed on Poland's frontiers. In short, the Potsdam Conference achieved little that was new or definitive.

However, the Conference could be considered significant in that it clearly demonstrated that relations between the Soviet Union and the Western Allies had deteriorated markedly between the Yalta and Potsdam Conferences. Co-operation over a common goal – the defeat of Hitler – had been replaced by growing suspicion and paranoia over peace-time aims, and there were clear signs of an increasing breakdown in trust between East and West. The death of Roosevelt in April 1945 worsened suspicions on both sides; Truman was liked less by Stalin and Truman's hard-line stance showed that he was less willing to 'baby' the Soviet Union.

The decision on reparations in particular was to have far-reaching consequences, hindering attempts to co-ordinate policy through the Allied Control Council. This concern was clearly and presciently expressed in a British government memorandum at the time:

'it is inconceivable that a Germany which is not treated as an economic unit could very long be treated as a political unit'.

From this point on, each Allied power began to govern its own zone in its own image and in pursuit of its own priorities.

The Potsdam Conference, in many ways, symbolised the end of one war and the beginning of another. In this sense, therefore, it was highly significant.

Denazification

What actions were taken to deal with former Nazis?

One of the principal agreements reached at Potsdam was that all vestiges of Nazism had to be destroyed and that the German people should be confronted with the full scale and horror of Nazi atrocities. Accordingly, the major Nazi war criminals faced trial in Nuremberg.

The Nuremberg trials

Twelve trials involving over a hundred defendants took place in Nuremberg from 1945 to 1949. The first trial, and the most famous, began on 20 November 1945 and involved the prosecution of 21 major Nazi war criminals. The International Military Tribunal (IMT), which sat in Nuremberg, was composed of two judges from each Allied country. The accused were refused the right to base their defence on the grounds that they were simply following orders or in terms of 'so did you', namely that the Allies too had committed war crimes.

The defendants were charged on four counts:

● conspiracy to wage aggressive war
● crimes against peace
● war crimes
● crimes against humanity.

Nuremberg was chosen as the venue for the trials both on a practical and symbolic basis. It was one of the few German cities still to have an intact courthouse, the Palace of Justice, where a major trial could be held. Moreover, the Nazi Party chief in Nuremberg, and one of those on trial, was Julius Streicher, one of the most rabid of Nazi anti-Semites. In addition, Nuremberg was the city of the annual Nazi Party rallies. As such, it was regarded as the spiritual home of Nazism. For these reasons, Nuremberg was chosen over Berlin as a fitting and logical location in which to judge Nazi atrocities.

On Tuesday 1 October, the IMT delivered its verdicts: eighteen were found guilty on one or more counts and three not guilty. Eleven were sentenced to execution by hanging; three others received life sentences and another four received prison sentences ranging from ten to twenty years in length. The executions were carried out in the early morning of 16 October, though Hermann Goering escaped his fate by taking a cyanide pill smuggled into his cell a few hours before he was due to be hung. Overall, as a result of the trials, in the Western zones more than 5,000 were convicted of crimes against humanity. Of these, just under 800 were condemned to death and 486 were eventually executed, despite loud German claims for clemency.

Verdicts	Defendents	
Execution	Frank, Frick, Goering*, Jodl, Kaltenbrunner, Keitel, Rosenberg, Sauckel, Seyss-Inquart, Streicher, Von Ribbentrop, Bormann**	
Acquittal	Fritzsche, Schacht, Von Papen	
Imprisonment and term	15 years	Von Neurath
	20 years	Doenitz, Speer, Von Schirach
	Life	Funk, Hess, Raeder

*Hermann Goering committed suicide before he was due to be executed.

**Martin Bormann was never found and was tried *in absentia*. He was sentenced to execution.

▲ **Figure 3** The Nuremberg defendants and the verdicts reached on each.

One of the intentions of the Nuremberg trials was to make the German people face up to the full horror of Nazi atrocities. However, many Germans questioned the legitimacy of the trials and the appropriateness of the verdicts reached, labeling Nuremberg as 'victors' revenge' based on questionable evidence. The participation of Soviet judges and prosecutors in particular was seen as further evidence of Allied hypocrisy.

Nevertheless, at the very time when many Germans preferred to forget their involvement with the Nazi regime as fast as they could, the trials served an important purpose: the documentation of Nazi crimes presented in Nuremberg ensured that the criminality of the regime could not be escaped and none of those accused could hide behind the defence of following orders. Ultimately, the Nuremberg trials may have contributed to the building of future democracy in Germany by denying the regime's supporters any opportunity to claim a martyr's fate. The trials made it clear that crimes committed by individuals in support of state ideology remained the responsibility of the individual.

However, by so clearly establishing the guilt of the Nazi leadership, the trials perhaps allowed many Germans to rid themselves of any feeling of collective guilt, claiming that they too were as much victims of the Nazi regime as anyone else. Indeed, the wider denazification process was partly intended to deal with this mindset.

Denazification: problems

Denazification was a very sensitive issue in post-war Germany. The Nazi legacy went much further than the obvious post-war physical destruction. Just as important an issue for the Allies was the extent to which Nazi ideology had permeated German life and how far Nazi indoctrination remained rooted in the German mindset. Those Germans who had lived through the years of the Third *Reich* felt very defensive over their participation in the Nazi state. Most, generally, tried to dissociate themselves from the Nazi regime and resented the 'prying' investigations into their past conduct. In particular, this issue inevitably raises fundamental issues of guilt. Additionally, denazification was problematic because of the difficulties of proof, of identifying the guilty and of determining appropriate punishments. Most Nazi Party members had thrown away their membership cards.

MILITARY GOVERNMENT OF GERMANY
FRAGEBOGEN
PERSONNEL QUESTIONNAIRE

WARNUNG. Im Interesse von Klarheit ist dieser Fragebogen in deutsch und englisch verfaßt. In Zweifelsfällen ist der englische Text maßgeblich. Jede Frage muß so beantwortet werden, wie sie gestellt ist. Unterlassung der Beantwortung, unrichtige oder unvollständige Angaben werden wegen Zuwiderhandlung gegen militärische Verordnungen gerichtlich verfolgt. Falls mehr Raum nötig ist, sind weitere Bogen anzuheften.

WARNING. In the interests of clarity this questionnaire has been written in both German and English. If discrepancies exist, the English will prevail. Every question must be answered as indicated. Omissions or false or incomplete statements will result in prosecution as violations of military ordinances. Add supplementary sheets if there is not enough space in the questionnaire.

A. PERSONAL
PERSONNEL

Name / Name — Zuname / Surname — Vornamen / Middle Name Christian Name — Ausweiskarte Nr. / Identity Card No.

Geburtsdatum / Date of birth — Geburtsort / Place of birth

Staatsangehörigkeit / Citizenship — Gegenwärtige Anschrift / Present address

Ständiger Wohnsitz / Permanent residence — Beruf / Occupation

Gegenwärtige Stellung / Present position — Stellung, für die Bewerbung eingereicht / Position applied for

Stellung vor dem Jahre 1933 / Position before 1933

B. MITGLIEDSCHAFT IN DER NSDAP

1. Waren Sie jemals ein Mitglied der NSDAP? Ja ___ Nein ___
2. Daten ___
3. Haben Sie jemals eine der folgenden Stellungen in der NSDAP bekleidet?
(a) REICHSLEITER, oder Beamter in einer Stelle, die einem Reichsleiter untersteht? Ja ___ Nein ___ Titel der Stellung ___ Daten ___
(b) GAULEITER, oder Parteibeamter innerhalb eines Gaues? Ja ___ Nein ___ Daten ___ Amtsort ___
(c) KREISLEITER, oder Parteibeamter innerhalb eines Kreises? Ja ___ Nein ___ Titel der Stellung ___ Daten ___ Amtsort ___
(d) ORTSGRUPPENLEITER, oder Parteibeamter innerhalb einer Ortsgruppe? Titel der Stellung ___ Ja ___ Nein ___ Daten ___ Amtsort ___
(e) Ein Beamter in der Parteikanzlei? Ja ___ Nein ___ Titel der Stellung ___ Daten ___
(f) Ein Beamter in der REICHSLEITUNG der NSDAP? Ja ___ Nein ___ Titel der Stellung ___ Daten ___
(g) Ein Beamter im Hauptamte für Erzieher? Im Amte des Beauftragten des Führers für die Überwachung der gesamten geistigen und weltanschaulichen Schulung und Erziehung der NSDAP? Ein Direktor oder Lehrer in irgendeiner Parteiausbildungsschule? Ja ___ Nein ___ Titel der Stellung ___ Daten ___ Name der Einheit oder Schule ___
(h) Waren Sie Mitglied des KORPS DER POLITISCHEN LEITER? Ja ___ Nein ___ Daten der Mitgliedschaft ___
(i) Waren Sie ein Leiter oder Funktionär in irgendeinem anderen Amte, Einheit oder Stelle (ausgenommen sind die unter C unten angeführten Gliederungen, angeschlossenen Verbände und betreuten Organisationen der NSDAP)? Ja ___ Nein ___ Titel der Stellung ___ Daten ___
(j) Haben Sie irgendwelche nahe Verwandte, die irgendeine der oben angeführten Stellungen bekleidet haben? Ja ___ Nein ___ Wenn ja, geben Sie deren Namen und Anschriften und eine Bezeichnung deren Stellung an ___

B. NAZI PARTY AFFILIATIONS

Have you ever been a member of the NSDAP? yes, no. Dates.

Have you ever held any of the following positions in the NSDAP?

REICHSLEITER or an official in an office headed by any Reichsleiter? yes, no; title of position; dates.

GAULEITER or a Party official within the jurisdiction of any Gau? yes, no; dates; location of office.

KREISLEITER or a Party official within the jurisdiction of any Kreis? yes, no; title of position; dates; location of office.

ORTSGRUPPENLEITER or a Party official within the jurisdiction of an Ortsgruppe? yes, no; title of position; dates; location of office.

An official in the Party Chancellery? yes, no; dates; title of position.

An official within the Central NSDAP headquarters? yes, no; dates; title of positions.

An official within the NSDAP's Chief Education Office? In the office of the Führer's Representative for the Supervision of the Entire Intellectual and Politico-philosophical Education of the NSDAP? Or a director or instructor in any Party training school? yes, no; dates; title of position; Name of unit or school.

Were you a member of the CORPS OF POLITISCHE LEITER? yes, no; Dates of membership.

Were you a leader or functionary of any other NSDAP offices or units or agencies (except Formations, Affiliated Organizations and Supervised Organizations which are covered by questions under C below)? yes, no; dates; title of position.

Have you any close relatives who have occupied any of the positions named above? yes, no; if yes, give the name and address and a description of the position.

C. TÄTIGKEIT IN NSDAP HILFSORGANISATIONEN

Geben Sie hier an, ob Sie ein Mitglied waren und in welchem Ausmaße Sie an den Tätigkeiten der folgenden Gliederungen, angeschlossenen Verbänden und betreuten Organisationen teilgenommen haben:

C. NAZI "AUXILIARY" ORGANIZATION ACTIVITIES

Indicate whether you were a member and the extent to which you participated in the activities of the following Formations, Affiliated Organizations or Supervised Organizations:

◀ The front page of a *Fragebogen* (personnel questionnaire).

The original plan to disallow important jobs to former Nazis began to unravel almost immediately because of the need for many experts, such as engineers and administrators, to rebuild German society. It was difficult to find people who had not been tainted in some way by association with Nazism.

Perhaps more fundamentally, this issue of denazification is inextricably bound to the continuing historical debate about the causes of the Holocaust and the extent to which the German people supported Nazi racial ideologies. In 1996, in his book, *Hitler's Willing Executioners*, the historian Daniel Goldhagen reignited a storm of controversy by arguing that anti-Semitism was deeply rooted in the German mentality and that Germans were unlike other Europeans in this respect. His book was written in response to Christopher Browning's *Ordinary Men*, published in 1992, which had concluded that many of the perpetrators of the Holocaust were acting more out of obedience to authority than as a result of any specifically German characteristic.

When visiting memorial sites such as Auschwitz–Birkenau, or a concentration camp such as Buchenwald, it is difficult not to conclude that the effectiveness of such horrific institutions owed much to German 'efficiency' and an 'order mentality'. However, this is far removed from arguing that the Holocaust grew out of a specifically German mindset. It is important for all students of the Holocaust to think beyond stereotypical generalisations about so-called national characteristics.

Fragebogen

This was a questionnaire containing 131 questions about each German citizen's activities and political affiliation during Nazi rule. The *Fragebogen* was designed as the main administrative tool for identifying former Nazis and was originally conceived as a crucial part of the process of 'cleansing' German society of the impact of National Socialist ideology. It was intended that all German adult citizens had to complete a *Fragebogen* but it was never applied in the Soviet zone and the whole process died under a mountain of paperwork – 16 million were issued in the Western zones.

Denazification: outcomes

The four occupying powers interpreted the process differently; there were many inconsistencies in application and in many respects each served national purposes.

- **The US zone** The Americans went about this process with great initial zeal and implemented denazification procedures more strictly than the other three Powers. They listed 3.5 million Germans as 'chargeable cases', one-quarter of the total population of their zone, though many were never brought in front of a denazification tribunal. The Americans wanted to convert the Germans to democratic attitudes but they also distrusted them. Their missionary zeal diminished as the Cold War developed and they quickly realised that Germans would be needed to build an anti-Communist West German state.

- **The British zone** The British, with much reduced resources, were more pragmatic and more lenient than the Americans. The *Fragebogen* questionnaire was much less used and the British were much more prepared to allow former Nazis to hold prominent positions, particularly since they were struggling to rebuild their zone's shattered economy.

- **The French zone** The French gave denazification a very low priority. Their main aim was to revitalise France's destroyed economy. Given that they had limited French manpower, they allowed former Nazis from other zones to work in their area.

- **The Soviet zone** The Soviets applied rigorous denazification measures. Many former Nazi civil servants, teachers and law professionals were purged. However, their approach was predicated on building a new Communist society. They held capitalist society to blame for the rise of Nazism. Therefore, though a number of Nazi war criminals were executed and Nazi properties confiscated, those former Nazis who were willing to conform to Communism, especially those in key professions, were not removed from public life.

Conclusions

The real problem in weeding out Nazism was that it was scarcely practicable in the circumstances of the post-war period. It was almost impossible to find competent Germans to fill posts in the zonal administrations who were not tainted in some way by Nazism. Denazification ended in March 1948 when many serious cases were still left untried. The coming of the Cold War had brought a halt to the process and it was clear that the measures had little impact.

Denazification met with considerable opposition from the Germans. They were more likely to see themselves as a victim than a perpetrator. Konrad Adenauer, in a speech in July 1946, argued that the measures had gone on for too long and went too far and that they threatened to build a nationalist backlash. He preferred that the issue be swept under the carpet. This 'turned away face' was typical of millions of Germans and persisted throughout the 1950s and early 1960s.

Universities and the legal profession were the least affected by denazification, and businessmen also were largely unaffected. In an opinion poll in October 1946, when the main Nuremberg Trial ended, only 6 per cent of Germans replied that it was 'unfair'; however, by 1950 this proportion had risen to just over 30 per cent. Clearly pro-Nazi sentiment persisted into the post-war period. A further poll in 1952 showed that 37 per cent of Germans thought that it was better for Germany not to contain any Jews, and 25 per cent admitted to having a 'good opinion' of Hitler. Perhaps the best that might be said of the whole process was that it was inadequate, but sufficient for a new society to be rebuilt.

WORKING TOGETHER

The Nuremberg trials and the issue of denazification were sensitive issues and the focus of much debate in post-war Germany. The trials were a significant aspect of the wider process of denazification. A class debate on this would help identify the most significant arguments on this issue, and would encourage the development of a balanced viewpoint, which is a key requirement at A-level. The class should be divided into two groups, one to argue for and one to argue against the following proposition:

'The process of denazification in post-war Germany was ill-advised and ineffective.'

Follow up the debate by writing your own balanced conclusion to the proposition.

Sovietisation in the East

How was Communism established in the Eastern zone?

Political, economic and social development in the Russian zone was modelled on the Soviet Union's version of Marxist–Leninism. It quickly became clear that Stalin intended to sovietise the Eastern zone, both as a buffer against the Western Allies and as a potential springboard to spread Communism throughout Germany. As previously outlined on page 191, at the end of April 1945, a number of senior German Communists, who had fled Nazi Germany after 1933 to go into exile in the Soviet Union, were transported to Berlin and other major cities in the Eastern zone. Their task was to establish Communist control in the Soviet zone of occupation. The leader of the group sent to Berlin was Walter Ulbricht. It was Ulbricht who became the first leader of the German Democratic Republic (GDR) when it came into existence on 7 October 1949.

Political developments

Stalin almost certainly believed that the sooner Communist control could be established in the East, the more susceptible a future united Germany would be to a Communist form of government. Ulbricht was charged with this goal. He had a window of opportunity. It was not until the beginning of July that Western forces took over their sectors of Berlin. Until then, the Soviet Military Administration in Berlin (SMAD) was in sole occupation of the city. Ulbricht, therefore, had approximately two months, unhindered by any Western presence, to establish Communist control. Ulbricht's strategy was based on a simple subterfuge: he would back the appointment of non-Communists as mayor in some Berlin districts but he would undermine and limit the influence of these figurehead mayors by ensuring that their deputies were committed Communists. His strategy was backed up by making sure that Communists were appointed as heads of police and education throughout Berlin.

Source C A statement by Walter Ulbricht, 1945.

> The first deputy mayor, the head of personnel and administration and the man who's in charge of education must be our chaps. And you've also got to find one comrade who's totally trustworthy. He's the one who takes over the police. It's got to look democratic, but all that really matters must be in our hands.

This process was well under way by the time the Western Allies took possession of their sectors of Berlin and there was really very little they could do to change these arrangements. Indeed, it is possible that for a period of time they were taken in by Ulbricht's subterfuge.

The formation of new political parties

In parallel to these developments, on 10 June the Soviet Union granted permission for the formation of anti-fascist political parties in the Soviet zone. Again, the Soviet Union was stealing a march on the Western Allies who did not begin this process until August and September. Their intention was clear: by allowing political activity the Soviet Union would be in a better position to support and legitimise the activities of the German Communists. Non-Communist parties were also formed but in Ulbricht's view this was largely window dressing and useful simply to give an appearance of true democracy at work.

Marxist–Leninism – The Communist ideology of Karl Marx as adapted by Lenin. Its goal was the creation of a classless society and the public ownership of all land and natural resources and production for the benefit of all members of society not the privileged few.

German Democratic Republic (GDR) – The formal title of the East German state which existed from 1949 until the reunification of Germany on 3 October 1990.

Walter Ulbricht (1893–1973)

Ulbricht was a German Communist politician much favoured by Stalin. He played a leading role in the KPD in the Weimar era. He spent much of the period of Nazi rule in exile in Moscow. He returned to Germany in April 1945 to help re-form the KPD and to establish a Communist-dominated administration in the Soviet zone of occupation. He was leader of the GDR until 1971.

What can you infer from Source C about the fundamental aim of Ulbricht's strategy and his method of achieving it?

The main parties to be licensed between 11 June and 5 July were the:

- German Communist Party (KPD)
- German Socialist Party (SPD)
- conservative Christian Democratic Union (CDU)
- German Liberal Party (LDPD).

Initially, the KPD had rejected close co-operation with other left-wing parties but this lack of popular support forced a change of plan. From the autumn of 1945, fully backed by the Soviets, the KPD put the SPD under intense pressure to merge the two parties. Otto Grotewohl, the SPD leader, agreed to a merger, hoping that the SPD's influence would have a mitigating effect on the Communists, forcing them to remain true to democratic principles and to the maintenance of individual liberties. On 21 April the KPD and SPD merged to form a united party: the Socialist Unity Party (SED).

Grotewohl's hopes that the SPD might play a leading role in the new Party, and that socialists throughout Germany would accept the merger, proved to be hopelessly naïve on both counts. The SPD in the Western zones, led by Kurt Schumacher, rejected the merger and in August 1945 Schumacher was elected 'western leader' of the SPD in opposition to Grotewohl. Moreover, the Communists quickly came to dominate the SED, sweeping to victory in the first local and regional elections in the Eastern zone in October 1946.

The formation of the SED also proved to be of great significance in the West. For the Americans and the British, the SED seemed little more than a tool of the Soviet Union and further reinforced their fear of a Communist takeover of Germany. It confirmed their growing belief that a merger of their two zones would provide the best means of blocking any Communist expansion. This union of the American and British zones to form Bizonia is discussed in more detail on page 208–10.

Economic developments

As outlined on pages 191–192, Germany's economic infrastructure had virtually collapsed by the end of the war. The scale of the damage and destruction and the logistical problems and cost of feeding and providing medical aid for the defeated population shocked even the victorious Allies. In addition to this, reparation demands and the basic costs of maintaining substantial armies of occupation were also competing economic priorities for the Allies. Just as important a factor in explaining post-war developments in the zones of occupation is an understanding of the ideological goals of the Allies. The Soviet Union in particular had a very clear ideological vision for shaping the economic development of its zone.

Reparations

The Soviet Union had no intention of putting German economic interests ahead of its own national self-interest. It determined to extract the maximum possible reparations from its zone, and probably about three times in excess of what had been agreed at Yalta and Potsdam. For the Soviet Union, the costs of occupation had to be extracted from the German nation. Whatever productive capacity that remained was seized, with entire factories and industrial plants being dismantled and transported back to the Soviet Union. Such large-scale removals were often haphazard and indiscriminate. Both the Germans and the Western Allies thought their demands insatiable. It is estimated that East Germany lost about one-third of its industrial base in this way. On top of this, there was extensive looting and confiscation at a personal level. The astonishing scale of this industrial expropriation was undoubtedly due to a combination of Stalin's desire for retribution laced with sheer opportunism and pragmatism on the ground and, together with the widespread rapes and poor Red Army discipline, did much to harm Soviet–German relations at a personal level.

Industry and commerce

The process of organising economic life in the Eastern zone according to the central planning model of the Soviet Union began almost immediately after the end of the war. The most important sectors of the industrial and commercial economy were progressively nationalised:

- **July 1945:** a centralised state banking system replaced private banks.
- **September 1945:** the nationalisation of heavy industry began.
- **June 1946:** over 200 major private companies were taken over and reorganised into 25 state-run enterprises called SAGs (German–Soviet Joint Stock Companies).
- **June 1947:** the German Economic Commission, controlled by the SED, was set up to co-ordinate economic development.
- **April 1948:** a large number of middle-sized private companies were taken over and reorganised into state-run organisations called VEBs (Public Enterprises); by the end of 1948 SAGs and VEBs together controlled about 60 per cent of East German business, and the private sector continued to be restricted through taxation and planning policies which heavily favoured state enterprises.

Agriculture

The first steps towards the collectivisation of agriculture began in September 1945 with the seizure of approximately 7,000 large estates, most belonging to the German Junker landowners, which were reorganised into state collective farms. In the early post-war years the state allowed small farmers and peasants to retain private smallholdings in order not to alienate this important social class group.

> **Collective farms** – Privately owned farms merged into very large state-controlled farms.

Social developments

The two great mass organisations of the future East German state were founded in the immediate post-war years: the Free German Trade Union Federation (FDGB) and the Free German Youth (FDJ). The FDGB replaced all independent trade unions. Membership was voluntary but in reality East Germans could not develop their careers without being a member. Like most East German state organisations, the FDGB was largely a vehicle for ideological control. As with the FDGB, membership of the FDJ, which was open to 14–25-year-olds, was voluntary, but educational opportunities and career advancement narrowed considerably for non-members. Its primary function was to cement loyalty to the state.

The secret police

The Soviets began very quickly to target their class opponents and to identify those who could be of particular use. As we have seen above, the industrial and agricultural elites had their businesses and properties seized. Thousands of German scientists and skilled technicians, particularly those who had worked on the Nazi atomic bomb programme, were also forcibly transferred with their families to the Soviet Union. An extensive secret police system was also begun, designed 'to know everything and to report everything worth knowing' (*The Russians in Germany, 1945–49* by Norman M. Naimark, 1995).

Arrests of so-called 'hostile elements' numbered over 120,000 in the years 1945–49, most of whom were imprisoned without trial and for indefinite terms. Those targeted ranged from suspected former Nazis to SPD members critical of Soviet policies, dissident youths, German prisoners of war and anyone loosely referred to as a 'class enemy'. The Soviet secret service, the NKVD, used former Nazi concentration camps such as Sachsenhausen in Berlin to imprison these 'hostile elements'. Known as Special Camp No 1, this was the largest of ten special camps in the Soviet zone of occupation. By the time the camp was closed in March 1950 about 60,000 people had been imprisoned there, of whom at least 12,000 had died. At Special Camp No 2, the former Nazi concentration camp Buchenwald, at Weimar, some 28,500 people were imprisoned. Of these, about one thousand were women. The living conditions in this camp were dreadful and one-quarter of the inmates died.

In many ways, therefore, the Soviet authorities initially used the remaining camps for the same purposes as the Nazis, later turning the major camps into memorials to Nazi–Fascist crimes. Most camps in the West were closed down and destroyed. Dachau, the largest camp in the western zones, was used as an SS prison until 1948 and then used as a refugee camp until 1964.

Conclusion

The rapes, plunder, reparations removals, land and property expropriation, arrests and deportations fatally undermined the Soviet Union's ability to win the majority of German hearts and minds in their zone of occupation, which had been the hope of Ulbricht and the other exiled German Communists who had returned after the war. The process of gaining control seemed more like a process of gradual strangulation than liberation. Already many alienated workers were migrating to the West. The compliance of the SED in this process significantly weakened its legitimacy in the eyes of many Germans in the Soviet zone. It is impossible to explain, therefore, the nature of life in the future East German state after 1949, and the state's ultimate death in 1989, without having an understanding of its difficult birth in these immediate post-war years.

Steps to Western unification

Why was there a merger of the Western zones?

We have already seen that as the war ended, the Allies could not agree what to do with a defeated Germany beyond temporarily partitioning the country into four occupation zones under the direction of an Allied Control Council. The Potsdam agreement had stated clearly that 'for the time being no central German government shall be established'. However, it was intended to restore administrative functions as quickly as possible in each zone and to treat the economy as a whole.

The decision to implement a zonal structure was not only a pragmatic one, given the extent and depth of the problems the Allies expected to encounter in Germany after twelve years of Nazi rule, but also reflected the deep-seated differences among the Allies over reaching a peace settlement with Germany, and about how a post-Nazi, united Germany would be governed. The expectation was that agreement would be achieved through meetings of the Council of Foreign Ministers.

However, the reality of zonal occupation was that Germany became fragmented, not united, as each of the victorious powers managed its zone of occupation for its own purposes and in its own self-interest. The major fragmentation occurred between East and West as the competing ideologies of democratic capitalism and Marxist–Leninism fought for primacy in Germany. But tensions also existed between the Western Allies, as the French pursued their own policies of retribution and resisted a formal merger of its zone with the British and Americans until June 1949.

Nevertheless, as early as spring 1946, the British and Americans had begun to explore how their common interests might best be served by combining their zones of occupation.

Political developments

The Western powers were more cautious than the Soviet Union in respect of licensing new German political parties. The process only began in September 1945, but even then new parties were restricted initially to participating in local elections. At first, so many new parties were formed it was feared that there was going to be a repetition of what had happened in the days of the pre-Nazi Weimar Republic. However, as in the Eastern zone, four major parties did emerge:

- the SPD
- the Christian Democrat CDU/CSU – see Chapter 7 for a broader discussion of this political grouping
- the KDP
- the Liberal Democratic LDP, later to become the Free Democrats (FDP).

Each of the Western powers, particularly the French, who felt that Germans were inherently anti-democratic, were slow to loosen their control of the political process. Nevertheless, by 1946 political development in the Western zones was well under way, with the SPD, led by Kurt Schumacher, and the CDU/CSU, led by Konrad Adenauer, developing as the dominant parties. Adenauer emerged as the Allies' favoured 'West German', shrewdly building for himself an image as a man of conciliation, repudiating the extremes of both right and left and working assiduously for reconciliation and a policy of western integration as a buffer to Communism. As will be seen in the next chapter, this earned Adenauer the nickname of the Chancellor of the Allies from his SPD rival Schumacher, who felt that Adenauer was placing his own political advancement ahead of promoting German unity.

Economic developments

It can be difficult to disentangle the various factors that pushed the Americans and the British towards merging their zones. Perhaps their common ideological fear that Stalin intended to achieve Communist domination in Germany and Western Europe was the prime motivating factor. However, it also became quickly apparent to both the Americans and the British that the sheer economic cost of propping up their zones of occupation necessitated common action. Added to this was George Kennan's analysis (see page 208) that Communism would be more likely to take hold in the West in conditions of economic want and misery. Economic imperatives, therefore, worked alongside political and ideological concerns in propelling the British and Americans towards a merger.

Kennan's 'Long Telegram', February 1946

George Kennan was an American diplomat with long experience of the Soviet state. He was firmly anti-Communist. This memorandum is often cited as the clearest expression of American anti-Soviet opinion in the early years of the Cold War.

Kennan argued that the Soviet Union was fundamentally expansionist and that it had to be opposed in order to protect the vital strategic interests of the United States. His views closely matched President Truman's growing distrust and suspicion of Stalin's intentions and were instrumental in moving opinion in Washington away from a policy of co-operation to one of 'containment' as expressed in the Truman Doctrine.

Kennan favoured political and economic methods of containment but his memorandum was seized upon by hard-liners in Washington who believed that the American public would only support the financial costs of defending democracy in Western Europe if they could be persuaded that the Soviet Union represented a global military threat to the United States' interests and, therefore, must be resisted militarily.

Kennan became a close advisor to James Byrnes' successor as Secretary of State, George C. Marshall, and was a key architect of the Marshall Plan.

The British in particular had their own significant economic problems:

- The costs of occupation were crippling the British; its zone comprised the industrial north and west of the country where the scale of the damage and destruction was perhaps at its worst.
- The situation was worsening month on month as a result of the added humanitarian cost of housing and feeding the flood of refugees and expellees from the East.
- The British also had wider financial problems: not only were they extensively in debt from the war but the Labour government was additionally burdened by financing a new welfare state in Britain and had committed itself to maintaining Britain's worldwide imperial commitments.

It made no sense to the British, therefore, to continue pursuing a policy of extracting reparations from its zone which could not even satisfy the costs of occupation. Both the British and Americans had come to the conclusion that if the march of Communism across Europe was to be halted, the western Germans had to be treated more as an ally than an enemy.

As early as spring 1946 the Truman administration had come to favour a merger with the British. According to General Clay, the commander-in-chief of the military administration in the American zone at the time, it had already been decided by the end of May 'to approach the British to learn of their readiness to unite their occupation zone with ours'.

The Bizone

The process towards a merger of the American and British zones, known as the Bizone, or Bizonia, moved relatively quickly as collaboration with the Soviet Union in the Allied Control Council proved increasingly impossible during 1946.

- **May 1946:** the reparations agreement decided upon at Potsdam broke down irrevocably when Clay halted deliveries of industrial goods from the American zone to the Soviet zone in frustration at the non-delivery of agricultural goods from the eastern zone; any pretence of treating Germany as a single economic unit was now gone.
- **6 September:** American Secretary of State James Byrnes announced the decision to merge the British and American zones under German civilian administration in a speech in Stuttgart. Many West Germans saw this as the first glimmer of hope that they would be given back control of their own domestic affairs.
- **1 January 1947:** the Bizone formally came into existence, uniting 40 million Germans in one zone.

The Bizone established beyond all doubt the economic division of the Western zones from the East, though it would take the French another eighteen months before finally deciding to merge their zone with the Bizone. The political division of Germany was accelerated in 1947 by two historic developments: the American decision to lead the West in resisting Communist expansion in Europe, enshrined in the Truman Doctrine, and the decision to back this up with dollars in the form of Marshall Aid.

The Truman Doctrine

The catalyst for the announcement of the Truman Doctrine was the political situation in Greece. In early 1947 the British government informed Washington that it could no longer afford to provide financial and military aid to the Greek government, which was fighting a civil war against Communist insurgents. The British withdrawal would leave this strategically important state susceptible to Communist takeover. For Truman, this threat was further evidence to support his growing belief that Western Europe was in danger of a Soviet-inspired Communist takeover. Kennan's thesis (see page 208) argued that the Soviet threat had to be 'contained'.

On 12 March 1947, in a speech to Congress, Truman declared that:

'it must be the policy of the United States to support free peoples who are resisting attempted subjugation by armed minorities or by outside pressures.'

This so-called Truman Doctrine demonstrated America's clear resolution to resist the spread of Communism beyond its current limits.

Just as the creation of the Bizone had signalled the intention of the United States to establish a western German economic union based on capitalist principles, the Truman Doctrine clearly implied the end of any meaningful political co-operation with the Soviet Union over the 'German problem'. From this point, the likelihood of a united Germany emerging from the ashes of the Third *Reich* was virtually zero. The United States had clearly rejected any return to its traditional isolationist foreign policy and had signalled that it would not abandon Western Europe; it was now fully committed to an anti-Communist interventionist path in Europe to fill the vacuum left by Hitler's defeat.

The Marshall Plan

The Marshall Plan was the economic complement of the Truman Doctrine. While the Truman Doctrine focused on military support, the Marshall Plan was an offer of purely economic aid. The Marshall Plan proposals were announced in a speech on 5 June 1947 at Harvard University by the new Secretary of State George C. Marshall. It is also referred to as the European Recovery Plan.

It was a package of aid amounting to $13 billion over four years. The offer of aid was open to all European nations, excluding fascist Spain, but including those Eastern European nations aligned to or under the influence of the Soviet Union, and the Soviet Union itself. The Organisation for European Economic Co-operation (OEEC) was set up in April 1948 to manage the distribution of Marshall Aid among sixteen recipient nations. Stalin rejected the offer of Marshall Aid as did the Communist-controlled Eastern bloc nations. His refusal cemented the economic division of Europe, just as the Truman Doctrine had signified its ideological and political division.

The currency reform

Between June 1947, when the Marshall Plan was announced, and June 1948, when a new currency was introduced in the Western zones, East–West relations moved remorselessly towards crisis point:

- The Council of Foreign Ministers, meeting in London during November and December 1947, became increasingly fractious and broke up without reaching any common agreement on Germany's future.
- Similarly, the Allied Control Council collapsed in acrimony when the Soviet delegation walked out of a meeting on 20 March 1948 after the Western Allies refused to share the details of their plans for a West German state. This effectively brought the existence of the ACC to an end.
- Between February and March, and April and May 1948, the United States, Britain and France, together with Belgium, Luxembourg and Holland, held a series of conferences in London agreeing in principle to the setting up of a federal form of government in Western Germany.
- The Soviet Union and the SED repeatedly and vociferously protested that the London conferences contravened the Potsdam Protocol and, therefore, were illegitimate.
- In response to the London conferences, the Soviet Union increasingly began restricting access to the western sectors of Berlin, either by imposing bureaucratic restrictions or temporarily closing road and rail links to the city. The geographical location of West Berlin, deep inside the Soviet zone, made it a very vulnerable pressure point for the Western Allies; the intention of the Soviet Union was to force the Western Allies into abandoning their plans for a Western political union.
- Crisis point was reached when the Americans and British pushed ahead with their plans to create a new German Central Bank and to replace the worthless *Reichsmark* with a new currency, the *Deutschmark*; currency reform was seen as the final prerequisite for political union.
- The Soviet Union refused to consider any possibility of currency reform sponsored by the West.
- The French formally agreed to join their zone with the Bizone on 17 June to form the Trizone, or Trizonia.
- The new currency was introduced into the three Western zones on 20 June.

The currency reform precipitated the first great Cold War crisis. On 24 June 1948, in retaliation, Soviet troops blockaded all road, rail and barge access to West Berlin. The Berlin Blockade had begun.

3 The Berlin Blockade, 1948–49

'What happens to Berlin, happens to Germany. What happens to Germany, happens to Europe.'

Vyacheslav Molotov, Soviet Union Foreign Minister, 1939–49.

Causes of the blockade

Why did the Soviet Union blockade Berlin?

Following the decision by the United States and Great Britain at the end of 1947 to proceed with a currency reform in their zones, after yet another inconclusive meeting of the Council of Foreign Ministers in December, the Soviet Union began to take counter-action against the West by bringing pressure to bear on its most vulnerable position: access to West Berlin. From January 1948 the

---

> ## KEY DATES: OCCUPATION AND DIVISION
>
> **1945**
>
> **17 July–2 August** The Potsdam Conference.
>
> **20 November** Nuremberg trials began.
>
> **1946**
>
> **21 April** The SED was formed.
>
> **1947**
>
> **1 January** The Bizone was formed.
>
> **12 March** Announcement of the Truman Doctrine.
>
> **5 June** The Marshall Plan was announced.
>
> **20 June 1948** The new currency – the *Deutschmark* – was introduced into the Western zones.

Soviet authorities increasingly began to interrupt and delay rail, road and barge traffic to West Berlin for both civilians and freight. Interference also occurred on air traffic. On 5 April a Soviet fighter first 'buzzed' then collided with a British transport plane as it approached Berlin-Gatow airport in the British sector. Both aircraft crashed, killing the Soviet pilot and twelve British and two Americans on the British plane. The implementation of the currency reform in the Western zones on 20 June precipitated a full-scale blockade, beginning on 24 June. The Soviet Union also stopped all water, fuel and food supplies from its own sector to the three Western sectors.

In simple terms the blockade can be explained as a retaliatory action on the part of the Soviet Union. The currency union was regarded by the Soviet Union as not only a clear provocation but also a direct repudiation of Four Power control in Germany (the Four Powers being the USA, the Soviet Union, Great Britain and France). The Soviet Union interpreted the currency reform not only as a virtual commitment to divide Germany, but also as an attempt to wreck the East German economy. The blockade, therefore, was intended at the very least to force the Western powers into renewed negotiations over the future of Germany. It was the first major confrontation of the Cold War.

The blockade can also be seen as an attempt to force an Allied withdrawal from Berlin and, in so doing, discredit Western policy towards Germany. This was a high-risk strategy designed to bring the whole of Berlin into the Communist orbit, and presented as a demonstration of the Soviet resolve to preserve German unity.

The blockade also needs to be understood in the context of Stalin's wider goal of maintaining a unified Germany under Communist leadership. This goal was looking less likely given the developments in the West. Stalin had been confident in the immediate post-war period that Britain would not have the resources, material or financial, or the political will to remain in Germany. He had also fully expected the United States to withdraw from Western Europe, believing the American population would not support either the costs of occupation or the potential for further conflict. Neither of these two outcomes had come about and it seems that the Soviet Union had almost come to see the blockade as a 'last throw of the dice' to regain the political initiative.

Of course, the situation in Berlin has to be seen not only as part of the German Question but also in the wider context of the Cold War. Berlin had become the front line in the emerging ideological confrontation between East and West, so the blockade can be seen as a trial of strength and will – a demonstration of Soviet resolve, just as the subsequent airlift was seen as a symbol of America's determination to contain Soviet expansionism.

Overall, the Berlin Blockade was a significant turning point in the superpower struggle which emerged following Hitler's defeat. Stalin needed to show his ability to exert pressure and Truman had to demonstrate that his doctrine was backed by actions as well as dollars. Most of all, the blockade was like a titanic prize fight with the prize being control of Berlin.

The Berlin airlift

Given the closure of all overland access to West Berlin, the only means of supplying West Berlin was by air through the existing three air corridors. The West correctly concluded that the Soviet Union would not risk all-out war by bringing down Western airplanes, just as the West did not feel it could risk war by breaking the land blockade by force.

The Berlin airlift was an immense logistical operation achieving a level of supply the Soviet Union had believed impossible. For the inhabitants of West Berlin it was almost as if wartime conditions had returned. There was an evening curfew;

no street lighting operated and the lack of gas and electricity meant that civilians lived after dark by candlelight. The following facts and figures give the merest indication of the massive scale of the eleven-month operation:

● Over 277,000 flights were made.
● Nearly 400,000 tons of foodstuffs, coal and supplies were transported.
● A new airfield was built at Tegel in the French sector by army engineers and Berlin volunteers in just 49 days.
● At the height of the operation, on 16 April 1949, an allied aircraft landed in Berlin every minute.

It was inevitable that there would be casualties – 39 British, 31 American and 13 German civilians lost their lives. Weather conditions could be treacherous, especially through the winter. The approach to Tempelhof airport in the American zone was particularly difficult for pilots given its inner-city location in a residential area. The sheer number and frequency of flights increased the likelihood of on-the-ground accidents. In the air, pilots faced additional problems. Soviet planes constantly 'buzzed' Allied transports, balloons were released into the air corridors, there was radio interference, and searchlights were even directed into pilots' eyes. The miracle is that so few died. Those who did lose their lives are commemorated by the Berlin Airlift memorial at Tempelhof airport in Berlin.

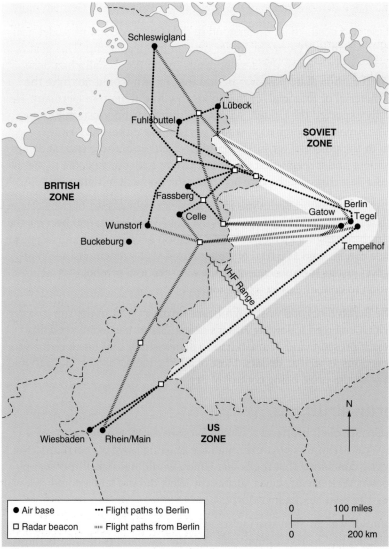

▲ **Figure 4** A map showing the details of the Berlin airlift.

◀ The Berlin airlift memorial at Tempelhof airport.

Consequences of the airlift

After eleven months, on 12 May 1949, the Soviet Union ceased the blockade. It was apparent that the Western Allies would not abandon Berlin and the failure to drive the West out of the city had not only become a major embarrassment but it also invalidated the whole purpose and premise of the blockade.

Perhaps the most obvious and concrete outcome of the blockade was the creation of two separate German states. The blockade had not caused this – the decision to move towards partition had been made in Washington and London through 1946 and this had been recognised, if not accepted, in Moscow at least from the creation of the Bizone at the beginning of 1947 – it had simply occasioned it. Certainly, as far as the French were concerned, the blockade had removed any final reservations they had had about merging their zone with the Bizone.

The blockade also confirmed a new world order. The superpower conflict was now established for decades to come. Though there would be periods of 'thaw' in relations between East and West, the blockade had provided an astonishing window through which to see how ideologically divided the post-war world had become, and how it would remain, until the collapse of the Soviet bloc in 1989–90.

The blockade also speeded up the development of formal Western defence arrangements. Britain, France, Belgium, the Netherlands and Luxembourg had already, on 17 March 1948, formed a European Defence Organisation (EDO), ostensibly to prevent any German resurgence which might threaten European stability, but in reality it was as much an anti-Communist alliance as it was an anti-German one. The blockade led to the realisation in the United States that the EDO would be too small and too regional to offer any effective defence against the Soviet Union. As a result, the North Atlantic Treaty Organization (NATO) was established in April 1949 as a political and military alliance extending well beyond the capabilities of the EDO.

> **NATO** – A collective Western defence alliance formed on 4 April 1949, intended primarily to safeguard the West from Soviet aggression. Its original members were: Belgium, Canada, Denmark, France, Iceland, Italy, Luxemburg, the Netherlands, Norway, the United Kingdom and the United States.

The lifting of the blockade was, of course, an enormous climb-down and humiliation for the Soviet Union. The blockade had failed; none of its goals had been achieved. The blockade had not brought the Western Allies back to the negotiating table over Germany; indeed it had confirmed rather than prevented partition. Neither had it succeeded in pushing the West out of Berlin. The city would remain divided into West and East, with their own administrations, separate currencies and totally dissimilar political and economic systems. The blockade cemented Berlin's importance as the frontline of the Cold War in Europe. West Berlin quickly became established as a capitalist 'thorn' deep inside the body of the Soviet bloc. Its symbolic importance during the period of German division, as an outpost of freedom and democracy still reverberates around the world even today.

Finally, the blockade had a significant impact in changing the relationship between Germans in the West and their occupiers. The bitterness of defeat had now been replaced by a more co-operative spirit; more friends than enemies. The Allied effort was seen as a great propaganda victory. General Clay had initially doubted that the Soviet Union would be so foolhardy as to mount a full-scale blockade 'because it would alienate the Germans almost completely'. His prophecy proved unerring.

Establishment of the Federal Republic of Germany

> **Federal Republic of Germany (FRG)** – This is the formal title of the West German state which existed from 1949 until the reunification of Germany on 3 October 1990.

Steps towards political unification continued throughout the duration of the blockade. A Parliamentary Council, chosen by each Land, was formed in August to draft a provisional constitution known as the *Grundgesetz* or Basic Law. This Council was chaired by Konrad Adenauer. The Basic Law was approved by the military governors of the three Western zones and the **Federal Republic of Germany (FRG)** was founded on 23 May 1949. The provincial city of Bonn became the West German capital.

The first national elections were held on 14 August 1949, resulting in a large turnout of 78.5 per cent, with the Christian Democrats emerging as the largest party, with just eight more seats than their socialist opponents (139 to 131). The first Chancellor of the new Federal Republic was Konrad Adenauer at the head of a CDU/FDP coalition. Theodor Heuss, the FDP leader, was appointed as the first West German President.

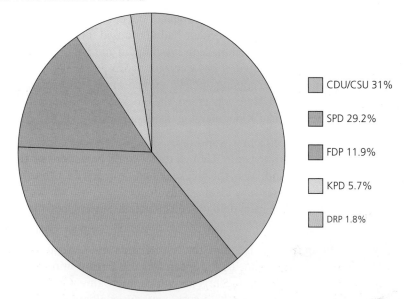

- CDU/CSU 31%
- SPD 29.2%
- FDP 11.9%
- KPD 5.7%
- DRP 1.8%

Figure 5 Election results, ▶ 14 August 1949.

Establishment of the German Democratic Republic

A similar political process occurred in the East. Already in December 1947 Ulbricht had called a People's Congress (*Volkscongress*), which included all-party delegates from all four zones, in order to win over opinion for a unified Germany. A second Congress held in March 1948 elected a German People's Council (*Volksrat*), containing 400 delegates, which was tasked with devising a new constitution for a united Germany. In reality, however, the SED was merely ensuring that it had a framework in place for a new East German state when, as was anticipated, the three Western zones merged to form a separate West Germany.

A constitutional framework was completed by March 1949 and elections for a third Congress in May 1949 included a ballot asking voters if they supported the creation of an East German state which would work for German unity. Two-thirds of voters supported this position. The German Democratic Republic was founded on 7 October 1949, the East German authorities having delayed taking this step until after the creation of the FRG in order not to be seen as leading the process of division.

The *Volksrat* became the provisional government with Wilhelm Pieck as President and Otto Grotewohl as Prime Minister. However, real power lay with Walter Ulbricht, who nominally held the post of Deputy Prime Minister but whose real authority came from his dominant position in the SED. East Berlin was chosen as the capital city of the GDR.

A divided Berlin

What was the political status of Berlin in a divided Germany?

Berlin's political status was complex and quite unique. Though the Allied occupation of Germany formally ended with the foundation of the FRG and the GDR in 1949, Berlin was not part of this arrangement and in 1949 it remained an occupied city separated into four sectors under the control of the four Allied powers. Sector boundaries remained in existence. The occupation of Berlin could only be ended by a Quadripartite Agreement to this effect (between Britain, France, the Soviet Union and the United States) and this did not happen until 1990.

The Basic Law, the constitution of West Germany, did not initially apply to West Berlin. Though West Berlin was represented internationally by West Germany, it did not become a 'state of the Federal Republic of Germany' until 1971 when there was a thaw in East–West relations and a new Quadripartite Agreement was signed on 3 September 1971 agreeing to this change in status.

West Berlin was administered by an elected Mayor and by the West Berlin Senate. Both the Mayor and the elected Senators had to be approved by the Allied Commission, which represented Britain, France and the United States, and the Commission had to approve all laws passed by the Senate. In reality, until 1971 the West Berlin Senate simply voted in without debate every new West German law and this was always approved by the Allied Commission.

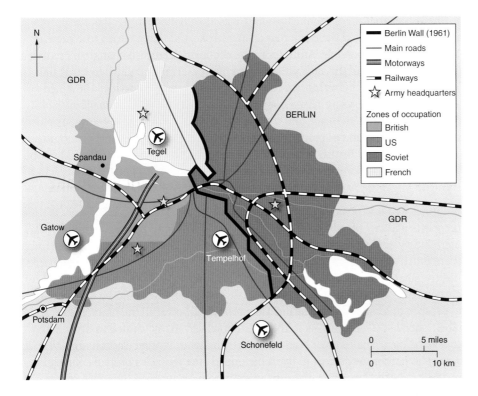

◀ **Figure 6 The division of Berlin.**

KEY DATES: THE BERLIN BLOCKADE

24 June 1948 The Soviet Union closed all overland access to West Berlin.

1949

4 April NATO was formed.

12 May The Berlin Blockade ended.

23 May The establishment of the FRG.

17 June The Trizone was formed.

7 October The establishment of the GDR.

Though the sector boundaries in West Berlin largely became meaningless and invisible, the boundary between the Soviet sector and the three Western sectors remained controlled. Nevertheless, up to 1961 it was relatively straightforward to cross between East and West on a daily basis and indeed some Berliners lived in one part of the city and worked in another and had family relatives in both parts.

As will be explored more fully in later chapters, this situation became a real problem for the East German state because Berlin was the one place from where an East German citizen could 'escape' to the West by entering West Berlin and then claiming refugee status. Though this was not an easy thing to do and the East German authorities were highly vigilant in trying to prevent this, many tens of thousands of East Germans fled in this way. This loophole was closed in 1961 by the building of the Berlin Wall.

Even after the erection of the Berlin Wall, all four of the former Allies insisted on retaining their right to send military patrols into each other's sector of Berlin. It also led to other anomalies. For example, the Russians insisted on their right to maintain a 24-hour honour guard at the Soviet War Memorial, which was located 400 metres beyond the Wall in West Berlin.

Conclusion: a divided Germany

What was the outlook like for the FRG and the GDR in 1949?

The partition of Germany, which unfolded in the years 1945–49, destroyed the German national state created in 1871. Perhaps this was the most significant aspect of the Nazi legacy. A racial and ideological war of conquest launched by Hitler in 1939 designed to establish a thousand-year *Reich* had succeeded only in making Germans and Germany into a pariah state and, ultimately, into a divided nation with the loss of its historic eastern territories. What did the future hold? According to Mary Fulbrook, 'many West Germans saw a potential new role in a new Europe' (*A History of Germany, 1918–2008*). If the price for this was a divided Germany, so be it. She argues that 'an economic upswing' was already happening, that the currency reform had eliminated the black market at a stroke and that a return to a 'normal' life seemed at last possible. Attitudes to the occupiers were also changing. Frederick Taylor had written of the sullen resentment many Germans had felt towards the Western Allies: 'Germans loathed the hypocrisy and the arrogance of the Allied assumption of superiority' (*Exorcising Hitler: The Occupation and Denazification of Hitler*). Yet, this had changed, and the people of West Germany now seemed valued as good democrats and as partners in the international struggle against Communism. The Americans and British had quickly come to realise that Germany could not be governed without Germans. West Germans would go forward into the 1950s actively trying to forget the past and to reconstruct a new type of 'democratic' German.

Fulbrook was less positive about the outlook for East Germans. Economic prospects without Marshall Aid looked relatively bleak and political repression was increasingly evident as the GDR turned into a fully fledged police state. Neither was there much affection for the Russians or their SED partners. However, there were positives here too. For those committed to a socialist path, who were prepared to participate in the vision of building a socialist utopia, there would be opportunities to prosper, at least in relative terms. Here too was a powerful intent to create a new, albeit 'socialist', Germany. As in the West, however, many wanted to draw a line under the past. The issue of Nazism was repressed or ignored in East and West. It would be harder in the East to live a life outside the tentacles of state control, but, in 1949 in both Germanys, the generation who had survived the rollercoaster of events of the previous twenty years were more than content to take a political backseat. In West Germany this generation was parodied in the 1950s as the *ohne mich* generation. It would not be until the 1960s that a new generation of young Germans would begin to ask awkward questions about the country's Nazi past.

Ohne mich – Literally meaning 'without me', this term reflects the view of many Germans throughout the 1950s that political activism was unnecessary as long as the federal government delivered on its social and economic promises. In many respects, it was a reaction against the deeply politicised Nazi era.

WORKING TOGETHER

A critical aspect of the specification is to consider the effects of Nazism on Germany. This is a demanding task and requires breadth of thinking. A fuller appreciation of the legacy of Nazism up to 1949 might best be achieved by working in pairs or in small groups to consider this issue. It is difficult to argue that there was any positive legacy, given the horrors inflicted on Europe by the Nazi state and the eventual partition of Germany arising out of its defeat in the Second World War. However, this is a broader debate you can return to after you have acquired a fuller perspective through studying the post-war history of the FRG. In some respects there is a philosophical dimension to this issue: can any good emerge from such evil?

It would be useful to consider the legacy by 1949. In your pairs or groups draw up an 'Impact' balance sheet divided into three columns: political, economic and social. Share your thinking with the rest of the class. By doing so you should be able to consolidate your understanding of the condition of Germany by 1949.

Look again at your notes on Section 1 of this chapter where you considered aspects of the Nazi legacy, to help you with this Working together activity.

Interpretations: Where does responsibility lie for the division of Germany?

The Potsdam Protocol agreed on 2 August 1945 envisaged a united Germany. Yet within four years two German states had emerged. The responsibility for this division is a key area of debate.

This is a complex issue and requires careful and balanced judgement. Clearly, what lay both at the heart of the Cold War and the division of Germany was mutual fear, suspicion and a breakdown of trust. At the height of the Cold War there was little doubt in the West that the Soviet Union alone was responsible for the partition of Germany. Naturally, the opposite premise was put forward by the Soviet Union. However, blame can be attributed more widely than this, as outlined below.

The USSR

The Soviet Union could be held responsible for the division of Germany because of Stalin's intransigence and obstructionism, which was a frequent criticism of Russian conduct in the Allied Control Council and at the Council of Ministers. It can be argued that the dash to 'sovietise' the East and Stalin's paranoia about future aggression from capitalists and fascists in the West was responsible for pushing the Americans and British towards a defensive posture, believing partition to be the best means of preventing a future united German state falling under Soviet control.

The USA

An analysis of the sequence of events by which the division actually occurred has led historians such as Mary Fulbrook to argue that the West 'repeatedly took initiatives to which Soviet measures came largely in response'. In other words, the United States, with British support, determined the direction and speed of developments.

Responsibility

What seems clear is that by mid-1946 the Western powers, the USA and Britain (and belatedly France), considered unity an impossibility, given their prevailing fear of Communism and the unpredictability of Stalin. They had come to believe that their security could only be guaranteed by the creation of a democratic, Western German state. The taking of the initiative by the Western powers to separate their zones of occupation from Soviet influence perhaps suggests they were chiefly responsible for the division of Germany.

Nevertheless, this judgement needs to be balanced, firstly, against the cumulative negative impact of Soviet obstructionism in their relations with the Western powers. The speed with which the Eastern zone was 'sovietised' did much to alienate the West, and contributed to their fears that Stalin intended to extend Communist control across the whole of Germany. In this respect, one can argue a case for Soviet responsibility. Secondly, French obstructionism also played a part. A dismembered Germany was France's primary aim in 1945. And thirdly, German responsibility needs to be considered. Hitler chose to destroy his own country rather than to surrender and both Adenauer and Ulbricht had motives to favour partition.

Great Britain

The British believed that Stalin was intent on European domination. This was not only the view of Conservatives such as Winston Churchill but also the view of Labour politicians. At a Cabinet meeting on 26 July 1948, Ernest Bevin, the British Foreign Secretary, put the British view succinctly:

'Over the past three years the Soviet Government had pursued a determined policy to bring the countries of Central and Eastern Europe under Communist control. The Soviet aim had always been to establish Communism in Germany.'

As far as the British were concerned, the best hope for the West in the face of this Soviet threat was to encourage the Germans themselves to create a Western democratic state.

France

Having been invaded by Germany three times in 70 years (1870, 1914, 1940) it is scarcely surprising that the French in 1945 vehemently opposed the restoration of a united and centralised Germany. Their prime aim was to annex key industrial areas of western Germany such as the Ruhr and the Saar and for Germany to be reduced to a series of small, impotent states, as had been the case before 1806. Given that the eventual solution to the 'German problem' was division, it is possible to argue that the French played a significant role in achieving this outcome.

Germany

At the most fundamental level, it could be argued that it was German actions which had divided the nation. Hitler had taken Germany into a disastrous war and chosen destruction rather than surrender. Hitler had led the Germans to ruin and opened the world to new global forces. Moreover, politicians such as Adenauer and Ulbricht saw their own political advancement better served by division than unity and, therefore, bear a certain degree of responsibility for the course of events. Of course, neither could openly reject unification as a goal but neither saw it as a preferred option.

Chapter summary

- Hitler committed suicide on 30 April 1945 and Germany surrendered unconditionally on 8 May. Germany's defeat was total; the country was utterly devastated.
- Defeat was followed by terror and retribution directed at most ordinary Germans. Nazi atrocities throughout the war allowed for very little sympathy for those Germans who survived the Nazi state.
- Germany was initially divided into four occupation zones. The intention to treat Germany as a single political and economic unit proved problematic right from the very beginning of the occupation.
- By spring 1946 joint arrangements for administering Germany were clearly not working and the Americans and British, driven by economic necessity and common fears about Stalin's expansionist goals, had begun discussions to merge their zones of occupation.
- The formation of the Bizone on 1 January 1947 confirmed that all pretence of treating Germany as a single economic unit was over.

- Political division was already well advanced by the beginning of 1947. The gradual strangulation of democratic, representative government in the East had begun with the forced merger of the KPD and SPD in April 1946, and in the West the announcement of the Truman Doctrine in March 1947 signalled the American intention to resist any extension of Communist control in Germany.
- Though both East and West continued to meet in the ACC and the Council of Foreign Ministers, by mid-1947 the separation of Germany into two spheres of influence was firmly established.
- By early 1948 East–West tensions began to focus on Berlin as the Soviet Union increasingly restricted the access of the Western Allies to their sectors of the city.
- The Berlin Blockade, from June 1948 to May 1949, occasioned the formal division of Germany, and symbolised the end of co-operation and the beginning of four decades of Cold War confrontation in Germany.
- The FRG came into existence on 23 May 1949 with Konrad Adenauer becoming its first Chancellor, a post he would hold until 1963; the GDR was founded on 7 October 1949. Walter Ulbricht would retain control of the GDR from its foundation until 1971.

▼ Summary diagram: Defeat, occupation and division

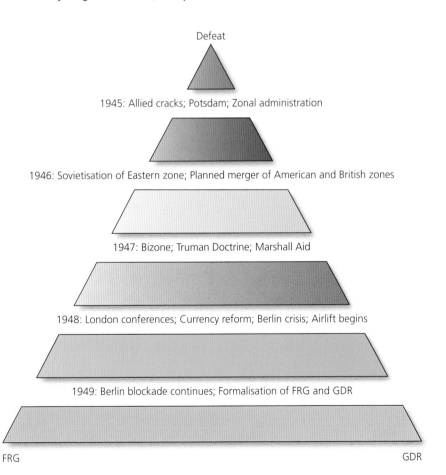

Defeat

1945: Allied cracks; Potsdam; Zonal administration

1946: Sovietisation of Eastern zone; Planned merger of American and British zones

1947: Bizone; Truman Doctrine; Marshall Aid

1948: London conferences; Currency reform; Berlin crisis; Airlift begins

1949: Berlin blockade continues; Formalisation of FRG and GDR

FRG   GDR

Working on interpretation skills: extended reading

The Berlin Airlift

Giles MacDonogh considers the reasons for the Berlin Airlift.

In January 1948, Albert Speer – one of the 'Spandau Seven' of Nazi bigwigs in Allied captivity – noted 'day and night transport planes roar over our building'. His fellow prisoners were aware the flimsy wartime alliance had collapsed and that the roads to Berlin had been closed. The Western Zones of occupation (American, British and French) were about to split off from the Soviet Zone or SBZ, paving the way for the creation of two, new German states: the *Bundesrepublik Deutschland* or 'BRD' (Federal Republic of Germany – FRG) and the *Deutsches Demokratisches Republik* or 'DDR' (German Democratic Republic or GDR). Those Anglo-American aircraft churning up the night sky were part of 'Operation Vittles', which attempted to provision the city after the Soviet authorities closed overland access to Berlin via their Zone on 24 June 1948.

The Russians hoped to force the Western Allies to abandon the former German capital, which lay 160 kilometres inside the SBZ and in which their continued presence was very largely governed by verbal agreement. No one earnestly believed the blockade would result in a new world war, and any military confrontation was scrupulously avoided. The Airlift officially ended when the Russians reopened the roads and rail links on 12 May 1949, but supplies continued to come in by air for several months more.

The pretext for the Soviet blockade was currency reform in the Western Zones and the introduction of the *Deutsche Mark*. It was hoped a new Mark would kick start the German economy. The Russians responded with their own *Ostmark* which Berliners swiftly baptised the '*Tapetenmark*' or 'Wallpaper Mark'. The Soviets rightly sensed that the London Conference in February 1948 had been a prelude to establishing a separate West German state and the foundation stone for the NATO military alliance directed against the Communist Bloc. That same February, Soviet-backed Communists staged a coup in Prague and murdered the foreign minister Jan Masaryk. East and West had been going their separate ways since American Secretary of State James Byrnes' Stuttgart Speech of 6 September 1946, if not before. From that moment the Allies had sought to win over the hearts and minds of the defeated Germans to their separate ideologies.

The 'Spandau Seven'

Seven of those tried at Nuremberg in 1946 received lengthy prison sentences. In 1947 the Allies transferred all seven from Nuremberg to Spandau prison in Berlin. Soldiers of each of the Allied powers shared guard duties. The last remaining of the seven was Rudolf Hess. He committed suicide in 1987 aged 93. He had been the sole remaining prisoner for 21 years. After his death Spandau prison was demolished to prevent it becoming a neo-Nazi shrine.

The bargaining counter would be food. The Russians refused to supply the city's Western Sectors and promptly removed the city's 7,000 cows thereby cutting off milk supplies. Next, the Russians cut off coal, gas, electricity and water. It was the British Air Commodore Reginald Waite who came up with the idea of supplying the starving Berliners from the air, but the idea was enthusiastically taken up by the American Byrnes-disciple and Cold Warrior General Lucius Clay. Later Lieutenant Gail Halvorsen suggested 'Little Vittles' and dropped sweets to Berlin children.

35

40

For eleven months Berliners relived their wartime nightmares, eating dehydrated food by candlelight and huddling together for warmth. There was one power station in the Western Sectors, working overtime to give Berliners a couple of hours of electricity a day. The Airlift was largely a propaganda battle and a number of Hollywood films were made including *The Big Lift* starring Montgomery Clift and an influential short documentary called *Operation Vittles*. As *Operation Vittles* puts it: fliers who had risked their lives to obliterate Berlin were going up again 'to keep the same city alive'. By the time the road and rail links reopened in May 1949, the Soviets had failed in both the propaganda battle and their attempts to drive the West from Berlin: on the 23rd, the Western Zones were merged to form the 'Trizone' and the Federal Republic. The Soviet-backed Democratic Republic was created in response on 7 October. The Cold War continued another forty years with Berlin remaining on the front-line. Following the erection of the Berlin wall in 1961, President Kennedy gave his most famous speech at Schöneberg Town Hall on 26 June 1963 in which he affirmed that all free men and women were now 'Berliners'.

45

50

55

Giles MacDonogh is an independent historian specialising in the history of modern Germany. Most recently he has written a social history of the Third Reich.

ACTIVITY

Having read MacDonogh's essay, answer the following questions:

Comprehension
1 What does the author mean by the following phrases?
- The 'Wallpaper Mark' (line 24)
- 'Little Vittles' (line 40)

Evidence
2 What evidence does the author use to support his view that East and West 'had been going their separate ways'?

Interpretation
3 Using the essay and your own knowledge, to what extent do you agree that the Berlin blockade was a failure for the Soviet Union?

Working on interpretation skills

The A-level practice question and extracts below offer three different interpretations of the responsibility for the division of Germany in 1949.

For each extract:

1 Identify the argument put forward.

2 Assess how convincing you find each interpretation and support your assessment with evidence from your study of this chapter.

3 Finally, write a paragraph in which you offer a balanced judgement of the relative merits of the three interpretations.

Using your understanding of the historical context, assess how convincing these three extracts are in relation to the responsibility for the division of Germany in 1949. (30 marks)

Extract A

One of the major reasons requiring a revision of American foreign policy towards Europe was the rise of Soviet imperialism. The United States, having fought to liberate Europe from German domination, could not tolerate domination of the continent (Germany included), by Moscow. Having emerged as the predominant power on the continent after the collapse of Hitler's Germany, the USSR was determined to take advantage of the power vacuum in Central Europe. Thus Germany, with its vital strategic position, became a major point of controversy. It was clear that by the end of 1945 Truman had become disillusioned by Soviet obstruction. Moscow's unbending attitude at Allied conferences, its determination to prevent Germany from being treated as a genuine economic unit, and to bring the Soviet zone within its satellite system, above all, the realization by the United States that a restored Germany was essential to the economic restoration of Western Europe, pushed Truman to revise American policy.

Adapted from 'American Policy towards Germany' by Wolfgang Schlauch, 1945, *Journal of Contemporary History*, Vol. 5, No. 4, (1970).

Extract B

The United States and Great Britain were primarily responsible for the division of Germany precisely because the United States determined the direction and speed of developments. A neutralized Germany, one exposed to Soviet influence, was unthinkable to the Americans already in 1945 because the reconstruction of Europe and Western access to German coal were amongst the most pre-eminent aims of American policy toward Europe. As it became clear in 1945–46 that American goals could not be achieved in co-operation with the Soviet Union, the United States seized the initiative to begin the integration of the Western parts of the country into the West, as well as to found the Federal Republic. Stalin believed in the possibility of an all-German solution longer than the United States did; as late as 1948–49 he had hoped to reverse the planned establishment of a German state in the western zones with the blockade of Berlin. US policies did much to split Germany, accelerate the division of Europe, and accentuate anxieties in the Kremlin.

Adapted from 'The Struggle for Germany and the Origins of the Cold War' by Melvyn P. Leffler, German Historical Institute, Washington, 1996.

Extract C

No one planned a divided Germany in May 1945, but few were deeply discontented with it. Some German politicians, notably Konrad Adenauer himself, even owed their career to the division of their country: had Germany remained a united country, an obscure local politician from the far western Catholic Rhineland would almost certainly not have made it to the top. But Adenauer could scarcely have espoused the division of Germany as a goal, however much he welcomed it in private. His chief opponent in the first years of the Federal Republic, the Social Democrat Kurt Schumacher, was a Protestant from West Prussia and a tireless advocate of German unity. He would readily have accepted a neutralized Germany as the price for a single German state, which was what Stalin appeared to be offering. And Schumacher's position was probably the more popular one in Germany at the time, which was why Adenauer had to tread carefully and ensure that the responsibility for a divided Germany fell on the occupying forces.

Adapted from *A History of Europe Since 1945* by Tony Judt, (Vintage), 2010.

Government and opposition in the FRG, 1949–89

This chapter focuses on political developments in the Federal Republic of Germany from its establishment in 1949 until the eve of reunification in 1989. It begins with an overview and analysis of the constitution and the main political parties, followed by a chronological survey of government throughout the period policies and actions, and the challenges they faced. The following areas are covered:

● The constitution, checks and balances
● Governments, parties and policies, 1949–89
● The pressures and challenges posed by extra-parliamentary opposition
● The state of West German democracy in 1989

Three key questions underpin this chapter:

● changes in and the development of political authority
● the nature and effectiveness of political opposition
● a focus on key individuals and groups across the political spectrum.

The overarching focus of this chapter might be summarised by the following question:

How did West German democracy develop in the years 1949–89 and what political challenges were faced by the state?

CHAPTER OVERVIEW

The democratic institutions that existed in Germany prior to the First World War were largely a sham; political authority essentially rested with the *Kaiser* and the social elites. The new Weimar constitution of 1919 was one of the most progressive in the world, yet it foundered on the rocks of economic depression and right-wing authoritarianism in the years 1930–33. To many, in Germany and abroad, Germans and democracy seemed temperamentally unsuited. Whether Bonn democracy could survive and prosper was, therefore, open to much doubt. That it not only survived but in many respects became a 'model' democracy, is the key theme of this chapter. Nevertheless, the path to a 'model' representative democracy was not uniformly smooth. Elements of continuity with the past persisted. Adenauer's 'conservative restoration' has been criticised as a thin veil of democracy covering an essentially unchanged authoritarian face. Such criticisms exploded in widespread radical protest in the 1960s and, for a minority, developed into terrorist activity in the 1970s. However, by the 1980s Bonn democracy had survived its challenges from right and left. The sub-theme of this chapter, therefore, is a consideration of political change and continuity.

1 The establishment of democracy, 1949–63

Konrad Adenauer became the first chancellor of the Federal Republic of Germany (hereafter FRG) at the age of 73 and only very reluctantly gave up office in 1963 at the age of 87. Considered the 'founding father' of West German democracy, a poll of the German people conducted by the German television station ZDF in 2003 ranked Adenauer as the 'Best German' ever. Adenauer was the individual to whom West Germans attributed their country's rapid political and moral re-birth. This section firstly explores the nature of the West German constitution and outlines the main political parties established by 1949, before going on to examine Adenauer's chancellorship.

The constitution

Why was Bonn democracy more successful than Weimar democracy?

The Basic Law (*Grundgesetz*), which came into force on 23 May 1949, established the FRG as a federal, parliamentary democracy. It was based on four key principles:

- The rule of law
- Democratic participation for all
- Federalism
- Social welfare

It operated through a bi-cameral parliament:

- The lower house: the *Bundestag* – elected every four years through universal suffrage; 50 per cent of its members were directly elected and 50 per cent through Party lists. Parties needed to win over five per cent of the vote to gain representation.
- The upper house: the *Bundesrat* – made up of representatives of each state, or *Land*; it had the power to approve and veto legislation.

The President of the Republic was a largely ceremonial head of state elected by *Bundestag* members and representatives of each *Land* parliament. The Chancellor was the head of government and was elected by the *Bundestag*. The Chancellor could only be removed from office by a constructive vote of no confidence in the *Bundestag*. The Federal Constitutional Court, modelled on the US Supreme Court, was designed to protect the constitution and had powers to settle disputes between the Federal government and the *Land* governments.

The Basic Law also set out the essential values of the state. It guaranteed freedom of expression, assembly, association and movement and included a statement identifying the fundamental basic human rights of each German. The Basic Law also committed the FRG to work to re-establish a united Germany. Moreover, it guaranteed West German citizenship for all people of German descent, which provided an enormous incentive for East Germans to flee the Communist GDR.

NOTE-MAKING

The constitution and the political parties

Though it is unlikely that you will be required to answer an essay question which focuses purely on the constitution and the nature of the political parties, a knowledge of both is essential to your understanding of political developments. The following tasks are suggested:

- **Safeguards**: produce a mind map outlining the main safeguards built into the constitution.
- **Constitutional framework**: construct your own flow chart showing how the constitution operated.
- **Party ideology**: for each party identify its essential ideology by drawing a line representing the political spectrum, ranging from extreme left to extreme right, and marking the approximate position of each of the parties on the line.

Bi-cameral – A democratic constitution operated through two chambers, or houses, of parliament.

First Past The Post (FPTP) – FPTP is a system of voting in single-member constituencies. The candidate who gains the most votes wins. All other votes count for nothing. The most well-known FPTP system operates in the UK.

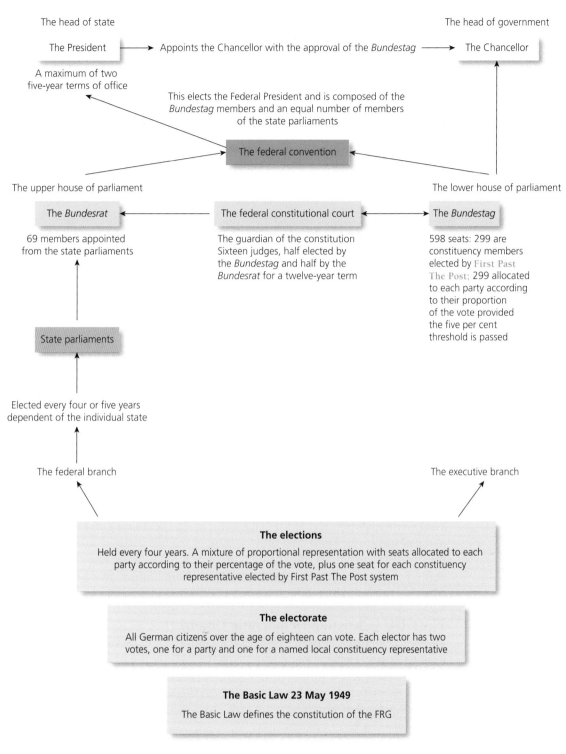

The head of state

The President $\longrightarrow$ Appoints the Chancellor with the approval of the *Bundestag* $\longrightarrow$ The Chancellor

The head of government

A maximum of two
five-year terms of office

This elects the Federal President and is composed of the
Bundestag members and an equal number of members
of the state parliaments

The federal convention

The upper house of parliament

The lower house of parliament

The *Bundesrat* $\longleftarrow$ The federal constitutional court $\longleftrightarrow$ The *Bundestag*

69 members appointed
from the state parliaments

The guardian of the constitution
Sixteen judges, half elected by
the *Bundestag* and half by the
Bundesrat for a twelve-year term

598 seats: 299 are
constituency members
elected by First Past
The Post; 299 allocated
to each party according
to their proportion
of the vote provided
the five per cent
threshold is passed

State parliaments

Elected every four or five years
dependent of the individual state

The federal branch

The executive branch

The elections

Held every four years. A mixture of proportional representation with seats allocated to each
party according to their percentage of the vote, plus one seat for each constituency
representative elected by First Past The Post system

The electorate

All German citizens over the age of eighteen can vote. Each elector has two
votes, one for a party and one for a named local constituency representative

The Basic Law 23 May 1949

The Basic Law defines the constitution of the FRG

▲ **Figure 1** The constitution of the FRG.

Checks and balances

The Basic Law was designed to avoid the flaws inherent in the Weimar constitution
which had facilitated Hitler's seizure of power. Political authority was to be exercised
through a democratic and federal structure protected by the Constitutional Court.
Substantial powers were given to the state (*Land*) parliaments, thereby limiting
federal powers. Creating a climate of political stability, therefore, was a primary
goal of the Basic Law. The main safeguards built into the new constitution are
summarised in the comparison chart on the following page (Figure 2).

Basic Law	Weimar constitution
Strong Chancellor: could only be forced out of office by a constructive vote of no confidence, which required a new Chancellor to be immediately voted in, thereby avoiding a leadership vacuum.	Weak Chancellor: could be forced out of office by a vote of no confidence or by losing the confidence of the President, which either required new elections or the appointment of a Presidential nominee; this occurred on several occasions from 1930, causing great instability in government.
Weak President: largely a ceremonial position.	Strong President: held substantial powers, such as Article 48, which allowed the President to rule by decree in times of emergency or government instability.
The five per cent rule: prevented extremist parties being elected to parliament.	Too many parties: led to political fragmentation and short-lived, weak coalition governments.
Extremist parties: any political parties not in line with the constitution could be banned.	Extremist parties: parties such as the NSDAP and KPD were able to participate in the political process, despite being openly anti-democratic and intent upon destroying the Weimar constitution.
Federal system: substantial powers given to the state (*Land*) parliaments in order to prevent the misuse of centralised powers.	The state (*Land*) governments had limited powers, leaving them vulnerable to centralised control; the Nazis abused this unequal allocation of political authority in consolidating their power after Hitler's appointment as Chancellor in January 1933.
Strong Constitutional Court.	Weak Constitutional Court.

▲ **Figure 2** Constitutional safeguards – the Basic Law vs the Weimar constitution.

In many respects, the Basic Law can be considered one of Germany's most substantial political achievements. Under the Basic Law, Germans have perhaps experienced the greatest political freedom of their history; it has become a successful constitutional model, widely exported, and has continued as the constitutional framework of the reunited German state.

Parties and policies

West Germany's political parties largely occupied the centre ground of the political spectrum. This is not only because of the five per cent rule, which prevented fringe parties from being represented, but also because the extremes of pre-war Nazism and post-war East German Communism greatly reduced the appeal of the far right and far left.

The CDU (Christian Democratic Union)

The CDU emerged out of the ashes of the Third *Reich* to become Germany's most successful political party, governing the FRG for the first two decades after its founding and for most of the last two decades of the twentieth century. Konrad Adenauer, the Party's first leader, envisioned the CDU as a conservative catch-all party that would attract a wide cross-section of the electorate.

The CDU is a centre-right political party espousing a Christian approach to politics, conservative on social issues, while advocating a social market model of the economy (see Chapter 8, page 255 for a fuller explanation of this concept). It has also been a strong supporter of European integration. It was founded in 1945 by a diverse group of conservative-minded political activists from the Weimar Republic era. At its core were Catholics from the former Centre Party, but it also included liberal and conservative Protestants, intellectuals, representatives of big business, and right-leaning trade unionists. Its traditional strongholds are in southwest and western Germany. The attitudes and values of these early Christian Democrats were largely determined by their personal experiences of Nazism and, despite their varied backgrounds, they shared a number of critical core beliefs that have shaped and guided the Party since its founding:

- They believed that the historic conflicts and divisions between Roman Catholics and Protestants contributed to the political fragmentation of the Weimar era, and were in part responsible for the rise of Adolf Hitler. To ensure that this could not happen again, the founders of the CDU were determined to create a political grouping open to all religious denominations.
- Most Christian Democrats by the end of the 1940s had reached a consensus that a social market economy was the best economic model for Germany.
- The Party's foreign policy was staunchly anti-Communist, pro-American and supportive of European integration.

The CDU, in alliance with the CSU (Christian Social Union), won clear victories in Germany's elections in 1949 and in subsequent elections in the 1950s. It owed its early success in great part to two men; Konrad Adenauer, Chancellor from 1949 to 1963, and Ludwig Erhard, considered the father of Germany's 'economic miracle' (*Wirtschaftswunder*), who served as Adenauer's economics minister and succeeded him as Chancellor in 1963.

The CSU (Christian Social Union)

The CSU is the sister party of the CDU. It operates only in Bavaria; the CDU operates in all the other states except Bavaria. Founded in 1946, the CSU originated from the Weimar-era Catholic Bavarian People's Party (BVP). It has always formed a common faction, or grouping, in the *Bundestag* with the CDU. The CSU is traditionally more conservative in its social policies than the CDU. Its most prominent, nationally known, politician was Franz Josef Strauss, leader of the Party from 1961 to 1988.

The SPD (Social Democratic Party)

Founded in 1875, the SPD is Germany's oldest political party. Much of its support came from the large cities of Protestant northern Germany and the industrial region of the Ruhr. After the Second World War, under the leadership of Kurt Schumacher, the SPD adopted a clear left-wing ideology, presenting itself as the party of the working class and the trade unions. The Party's programme included a number of Marxist elements, in particular advocating the nationalisation of major industries and a system of centralised economic planning.

Schumacher was a strong nationalist. He rejected Adenauer's western-oriented, pro-American foreign policy in favour of prioritising the reunification of Germany, even if this meant some kind of accord or arrangement with the Soviet Union.

The SPD's policies, however, proved unappealing to many Germans, a majority of whom were instinctively attracted to Adenauer's conservatism. Schumacher's death in 1952 and a string of electoral defeats, particularly in 1957 when the CDU acquired more than 50 per cent of the popular vote, led the Party to re-think its political platform in order to make itself more electable. Its new Bad Godesberg Programme was formulated in 1959.

The FDP (The Free Democratic Party)

The FDP was much smaller than the CDU or the SPD but it exercised a position of great influence in West German politics. Its electoral support, averaging 9.6 per cent between 1949 and 1989, meant that it had enough seats in the Bundestag to make or break a government. It served as a coalition partner to either the CDU or SPD throughout the lifetime of the FRG, with the only exceptions being the periods 1957–61 and 1966–69.

Social market economy – A mix of free market capitalism, guided by strong government regulation, and comprehensive social welfare policies; a middle way between socialist planning and laissez-faire economics—a political doctrine which argues that government should intervene as little as possible in economic affairs.

'Economic miracle' – The term used to describe West Germany's astonishing economic boom of the 1950s and early 1960s (see Chapter 8, pages 255–6).

Bad Godesberg Programme – At its 1959 Party conference in the German town of Bad Godesberg, the SPD abandoned its socialist economic policies and adopted the principles of the social market economy. It also abandoned its anti-Americanism and espoused the CDU's Western position. The SPD now also presented itself as a catch-all party, albeit of the left.

WORKING TOGETHER

Coalition government

Go back to Chapter 6, page 136 to remind yourself of the reasons for the failure of Weimar democracy in order to prepare yourself for this activity.

Coalition government is often cited as a reason for the failure of Weimar democracy, yet coalitions seemed perfectly compatible to the working of Bonn democracy. Working in groups, discuss why coalitions operated successfully in the Federal Republic but less so in the Weimar Republic. Present your findings to the rest of the class by giving your reasons in order of priority. Compare the priority order given by each group. Can you reach a consensus opinion as a class about your rank ordering of reasons?

Secular – In this context, a political party with no connections to organised religion or religious groups; not concerned with spiritual or religious matters.

The FDP was founded in 1948 under the leadership of Theodor Heuss, who served as the first President of the FRG from 1949 to 1959. The Party held a liberal view of politics, distinct from the two major parties. Unlike the SDP in 1949, it was a pro-business party, supporting the free enterprise social market economy and, unlike the CDU/CSU, it presented itself as a purely secular party. Its overarching guiding principle was its determination to protect individual freedoms. The long time that the FDP served in government was significant in contributing to the continuity and stability of the FRG's political development.

Conclusion

The CDU/CSU was so successful in the first decade of the FRG's existence that by the end of the 1950s most of the small regional and splinter parties had either disbanded, unable to reach the five per cent threshold, or had amalgamated with the larger parties. Two parties in the 1950s were banned as anti-constitutional, the neo-Nazi Socialist Reich Party (SRP) in 1952, and the KPD in 1956.

NOTE-MAKING

Your notes should focus on two main aspects. Firstly, Adenauer's main achievements in office, and secondly, the reasons for the gradual diminishment of his political authority and influence from 1957 to his resignation in 1963. The following basic framework is suggested:

● Adenauer's main legislative achievements:
  – 1949–57
  – 1957–63
● The reasons for the diminishment of Adenauer's political authority after 1957

Konrad Adenauer as Chancellor, 1949–63

How successful was Adenauer as Chancellor?

The elections held on 14 August 1949 saw twelve parties elected to the *Bundestag*: a near equal number of CDU and SPD members, with a further third of the *Bundestag* divided between ten smaller parties, of which the FDP was the largest. The CDU obtained 31 per cent of the vote. Refusing to consider working with the SPD, as favoured by many in his own Party, Adenauer formed a government coalition with the support of a number of small parties and the FDP, securing a majority of just one – 202 out of 402 votes – for his election as Chancellor. It seemed at this point that there was a danger of a return to Weimar instability, with the larger parties dependent on coalitions with smaller, often single-issue or regional, parties.

Party	Percentage of the vote	Deputies
CDU/CSU	31	139
SPD	29.2	131
FDP	11.9	52
KPD	5.7	15
DRP	1.8	5
DP	4.0	17
BP	4.2	17
ZP	3.1	10
Others	9.1	16

▲ **Figure 3** The 1949 *Bundestag* election results.

DRP: The German Right Party (neo-Nazi); DP: The German Party (Conservative)
BP: The Bavarian Party (Bavarian separatist); ZP: The Centre Party (Catholic)

1949–57

This period was the most dynamic and most successful of Adenauer's long period in office. His first two chancellorships from 1949–57 achieved a great deal in terms of Germany's international rehabilitation, particularly the effective return of German sovereignty by the Bonn Convention of May 1957 and, in the same year, the signing of the Treaty of Rome which inaugurated the European Economic Community (EEC). Adenauer's policy of European integration and his rapprochement with France are discussed more fully in Chapter 8.

◄ Ludwig Erhard with his book, *Prosperity for All*, 1957.

Economic recovery was Adenauer's most significant domestic success, sweeping away rationing, import controls and bureaucratic regulation as well as achieving an astonishing average eight per cent growth per annum. The rapid upturn in the economy is most associated with Ludwig Erhard, Adenauer's Economics Minister from 1949 to 1963. Erhard's economic miracle fuelled a consumer revolution. Despite relatively low wages, West Germans favoured material goods rather than savings, perhaps influenced by their memories of the hyperinflation in the Weimar period or the restrictions of the Nazi years as Hitler focused on a 'war economy'. Advertisements and radio broadcasts urged people to spend, further promoting high domestic consumption. Living standards rose 58 per cent between 1953 and 1960, more than double the 25 per cent increase in the UK. This rise is shown through the building of modern apartments with central heating and the increase in modern kitchen appliances. This led to a 'virtuous cycle', improving everyday life and increasing leisure opportunities which continued into the 1960s as growth progressed.

Achievement can also be measured in other ways, and might be summarised under the 5 Rs:

- **Reconstruction**
  The 1950 Construction Law provided grants and subsidies for a massive house-building programme; 4 million new homes were built by 1957.
- **Reintegration**
  Millions of refugees and expellees were gradually dispersed from 'holding camps' and integrated into work and accommodation.
- **Restitution**
  Compensation was paid to individual victims of Nazi crimes, and particularly to Jews. Grants and pensions were made available to German

civilians who had suffered significant losses, particularly to property, as a result of the wartime bombing campaign through the 1953 Equalisation of Burdens Act.

● **Restoration**

The 1951 '131 Law' allowed former Nazis to be employed as civil servants, leading to the re-employment of over 150,000 Germans who had previously lost their jobs as a consequence of the denazification actions.

● **Labour relations**

The 1949 Collective Bargaining Law established ground rules for labour relations between the government and trade unions, effectively de-politicising the unions by focusing industrial relations on enhanced productivity rather than wealth redistribution through pay bargaining; low wage demands and a low strike record were characteristic of Adenauer's time in office. Co-determination was also introduced as a key principle designed to establish non-confrontational industrial relations.

'Chancellor democracy'

Adenauer's style of leadership has been called 'chancellor democracy' because of the dominating personal authority he wielded in government. Indeed, opinions about Adenauer's personality and manner are quite polarised. His apologists praise him as a clear-sighted, practical politician, tough and uncompromising and clear in his assessment of the art of the possible. His critics see him as a dogmatic, dominating, arrogant leader, intolerant of contrary opinions and witheringly dismissive of those who opposed him. He was certainly convinced of the need for firmness to make the new democracy work. Although he always took care to operate within his constitutional limits, he was certainly uncompromising in the correctness of his own opinion. Equally controversial was the large number of former Nazi sympathisers or 'fellow-travellers' who found their way into his governments.

By the mid-1950s other factors were emerging to ensure his continued success:

● The CDU had developed an efficient party organisation; Adenauer was astute in ensuring that the Party was seen to appeal to a wide cross-section of German society, and particularly to represent the views of particular influential interest groups such as the expellees. The CDU became genuinely trans-regional in appeal.

● This was in stark contrast to the SPD. Its former political strongholds were now in East Germany whereas the staunchly conservative regions of Bavaria and the Rhineland were in the West. Moreover, the actions of the Communists in the East had created an anti-socialist backlash in the West no matter how vociferously Schumacher, the SPD leader, condemned such actions.

● Schumacher's constant criticism that Adenauer was sacrificing German unity on the altar of Western and European integration backfired on the SPD. It was clear that for most West Germans, money in their pocket and the security of American support was of greater importance in the midst of the Cold War than demands for unity.

● Similarly, West Germans preferred new models of European co-operation such as the Council of Europe and the European Coal and Steel Community promoted by Adenauer, to Schumacher's denunciations. Schumacher's sudden death in August 1952 brought in a more moderate SPD leader, Erich Hollenhauer, but he had neither the experience, charisma nor the policies to challenge Adenauer's dominance.

● By 1955 Adenauer had brought a return of sovereignty, obtained membership of NATO and, in 1956, re-introduced a new German military force, the *Bundeswehr*.

Co-determination – Shared decision making between management and labour, through their union representatives; designed to promote good industrial relations through co-operation rather than confrontation.

The Council of Europe – Founded in 1949, the Council was set up to promote legal and judicial co-operation between all countries of Europe. Perhaps its best known institution is the European Court of Human Rights.

The European Coal and Steel Community (ECSC) – Set up by the Treaty of Paris in 1951 by Belgium, France, Italy, Luxemburg, the Netherlands and West Germany, the ECSC was the first step towards the creation of the European Union.

Bundeswehr – This is the name given to the German armed forces established on 12 November 1955 as part of the FRG's admission to NATO. German rearmament was a controversial issue, both within and outside of Germany, but accepted as a necessity by the occupying powers as the Cold War deepened. The *Bundeswehr* was portrayed as a citizens' army to emphasise that it remained under political control.

It is hardly surprising that this record of achievement and the feel-good factor it generated transferred itself into electoral success. The 1953 election increased the CDU's lead over the SPD from 400,000 to 4.5 million votes. Campaigning on the slogan *Keine Experimente* (No Experiments), the 1957 election saw Adenauer at the peak of his domestic popularity, winning 277 seats and taking 50.2 per cent of the popular vote; a margin of 96 seats and 18.4 per cent over Ollenhauer's shattered SDP, enabling the CDU to rule as a single party for the next four years. For *Der Alte* (The Old Man), the Germans' affectionate nickname for Adenauer, there seemed no end to his popular appeal.

1957–63

Adenauer's third and fourth governments were characterised by a gradual diminishment in his political authority, despite an economy that continued to boom. A series of self-inflicted political miscalculations and scandals, and a prolonged fall out with Erhard (whom Adenauer once dismissed as a 'pudding') largely over the detail of economic policy priorities, dominated his later years. Adenauer seemed increasingly out of touch with the *Zeitgeist*.

Political wranglings

Adenauer's first miscalculation came in 1959. Theodor Heuss was retiring as President and Adenauer was keen to prevent the SPD nominee, Carlo Schmid, from being appointed. He calculated that the best means of doing so was to persuade Erhard to stand for the Presidency. This would serve a second, ulterior, purpose for Adenauer: his rift with Erhard had become so wide that by 'promoting' him to the Presidency he would, in this way, block Erhard's ambition to succeed him as chancellor. However, Erhard recognised Adenauer's subterfuge and refused. At that point, and to the amazement of most West Germans, Adenauer announced his own nomination for the Presidency largely, it seems, to use this position to refuse any proposal for Erhard to become chancellor. After eighteen days of internal party feuding, a lack of support for his nomination forced Adenauer to withdraw, making him look not only a fool in the eyes of many Germans but also to be self-seeking and vindictive.

A second error and blow to his personal prestige occurred in August 1961 at the time of the building of the Berlin Wall. Instead of travelling to Berlin to show solidarity with West Berliners, Adenauer chose to stay on the campaign trail for the September federal elections. Even more damaging, on 14 August, the day after the city was divided, Adenauer launched a personal attack against the SPD mayor of West Berlin, Willy Brandt. The West German press roundly condemned Adenauer, not only for his arrogance in suggesting that Brandt was unfit for high office, but also for his seeming attempt to deflect attention away from the building of the Wall.

1961 election

These errors of judgement were reflected in the outcome of the 1961 election. The CDU lost its absolute majority, losing about 1 million votes; the SPD gained 1 million and the FDP increased its vote by 50 per cent. Coalition negotiations proved difficult as Adenauer refused to make way for Erhard, who was supported by many CDU members concerned that Adenauer was becoming a political liability. Eventually, Erich Mende, the FDP leader, agreed to support an Adenauer-led CDU/FDP coalition but only after Adenauer had agreed, in a secret letter to Mende, to resign after about two further years in office.

WORKING TOGETHER

The 1957 election

At this point, it would be useful to explore the reasons for Adenauer's overwhelming election success in 1957. Working in pairs or small groups, focus on one or two of the following suggested factors or explanations:

- Adenauer's individual qualities
- CDU organisational strengths
- SPD weaknesses
- Economic recovery

Research and develop your explanation and then feed back to the rest of the class.

As a consolidation exercise, try writing a newspaper editorial dated 16 September 1957 (the day after the election) explaining Adenauer's success. Your editorial strapline could be: 'No Experiments' Sweeps *Der Alte* to Third Term Success!

Zeitgeist – Literally meaning the 'spirit of the times', it refers to the outlook, tastes and characteristics of a particular period or generation. In this context, Adenauer's political outlook no longer represented the dominant mood of a new generation as Germany entered the 1960s.

The *Spiegel* affair

Der Spiegel was West Germany's most popular news magazine with a circulation of about 5 million. It was relatively liberal and left-leaning in its political outlook. In 1961 it had published an article suggesting that Strauss, the CSU Defence Minister, had used his position to win a lucrative construction contract for a friend's company. Strauss was something of a hate figure for the left-wing press; the long-standing leader of the CSU and Defence Minister, he was profoundly conservative, anti-Communist and nationalist in his thinking. A subsequent investigation found Strauss not guilty but the relationship between Strauss and the magazine's owner, Rudolf Augstein, remained very antagonistic.

On 8 October 1962, the magazine printed an article critical of the *Bundeswehr* (see page 230), claiming that it was not capable of putting up any meaningful resistance to a potential Russian attack. This was seen as a pretty loosely veiled attack on Strauss. What followed, to many liberal and left-wing commentators, seemed like a re-occurrence of the worst excesses of Nazism. The *Spiegel* offices were raided by the police on 26 October. Large volumes of papers and documents were seized. Augstein was accused of treason and he, and nine others, and the author of the article, were arrested. The *Spiegel* offices were not allowed to reopen until 26 November. The popular protests which grew out of this affair seemed, in hindsight, to foretell the beginnings of a widespread protest culture in West Germany, which is explored more fully in Section 3 (page 244).

▲ Documents being removed from the offices of *Der Spiegel*.

Clearly Adenauer was not prepared to go gracefully into the twilight of his career. He was badly tainted by the fallout from the *Spiegel* affair (see above) in 1962 which pushed his coalition partnership with the FDP to breaking point: five FDP ministers resigned complaining that Strauss, the CSU Defence Minister, had not consulted the FDP Justice Minister about the action against the *Spiegel* magazine. After attempting, and failing, to form a coalition with the SDP, Adenauer was forced to grovel to the FDP, which agreed to return to the coalition but only on condition that Strauss was sacked, and Adenauer himself had to reaffirm that he would leave office by October 1963. Adenauer very reluctantly agreed to both demands, resigning on 15 October 1963, stepping aside for Erhard to take the chancellorship.

Conclusion: the state of German democracy in 1963

The political fragmentation feared in 1949 did not occur. This contrasts significantly with the early years of Weimar. The safeguards built into the constitution, particularly the five per cent rule, contributed to the political stability of the FRG. Moreover, a number of the smaller parties were absorbed by the larger parties, such as the right-wing conservative German Party (DP), which effectively had merged with the CDU by 1961, and some single-issue parties, such as the All-German Bloc/League of Expellees and Deprived of Rights (GB/BHE), which had gained 27 seats in 1953, failed to reach the electoral threshold in 1957 and dwindled away.

Undoubtedly, economic success was a key factor in moving formerly undemocratic Germans to support Bonn democracy, contrary to the way in which economic weakness had led many to drift away from Weimar democracy. Erhard's ability to deliver the goods and put 'a refrigerator in every household' provided a powerful incentive to stick with democracy. The 1950s *ohne mich* generation (see page 216), politically apathetic in many ways, remained content to support a political system that was successful in filling shop windows with food and consumer durables. An additional factor in swaying West Germans towards democracy was Adenauer's fundamental anti-Communist position and his policy of Western integration. Anti-Communism provided an alternative ideological pathway leading West Germans towards accepting democratic values and institutions. It can also be argued that the reintegration of Nazis into key positions in society, Adenauer's so-called 'conservative restoration', though morally dubious, was essential to the survival of democracy. Many of Germany's most able individuals in all walks of life had either worked for or conformed to the Nazi state. It would have been much more difficult to build a new state without the integration of former Nazis and those in some way tainted by their involvement with the former regime. In this sense, it is possible to argue that the end justified the means.

Adenauer's legacy as the 'founding father' of West German democracy offers a number of clues to explain his longevity in office as a committed opponent of both Communism and Fascism. He set clear and simple goals to ensure that Bonn democracy did not go the same way as Weimar democracy:

- He committed the FRG to full co-operation with Western Europe and the USA; he was convinced that Germany could only regain its lost political and moral esteem as part of a larger Europe, with the backing of the United States.
- He set the FRG on a course of economic recovery through a social market economy ably managed by Erhard.
- He determined to compensate the surviving victims of the Nazi terror and to rehabilitate those compromised by their involvement with the Nazi regime.
- He determined to provide political stability even at the cost of cementing German division; he aimed to do the next best thing to German reunification: to build a stable, prosperous state that would undermine the GDR by acting as a magnet of freedom and prosperity for East Germans.
- He was no puppet of the West; he built a reputation for straightforward dealing and a sure feeling for what was possible and when.

As Mary Fulbrook has written, 'the period is an exceedingly difficult one to evaluate'. Source A explores this dilemma.

Source A *A History of Germany 1918–2014*, fourth edition by Mary Fulbrook, (Wiley Blackwell), 2015, pp. 156–57.

It is a period which has provoked heated debates between Germans. From one point of view, it can be pointed out that many former Nazis received minimal, if any, punishment for their crimes or complicity in an evil regime. It can be pointed out that there was a massive wastage of talent, as thousands of courageous people who had refused to compromise with the Third Reich found their paths to post-war careers blocked, as positions were retained or refilled by Nazi time-servers. It can be pointed out that the chance of a fundamental restructuring of German society was missed, as neither structure nor personnel were radically changed in an era of conservative 'restoration'. Against all this, it can be asserted that without the integration of former Nazis, and without the startling economic success, Bonn democracy might have had as little chance of success as Weimar democracy. The argument can be mounted that the end, retrospectively, might have justified the means.

WORKING TOGETHER

Adenauer's longevity in power

Only one German Chancellor has held office for longer than Konrad Adenauer: Helmut Kohl, who served for sixteen years from 1982 to 1998. His longevity owed a great deal to one main factor: the process of German reunification. The reasons for Adenauer's longevity, particularly considering that he was already 73 years old when he first became Chancellor, are perhaps more complex. Work together as a class to suggest reasons why he remained in power for so long. Look again at your Working together activity on the 1957 election (page 231) as a starting point. You could follow this up by producing a part-obituary for Adenauer, dated 20 April 1967, the day after he died, writing two paragraphs praising his virtues and explaining his longevity as German Chancellor.

Assess how convincing the argument in Source A is in relation to the stability of Bonn democracy.

Adenauer's foreign policy

Though this part of your specification does not cover foreign policy issues directly, it is worth having a basic understanding of Adenauer's foreign policy, which was fundamental to his political ideology. Adenauer based his policy on Western integration or *Westpolitik*. He argued that Germany had to align itself with the West in order to achieve future unification from a position of strength. Consequently, through the 1955 Hallstein Doctrine, he refused to deal with any country which recognised the German Democratic Republic. Adenauer was deeply suspicious not only of Communism, but also of nationalism. For Adenauer, therefore, another key strand of his policy was Europeanism and, in particular, a rapprochement with France within a European political and economic framework. In this way, Germans might once again 'hold their heads high' (*wir sind wieder wer*).

The Hallstein Doctrine, December 1955

The Hallstein Doctrine, named after Walter Hallstein, a state secretary at the West German foreign ministry responsible for the policy's public announcement, was central to West German foreign policy in the 1950s and 1960s. It stated that if any nation, other than the Soviet Union, established diplomatic relations with the GDR, West Germany would withdraw diplomatic relations with that country. It was initiated as a result of the Soviet Union's formal recognition of the GDR as a sovereign state in 1955, which threatened to undermine Adenauer's claim that the FRG was 'the sole legitimate state organisation of the German people'. Adenauer was concerned that if other nations followed the Soviet Union's example, it would weaken his argument that his policy of Western integration would do no harm to the cause of future German unity. It was a crude threat but was one that worked very well.

Analysis: Adenauer's guiding principles

The extent to which key individuals shape events, or are shaped by them, is often a matter of interpretation. Historians disagree over the impact and influence of prominent individuals. We can often learn a great deal about an individual by how they present themselves and their reasons for their actions. Read the sources below from Konrad Adenauer and work through the activities which follow.

Source B Adapted from a speech by Adenauer in Cologne, October 1945.

The winter ahead of us will be very hard. We – you and we – will do everything in our power to create conditions that are at least tolerable. It will not be possible to do this to the extent you and we would like. But – and I am now addressing myself not to this hall alone but to all the citizens of Cologne – I ask all our fellow-citizens always to remember this: the guilty, those responsible for this unspeakable suffering, this indescribable misery, are those accursed men who came to power in the fatal year 1933. It was they who dishonoured the German name throughout the world and covered it with shame, who destroyed our *Reich*, who systematically and deliberately plunged our misguided and paralysed people into the deepest misery.

Source C Adapted from a speech by Adenauer in Bern, Switzerland, March 1949.

We live in disturbed times. New problems arise every day. Despite the number and variety of problems, every responsible person must realize that for the present and coming generation there is now only one main problem, and it is this: the world has seen the formation of two power-groups. On one side there is the group of powers led by the United States and united in the Atlantic Pact. This group defends the values of Christian and Western civilization, freedom, and true democracy. On the other side there is Soviet Russia with her satellites. The attempt by the Allies to govern from outside, guided by their own self-serving political and economic agenda, was bound to fail. The Marshall Plan brought the turning point; it will remain for all time a glorious page in the history of the United States.

Source D Adapted from Adenauer's Memoirs, July 1952.

I am a German, but I am also, and always have been, a European and have always felt like a European. I have therefore long advocated an understanding with France; I did so, moreover, in the 1920s, during the severest crises, and also in the face of the Nazi government. I always urged a reasonable understanding that would do justice to the interests of both countries. General de Gaulle recognized this in his speech at Saarbrucken in August 1945: 'Frenchmen and Germans must let bygones be bygones, must work together, and must remember that they are Europeans'. These words gave me great hope for Germany and for the realization of my hopes for a united Europe. A union between France and Germany would give new life and vigour to a Europe that was seriously ill.

ACTIVITY

Comprehension

1 Source B: What does Adenauer mean by 'the fatal year 1933'?
2 Source C: Why does Adenauer refer to the Marshall Plan as 'a glorious page in the history of the United States'?
3 Source D: What events in the 1920s is Adenauer recalling when he refers to 'the severest crises'?

Evidence

Using the material from this chapter, Chapter 5 and your own knowledge:

4 Source B: What supporting evidence can you provide for Adenauer's statement that conditions in 'the winter ahead of us will be very hard'?
5 Source C: Provide evidence to support Adenauer's claim that Germany's main problem was 'the foundation of two power-groups'.
6 Source D: What evidence can you provide from Adenauer's period in power in the years 1949–63 that he pursued his vision of a 'united Europe'?

Interpretation

7 How does Adenauer present himself in these three sources?
8 Using the sources and your own knowledge, identify Adenauer's fundamental guiding principles in his political career in the years 1939–63.

KEY DATES: KONRAD ADENAUER AS CHANCELLOR, 1949–63

23 May 1949 Becomes Chancellor.

14 August 1949 First West German elections.

6 September 1953 Election: CDU/FDP coalition retained power.

September 1955 The Hallstein Doctrine was announced.

25 March 1957 The Treaty of Rome, inaugurating the EEC.

15 September 1957 Election: CDU secured an overall majority.

13 August 1961 Berlin was divided.

17 September 1961 Election: CDU/FDP coalition was formed.

October 1962 The *Spiegel* Affair.

15 October 1963 Adenauer resigned.

2 The search for consensus, 1963–89

Adenauer's resignation signalled the beginning of the end of a period of twenty years of conservative ascendancy in West German politics; it was followed by a period in which political power was shared between the CDU and the SPD in coalition with the FDP, except for the years 1966–69 when a Grand Coalition comprised of the CDU and SPD was in office. From 1969 to 1982 the SPD emerged as the single most dominant party until Helmut Schmidt was unseated by a constructive vote of no confidence, the only time in the history of the FRG that this constitutional device was used. These years demonstrated that the Federal Republic could operate in conditions of relative stability under what was in effect a three-party system. The emergence of the Green Party in the 1980s briefly threatened a four-party system, but support for the Greens was never strong enough to make them a viable coalition partner. Although political stability was sustained, this three-party consensus was challenged by the extra-parliamentary opposition of the 1960s, the urban terrorism of the 1970s and the environmental and peace movements of the 1980s.

▲ Some of the chancellors of the Federal Republic. Clockwise from top left: Konrad Adenauer; Kurt Georg Kiesinger; Willy Brandt; Helmut Kohl; Helmut Schmidt.

Ludwig Erhard (CDU), 1963–66

Why was Erhard's chancellorship so short-lived?

When Erhard replaced Adenauer it seemed that his intention was to press ahead with few changes of policy or direction. However, a series of unexpected events conspired against him. His period as chancellor is often considered a relative failure in comparison to his time as Economics Minister under Adenauer. Indeed, Mary Fulbrook characterised him as being 'less adept at politics than at economics'. Nevertheless, Erhard's reputation as the 'father' of the economic miracle, and his promise to cut income tax and increase social welfare spending, ensured that the CDU/CSU, in coalition with the FDP, were successful in the 1965 election.

A number of factors undermined Erhard. The persistent sniping and public criticism from Adenauer, now in post as Party Chairman, was a contributing factor. He was a constant irritant to Erhard, bitter and ungracious in his 'retirement'. Heightening left-wing student radicalism – see Section 3 (page 244) for a fuller discussion – was also an indication that a new political generation was emerging who would not allow Erhard to remain in his 1950s comfort zone. The emergence of the right-wing National Democratic Party (NPD), threatening an electoral breakthrough at federal level, also increased political uncertainties.

However, it was the economic situation that most undermined his credibility. In October 1966, Erhard presented a package of financial proposals to tackle the 1965 economic recession, but this was rejected by his FDP coalition partners. The subsequent resignation of the FDP cabinet ministers was the final nail in his chancellorship's coffin. Erhard's damaged legacy – the lack of integrity shown by Adenauer and Strauss at the time of the *Spiegel* affair – combined with a set of unpropitious circumstances – left-wing criticism; right-wing resurgence and economic recession – created sufficient political turbulence to change the mould of West German politics. Erhard resigned in November 1966, making way for a Grand Coalition between the CDU/CSU and the SPD. The SPD's participation in government signalled the beginning of a new political era.

Georg Kiesinger (CDU) and the Grand Coalition, 1966–69

How successful was the Grand Coalition?

In the early years of the Federal Republic Kiesinger had been an eloquent supporter of Adenauer. From 1958 to 1966 he was the first Minister-President of the newly formed *Land* of Baden-Württemberg; his talents as a mediator and conciliator proved important in establishing this new *Land*. It was precisely this talent that brought him to the chancellorship. He was relatively untainted by the war of succession that had broken out in the CDU on Adenauer's resignation and which rumbled on throughout Erhard's time in office.

The Grand Coalition which Kiesinger headed was something of a marriage of convenience between an ailing CDU/CSU and a resurgent SPD. The CDU/CSU had eleven ministers to the SPD's nine. It was a highly talented team of ministers, including Willy Brandt as foreign minister and deputy chancellor. Given the talent in the coalition, and its unchallengeable majority in the *Bundestag*, Kiesinger's role was largely that of mediator and facilitator, which he managed with great skill. His chancellorship was also able to steer a

The National Democratic Party of Germany (NPD) – Founded in 1964, the NPD was the most neo-Nazi party to emerge since 1945.

The Weimar legacy

The recession in the mid-1960s was relatively mild, largely caused by overproduction. Inflation was running at 4 per cent per annum in 1966, driving up prices and wages, and unemployment had reached 700,000, in contrast to the labour shortages of the 1950s. Erhard proposed a number of modest measures to tackle this economic dip: spending cuts of 10 per cent, small rises in interest rates and taxes. He even suggested an extra hour on the working week, which did not, however, go down well with the trade unions. The FDP baulked at any suggestion of increasing taxation, preferring greater cuts in government spending. In order to understand the level of public anxiety about what was a relatively minor economic slowdown, it is important to remember how frightened West Germans were of even the slightest whiff of economic crisis. The spectre of 1923 and 1929–32 ran very deep in the German psyche. The fear that the economic slowdown might force the Bonn Republic to go the same way as the Weimar Republic proved a very strong impetus to form a Grand Coalition to stabilise the state.

Ostpolitik – Brandt's desire to build more positive relations with the GDR coincided with a growing receptiveness in the USSR for East–West co-operation (*détente*). Brandt's policy became known as *Ostpolitik*. This was a strategy to seek German unification through rapprochement – a belief that a sustained period of contact over many years and at many levels would bring East and West together. This was a dramatic initiative, overturning the Hallstein Doctrine and leading to the negotiation of a whole series of new Eastern treaties in 1969–70. So controversial was this development that the 1972 *Bundestag* election was essentially a referendum on *Ostpolitik*. This policy won Brandt the 1971 Nobel Peace Prize.

KEY DATES: 1965–69

19 September 1965 Election: CDU/FDP coalition retained power.

1 December 1966 Kiesinger succeeded Erhard as chancellor. Grand Coalition was formed.

May 1968 The Emergency Laws were passed.

28 September 1969 Election: SDP/FDP coalition was formed.

Willy Brandt

Brandt was born Herbert Frahm. As an active Social Democrat he was forced to leave Nazi Germany in 1933, fleeing to Norway and adopting the name Willy Brandt, which he kept for the rest of his life. In 1940, at the time of the Nazi invasion of Norway, he had been a member of the Norwegian army. He spent a short time as a prisoner of war before escaping the country to neutral Sweden.

pragmatic middle-way between the increasing student agitation on the left and the rising NPD on the right. He refused pressure for a legal ban on the NPD and allowed the re-formation of the Communist Party (DKP). Both of these decisions kept the mainstream political debates within the framework of the constitutional system, thereby to some extent limiting extra-parliamentary opposition at a time of increasing political agitation, in stark contrast to the political apathy of the 1950s.

The Coalition did come under fire from left-wing students for an amendment to the constitution in May 1968 allowing a committee of the *Bundestag*, with representatives from each *Land*, to take emergency measures at times of extreme civil unrest. The fear that this might become another Article 48, weakening the democratic process, proved unfounded. Indeed, it can be argued that these Emergency Laws were symbolic of the increasing democratic maturity of the Republic, signifying its confidence that such powers could be exercised legitimately to protect civil liberties, not to undermine them.

The Coalition achieved a great deal of unanimity on economic matters, successfully achieving its most urgent task, which was to reverse the economic recession, as is discussed in more depth in Chapter 8. It also implemented a degree of social modernisation, liberalising the criminal law, including the de-criminalisation of adultery and adult homosexuality. The Coalition was much more divided on foreign policy, with the SPD and the left-liberal wing of the FDP favouring a new *Ostpolitik* in contrast to the CDU's preference for maintaining the status quo in the Republic's relations with East Germany and the Soviet Union. The SPD also grew increasingly frustrated with the CDU over welfare reform, feeling that Kiesinger was dragging his heels in pushing through modernisation.

For a time the Grand Coalition seemed very popular and Kiesinger expected that the CDU would be the biggest beneficiary in the 1969 elections. The CDU did indeed emerge as the strongest individual party with 46.1 per cent of the vote but the FDP preferred a progressive coalition with the SPD; together they had 48.5 per cent of the vote. For the first time in the history of the FRG, a socialist party was in power.

The SPD 'Social-Liberal' era, 1969–82

Did the 'Social-Liberal' era represent a significant turning point in West Germany's political development?

In these fourteen years the Social Democrats introduced a number of controversial measures, yet were re-elected three times. This long period in office was evidence of a fundamental, long-term shift in German political culture given that Social Democrats in Imperial and Weimar Germany were often perceived as threats to middle-class, bourgeois values. Brandt took office in 1969, burning with missionary zeal until his resignation from the chancellorship in 1974. He was succeeded by the less charismatic, but extraordinarily able Helmut Schmidt, who remained as chancellor until 1982.

Willy Brandt (SPD), 1969–74

Brandt swept into power in 1969 offering a new vision; he believed that the Federal Republic urgently needed renewal and reform. Brandt had the common touch, hating empty rhetoric and ideological posing; Adenauer was aloof, arrogant and filled with his own self-importance. The two men could not have been more different, and neither much respected each other. During the

1961 election campaign Adenauer had insulted Brandt, the SPD's candidate for chancellor, referring to him as '*Herr Brandt alias Frahm*', implying that he was a traitor (see text box). The CDU often referred to Brandt's illegitimate birth and even went so far as to allege that he had 'shot at Germans' during the war. There is little doubt that Brandt was determined to take the Republic in a radically different direction from that taken by Adenauer.

Source E An extract from Brandt's first speech as chancellor to the *Bundestag*.

We want to dare to be more democratic. We will make government more transparent and be more forthcoming with information. We want to create a society which offers more freedom and demands more co-responsibility. The government stands for dialogue; it looks for a critical partnership with all those who carry responsibility. If we want to do what has to be done then we need to make use of all active forces in our society. In our Federal Republic we are being faced with the necessity of comprehensive reforms. We need people who are critical, who want to take decisions and carry responsibility. The self-confidence of this government will reveal itself as tolerance. It will value the kind of solidarity which expresses itself in criticism. We are not chosen, we are elected. This is why we are seeking a dialogue with all those who care for this democracy. Over the last years some in this country have had fears that the second German democracy might follow the course of the first. I never believed this to be the case. Today I believe it less than ever. No: we are not standing at the end of our democracy; we are only just about to begin.

> What criticisms of the CDU era are implied in this extract (Source E)? What is Brandt offering that is different?

Brandt's government carried out a series of wide-ranging, progressive liberal reforms.

Education

Reforms were made in the education sector aimed at greater egalitarianism and an expansion of opportunity:

- The school leaving age was raised to sixteen.
- The 1971 Educational Support Law provided grants for students from poorer families for continuing higher education; this established the fundamental principle that all students, whatever their background, had a legal right to adequate financial support.
- Expenditure on school buildings and research was increased.

Employment

A series of changes were made, aimed both to broaden opportunities and responsibilities, and to supplement funding. For example, spending on job creation schemes increased, particularly in West Berlin where tax incentives were offered for those prepared to re-locate; the social housing budget was increased by just over one-third; a new Factory Law was passed in January 1972 giving workers a greater say in management decisions.

Social welfare

Spending was significantly increased on a range of welfare benefits: pensions rose by about five per cent overall, sickness benefits by nearly ten per cent; family, health, accident and unemployment allowances all went up.

Liberalisation

The SPD's modernising agenda was very apparent: the voting age was lowered to eighteen years of age; censorship and laws against homosexuality and abortion were relaxed; the criminal law was overhauled, limiting overall sentences and promoting rehabilitation rather than punishment.

Conclusion

Any assessment of Brandt's chancellorship has to be seen in the context of the economic and social challenges which confronted the FRG in the early 1970s. Brandt's critics on the right accused him of reckless public spending, creating an inflationary spiral, leading to wages and pensions rising beyond what the nation could afford. Indeed, in 1971 he had to backtrack, being forced to re-call the *Bundestag* in July to implement emergency anti-inflationary measures. Brandt was in a difficult position, pushing through cuts his own left-wing opposed. He faced further opposition in his own party from the *Jusos*, the younger, radical SPD members, angered by his anti-terrorism measures which, in their view, went too far in restricting individual liberties. The 1973–74 oil crisis further weakened the economy, contributing to the growth of inflation and unemployment. *Ostpolitik*, too, had many detractors on the right and among older Germans.

Conversely, Brandt's supporters strongly defend his record in government. For many, he represented a new German spirit: compassionate, decent and brave, willing to compromise without abandoning his principles. He had promised to 'risk more democracy', reform and expand education, reduce the voting age, improve the welfare state, reform family and criminal law and extend workers' rights – all of this he achieved. At a time of global economic difficulties, the FRG's economic performance was significantly better than most other industrialised nations. The 1972 election, which was fought almost exclusively on Brandt's policy of *Ostpolitik* and his government's economic record, was a triumph for Brandt, giving the SPD its best result ever.

Clearly, opinions of Brandt's achievements are mixed. Though he styled himself as the 'Chancellor of domestic reform', he has been criticised for making *Ostpolitik* his primary focus. As damaging for his reputation were the circumstances of his resignation from office over the Guillaume affair in May 1974. Some have described his chancellorship as a 'shambles', stumbling from one crisis to another with limited direction; others see Brandt as representative of a new Germany and of a new German, symbolising the transition of Germany into a new, more liberal era. Like Adenauer, he was a leader who excited equal and opposite reactions.

The Guillaume affair

Günter Guillaume was a confidant and close advisor of Brandt. He had arrived in the FRG as a refugee from East Germany in 1956. He joined the SPD in 1957 and in 1970 he was appointed to a post in the Federal Chancellery with access to sensitive state documents. He was revealed as an East German spy in April 1974. Sentenced to thirteen years in gaol, Guillaume was exchanged to East Germany in 1981 for Western spies and received in the GDR as a returning hero. The Michael Frayn play *Democracy* is based on the Brandt–Guillaume relationship.

WORKING TOGETHER

Willy Brandt was German chancellor in momentous times. It is worth pausing at this point in your breadth study to assess his part in guiding the FRG through such a turbulent period. Hold a class debate to assess his success as a key individual, with one group arguing for Brandt, and another against. Use the following motion to discuss:

'This class believes that Brandt succeeded in promoting a fairer democratic society.'

As part of your overall consideration of breadth you could follow this up on your own by writing a response to this statement:

'Willy Brandt has a greater claim to be recognised as the "father of modern Germany" than Konrad Adenauer.'

Helmut Schmidt (SPD), 1974–82

Schmidt succeeded Brandt on 16 May 1974, remaining chancellor in coalition with the FDP after the 1976 elections; he was re-elected again in 1980. A more conservative-minded Social Democrat than Brandt, he was confronted with difficulties on several fronts: economic crises, acts of terrorism and opposition from his coalition partners and from within his own party. From the start of his eight years as chancellor he knew that he would be in for a bumpy ride: 'I was quite aware of that. It was a sea change. It was an ebb tide after a flood tide.'

The terrorism of the 1970s, covered in more detail in Section 3 (see pages 246–7), was a serious challenge to West Germany's image of a politically stable, model democracy. The terrorists pushed the state towards a Catch 22 position: it found itself taking authoritarian actions simply to defend itself from a violent minority, which justified its own position by claiming that the FRG was a neo-Fascist, authoritarian regime hiding behind a sham democracy. In 1972 Brandt had already enforced tough anti-terrorist regulations, imposing new, open-ended police and judicial powers to deal with political terrorism, such as issuing threats against politicians, and tightening up laws against drug dealing and possession of weapons. Schmidt continued this hard line, coming under criticism for what seemed a witch-hunt against anyone suspected of left-wing sympathies in public employment. The dismissal of many public sector employees labelled as 'unreliable' produced further uneasiness about the over-powerful state.

Schmidt also came under fire from his own left wing and from environmental groups and peace protestors critical of his pro-nuclear power policy, and of his decision in 1979 to allow the United States to station short-range nuclear missiles on German soil. These issues caused a deep split in the SPD, which partly explains its poor showing in the 1983 election as many former SPD voters defected to the newly formed Green Party.

Schmidt's reputation is strongest as an astute manager of the economy throughout the difficult dips and slumps of the 1970s. His relationship with his coalition partner, the FDP, mirrored the economic fluctuations of the period as disagreements developed between them over how best to balance the federal budget. The increasingly right-wing FDP preferred to see limits to public spending further than Schmidt was prepared to support. Indeed, it was this issue which led the FDP in 1982 to switch its allegiance to the CDU, forcing Schmidt out of office through a constructive vote of no confidence and replacing him with the CDU leader Helmut Kohl.

Assessments of Schmidt

Just as Adenauer is personally associated with the *Zeitgeist* of the 1950s, so Schmidt is feted as 'the Achiever', a pragmatist blessed with managerial gifts and decisiveness who guided the Federal Republic through the troubled 1970s. He is regarded as an innovator, particularly in financial affairs, promoting European and Western initiatives to counter global economic problems. His supporters praise his powers of critical analysis and objectivity as opposed to Brandt's emotional socialism. His prestige soared due to his firm handling of the wave of terrorism that peaked in 1977.

Nevertheless, he is not without his critics from within his own party as well as from his political opponents. At times he seemed more popular among the German public than within sections of his own party; in 1980–82 particularly he seemed caught in the middle between his own rebellious left wing and his coalition partner the FDP, which was becoming increasingly conservative in economic matters. Two new books published in 2014 also chip away at Schmidt's highly regarded reputation. Sabine Pamperrien's biography, *Helmut Schmidt and the Lousy War*, casts doubt on his anti-Nazi record by suggesting that he was 'temporarily contaminated' by Nazism. Another book by the veteran German journalist Klaus Harpprecht has referred to long-term marital infidelities. Overall, however, Schmidt's reputation remains high, praised by the newspaper *Hamburger Morgenpost* as 'the most popular German of today'.

> **Catch 22** – A contradictory or self-defeating situation or course of action.

KEY DATES: 1972–82

19 November 1972 Election: SPD/FDP retained power.

October 1973 Oil crisis.

16 May 1974 Brandt resigned; succeeded by Schmidt.

3 October 1976 Election: SPD/FDP coalition retained power.

5 October 1980 Election: SPD/FDP coalition retained power.

1 October 1982 Schmidt was removed from office by a constructive vote of no confidence; succeeded by Kohl-led CDU/FDP coalition.

Helmut Kohl (CDU), 1982–89

How successful was Kohl in restoring the political dominance of the CDU?

The use of a constructive vote of no confidence to remove Schmidt from office led to further unease about the democratic system being manipulated by a small party in pursuit of its own political agenda. However, people's fears proved unfounded and there was no constitutional crisis. In effect, this constitutional safeguard worked effectively. To deflect criticism and any perceptions of constitutional manipulation, Kohl made use of the same device to make possible an early general election in 1983, which he duly won, thereby achieving a popular mandate for the change of government. The election held on 6 March 1983 returned a 58 seat majority for the CDU/FDP coalition, the CDU gaining 48.8 per cent of the vote and the FDP 7.0 per cent. This change of government became known as *die Wende*, 'the turning point', indicating the end of SPD rule and the return of conservative ascendancy.

Traditional conservatism

While the SPD entered a period of re-evaluation and forward-planning, split between its left- and right-wing factions and losing votes to the Greens, Kohl tended to look backwards to restore the CDU's political dominance and authority. He returned more closely to Erhard's version of social market economics, reducing the government's role in the economy. In economic terms, therefore, *die Wende* represented a return to tried and tested policies rather than innovative new ideas. It was not until the latter years of the decade that the German economy began a modest revival, though Kohl never really got to grips with the problem of unemployment.

Kohl also pushed ahead with traditional CDU policies, putting himself in the forefront of closer European economic and monetary integration. He continued *Ostpolitik* as the basis of the FRG's relationship with East Germany and became the first West German chancellor to host a visit by an East German Head of State: Erich Honecker, in 1987. In some respects this was a natural consequence of many years of closer West–East recognition but the visit was still controversial for many, seeming to confirm the view that German division was a permanent situation. Equally controversial was Kohl's decision to allow the United States to press ahead with stationing mid-range nuclear missiles on West German soil.

Social problems

Like Margaret Thatcher in Britain, Kohl preferred less government regulation and lower taxes as the best means of ensuring rising living standards, wealth creation and social improvement. This ignored, however, Germany's problem of a growing underclass of the socially deprived. Much of the continuing problem of unemployment affected Germany's remaining *Gastarbeiter*, numbering about eight per cent of the population. Though overall this was a relatively small number, many German cities had areas where these immigrant labourers and their families numbered up to 50 per cent of the population. His desired solution, expressed largely in private, was to encourage these groups to leave Germany, particularly the Turks who he believed did not integrate well. However, this was politically very contentious. Many *Gastarbeiter* were by now second generation immigrants and beginning to think of Germany as their home, though it would take another generation before, for example, young men of Turkish background would choose to represent Germany, rather than Turkey,

Gastarbeiter – Literally 'guest worker'. The term refers to the foreign and migrant workers who moved to West Germany in the late 1950s and early 1960s as manual, unqualified labour to fill the employment shortages created by the economic miracle. Turkish workers, for example, arrived in large numbers after 1961.

in professional football. This potential social fracturing was worsened in the last years of the decade with the arrival of many ethnic Germans from Eastern Europe and the Soviet Union as the Iron Curtain began to disintegrate. The arrival, in the summer and autumn of 1989, of hundreds of thousands of East German refugees would completely change the political situation in West Germany.

Corruption

The credibility of Kohl's government was also undermined by recurring incidences of sleaze, corruption and misjudgement. Most notable among these were the so-called Flick affair and the Bitburg controversy. This loss of credibility was reflected in a weaker showing in the 1987 election with the CDU vote falling to 44.3 per cent, the party's lowest percentage of the popular vote since 1949. The coalition was saved, however, due to a strong vote for the FDP of 9.1 per cent, resulting in a coalition majority of 45 seats. Despite an up-turn in the economy, Kohl's popularity rating continued to decline and most expected his lame duck government to limp towards defeat in the 1991 elections. However, Kohl was saved by the collapse of the East German government in 1989, an event so unexpected but so momentous it not only saved Kohl's career, it utterly changed the landscape of German politics and was arguably the most momentous political event of the late twentieth century.

Party	1965	1969	1972	1976	1980	1983	1987
SPD	39.3	42.7	45.8	42.6	42.9	38.2	37.0
CDU/CSU	47.6	46.1	44.9	48.6	44.5	48.8	44.3
FDP	9.5	5.8	8.4	7.9	10.6	6.9	9.1
KDP/*Deutsche Kommunistische Partei*	-	-	0.3	0.3	0.2	0.2	-
Greens/*Bundnis 90*	-	-	-	-	1.5	5.6	8.3
NPD	2.0	4.3	0.6	0.3	0.2	0.2	0.6
Others	1.6	1.1	-	0.3	0.1	0.1	0.6

▲ **Figure 4** West German election results: share of votes (%). From *Cassell's Dictionary of Modern German History,* by T. Kirk (2002).

KEY DATES: 1982–89

6 March 1983 Election: CDU/FDP coalition retained power.

May 1985 Bitburg controversy.

7–11 September 1987 State visit of Erich Honecker.

25 January 1987 Election: CDU/FDP coalition retained power.

9 November 1989 The opening of the Berlin Wall.

The Flick affair

Count Lambsdorff, the FDP Finance Minister, exempted the Flick Corporation, one of Germany's largest businesses, from tax payments in return for financial contributions to the FDP. He was forced to resign in 1984, effectively for accepting bribes, and was convicted of tax evasion in 1987.

The Bitburg controversy

As part of the state visit to West Germany by the American President Ronald Reagan in 1985, Kohl arranged for a ceremony of reconciliation to take place at a small military cemetery at Bitburg to mark the fortieth anniversary of the end of the Second World War. This raised a storm of controversy, both in Europe and in the United States. The cemetery contained the graves of 49 members of the Waffen-SS and was interpreted as part of Kohl's attempt to rehabilitate as many Germans who had served in the Third *Reich* as possible. A visit to the former concentration camp at Bergen-Belsen, a Holocaust memorial site, was belatedly added to Reagan's itinerary, but this was seen as little more than a desperate face-saving attempt to deflect controversy and to placate outraged world Jewish opinion.

3 Extra-parliamentary opposition

This section focuses on the final three decades of the Federal Republic, a period when the relative political apathy of the 1950s was replaced by a turbulent period of transition as a new political generation took to the streets to protest against what it perceived to be the limitations of Bonn democracy. The 1970s saw the emergence of left-wing political extremism as the ultra-radical fringes of the 1960s student movement turned to terrorism. By the late 1970s extra-parliamentary pressure had re-focused itself in the peace and environmental movements, which, in the 1980s, formed the core of a new political force: the Green Party.

Student protest

How effective was extra-parliamentary opposition in re-shaping West German political life?

Right-wing dissent grew in West Germany in the mid-1960s with the onset of economic depression. However, the neo-Nazi NPD failed to make any significant electoral breakthrough. The most widespread dissent occurred on the left, in parallel with wider left-wing student protest throughout the Western world. Young Germans, having grown up in a highly regulated, relatively authoritarian and materialistic society, which seemed to have collective amnesia about its Nazi past, began to question the values of the state and the values of their parents. Moreover, for many of this generation, Germany, in a phrase common at the time, seemed to be an 'economic giant, but a political dwarf' – rich in terms of wealth but poor in terms of political consciousness. A number of short-term factors combined with these longer-term concerns to spark widespread student protest:

- A major expansion in higher education provoked criticisms of overcrowding, poor teaching and right-wing bias: many professors and lecturers, in the eyes of the students, seemed to be relics of a past that did not belong to them.
- The development of a youth culture predicated on affluence provoked an opposite reaction from many left-wing students critical of the shallowness of middle-class West German values.
- The anti-Vietnam War protests in the USA manifested themselves in West Germany as protests against the Americanisation of German culture and in criticisms of the United States' failure to prevent the division of Berlin.
- Intellectually, many left-wing German students were encouraged to activism by the in-vogue, neo-Marxist view that a society made by people could be changed by people, and that the only real and permanent change grew out of protest.
- The formation of the Grand Coalition in 1966 seemed to confirm the worst fears of many young Germans that true parliamentary opposition was disappearing; the accidental shooting by police of a student protestor, Benno Ohnesorg, on 2 June 1967, sparked an explosion of extra-parliamentary opposition.

The APO

The APO (Opposition Outside of Parliament) was a loose alliance of left-wing students, trade unionists and intellectuals. Its aim was to co-ordinate radical protest through strikes and demonstrations with the goal of making West Germany a more open, tolerant and free society. It was hugely idealistic, motivated by the seeming disappearance of true parliamentary debate, given that the two main political parties were now in a Grand Coalition. In the view of the APO, effective in-parliament opposition to the government no longer operated, hence the need to take to the streets.

The high point of the movement was in 1968 (former members of the APO are often referred to as '68ers') with extensive campaigning against the Emergency Laws. The movement declined towards the end of the decade as its membership fractured, some supporters attracted to the SPD by Brandt's victory, some to the newly formed Communist Party (DKP), and some moved into the emerging environmental movement. A few extremists turned to terrorism.

The SDS

Originally affiliated to the SPD, the SDS (German Socialist Students Union) was expelled in 1961 because of its opposition to German rearmament, which the SPD had accepted in its Bad Godesberg conversion in 1959. Its most well-known leader was Rudi Dutschke. The SDS was a fundamental part of the wider APO movement, taking an important lead in street protests.

▲ An SDS poster. It reads 'Everyone's talking about the weather. Not us.'

What is your interpretation of the message of the poster?

Rudi Dutschke

Dutschke was the best known and most charismatic of the SDS student leaders. On 11 April 1968 he was shot in the head and shoulder by Josef Bachmann, a Berlin house painter. The SDS blamed the attack on the lurid anti-student articles appearing in the right-wing Springer press, which Bachmann cited as influencing his actions. Dutschke survived the attack but died on Christmas Eve 1979 due to brain damage related to his injuries. His shooting and death has become symbolic of the deep left-wing student disillusionment with the politics of the day.

The Axel Springer press – The Springer press was founded by Axel Springer in 1946, becoming West Germany's largest press organisation, and incorporating the mass circulation tabloid *Bild* and the influential broadsheet *Die Welt*. Springer's arch-conservative views found expression in his newspapers, attacking the 1960s student movement in a series of inflammatory articles.

Urban terrorism: The Red Army Faction (RAF)

The RAF emerged from extremist elements of the APO. It is often referred to as the Baader-Meinhof gang, named after two of its most prominent members: Andreas Baader and Ulrike Meinhof. These two, along with Gudrun Ensslin, Jan Carl Raspe and Holger Meins formed the core of the first generation of terrorists. Baader, proclaiming that 'violence against property' was a legitimate democratic action, was imprisoned for his role in setting fire to two department stores in 1968, briefly released in 1969 and re-imprisoned in 1970. He met Ulrike Meinhof, a journalist, while in prison. She was to help him collaborate on a book, but went further and helped him escape in 1970. Baader and other founding members of the group were re-imprisoned in 1972. The group was never larger than 60 people.

Aims and objectives

The RAF opposed what it perceived to be the Fascist-leaning bourgeois values of West German society. It supported Communist ideals and opposed capitalist 'exploitation'; it attacked the Vietnam War as an American imperialist action, supported 'freedom' movements such as the Palestine Liberation Organization (PLO) and denounced Western exploitation of the Third World. The RAF was a West German manifestation of the wider, global terrorist movement that emerged in the 1970s. It had a life span beyond the 1970s, remaining active until 1993 and not officially disbanding until 1998.

Actions

The RAF at first focused on robberies and attacks on property. At this juncture, the RAF even had a degree of public sympathy as Robin Hood villains, protecting the powerless by its attacks on symbols of capitalist exploitation. The hysterical reporting of their actions by the right-wing press contributed to this thin veneer of democratic legitimacy. The most notable of these right-wing attacks came from the Axel Springer group which controlled about 80 per cent of West Germany's popular press. Its sensationalist headlines and language reminded many of the excesses of the 1930s Nazi press. Others criticised what they saw as an excessive police response to anyone remotely connected with dissent. The film *The Lost Honour of Katharina Blum*, based on a short story by the contemporary novelist Heinrich Böll, reflects this view of an over-powerful state, the loss of individual freedom and manipulation by the media.

However, sympathy quickly evaporated once crimes against property developed into a campaign of violence against the state, including bomb attacks, kidnappings and murder. The terror attack by the Palestinian group Black September, which had links with the RAF, against Israeli athletes at the 1972 Munich Olympic Games further alienated public opinion. This led to more vigorous anti-terror policing, the imprisonment of the main RAF leaders and a consequent reduction in terrorist actions.

The German Autumn

In May 1976 Ulrike Meinhof committed suicide in prison. This precipitated a second wave of RAF activity in 1977 known as the German Autumn, with prominent 'establishment' members of German society being kidnapped and murdered. Arab supporters of the RAF also hijacked a German airliner, an action known as the Mogadishu incident. Isolated RAF attacks persisted into the 1980s but by then much of the movement had been neutered. Left-wing activists in the 1980s turned to more peaceful forms of protest, focusing on nuclear power and environmental issues.

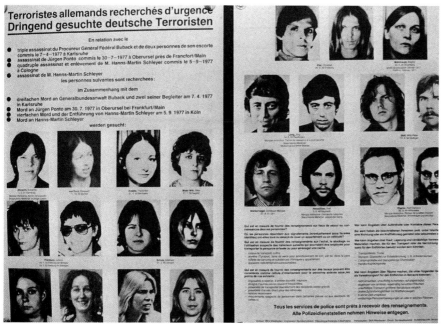

▲ RAF wanted poster. The French and German headline translating to 'Urgently wanted German terrorists'.

The existence of the RAF raises all kinds of questions about the relative strengths and weaknesses of Bonn democracy: some see the RAF as evidence of its limitations; others as evidence of how strong and deep-rooted the democratic system had become in such a short time, showing itself capable of resisting and surviving terrorist attacks.

Environmentalism

How and why did the Green movement develop?

Beginning in the late 1960s, ecological concerns became very widespread in West Germany. In the aftermath of the oil crisis of 1973–74, regional political groups concerned with environmental issues, such as pollution in the Baltic Sea and the Rhine and Main rivers, and the damage to the country's forests from acid rain, began to put up candidates in local and regional elections. In 1980, following the accident at the Three Mile Island nuclear plant in the USA in 1979 and the NATO Dual Track Decision in the same year, a number of ecological groups, alternative action movements, and various women's rights organisations banded together at the national level to form the political party that came to be called the Greens (*Die Grünen*).

The Green Party

Although the political views of the various groups in this new party were widely diverse, all agreed that the continuous expansion of the economy was detrimental to the environment and that disarmament was necessary if mankind was to survive. From the early 1970s environmentalists had also begun to question the seemingly widespread pro-nuclear power consensus. Many of those campaigning to prevent nuclear power stations being built in their own backyard shared the broader feeling of the protest movements of the 1960s that the authorities were not only not listening to their protests, but were actually not interested in wider consultation. The environmental movement was, therefore, another aspect of protest against what was perceived to be an authoritarian, arrogant and, in part, corrupt government that paid lip-service to democratic processes.

The Mogadishu incident

In October 1977 the RAF kidnapped Hans-Martin Schleyer, the President of the West German Employers' Association, in an attempt to blackmail the government into releasing eleven RAF prisoners, including Baader. In support of this demand, on 13 October an Arab terrorist group with links to the RAF hijacked a Lufthansa aeroplane flying from Mallorca to Frankfurt full of German holidaymakers. The plane was flown to Mogadishu in Somalia via Rome, Dubai and Aden. Schmidt refused to give in to the terrorists' demands and on 17 October the GSG9, a special West German anti-terrorist police group, successfully stormed the plane freeing all 91 hostages. Schleyer was subsequently murdered and the imprisoned terrorists, including Baader, committed suicide in their cells. Schmidt was highly praised for his refusal to give in to blackmail.

Three Mile Island nuclear accident, 1979

The Three Mile Island power station in Pennsylvania, United States was the location of America's worst nuclear accident: a partial meltdown occurred in one of the plant's two nuclear reactors. The Three Mile Island accident gave the world its first glimpse of the possibility and dangers of a nuclear accident and prompted much anti-nuclear action around the world.

NATO Dual Track Decision, 1979

In 1976–77 the Soviet Union began deploying SS20 medium-range nuclear missiles in East Germany. In retaliation, NATO adopted what it called the Dual Track approach, a decision to deploy its own medium-range nuclear missiles in West Germany. Schmidt was the driving force in gaining *Bundestag* approval of this controversial decision. Many Germans were against nuclear proliferation; Schmidt's decision prompted the development of a broad-based peace movement with many Germans anxious to avoid the doomsday scenario of Germany becoming a nuclear battlefield in a Third World War.

The Greens' support for radical peace movements and their demand that the FRG withdraw from NATO initially prevented many West Germans from taking the Greens seriously as a political force. In the *Bundestag* elections of 1980, they gained only 1.5 per cent of the vote, not enough to win any parliamentary seats. In the 1983 elections, however, benefitting from disaffected SPD supporters switching to the Greens, they broke the 5 per cent barrier and won 27 seats in the *Bundestag*.

Differing ideological viewpoints within the Greens soon began to undermine the Party's effectiveness in the political process. Two different factions emerged: the dogmatic fundamentalists (*Fundis*), who were unwilling to make any compromises on policy in order to win political allies; and the realists (*Realos*), who were ready to enter into a coalition with the SPD at the local and *Land* level in order to put environmentalist ideas into practice.

Another cause of disagreement within the Party organisation of the Greens was the principle of rotation of seats in the *Bundestag* and in *Land* parliaments. This policy required members to give up their seats after only half a term so that other Green candidates would have an opportunity to participate in the political process. As a result, experienced Green politicians who understood the workings of parliament were forced to give up their seats and had to make do with subordinate work in the Party. Such unrealistic policies caused numerous talented Green politicians to withdraw from active politics, or to leave the Party altogether. In 1984 a Party leadership consisting only of women was elected, giving the Greens an unpopular image of practising unbalanced reverse discrimination.

Although the *Realos* among the Greens subsequently participated in *Land* governments as cabinet members, the Party remained on the periphery of politics during the remainder of the 1980s. Nevertheless, the Greens positively influenced the views of the German people, raising awareness about the environment and the protection of natural resources. The wider peace movement of the 1980s was also influential in mobilising protest against an unpopular nuclear weapons policy, and in raising awareness of the Holocaust and the search for an appropriate state response to this chapter of Germany's recent past. Perhaps its most significant achievement was to show that non-violent, active civil disobedience could have a positive impact in raising the level of public debate about government policy and, to some extent, recaptured the protest movement from extremist factions such as the RAF.

What was the state of West German democracy in 1989?

The West German political system continues to be the subject of much debate. Those who argue in support of the FRG as a strong democracy focus on its relative political stability. This interpretation views the Federal Republic as a model democratic state, notable for its orderly, smoothly functioning succession of governments and lack of significant political crises, particularly when compared with the weaknesses and failures of Weimar democracy. Another interpretation views the Federal Republic as a fundamentally unequal democratic state, notable for the disproportionate political and economic power wielded by establishment elites, which led to so much extra-parliamentary opposition. Source F offers an overall judgement of the nature of West German political development.

Source F Adapted from *A History of Germany, 1918–2014*, fourth edition by Mary Fulbrook, (Wiley-Blackwell), 2015, pp. 210–11, 236.

The West German political system became established as a system capable of gradual transformation and attracting at least passive assent on the part of a majority of its citizens. That there are critiques of the shortcomings of West German democracy paradoxically substantiates the extent of that democracy's success: it is possible for articulate citizens to analyse, debate and argue in the interests of improving the state and society in which they live. While there was a wide range of dissenting opinions of one form or another in the Federal Republic, there was nothing which remotely resembled the extent of anti-system opposition to parliamentary democracy in the Weimar Republic. The reasons for this are various, but one key factor has to do with the relative material success of West German capitalist democracy. For the Federal Republic's first forty years there was no mass discontent to provide a popular basis for extremist parties. On the other hand, it is quite clear that social tensions – particularly in relation to *Gastarbeiter* – and fear of the impact of immigrants (including, in 1989–90, East Germans) on unemployment and housing, could quite easily lead a substantial minority of West Germans to sympathize with or support right-wing views and groups.

What overall judgement is reached by Mary Fulbrook (Source F) about West German democracy? How does she qualify her judgement?

WORKING TOGETHER

A 25-year-old in 1968 would have been born in 1943. This generation, reaching political maturity in the later 1960s, would have had no substantive, direct personal experience of the Nazi or Weimar era, and would, therefore, have had a radically different mindset from that of their parents and grandparents. Similarly, it would be a truism to say that the Germany of 1968 would have differed considerably from that of 1938.

In order to gain a fuller understanding of this new generation's mindset, split into groups and begin to itemise its concerns and grievances in the 1960s. Write each one on a sticky note. Each group should then fasten these to the wall or whiteboard. Compare the points raised by each group. Discuss what seem to be the key issues. As a follow-up, devise your own flow diagram of these issues, making links and connections between them.

KEY DATES: EXTRA-PARLIAMENTARY OPPOSITION

2 June 1967 The shooting of Benno Ohnesorg by police.

11 April 1968 Rudi Dutschke shot by Josef Bachmann.

May 1976 Ulrike Meinhof committed suicide.

October 1977 The Mogadishu incident; Andreas Baader committed suicide.

January 1980 The foundation of the Green Party.

Chapter summary

- The Basic Law was the founding document of the constitution of the Federal Republic of Germany.
- The checks and balances built into the constitution were instrumental in safeguarding Bonn democracy.
- With one exception only, between 1957 and 1961, all West German governments were coalitions.
- The period 1949–66 was one of conservative ascendancy, led by the CDU Chancellor Konrad Adenauer until 1963, and Ludwig Erhard until 1966.
- The Grand Coalition, led by CDU Chancellor Georg Kiesinger from 1966 to 1969, marked the first entry of the SPD into government.
- From 1969 until 1982, Willy Brandt and Helmut Schmidt led an SPD era throughout which West Germany faced recurrent economic recession and an extra-parliamentary opposition that turned increasingly to terrorism.
- The appointment of the CDU Chancellor Helmut Kohl was seen as a turning point (*die Wende*), a return to the tried and tested values of a social market economy and less government regulation.
- The terrorism of the 1970s largely receded in the 1980s, being superceded by an environmental movement that led to the foundation of the Green Party in 1980.
- By the end of the 1980s West German democracy was securely founded; the FRG lay at the heart of a powerful European community, sufficiently confident and vital to lead the reunification process as the East German government crumbled in the summer and autumn of 1989.

▼ Summary diagram: Government and opposition, 1949–89

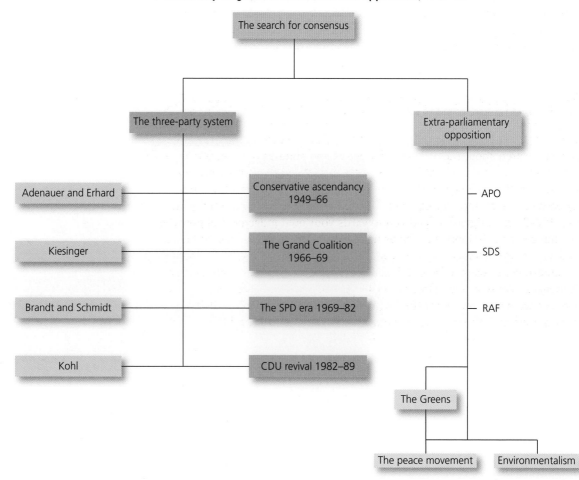

Working on essay technique

Developing conceptual depth in essays

The guidance on essay writing up to this point has focused on the basics of essay organisation and how to develop balanced answers, both of which are essential requirements for producing a good essay.

For an outstanding essay, additional depth and precision, and greater conceptual understanding are expected, such as:

- precise details (names, dates, specialist terminology, etc.)
- clear planning, including a substantial conclusion that leads to a judgement
- clear understanding of the topic shown by linking aspects, not treating every aspect as separate
- breadth of knowledge and understanding.

Consider the following A-level practice question:

'The social turmoil of the late 1960s suggests that the CDU governments in the years 1949–69 had made little progress towards achieving a stable political consensus.' Assess the validity of this view. (25 marks)

Follow the same steps outlined in the essay writing guidance on page 186. This question has a main focus on 'similarity and difference' in respect of political development over two decades.

Your opening paragraph is crucial in setting out your understanding of the question and signposting your argument. The following paragraphs should take the reader step by step through the development of your argument. Finally, your concluding paragraph should offer a clear judgement that had been supported by 'well-selected, specific and precise' evidence throughout.

Working on interpretation skills

The SPD was in power for less than one-third of the lifetime of the FRG. Much has been written about the different characters and abilities of its leadership and the extent to which the role of its key leaders influenced the Party's electoral success. One of the key goals of your breadth study is to consider the interplay between cause and consequence. The following extracts and activity on pages 252–3 are designed to lead you towards your own judgement of how the SDP changed and developed in the years 1949–82. In so doing, you will need to balance your judgement of each leader's individual strengths, weaknesses and achievements against the political developments and circumstances they experienced. We have seen already in this part of our study that Konrad Adenauer seemed to represent the *Zeitgeist* of West Germany in the 1950s. How representative of their times were Schumacher, Brandt and Schmidt?

ACTIVITY

The extracts below and on page 253 offer three interpretations of the key SPD leaders in the years 1949–82. Using your understanding of the historical context, assess the effectiveness of each leader.

Having read the extracts:
- Identify the strengths and weaknesses of Schumacher, Brandt and Schmidt.
- Assess how convincing you find each interpretation and support your assessment with evidence from your study of this chapter.

Now answer the following A-level practice question:

Using your understanding of the historical context, assess how convincing the arguments in these three extracts are in relation to the effectiveness of SPD leaders in the years 1949–82. (30 marks)

Extract A

The Socialist leader Kurt Schumacher had been a resolute anti-Nazi. Arrested in July 1933 he spent most of the next twelve years in concentration camps, which permanently damaged his health and shortened his life. Gaunt and stooped, Schumacher, with his personal heroism and his unswerving insistence after the war on Germany's obligation to acknowledge its crimes, was not just the natural leader of the Socialists but the only national politician in post-war Germany who might have provided his fellow Germans with a clear moral compass [a strong personal sense of what is right and wrong]. But Schumacher, for all his many qualities, was curiously slow to grasp the new international regime in Europe. He disliked and distrusted communists and had no illusions about them; but he seems seriously to have believed that a demilitarized Germany would be left in peace to determine its fate, and that such circumstances would be propitious for the Socialists. He was thus virulently opposed to Adenauer's Western orientation. The trouble was that Schumacher's Social Democrats had nothing practical to offer instead. By the mid-fifties, with West Germany firmly tied into the Western Alliance, and with the Socialists' doom-laden economic prophecies demonstrably wrong, the SPD was out-in-the-cold. Only in 1959, seven years into the drab leadership of Ollenhauer, did a new generation of German Socialists formally abandon the party's seventy-year old commitment to Marxism and compromise with West German reality.

Adapted from *Postwar, A History of Europe since 1945* by Tony Judt, (Vintage), 2005.

Extract B

What Brandt offered to do was to integrate all those political forces who were discontented with Konrad Adenauer, with the long rule of Christian Democracy over German politics, with the stifling authoritarianism of the 1950s and with the lack of serious debate about National Socialism. He offered to renew the FRG for those who felt marginalized in Adenauer's state. At the end of the 1960s there was a strong feeling in large sections of German society that what was needed was a new beginning, and this was precisely what the young, popular and good-looking mayor of Berlin had to offer. The 1960s have been described as a 'hinge decade' [a period of ten years during which one era leads into another], in which the modernization of West German society, which had begun in the 1950s, accelerated and brought a break with many traditional aspects of German society. Willy Brandt symbolized that break in both foreign and domestic policies. What he stood for was a new vision of the nation, a more democratic nation, for sure, but also a nation which would no longer orient itself towards the old *Reich* founded by Bismarck in 1871. When he talked about 'our country' he meant, first and foremost, the FRG, and was willing to accept the division of Germany as the outcome of German history in the first half of the twentieth century.

Adapted from *Germany* by Stefan Berger, (Bloomsbury Academic), 2004.

Extract C

If Brandt represents the beating heart of German Social Democracy, Helmut Schmidt represents its more coldly calculating brain. A brilliant organizer and manager, who served as SPD Bundestag leader, Defence Minister, Finance Minister and 'Super Minister' of Finance and Economics before replacing Brandt as chancellor in 1974, Schmidt enjoyed one of the most successful careers in post-war German politics. All his success, however, could not win him the kind of deep admiration and affection that Brandt enjoyed. His reputation for hard-nosed politics, his determinedly realistic demeanour, even his success at attracting support from voters of the centre-right, all made him appear a bit too 'establishment' for the German Left that had cheered Brandt's idealistic [socialism]. That his chancellorship corresponded to the dismal 1970s, where ... the great hopes for social improvement gave way to the sombre reality of oil crises, driving bans, and budget cuts, further diminished his appeal in many traditional SPD circles. The final blow to his popularity within his own party came with his support for stationing the Pershing II and Cruise Missiles in Germany after 1979. What Schmidt saw as a necessary step in preserving the Atlantic Alliance, while also maintaining some momentum for *Ostpolitik*, many in the SPD saw as war mongering. The split he caused within the SDP partly led to the FDP's defection in 1982 and continues to overshadow his reputation.

Adapted from 'Building a Social Democratic Hall of Fame' by Ronald J. Ranieri, www.h-net.org, October 2005.

8

Economy, society and reunification, 1949–91

The first two sections of this chapter focus on economic and social change in the Federal Republic of Germany from 1949 to 1989. The final two sections examine the process of reunification from 1989 to 1990, and the transition to a new, united German state up to 1991. The following areas are covered:

- Economic developments, from the economic miracle of the 1950s to 1989
- A survey of social and cultural developments, and an assessment of the legacy of Nazism
- The drive to unification, including the role of Helmut Kohl and the problems of transition
- An overview of the condition of Germany by 1991, interweaving elements of political, economic and social change

A number of breadth issues run through this chapter: the nature and course of economic development and change; the extent of social and cultural change; and the role of key individuals and groups, particularly in relation to German reunification. Themes of change and continuity and cause and consequence underpin the chapter, which might be expressed through the following question:

What patterns of economic and social development can be identified in the FRG between 1949 and 1989, and what factors brought about the reunification of the two German states?

CHAPTER OVERVIEW

The Germany of 1989 was in many ways unrecognisable to that of 1949. For the majority of West Germans the misery of the post-war years was eliminated by an unanticipated, and almost unprecedented, economic recovery, which underpinned not only social stability but also the acceptance of democratic institutions. Those who had doubted the German mentality to make democracy work were proved spectacularly mistaken. Just as remarkable was the evolution of German society from its very traditional, highly paternalistic roots in the 1950s, to one in which social and political change was spearheaded by a post-Auschwitz generation, in which the young, and women, took leading roles.

German reunification, which was not on the political radar in 1987–88, suddenly exploded on the European and world scene in 1989. To a large extent, pressure 'from below' exerted by citizens in both West and East Germany drove the process of unification at a dizzying speed. Politicians in Germany and abroad struggled to keep abreast of the popular will. If Germany had been at a crossroads in 1949 and in 1969 it was even more so in 1991. Reunification had been accompanied by a heady mix of political idealism, hope and aspiration which would present the Germans and their leaders with significant challenges in the years to come.

1 Economic developments, 1948–89

The record of the West German economy during the four decades before unification shows significant achievement. The first decade, the 1950s, was that of the economic miracle. The 1960s saw consolidation and the first signs of trouble. The 1970s brought the oil shocks, the generous social welfare programmes, the rising deficits, and finally a loss of control. In the 1980s, new policies at home and a more stable environment abroad combined to put West Germany back on the path of modest, though sustained, growth.

The CDU era, 1949–69

How and why did the CDU management of the economy change in the mid-1960s?

Germany's post-war economic and political leaders viewed the economy as more than just an instrument for prosperity; it had to safeguard democracy and support a stable society. The economy had to be a vehicle for social harmony as well as economic progress. The intention was to establish an economic system that would provide equal opportunity for all and which would prevent the creation of underprivileged and 'outsider' social groups with no stake in the system. The most prominent individual to shape this new vision, radically different from the Third *Reich*, was Ludwig Erhard.

Erhard's first step was to reform the currency, replacing the *Reichsmark* (RM) with the *Deutschmark* (DM). This change, on 20 June 1948, was carried out in co-operation with the Western Allies. He also took the opportunity to abolish many Nazi, and Allied, rules and regulations in order to establish the basis of a new and free economy. The currency reform worked brilliantly. It created a widely accepted and valued legal tender. It provided the foundations for the West German economy and of the West German state.

The social market economy

The label 'social market' is significant. The term 'market' is important to distinguish it from the Nazi model of centralised control; the term 'social' is emphasised because West Germans wanted not only a competitive economy but one that would also provide a safety net for the more vulnerable and less privileged in society.

The kick-start and stimulus needed for the German economy also came from a number of external sources, particularly investment funds under the European Recovery Programme and the Allies' need for increased West German industrial production necessitated by the outbreak of the Korean War in 1950. The German readiness to work hard for low wages until productivity had risen was another important factor. However, the fundamental component for success was the revival of confidence caused by Erhard's reforms and by the introduction of the new currency.

The economic miracle

The West German boom that began in 1950 was truly astonishing. The growth rate of industrial production was 25 per cent in 1950 and 18.1 per cent in 1951. Growth continued at a high rate for most of the 1950s despite occasional minor slowdowns. By 1960 industrial production had risen to 2.5 times the level of

NOTE-MAKING

The important task in your notes in this section is to identify patterns, trends and turning points over 40 years. Changes in economic development can sometimes be linked to changes in government and changes in government policy – indeed, both Erhard and Schmidt lost office partly as a result of disputes over their handling of the economy, with their successors adopting different approaches to the economic issues of the day. Use the following headings to enable you to gain an appreciation of change and continuity, and the impact of different government approaches to the economy:
- The triumph of the social market economy, 1949–65
- Slowdown and stabilisation: the beginnings of intervention, 1966–69
- Balancing spending and recession, 1969–82
- *Die Wende* – a return to social market principles, 1982–89

Alongside this, consider identifying patterns of change and continuity decade by decade, as outlined in the opening paragraph to this section.

LOOK AGAIN

Remind yourself of the political context and wider consequences of currency reform in Chapter 6, page 210.

West Germany experienced a consumer boom in the 1950s, which included more foreign holidays, particularly to Italy. These shoppers are picking up some chianti in a West German supermarket in 1959 – the demand for Italian wine in West Germany more than doubled in the 1950s.

Gross Domestic Product (GDP) – The total value of all the goods and services produced by a nation's economy in one year.

LOOK AGAIN

It is important to remind yourself of the context of Germany's astonishing economic rejuvenation in the 1950s. Look again at the opening sections to Chapter 6 about the state of Germany in 1949.

Keynesian – John Maynard Keynes, a professor of economics at Cambridge, argued that governments should spend their way out of recession. His ideas contradicted orthodox economic thinking in the 1930s but gained considerable support after 1945.

1950 and far beyond any that the Nazis had reached during the 1930s in all of Germany. Gross Domestic Product (GDP) rose by two-thirds during the same decade. The number of people employed rose from 13.8 million in 1950 to 19.8 million in 1960, and the unemployment rate fell from 10.3 per cent to 1.2 per cent in the same period.

The economy did not grow as fast or as consistently in the 1960s as it had during the 1950s, in part because such rapid growth could not be sustained, in part because the supply of fresh labour from East Germany was cut off in 1961 by the building of the Berlin Wall, and in part because the *Bundesbank*, West Germany's central bank, concerned about a potential overheating of the economy, intervened to slow growth by limiting the money supply. The economy experienced its first minor recession in 1965.

As a result of the slowdown Kiesinger's Grand Coalition modified Erhard's *laissez-faire* social market philosophy. Karl Schiller, the new Economics Minister, argued strongly for legislation that would give the federal government greater powers to intervene in economic policy, and in 1967 the Law for Promoting Stability and Growth (the Stabilisation Law) was passed allowing greater co-ordination of federal, *Land* and local budget planning. This law was an important fine-tuning of the social market economy and more suited to a new era of global economic uncertainty. Schiller was more of a Keynesian than Erhard, and his Stabilisation Law meant that West German governments now had greater authority to direct the economy at times of recession and slowdown.

The Grand Coalition was remarkably successful in reversing the recession. Full employment was largely restored, economic growth resumed and a positive trade balance was achieved.

Participation in the EEC/EU

The growth of European integration had a major positive impact on the economy of the FRG. European economic integration began in 1951 when trade restrictions on coal and steel were dropped between Belgium, France, Italy, Luxemburg, the Netherlands and West Germany (the 'six'). Integration took a big step forward in the 1957 Treaty of Rome, by which the 'six' formed the European Economic Community (EEC) to establish a common or single market. Restrictions on trade and the movement of labour within the EEC continued to fall until the eventual formation of the European Union (EU) in 1993. A combination of political and security considerations, as well as economic benefits, lay behind the steps to integration: particularly the need for a rapid development in standards of living and economic performance as security against Communist expansion in a Europe divided by the Cold War. The main economic benefits to West Germany of closer European integration were:

- cheaper products, by the elimination of trade barriers within the EEC
- easier access through the EEC to foreign markets for West German exports
- savings achieved through common policies on agriculture and transport
- easier flow of skilled labour around the EEC.

By 1969 a common market had been pretty well achieved. A summit meeting held in the Hague in 1969 by the Heads of State of the 'six' decided on a further process of expansion towards closer European union. For Adenauer and his successors, economic integration had always been seen as a step towards longer-term goals: monetary union – the adoption of a common European currency; and political union – the creation of a single European state. Progress towards these goals was almost non-existent throughout the 1970s and 1980s, but by the end of the 1980s the Western European economic system had proved clearly superior to the command economies of the Soviet Union and the Eastern bloc, which was an important factor in leading to reunification.

> **Command economy** – A command, or planned, economy, as existed in the Soviet Union, is one in which the state rather than the free market or private business organises all aspects of the economy.

The SPD era, 1969–82

How successful was the SPD in dealing with the recurring economic crises of the 1970s?

Schiller's success in the Grand Coalition helped to give the SPD an electoral victory in 1969, forming a new coalition with the FDP. The SPD/FDP coalition expanded the West German social security system, substantially increasing the size and cost of the social budget. Social programme costs grew by over ten per cent a year during much of the 1970s. This increased government spending worsened inflation in the short term and, in the longer term, made it more difficult for all future German governments to balance their budgets.

Schiller himself resigned in June 1972, unable to break the inflationary spiral caused not only by increased social spending but also by a 'strong' *Deutschmark*: overseas currency speculators increasingly converted 'weaker' US dollars into Deutschmarks; this increase in the money supply prompted German banks to increase their lending, which led to higher prices, which in turn led to increased wage demands from German workers. Schiller, a member of the more right-wing FDP, was prevented by the SPD left-wing from making public spending cuts to balance the federal budget. His successor, Helmut Schmidt, immediately formed a Super Ministry to deal with the crisis by combining the posts of Minister of Finance and Economics, and promptly found it necessary to implement the cuts he had criticised Schiller for proposing!

Schmidt encountered great problems. Already facing inflationary pressures and spiralling import costs, at the end of 1973 the Organization of Petroleum

> ### Exchange rates
>
> In August 1971 the United States, concerned about its own weak economy, partly caused by an over-priced dollar on the international currency market, abandoned the system of fixed exchange rates which had operated since the end of the Second World War. This allowed the dollar to float against other international currencies, which prompted speculators to make profits by converting dollars into stronger currencies such as the *Deutschmark*. In general terms, this freeing-up of the international currency market caused an increase in the money supply, meaning it was easier to borrow, which worsened inflation not just in Germany but in all Western economies.

Exporting Countries (OPEC) imposed a huge increase in crude oil prices. Oil prices had been virtually unchanged since the 1950s. As a direct short-term measure, Schmidt introduced a temporary ban on Sunday driving.

Source A Helmut Schmidt, adapted from an interview in *The Guardian*, 22 December 2013.

During the Yom Kippur War the Saudis decided to squeeze the West by limiting their exports of oil, thereby allowing the prices to increase fourfold within a year. There was another increase at the end of the 1970s by which time oil prices were 10 to 20 times higher than they had been in the 1960s. This situation created a worldwide depression. In my view, it only needed one more step to lead to a worldwide depression.

> According to Schmidt in Source A, why were the oil crises of the 1970s so serious for West Germany?

The impact of the 1970s oil crises

OPEC was founded in 1960. By the 1970s it was dominated by Arab oil-producing countries. There were a series of energy crises between 1967 and 1979 caused by political problems in the Middle East but the most significant started in 1973. On 6 October (Yom Kippur in the Jewish calendar) Egypt and Syria attacked Israel. OPEC introduced an oil embargo on the United States and other countries who provided military support to Israel, and raised crude oil prices from $3 per barrel to $12 by 1974. Effectively, OPEC was using oil price increases as a political weapon against Israel and its allies. A further hike in prices occurred in 1979 following the loss of oil production as a result of the Iranian revolution which deposed the Shah of Iran. Oil prices fell in the 1980s as other countries increased their production when the Iran–Iraq war began in 1980.

The initial impact of the oil crisis on the FRG was substantial. Unemployment reached 1 million by 1975 and in the same year GDP fell by 1.4 per cent, the first time since the founding of the FRG that it had fallen so sharply. However, by 1976 the worst was over. Schmidt increased public spending and reduced taxation in order to create jobs. West German growth resumed and the inflation rate began to decline. Schmidt began to be known as *der Macher* (the achiever). The 1976 election campaign was largely fought and won on his government's positive economic record.

The economy slowed again in 1977 and further public sector investment was required to drag the economy into recovery. This policy was moderately successful, creating 160,000 additional jobs by 1977–79 but only at the cost of a larger budget deficit: rising from 31.2 billion DM in 1977 to 75.7 billion DM in 1981. The economy continued expanding through 1979 and 1980, helping the government win re-election in 1980. However, the upturn proved to be uneven and by early 1981 Schmidt once again faced decreasing growth and rising unemployment and inflation, falling from office in 1982 when the FDP lost confidence in Schmidt's economic strategy and withdrew from the coalition.

Overall, the FRG was able to weather the global financial storm far better than almost all other developed countries, keeping inflation to an average 4.7 per cent in the years 1973–79 compared to a western European average of 11.7 per cent, and unemployment rates never went above eight per cent. Schmidt also won much recognition for promoting European and Western co-operation in tackling common economic problems. Together with French President Giscard d'Estaing in 1975 he established regular meetings between the most important economic nations (the so-called G8). He was also instrumental in setting up the European Exchange Rate Mechanism (ERM) in March 1979 to promote monetary stability and to prevent damaging fluctuations in the value of European currencies.

The economy under Kohl, 1982–89

To what extent did the West German economy benefit from Kohl's return to social market principles?

As part of *die Wende*, Kohl began to implement policies to reduce the government role in the economy and to return more closely to the principles of the social market economy. Kohl won an election mandate for his new course in March 1983, with the SPD experiencing its worst defeat since 1961. Within its broader policy, the new government had several specific objectives:

- To reduce the federal deficit by cutting expenditure as well as taxes: annual budget increases were held at three per cent and, to avoid revenues falling too quickly, tax cuts were phased in over seven years.
- To remove many government restrictions and regulations.
- To improve flexibility in the labour market and to reduce employment, which was still over 2 million in 1983; Kohl introduced early retirement schemes and retraining programmes.
- To reduce the role of the state in the economy: the government carried through a series of privatisation measures, selling almost 10 million DM in shares of a range of state-owned institutions such as Volkswagen and Lufthansa; as a result of such measures the state role in the West German economy shrank from 52 per cent to 46 per cent of GDP between 1982 and 1990.

Limits

Although the policies of *die Wende* reinstalled a measure of confidence in the West German economy, progress came unevenly and haltingly. It would have been politically very unpopular to slash welfare spending, therefore the social budget remained high, and many government subsidies, such as those for farming and heavy industries, continued. During most of the 1980s the figures for growth and inflation improved but only slowly, and the figures on unemployment barely moved at all. There was little job growth until the end of the decade.

It also remained true that West German growth did not again reach the levels that it had managed in the early years of the FRG. There had been a pattern of a steady decline in the growth rate since the end of the 1950s, and a gradual increase in inflation except during or after a severe downturn. Global statistics also showed an overall decline in economic output and vitality: the West German share of total world production had grown from 6.6 per cent in 1965 to 7.9 per cent by 1975, but by 1987 it had fallen to 7.4 per cent, largely because of the more rapid growth of the economies of Japan and other Asian states.

Positives

By the late 1980s the West German economy began to grow more rapidly. The growth rate for GDP rose to 3.7 per cent in 1988 and 3.6 per cent in 1989, the highest levels of the decade, and the unemployment rate began to fall.

Overall, the results of the late 1980s appeared to justify the policies of *die Wende*. Tax rate reductions were producing greater revenues; although the public sector deficit had gone above the 1 trillion DM mark the public sector was growing more slowly than before. The year 1989 was the last year of the West German economy as a separate institution. From 1990 the West German economy began to reorient itself towards economic and political union with what had been East Germany, generating a whole new set of positive and negative distortions in the economy as the state turned its priorities to the costs of reunification.

ACTIVITY

In order to strengthen your overview of economic developments between 1945 and 1989, and to gain a visual perspective of change over time, produce two line graphs identifying fluctuations in the West German economy. Some additional research beyond this text may be needed to obtain a spread of statistics.

The first graph should focus on economic growth. Your horizontal line should be labelled 'Chronological range' and should be divided into years from 1945 to 1989; your vertical line should be labelled 'Growth range', extending from 0 to 25 percentage points, with 0 being 1949. Some approximation may be necessary but your aim is to identify the overall pattern of change.

The second graph should focus on unemployment. Again, your horizontal line is the 'Chronological range', and your vertical line is the 'Unemployment total', measured in units of hundreds of thousands.

KEY DATES: ECONOMIC DEVELOPMENTS, 1948–89

June 1948 Currency reform.

April 1951 The establishment of the European Coal and Steel Community (ECSC).

March 1957 The Treaty of Rome.

August 1961 The construction of the Berlin Wall.

June 1967 The Stabilisation Law.

December 1969 The Hague Summit.

October 1973 The first oil crisis.

January 1979 The second oil crisis.

March 1979 The European Exchange Rate Mechanism (ERM) was set up.

March 1983 Kohl implemented *die Wende*.

2 Social and cultural developments

This section offers an overview of social and cultural change throughout the four decades of the FRG. This is necessarily broad in scope and designed to provide a sense of change and continuity commensurate with a breadth study. The narrative is initially organised on a chronological basis, giving a sense of development from decade to decade, and subsequently followed by a number of thematic aspects.

Standards of living and social tensions

How did German society change and develop in the years 1949–89?

The first years after the Second World War were years of bitter poverty for the Germans. As we have seen, their land, their homes and their property lay in ruin. Millions of Germans had been expelled from Central and Eastern Europe with little more than the clothes on their backs. Tens of millions did not have enough to eat or to wear. Money had little effective value. Ballpoint pens, nylon stockings and cigarettes served as the accepted legal tender of the time. The outlook for the survivors was extremely grim: research carried out by the Western occupation forces in the immediate post-war years suggested that, on current projections, the average German would be able to buy a plate every five years, a pair of shoes every twelve years, and a suit every 50 years.

The 1950s

The economic miracle made a mockery of such pessimistic projections. By 1952, 450,000 houses were built, wages and salaries rose over 80 per cent between 1949 and 1955, and an insurance-based health and social welfare system had been an integral part of the social market economy since its inception in 1949. Pension entitlement was given a considerable boost in 1957, just before the national election, when Adenauer's government introduced a new Pension Act, establishing index-linked state pensions and increasing pensions by almost 75 per cent.

The first fifteen years of the FRG were characterised by almost unbroken advances in material well-being and affluence for many Germans. As real incomes began to rise from 1952–53, consumer demand increased in pace with the economy as a whole. Perhaps the greatest and most enduring symbol of West German growth and affluence is the car industry. BMW, based in Munich, Mercedes in Stuttgart, VW in Wolfsburg and Opel in Russelsheim produced hundreds of thousands of vehicles from seemingly never still production lines.

Nevertheless, there was a rather brittle, somewhat superficial quality to life in the 1950s which suggested a society, if not in denial, then blinkered in terms of its refusal to enter into any open discussion about its immediate past. In hindsight, it can be observed in the intensity with which an entire generation focused almost exclusively on work and material enrichment. You could see it in the tension of family life; the war had created a communication gap between wives and husbands, neither volunteering their experiences of home and battle front beyond banal generalisations. Often relatively cramped housing conditions and long hours at work added to the separation and strain. If there was a distance between husbands and wives, there was an even greater gap between the generations. Young people growing into adulthood in the 1950s increasingly began to question the health of a society that refused to talk about the past and which encouraged the pretence of happy families.

NOTE-MAKING

This is inevitably a wide-ranging section of study where you need to acquire a sense of change and continuity and similarity and difference in social and cultural trends. Perhaps the easiest approach is to organise your notes chronologically in order to obtain the bigger picture. Focus on identifying the key characteristics of each decade – perhaps by considering the state as developing through life stages – and finish this off by producing a comparison chart of West German society at the start of the 1950s and how that society had changed by the later 1980s:

- The 1950s: renewal and rebirth: first steps
- The 1960s: adolescent crisis
- The 1970s: growing pains: progressive and traditional values in conflict
- The 1980s: entering maturity: a search for identity

LOOK AGAIN

Look again at the opening to Chapter 6 to remind yourself of the condition of Germany in 1945. It is important to remember this context when evaluating subsequent developments in the Federal Republic. Zero Hour, or *Stunde Null*, was how Germans characterised the utter devastation and hopelessness facing the survivors of the Third *Reich*.

The 1960s

The 1960s proved to be a decade of transition. By its end the CDU monopoly of power had been broken and a new generation, angry at the bland conformity of West German society and a seemingly self-satisfied, materialist way of life, had taken to the streets to voice its complaints, and the older generation was pushed out of its collective, complacent amnesia about the Nazi legacy. According to Mary Fulbrook, 'by the late 1960s there was a political polarisation of new left against "bourgeois materialist" right, of young against old'.

The Nuremberg Trials in 1945–46 had been criticised as 'victors' justice' by the Adenauer generation, but the 1960s saw the first genuine debates about German war crimes:

- The trial of Adolf Eichmann in Israel in 1961 brought the Holocaust directly and indelibly into the wider public domain; it could no longer be denied.
- In 1963, the Frankfurt trials, bringing many Auschwitz perpetrators to justice, broadened the debate about German war crimes that had been closed throughout the 1950s.
- Also in 1963, a play written by Rolf Hochhuth, entitled *The Deputy*, criticised the Pope's silence in the face of the extermination of the Jews and opened up a wider, and highly divisive, discussion about the role of the 'bystander', the German who acquiesced in Nazi crimes by their inaction.

By 1966, the FRG was entering an early-life crisis. Student protest, anti-Vietnam War demonstrations and the emergence of alternative political movements, including the far right NPD and the Communist DKP, all signalled a new desire to come to terms with the past and an idealistic demand for greater openness in German society.

The 1970s

This decade is sometimes referred to as that of the two-thirds society. As seen earlier in this chapter, and in Chapter 7, economic recession and terrorism dominated this decade. The increase in the number of the long-term unemployed to around 2 million of the working-age population by the end of the decade raised fears of a new wealth gap, with an underclass of guest workers predominating in this bottom one-third of society. In addition, the government's repressive response to the growth of terrorism under both Brandt and Schmidt raised fears that increasing government and police powers threatened to undermine the liberal fabric of the state, and hinted at a return of authoritarian tendencies. The 1972 Decree on Radicals in particular aroused criticism among civil rights advocates; it gave government the power to sack many thousands of public sector employees if found guilty of left-wing connections. By the end of the decade, close to 10,000 West Germans were under police surveillance as terrorist sympathisers. To many this seemed an over-reaction, and cast a shadow over a state that in other respects had developed into a model progressive, democratic society.

The 1980s

By the 1980s West Germany had acquired a cosmopolitan appearance, clearly influenced by the broader cultural Americanisation of Western society. Nevertheless, old and new cultural forms co-existed, with many local and *Land* traditions persisting. Germany's wider transformation and rehabilitation from a post-war pariah state to one that was internationally oriented was remarkable. Young Germans may have been resolutely materialistic yet they were also strongly idealistic, attracted to environmentalism and Green politics.

Green politicians arriving for work in the *Bundestag* wearing knitted sweaters and casual trousers rather than the de rigueur suit and tie symbolised this generational difference. Those 'blessed by a late birth' (too young to be tainted by Nazism) were self-assured and confident in their modern identity as both proud Germans and proud Europeans.

There were continuing social tensions in the 1980s, often linked by the persistence of unemployment and concerns over immigration. **Structural unemployment**, remaining at roughly ten per cent, was a spectre that refused to go away and led to a growing debate over immigration which scratched away at the veneer of tolerance in West German society. A 1982 opinion poll found that two-thirds of West Germans believed that there were too many foreigners in the country. Though social stratification and class differences were generally becoming outwardly less visible, a significant gap had opened up between the top 30 per cent, a university-educated, salaried and aspirational middle class intent on creating a leisure society, and the unskilled, foreign immigrants who constituted about a quarter of the 'bottom' 15 per cent in German society, populating the poorer areas of German cities.

Though many guest workers had sunk German roots, few ethnic Germans considered them worthy of German citizenship. Kohl's government went along with this anti-immigrant mood, though its efforts at promoting repatriation met with little practical success. By 1990 West Germany's population of guest workers and their families totalled a substantial minority of about 6 million.

The effect of the Nazi legacy

The greatest legacies of Nazism were division, the loss of national self-esteem and guilt. The first of these disappeared in 1990, though many difficulties associated with reunification still persist; the rehabilitation of the nation was achieved gradually and self-esteem was much restored in the two decades after division, but the issue of guilt persisted throughout the life of the Federal Republic and beyond. Indeed, a fourth national Holocaust memorial was unveiled in Berlin in 2014.

The legacy of Nazism is a complex, multi-layered issue and is one which still provokes polarised reactions. Inextricably entwined with this debate is the nature of the German character and the strength of German democracy. The central question in 1949 among Germans and the Allies alike was whether the Federal Republic could provide a stable democracy, or whether Weimar conditions would re-surface, resulting in the re-appearance of authoritarian or semi-authoritarian government and institutions, and lead to a revival of Nazism. Whether Nazism originated in the nature and soul of the German character, or whether it was an 'exceptional' blip in German political development, is a question which refuses to go away.

The Nazi restoration

In the decades following 1949 the West German state did indeed prosper and a stable, liberal democracy did emerge, strong enough to weather a number of political, economic and social crises. Nevertheless, the incompleteness of denazification, which kept many high-ranking former Nazis in prominent political, business and public roles, meant that the National Socialist legacy was kept alive as a painful, chronic ulcer on the national identity. Despite a Reparations Treaty, accepted in 1952 by the new state of Israel, under which it received 3.5 billion DM in compensation for the Holocaust, any meaningful national debate about the crimes of the Nazis was prevented by Adenauer's inclination to sweep the issue under the carpet.

> **Structural unemployment** – A more permanent form of unemployment caused by underlying changes in the economy.

This situation was exacerbated by the sheer number of ex-Nazis who held high office in post-war West Germany. Prominent among these was Hans Globke, Adenauer's chief of staff in the years 1953–63. Globke had been one of the authors of the 1935 Nuremberg Laws. Another was the German president from 1959 to 1969, Heinrich Lübke, who had worked for the Nazis building prison camps with slave labour; he was forced to resign when this became public knowledge. Georg Kiesinger, chancellor of the Grand Coalition, had been an NSDAP Party member from 1933 to 1945, allowing his student critics to brand him a 'regime conformist'.

Greater openness

This cloak of silence was to be challenged in the 1960s. A new generation demanded a much more open confrontation with the National Socialist past, which was initially pushed centre-stage in the middle of the decade by the series of Auschwitz trials held in Frankfurt between 1963 and 1968, in which 22 police and SS functionaries were found guilty of war crimes. The extent of the damning documentation released, and the harrowing nature of the witness testimonies given, raised the public discussion of Holocaust crimes to unprecedented levels. The left-of-centre era under SDP leadership between 1969 and 1982 signified a new, more open political culture, akin to a second re-birth for the Republic.

By the 1980s the debate over the Nazi legacy had tempered but not disappeared. Kohl's controversial meeting with Ronald Reagan at Bitburg in 1985 demonstrated that sensibilities surrounding the legacy simmered on. Kohl's attempts to rehabilitate the 'honourable' *Wehrmacht* by separating them from the SS and complicity in Nazi crimes raised further controversy. Another manifestation of the continuing debate about the origins of National Socialism appeared in the late 1980s in the so-called 'historians' dispute', with some conservative academics, such as Ernst Nolte, arguing that Nazism and its crimes had grown out of opposition to the greater crimes of Soviet Communism. The economic malaise of the 1980s fanned neo-Nazi outbursts over immigration issues, threatening to undermine social stability.

The emotional legacy of Nazism persisted, therefore, throughout the life of the Federal Republic, not so much in failing to recognise the crimes of Hitler's regime but in the persistent belief of many Germans who had experienced the Third *Reich* that they too were victims, with no or little complicity in the regime's crimes. It was not until the 1990s, following reunification, that a more nuanced, less black and white debate over guilt was to take place. However, on balance, it is clear to see that the post-Hitler generation was a different German people, fundamentally democratic in outlook and European in character.

Conclusion

By 1989 German society seemed once again at a crossroads, as it had been in 1949 and 1969, caught between an emerging Green, progressive consensus, criticised by conservatives as pacifist and romantic, and a new CDU/CSU era signalling a desire among moderate centre-right Germans for a slowing down of the pace of social change and turning to introspective bouts of nostalgia for a lost homeland. This was symbolised by the astonishing popularity in 1984 of an eleven-part television series: *Heimat: A German Chronicle*, which dramatised twentieth-century German history as experienced in the rural, small-town Rhineland. However, alongside this continuing quest to define German national identity in the post-war era was an unwavering commitment in support of the European dream. The belief that European identity and national identity could exist side by side, something the British have always struggled to accept, was widespread among the German political elites, whether right- or left-wing.

Source B offers a broad overview of the state of the German nation at the end of the 1980s.

Source B From *German History in Modern Times* by William W. Hagen, (Cambridge University Press), 2012, pp. 382, 384.

On the eve of the Berlin Wall's fall on November 9, 1989, unemployment, unresolved questions of German national identity, disputes over immigration, and indecisiveness over Communism's deepening crisis in the neighbouring Soviet empire clouded West German skies. Conflicts between Greens and Social Democrats weakened opposition to Chancellor Kohl's CDU-FDP government.

If the centre-right parties sometimes posed as 'more German' than the moderate left parties, they were not reluctant to pride themselves on their internationalism. To be 'citizens of the world' – that is, cosmopolitan – was a badge of honour. Well-educated, young West Germans travelled the world extensively, commonly spoke foreign languages fluently, and scorned narrow provincialism. In 1989, the Federal Republic embodied a new, multiform and conflict-beset German nation.

> To what extent does Hagen in Source B offer an optimistic view of West Germany in 1989?

Cultural developments

What cultural trends can be identified in the years 1949–89?

It is difficult to reach definitive judgements about social and cultural trends when studying such recent history. Nevertheless, it is possible to begin to discern some broader changes in behaviour and morals.

The position of women

The Basic Law declared that men and women were equal but in the 1950s there was initially little perceptible change from the prevailing pre-war values of *Kinder, Kirche, Küche*, the stereotypical, traditional female roles of children, church and kitchen. Women, for example, could still be dismissed from civil service jobs when they married. Despite the post-war shortage of males, marriage remained West German society's ideal, with employment and social welfare models all based on the male as the natural breadwinner.

This pattern persisted through to the mid-1960s, when conformism began to shatter as young women, within the context of the broader generational revolt of this decade, began to demand meaningful emancipation from their perceived subservient gender role. The SPD era saw significant gains for women as a coherent women's movement blossomed. Women achieved equal rights in marriage in 1977 and divorce instigated by women became easier; abortion was largely legalised in 1976. Progress in education was slower. The percentage of women going into higher education increased only gradually from 31 to 41 per cent between 1970 and 1989, and was only beginning to equal male numbers by the early 1980s. Overall, the persistence of a traditional, patriarchal family and work structure was relatively marked in West Germany; it was only in 1980 that a separate federal office was created responsible for women's affairs.

Youth

We have seen already how the 1950s was a period when the searching questions about Germany's Nazi past were largely avoided. To a certain extent this was true of German youth in the 1950s. The traditional view of this period being a rather static time in youth culture is beginning to be challenged as more oral history is being examined, but it seems apparent that this was an essentially apolitical period of time for German youth. The onslaught of

Americanisation and the pre-dominant culture of consumption caught young people in a rising tide of new opportunities – rock and roll, motorcycles, Hollywood films and vacations abroad – all of which surfaced as distractions from the more immediate past. There was also a rising secularism among youth evident in the declining membership of young people in Church organisations. For example, Catholic youth groups in the 1920s had about 1.5 million members; by the early 1960s this had shrunk to about 500,000.

By the 1960s and 1970s West German youth, as discussed above, had developed a distinctive political voice, though it is difficult to know with any certainty why some of the stridently anti-materialist youth of the 1960s should embrace the terroristic violence of the 1970s. Although the middle decades of the Federal Republic witnessed, as in West German society as a whole, a decline in class and religious differences among young people, young people were increasingly seeing themselves as West German. Expectations of a re-united Germany had dwindled and fallen off the political radar of the young, especially after Brandt's series of treaties in the early 1970s seemed to confirm and further legitimise the post-war boundaries in Europe. Interestingly, in the aftermath of these changes, West Berlin, isolated within the East, began to develop a distinctive youth sub-culture of its own. Heavily subsidised but still rather neglected by the Bonn government, West Berlin attracted a significant number of young men taking advantage of the exemption of West Berliners from military service. The city gained a reputation as a refuge for 'alternative' youth looking to escape the West German fixation with making everything economically viable. Berlin has carried this reputation through to the present day, advertising itself as Europe's alternative scene and party capital.

By the 1980s, West German youth had become enormously cosmopolitan and varied in their attitudes, but the strength of the peace and environmental movements in this decade serves to remind us that many young West Germans were acutely conscious of their country's continuing position on the front line of the Cold War. If a war were to be fought, it would be in their backyard. Well-fed, well-travelled, expensively but casually clothed, increasingly vegetarian or alternative in their lifestyles, even West Germany's youth was modified and shaped by its post-war political heritage.

Religion

The post-war division left roughly an equal number of Roman Catholics and Protestants in West Germany. Freedom of religion was guaranteed by Article 4 of the Basic Law. Most West Germans continued to pay a voluntary Church tax in the post-war era, though this consensus began to falter in the 1980s as Church membership began to decline; almost 1 million Catholics and about 1.2 million Protestants left the Church in this decade, with many beginning to withdraw from paying Church tax. This reflected not only similar trends throughout Western society, but also the development of an increasingly materialist and secular West German society.

Literature

Perhaps the two greatest literary figures in the life of the Federal Republic were Heinrich Böll (1917–85) and Günther Grass (1927– 2015). Böll was the most significant of the *Trümmerliteratur* (literature of the rubble) group of writers. This group was the mouthpiece of a generation of writers trying to come to grips with the crimes of the Nazi era and the psychology and values of the new Republic. Böll, a devoted, anti-war Catholic, was the focus of much criticism from conservative Germans for his liberal views on religious and social issues.

Yet he was also unafraid to criticise what he saw as the moral decay of an over-materialistic and over-authoritarian West German society. In many ways Böll was Germany's outstanding literary voice of the 1960s and 1970s. He was awarded the Nobel Prize for Literature in 1972. His work is a starting point for a critical understanding of the moral and ethical dilemmas facing the post-Nazi generations.

Günther Grass occupied a more centre-left political position than the liberal Catholic Böll, but was also a stern critic of West German society. His most famous work is *The Tin Drum*, published in 1959, part of a trilogy in which he explores Germany's Nazi past. Grass spoke out against all forms of fanaticism and totalitarianism. He was active in politics in the 1960s, campaigning for the SPD and working as a speechwriter for Willy Brandt, and in the 1970s and 1980s he was a supporter of the peace and environmental movements. In 1999, Grass too was awarded the Nobel Prize for Literature.

Sport: The Miracle of Bern, 4 July 1954

West German sporting development paralleled its economic and political revival. Sport has often been seen as a measure of national health and West Germany's pantheon of sporting achievement cannot fully be told in this brief overview. West Germany enjoyed great success in particular in field and track athletics and in the 1980s produced two of the world's finest ever tennis players: Boris Becker and Steffi Graf. However, it is for its achievements in football that West Germany was most renowned, winning the World Cup in 1954, 1974 and 1990. It was the first of these victories, achieved in the Swiss capital Bern, which overshadows almost every other German sporting success.

Academic studies have been written about the effect of this victory on the German psyche. Never before or since has there been such a big discrepancy between the two teams in a World Cup final. The underdog West Germany was up against the great Hungarian side of the 1950s, undefeated in thirty games over four years. The West German team had already been beaten 8:3 by Hungary in the first round, and within ten minutes of the start of the final, Hungary led 2:0. Germany managed two goals before half-time to level the match and scored the winning goal six minutes from the end of full-time.

The impact on the nation was immense. The writer Friedrich Delius commented: 'a guilt-ridden, inhibited nation was suddenly reborn'; the historian Joachim Fest called it 'the true birth of the country'. According to Franz Beckenbauer, the most famous, sublime West German footballer of the 1960s and 1970s:

'For anybody who grew up in the misery of the post-war years, Bern was an extraordinary inspiration. The entire country regained its self-esteem.'

The Miracle of Bern was iconic, encapsulating in 90 minutes the revival of a nation. The 2003 film of the same name is a magnificent portrait of post-war Germany, a must-watch film for a student of this period. The victory spawned a popular saying of the time: 'We are something again', and the words of the German radio commentator, Herbert Zimmermann, as the Germans scored their third goal, have become the most famous in German sporting history: 'Rahn shoots. Goal! Goal! Goal! Goal! Germany leads 3:2 … call me mad, call me crazy!'

KEY DATES: SOCIAL AND CULTURAL DEVELOPMENTS

1954 The Miracle of Bern.

1959 *The Tin Drum* by Günther Grass was published.

1963 The Frankfurt trials began.

1972 The Decree on Radicals.

1977 Equal marriage rights for women.

1984 *Heimat* was televised.

3 The drive to reunification

Reunification had a momentum of its own. One historian, Lothar Kettenacker, in his book *Germany since 1945*, argues that for the politicians involved it was more 'crisis management' than 'rational determination'. Kettenacker suggests that East Germany was like a 'downhill train out of control'. This section outlines the context and background to reunification before going on to consider the process itself, and particularly the role played by the West German chancellor Helmut Kohl. The section ends with an assessment of the impact of reunification on Germany by 1991.

The situation in East Germany

What were the underlying weaknesses of the East German state?

On 10 December 1989, one month after the opening of the Berlin Wall, the *Sunday Times* newspaper ran a feature under the headline 'House of Cards', reporting the chaotic situation in East Germany in the days immediately following the collapse of SED control. A 34-year-old construction engineer and Party member, Kurt Hagewald, was asked whether the Party (the SED) could survive: 'No, it cannot recover. To save our skins, we have opened the Wall, and now we cannot close it. We thought we were the alternative to capitalism, but the leaders betrayed us. It should be dissolved'.

All East Germans had known that their system was corrupt, that former leader Erich Honecker and his entourage, for example, had well-appointed private homes, luxury cars and soft toilet paper, but the extent of the corruption which was emerging, among even relatively minor officials, took people by surprise and emotions were running high. The fear in West German political circles was that this outpouring of anger against state officials could become a *Volkszorn*, an outpouring of popular fury, turning the so-called 'peaceful revolution' into a wave of bloody retribution. The term *Volkszorn* also had dark connotations for many Germans: it was used by the Nazis to describe their pogroms against the Jews.

▲ Crowds of people at the new border crossing at Bernauer Strasse, 12 November 1989.

The speed of events following the opening of the Berlin Wall took everyone by surprise, not least those actively involved in driving those events. Indeed, K. Jarausch, in his book *The Rush to German Unity*, argues that this was the most striking feature of the whole process. No one in November 1989 envisaged how quickly the reunification momentum would pick up speed; however, as Source C below indicates, 'reunification' itself was ceasing to be a taboo word in both East and West Germany.

Source C Adapted from an article in the *Sunday Times*, 10 December 1989.

Interviewed last Friday by the East German newspaper 'Der Morgen', Willy Brandt was quoted as saying: 'The existence of two German states remains a basic consideration'; however, Eberhard Diepgen, a former Conservative mayor of Berlin, declared that 'sooner or later the people of East Germany will decide for unity'.

Diepgen's looks the more realistic assessment. Although the communist party has publicly accepted responsibility for 'the worst crisis in the history of the German Democratic Republic', it was a typically mistaken analysis. The communists are responsible for the entire history of the GDR, its very existence and its lack of democracy. Now democracy is about to destroy it. The Communist party and the state it created were identical, and the people's revenge will not be only against the party.

> What differences of opinion are expressed by Brandt and Diepgen (Source C)? What conclusion is reached by the author of this article?

The causes of East German collapse

It is a matter of considerable historical debate whether the GDR was doomed to fail from the beginning. Though a detailed study of the collapse of East Germany falls outside of the strict limits of your studies, it is useful to have an understanding of the main causes of its dramatic collapse. This is developed on page 271 but a summary is provided here.

- It is possible to argue that the GDR was living on borrowed time ever since the building of the Berlin Wall in 1961. Since it could only hold on to its citizens by walling them in, it had, therefore, no hope of long-term survival.
- The collapse of Communism in Eastern Europe and the liberalising policies from 1985 of Mikhail Gorbachev in the Soviet Union severely undermined the fabric of East German Communism.
- As the momentum towards *détente* in East–West relations gathered pace in the late 1980s the external factors dividing Germany began to disintegrate, leading, albeit tentatively at first, to a climate of international approval for reunification.
- The Civic Revolution in the GDR – its so-called 'democratic awakening', suggests that the SED's refusal to tolerate loyal criticism meant that its critics had little alternative but to pursue a 'revolution from below'.
- Domestic sentiment in West Germany, fed by *Ostpolitik* since the late 1960s, supported the East German protesters, hoping that their actions would lessen division between the two Germanys.
- The opening of the border between Hungary and Austria in May 1989, allowing East Germans to travel to the West via Hungary, opened the floodgates to an exodus that had been closed off by the Berlin Wall since 1961.

Once the borders were opened there seemed little prospect that the GDR could survive. By this point all the ingredients for a chain reaction were in place: civil unrest, a Soviet regime unwilling to intervene in East German internal affairs, and swelling emigration. It was left to the politicians in both East and West Germany to try to manage the pace of change demanded by the people on the streets. This task was increasingly taken up by Helmut Kohl.

The Civic Revolution

The Civic Revolution is the umbrella term for the nationwide protest movements which developed in East Germany in the late 1980s. A variety of groups had been formed demanding reform and change: the Civic Movement, New Forum, Democracy Now, Democratic Awakening, assorted feminist groups and the Greens. A defining point in the Civic Revolution occurred on 9 October 1989 when 70–100,000 protesters defied the *Stasi* to gather on the streets of Leipzig; the protest rocked the state and set in motion the final and decisive month of the 'revolution from below'.

Stasi – The Socialist Unity Party of Germany (SED) governed the GDR for 40 years without ever being legitimised in a democratic election. The SED maintained its position of power through a huge security apparatus. The cornerstone of this system was the Ministry for State Security (MfS), better known as the *Stasi*, which was founded in 1950.

The role of Helmut Kohl

How important was Helmut Kohl in the drive to unification?

Unification was a long way from the minds of those in East Germany who voiced their dissent in the autumn of 1989. Groups within the Civic Movement wanted to deal with shortcomings in the GDR; ultimately they wanted public debate and democratic decision-making by a responsible and accountable government. Yet what they got, within a year, was unification with the capitalist West, on the terms of the West.

Why this occurred had much to do with the energetic intervention of Helmut Kohl. In 1989 Kohl's chancellorship was going nowhere fast, characterised by political scandal and growing electoral support for the left- and right-wing elements of German politics. The German Question was thrust at him from out of the blue; the political and economic problems resulting from the collapse of East German government authority threatened to push both East and West Germany into crisis.

Perhaps the most significant of these problems, and the most important factor which led Kohl to move as quickly as he did towards unification, was the dire economic state of the GDR. From the summer of 1989, and in ever-increasing numbers from the opening of the Berlin Wall, GDR citizens continued to leave for the West for better material prospects. It was becoming clear with each passing month that the GDR could not survive economically on its own for very long. The loss of skilled labour, the disruption of production, the collapse of local administration and the associated social and psychological impact of collapse were all contributing to a growing crisis in the GDR which the government could not control.

There were also other factors pushing Kohl to action besides the economic meltdown in the East:

- The far-right, so-called 'Republicans' within West Germany, already making the political headlines for their anti-immigration agenda, had put re-unification at the top of their campaign priorities.
- The Bavaria-based CSU was also putting increasing pressure on its sister party to harness the re-unification momentum.
- Something needed to be done to limit the growing refugee crisis hitting West Germany: in November 1989 alone 133,000 East Germans came to the West; if this flood was maintained, West Germany's welfare system would be overwhelmed.
- On a pragmatic level, Kohl faced elections in 1990 and his poll standing was already low; politically, he could not afford to be seen as apathetic towards the East German crisis.

If Kohl was to deliver unification he would have his work cut out to convert a powerful number of opposition voices, both at home and abroad:

- Left-wing opinion in Germany was opposed to a Western-led, capitalist takeover of the East; even Willy Brandt expressed doubts.
- A new leadership had assumed power in East Germany on 13 November under the chairmanship of Lothar Maiziere of the CDU, with Hans Modrow, a moderate SED reformer as Prime Minister, which was resistant to a Western takeover and was determined to find a third way, guaranteeing the survival of a separate East German state.

- Mikhail Gorbachev, the Russian leader, was anxious to slow down the whole process, insistent that any unification should occur only as part of a wider European rapprochement; he was also under fire from the old guard in the Soviet Union, deeply suspicious of his attempts to reform Communism.
- The British and French, despite their long public support for German re-unification, privately warned George Bush, the American President, and Gorbachev that they opposed any swift process of unification; Margaret Thatcher told Gorbachev bluntly that Britain did not want German reunification.
- Germany's smaller neighbours too were naturally anxious about any revival of Germany as a potentially expansionist Great Power.

Kohl's decision to take the initiative was, therefore, both a leap of faith and a leap in the dark. As already suggested, there continues to be considerable debate about Kohl's motivation. His Ten-Point Plan, announced on 28 November 1989, outlining a tentative five-year process towards German confederation, took everyone by surprise; he had not even consulted his FDP coalition partners. Some have praised him as a visionary statesman, others have seen him as a pure opportunist, salvaging his own political career by harnessing himself to a populist bandwagon. Probably it was something of both. Kohl, however, saw perhaps faster than most that a quick solution was essential if chaos in Germany was to be avoided. He was under immense pressure to act as Communism collapsed in the East.

WORKING TOGETHER

Kohl's Ten-Point Plan outlined a process which he envisaged taking five years or more to complete, with point 10 being the final goal. Divide into groups to consider the steps within this process. As a first task, are you able to bracket any points together as linked, or connected, developments?

Secondly, as outlined above, Kohl undoubtedly anticipated opposition, particularly from:

- Germany's left-wing
- the USSR
- Great Britain
- France
- Germany's smaller neighbours: Holland, Belgium, Denmark, Czechoslovakia, Poland
- Modrow and the East German reform movements.

Look more deeply at each of these factors. Without looking at the narrative that follows, discuss which factors you think might present Kohl with his greatest obstacles. It could be that one person is allocated to research an individual factor, reporting back to the whole group. The purpose of the activity is to reinforce in your mind the complexity of the situation facing Kohl. There can be a tendency to assume, with hindsight, that reunification in 1990 was inevitable, given the situation of collapse in East Germany at the time, but this was far from the case; there were a number of factors working against this outcome.

The rush to unity

Why was German reunification achieved so quickly?

As outlined already, the rapidity with which unification came about astonished all participants and, at times, seemed beyond their control. Rudolf Seiters was a key German negotiator during the reunification process. Source D is from an interview he gave to 'Spiegel Online' in March 2009.

Source D Rudolf Seiters, interviewed on 'Spiegel Online', March 2009.

The decisive day was 19 December 1989, when Chancellor Helmut Kohl addressed hundreds of thousands of people at Dresden's *Frauenkirche* (Church of Our Lady). There was an unbelievable atmosphere. Black-red-and-gold German flags were fluttering everywhere. In my entire political life, I have never known a state leader to leave a visiting leader alone with his population. That clearly happened because they expected Helmut Kohl to generate applause while they feared the SED would be greeted with catcalls. It was then that we realized that this regime was nearing its end. We saw a realistic chance for German unity.

> Why did Seiters (Source D) believe that 19 December was a turning point?

Acceleration

Kohl's rapturous greeting in Dresden helps explain his decision to reconsider his timetable for unification; Dresden convinced Kohl that unification was possible, and desirable, in a shorter time period than originally envisaged. This feeling was reinforced when the Brandenburg Gate was symbolically opened on 22 December; a festival spirit was manifest as both East and West German politicians made positive speeches and walked together through the breach in the Wall. Furthermore, President Bush provided unlimited support and encouragement. In order to limit the fears and worries among Germany's neighbours about the future political orientation of a reunited Germany, Kohl always spoke of German unity within the context of the European Union. He viewed German unity and European unity as two sides of the same coin.

If momentum was added by the events in Dresden and Berlin in December, a further acceleration occurred in February. Elections had been scheduled in the East for March 1990. On 1 February Kohl met with the leaders of the East German CDU and the parties which looked to ally themselves with it. After what Kohl called a 'difficult meeting' – Kohl had been critical of the East German CDU 'dancing to the tune' of the SED for the past four decades – these parties formed a right-of-centre Alliance for Germany. Kohl threw himself into the campaign to get them elected.

Following this meeting Kohl travelled to Moscow. Gorbachev was increasingly coming to the view that European stability would be better served by unification; West German economic aid to a financially insolvent Soviet Union, with more promised, was an added factor in explaining his diminishing opposition to unification. Kohl returned to Germany convinced that he had Gorbachev's support in principle, and added further momentum by announcing that a currency reform would follow the March elections should the Alliance be successful.

The 18 March election, 1990

There were roughly three political groupings, or camps, in the GDR by this point:

- The **PDS**: largely isolated from the other groupings; it stood on a left-wing platform, proclaiming the virtues of socialism, though distancing itself from the former SED; it favoured the continuation of a separate East Germany.
- Bündnis 90, and a number of smaller, linked parties wanted to hold on to elements of GDR separatism; it feared that the rabid consumerism of West Germany would destroy the East's socialist achievements.

> **The Party of Democratic Socialism (PDS)** – Founded on 16 December 1989, this party was the legal successor to the SED.

● Much the larger camp consisted of the main GDR parties: the Alliance, the SPD and the League of Free Democrats (Liberals); all promoted unity, merely disagreeing on aspects of process, with the Alliance and the Liberals favouring the fastest practical route – unification under Article 23 of the Basic Law – while the SPD favoured a new constitution, which was a much slower and more complicated process.

Kohl used the election to push his unification agenda. The main theme of his six major campaign speeches promoted prosperity through unification. He promised to 'build a flourishing land together' and, against the advice of the German Federal Bank: 'we want savers to know that when the change in currency comes it will be at one-for-one for them'. His opponents accused him of attempting to bribe the voters, and of being even more economical with the truth when he criticised the SPD as long-term partners of the Communists. The election returned an overwhelming mandate for Kohl and unification. The Alliance won 40.8 per cent of the vote, nearly twice as much as the second-place SPD, in a 93.4 per cent turnout, higher than any West German election.

The currency union

The Currency Union Treaty was signed on 18 May 1990 and took effect on 1 July. Problems occurred in the run-up to the union. West Germans travelled to the East to snap up bargains, particularly in food stuffs, leading to shortages; East German shops began to fill with West German goods at prices Easterners could not afford. Many of the longer-term economic problems following reunification have been attributed to the unrealistic 1:1 currency union. Although West German investment in the East almost doubled from DM 48.3 to 88.3 billion in the years 1990–92, and real income increased by 28 per cent between 1989 and 1991, East Germans were generally worse off due to higher prices for food and services. As a consequence of the 1:1 union, much of East Germany's production became uneconomic. The currency union was, indeed, a symbolic and practical act but flawed in its over-generous detail; it was as much an act of political calculation as it was an economic necessity.

Overcoming international barriers

Even given the compelling economic argument for reunification, and the committed leadership of Kohl to reach that goal at the earliest opportunity, it is doubtful that unification could have occurred as it did without the support of Mikhail Gorbachev. The 'miracle of Moscow' in February was followed up by Kohl with another face-to-face meeting with Gorbachev in the Caucasus that took place 14–16 July. Much has been written of their easy personal relationship and, if not crucial, this was certainly a significant factor in enabling co-operation. Nevertheless, Gorbachev struck a hard bargain for his support for unification. Kohl had to agree to domestic troop reductions, to provide considerable financial and technical aid to the Soviet Union, and to pay for the removal of Soviet troops from former GDR territory by 1994. Ultimately, of all the factors enabling unification, it came down to convincing the Soviet leader to agree, and Helmut Kohl did the trick.

Conclusion

Kohl seized the opportunity that history gave him. He was able, through genuine belief, to convince the people and the main international players, that a united Germany would not be a threat, that it would be deeply embedded in the European ideal and that there was nothing to fear. He was convinced that Germany could be an integral element of a more united Europe.

There is no doubt that Kohl's accomplishments in moving Germany towards unity are indisputable, but he would not have been able to do so without favourable international circumstances. In that sense, he was lucky. The precedent set by **Solidarity** in Poland showed what was possible; the

Solidarity – Founded in September 1980 in Gdansk, Poland by Lech Walesa, Solidarity was the first free trade union in a Warsaw Pact country. Solidarity led the opposition to Soviet Communist control in Poland throughout the 1980s.

Hungarian decision to be the first to open its borders to East German refugees provided a catalyst. The consistent support of President Bush was crucial. The European 'project', begun by Adenauer four decades earlier, was equally crucial. By placing German unification at all times in the broader European context, Kohl was able to overcome the reservations of the British – Margaret Thatcher was particularly hostile and uncompromising – of Andreotti in Italy, and Mitterrand in France. Kohl's insistence that the two Germanys were a fundamental part of the decision-making – 'Two Plus Four', not 'Four Minus Two' – was an important tactical decision.

The final 'Two Plus Four' Treaty was signed on 12 September and the new united Germany came into official existence on 3 October 1990.

The 'Two Plus Four' agreements

This agreement, also known as the Treaty on the Final Settlement With Respect to Germany, was the final peace treaty negotiated between the Federal Republic of Germany and the German Democratic Republic (the 'Two'), and the four powers that occupied Germany at the end of the Second World War: the USA, the Soviet Union, Great Britain and France (the 'Four'). The four Allied Powers renounced all their rights in Germany, allowing a united Germany to become a sovereign state. In return, Germany agreed to limitations on its armed forces, promised to keep the six former states of East Germany a nuclear weapon-free zone, confirmed its 1945 borders and renounced any future territorial claims beyond those existing borders.

KEY DATES: THE DRIVE TO REUNIFICATION

9 November 1989 The Berlin Wall fell.

28 November 1989 Kohl announced his Ten-Point Plan.

19 December 1989 Kohl's speech in Dresden.

22 December 1989 The symbolic opening of the Brandenburg Gate.

10 February 1990 Kohl met Gorbachev in Moscow.

18 March 1990 The East German elections.

18 May 1990 The Currency Union treaty.

14–16 July 1990 Kohl met Gorbachev in the Caucasus.

12 September 1990 The 'Two Plus Four' treaty.

3 October 1990 German reunification.

WORKING TOGETHER

There is considerable historical debate about the role and motivation of Helmut Kohl in pursuing the unification process.

Consider the factors listed below which can be used to support the argument that Kohl was primarily responsible for German unification. In groups, try to agree a rank order for these factors, from the most to the least crucial. If you think that some are of equal importance or need to be linked together then try to accommodate this in your rank order. Present your thinking to the class as a whole. Is there any common agreement?

● Kohl maintained the policy of *Ostpolitik*.
● Kohl acted with initial and calculated caution.
● Kohl quickly recognised the force of the popular will.
● Kohl quickly understood the seriousness of the economic collapse in the GDR and the impact of East German migration on the FRG.
● Kohl seized the initiative through his Ten-Point Plan and made reunification a topic of practical politics.
● Kohl refused to back Modrow's third-way initiatives.
● Kohl campaigned in the March 1990 elections to help build what Jarausch (page 268) called a 'blinding national euphoria' in favour of unification.
● Kohl insisted on a 1:1 currency conversion.
● Kohl stood up to Margaret Thatcher.
● Kohl won George Bush's support, building on his excellent personal relationship with Ronald Reagan.
● Kohl won Gorbachev's backing (and in so doing weakened French and British opposition) for a reunited Germany being a member of NATO (a US demand) and the EC.
● Kohl steered the 'Two Plus Four' talks towards agreement by accepting arms limitations and existing borders.

All of these factors focus on Kohl himself and his actions. In order to balance the argument, identify, as a class, a range of other contributing factors. Do these seem more compelling as explanations for why unification occurred as it did and when it did?

The political, economic and social condition of Germany by 1991

What was the impact of reunification on Germany by 1991?

Germany was transformed in the space of a year, between the opening of the Wall on 9 November 1989 and 3 October 1990, the Day of German Unity, when the FRG and the GDR officially merged, now an annual public holiday in Germany. Unification not only fundamentally re-shaped Germany but also the centre of Europe, as Cold War certainties were replaced by a new and fluid European and world order. The process took place in the full media spotlight, suggesting that unification took place through a sequence of planned, logical steps, but it was, in reality, a process that left all leaders desperately trying to control events and all participants reeling from the pace of change.

Source E From *The Rush to German Unity* by Konrad H. Jarausch, (Oxford University Press), 1994, p. 197.

The joint country was smaller and less threatening than before the world wars. But the increase of 41,817 square miles made it the third largest state on the continent with about 137,931 square miles. Reunification of the divided city restored Berlin as a metropolis of 3.5 million and moved the centre of gravity toward the East. The addition of 16.34 million people pushed the German population up to 78.42 million, the most numerous in Europe. GDR accession made the populace younger (17 per cent under fifteen), more Protestant (42 per cent), and more atheist than it was in the old FRG. The gain of another 12 per cent in output increased the joint GNP to about $2 trillion (by 1992). Though GDR trade disintegrated, the new Germany remained the second biggest exporter in the world, after the US, but before Japan.

Reunification: the problems of transition

The problems of living standards, institutional arrangements and personal attitudes all proved much more difficult than anticipated. The obstacles to a neat transition constantly multiplied, and the costs rose inexorably. The most significant problems of transition are outlined below:

● The economic decline of the East lay at the root of many difficulties. Industry was much more run down and antiquated than anticipated, pollution much more widespread and endemic.
● The 1:1 currency conversion rate was politically pragmatic but economically damaging.
● The decision to restore property to Germany's pre-division owners hindered recovery, slowing re-building until legal disputes were solved.
● Kohl's administration consistently underestimated the costs of reunification, pushing the new Germany into deficit and depression. This was only belatedly acknowledged in March 1991 by the launch of an Eastern recovery programme, which imposed a temporary solidarity tax, the *Soli*, under which some tax payers were charged up to an additional 7.5 per cent of their yearly tax bill. This tax is still being paid and is the subject of heated debate in Germany.
● Higher education institutions proved difficult to re-construct; in places, whole academic departments needed democratising, a process that led to many staff being fired and even whole departments re-peopled by Western academics, leaving much confusion and bitterness in its wake.
● Psychological reconciliation was difficult. Many Easterners felt a loss of identity, commonly expressed in the phrase: 'living in two worlds, but not feeling at home in either one'. The physical walls may have been disappearing but the mental walls remained. Easterners (*Ossis*) resented

Besserwessis – Westerners (*Wessis*) who thought they knew better; Westerners could not understand why *Ossis* were not more grateful.

- Investigations into those who had collaborated with the *Stasi* caused much dissension, and seemed to some extent to parallel the denazification disputes in the immediate post-war years.
- Excessive expectations among Easterners, coupled with widespread resentment among Westerners of the sacrifices expected of them, caused domestic conflict and permeated the whole political agenda of the new Republic.
- Inner conflict was also apparent in the expectations of the European and world role to be played by the new Germany. Kohl and his contemporaries were very concerned to avoid accusations of a renewed power mentality (*Machtversessenheit*), which would once again raise the spectre of *Weltpolitik* or *Lebensraum*.

In search of identity

What was it to be German in 1991? This question was re-triggered by unification and remains pertinent. The German right-wing promoted unification as an opportunity for a new patriotism; the left-wing felt more disquiet, fearing the rise of xenophobia and a new nationalism. Women's groups feared a return to a more male-dominated society. An overarching issue was whether Germans should be primarily German or European in outlook, a debate which is as strong in Germany today as it was in 1991.

The question of where to locate the new capital, in Bonn or Berlin, illustrated the dilemma over identity. Berlin was the traditional centre and the historic capital; Bonn was the city that symbolised a democratic break with a difficult past. The issue was debated in the *Bundestag* in June 1991 in an open, free debate with members allowed to vote as individuals. The outcome was unexpected: Berlin won by fifteen votes. Historical continuity won out.

Who could live in Germany was another difficult dilemma. The Basic Law defined citizenship in terms of ethnic descent and disallowed an immigration policy. The West faced not only an influx of *Ossis* but Germany also became a magnet for Eastern European refugees, worsening housing shortages and increasing welfare spending. The resentment this caused began to manifest itself in the growth of right-wing sentiment. This sense of being overwhelmed by the consequences of unification are still prevalent today.

Reunification: the strengths of transition

West Germany's most important legacy to a re-united nation, sometimes referred to as the Berlin Republic, was a smooth-functioning, transparent parliamentary democracy, with a sense of legitimacy and economic prosperity. The fears that a united Germany might again prove vulnerable to a return of traditional right-wing German nationalism proved unjustified, in 1991 as now. Kohl's CDU received a higher percentage vote in 1990 than the Nazis had gained in the two elections held in 1932, and even in the manipulated election of March 1933. The political system already in 1991 had sufficient robustness, fairness and openness for Germans to face the transition to a unified nation with confidence. A new Germany had emerged from the rush to unity with deep democratic roots, firmly embedded in the Atlantic Alliance and in the supranational confederation of states that is the European Union.

Unification, given almost heroic status by contemporary media coverage, has been a triumph mixed with uncertainties. Germany is no longer the country of Bismarck, the Kaiser or of Hitler; the attempts at European hegemony of 1871, 1914 and 1939 are the stuff of history books. Yet, to some extent, the stereotype of Germany as a nation intent on European domination, now through its position in the EC, refuses to go away in the minds of some Europeans, despite the Third

German Republic being a stable and democratic state. Germany's success in sport (their football teams always win on penalties) and car manufacture (ahead of everyone else because they are 'Vorsprung durch Technik') might further nurture the stereotype of German efficiency and *macht* (power), but Germany is firmly a 'normal' state of the present, not an exceptional state of the past. The events of 1989–91 may have left not only Germans, but also the German state, still searching for a twenty-first-century identity, but the 25 years after reunification have opened a new chapter in Germany's history, one which is unlikely to be as troubled as the 120 years preceding 1991. The events of 1989–90 resolved the German Question, though the European Question remains open!

Conclusion

A reunited Germany is today a country of greater self-confidence and assurance than at any time since 1991. Concerns remain over the continuing costs of unification and the rise of *Ostalgia* illustrates that tensions between *Wessis* and *Ossis* still persist; the problems of the Euro and of the future of the European Community to some extent mirror the dilemma over Germany's own future direction. Its current chancellor, Angela Merkel, is paraded as the 'most powerful woman in the world', yet no one thinks any longer that such a claim could lead to German power being applied in ways seen in the Second and Third *Reichs*.

Germans may be allegedly humourless and paragons of efficiency, but the nation is in many ways a beacon of hope. Potsdamer Platz in the new heart of Berlin, and developments around Alexander Platz symbolise a coming together of East and West. The great Holocaust Memorial sites around central Berlin are magnificent testimonies to the desire of this present generation of Germans finally to come to terms with their troubled past. In the east, a revived Leipzig celebrated its 1,000-year anniversary in 2015, and Weimar is beginning to recover its historic place as Germany's literary centre; in the west, the Ruhr remains an industrial powerhouse despite pockets of inequality and unemployment; Munich in the south-east, prosperous and affluent, is increasingly cosmopolitan and, albeit very tentatively, is beginning to acknowledge its Nazi past; in the south-west, Freiburg in the Black Forest region is one of the world's great eco-capitals. Unity and division, the overarching themes of this book, seem to be receding issues in today's Germany.

Ostalgia – A German term referring to the wave of sentimental nostalgia in recent years for aspects of life in the former East Germany.

Ordinary lives

It is easy for the sixth form historian to become weighed down with facts, dates and events to the point where people become lost. At its simplest and best, history is the story of people and their times. We met Gerda Schulz in Chapter 6, aged seventeen in 1945. Her father, Albert, was born in 1900 in the state of Pomern, now part of Poland. He married Frieda. Gerda's grandparents, of whom she knew very little, were citizens of Bismarck's *Reich*, the first independent Germany. These three generations experienced the traumatic times covered in this breadth study, and their stories are history in the raw, serving to remind us that great events impact on ordinary lives. Albert served in, and survived, two world wars. His family lost all their savings in the 1923 hyperinflation and he lost his job in the Great Depression. Gerda's family moved to western Germany in the 1930s but her mother's nine brothers and sisters remained in the east. The fate of Frieda's brothers is unclear, but none survived the war; one sister died of natural causes in 1941, one committed suicide in 1945 to avoid Russian rape, one emigrated to the USA immediately after the war and one remained in Berlin, married a Communist, but left him and all her possessions two days before the Berlin Wall was built to seek refuge in West Berlin. She never saw her husband again. Gerda left for England in 1949 to seek a new life as a nurse in the NHS in Barnsley, remaining in England until her death in 2012, a period of 63 years. The family she left behind experienced the 1950s economic miracle and sent her food parcels and German consumer goods every Christmas. She became a British citizen but never felt British. Ordinary lives; exceptional times.

Chapter summary

- The West German economy sustained an astonishing period of growth from 1949 to the mid-1960s; the so-called 'economic miracle'.
- Despite a series of economic downturns and unfavourable global circumstances in the 1970s and 1980s, the Federal Republic achieved higher rates of growth and experienced lower rates of inflation and unemployment than most of its European neighbours.
- Standards of living were consistently high throughout the lifetime of the Republic.
- The 1960s can be viewed as a significant turning point: a decade of astonishing social ferment and mid-life crisis.
- By the end of the 1980s West Germany had become a remarkably stable, self-confident state: an assured democracy capable of self-criticism and social debate over its inner tensions, yet also profoundly European and internationalist in outlook.
- Progressive social change was apparent both in the role of women and of young people, particularly manifested in the expansion of higher education which had begun in the 1960s and in the growth of environmentalism.
- Though the practical legacies of Nazism had largely been eradicated by the 1980s, its emotional legacy, and particularly the issue of guilt, was to persist throughout the Republic's lifetime.
- Chancellor Helmut Kohl was instrumental in steering the process of unification in 1989–90.
- The pace of reunification, and the nature of the compromises made in achieving unity, left a legacy of problems of transition for the new German state.
- Reunification was achieved remarkably peacefully; by 1991, the pariah, divided nation of 1949 had become Europe's best hope for a continent founded on co-operation and peace.

▼ **Summary diagram:** Economy, society and reunification, 1949–91

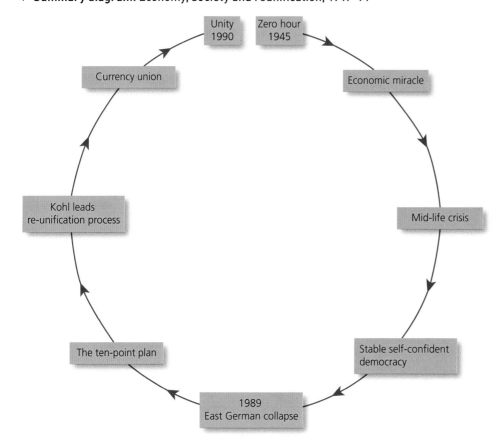

Working on interpretation skills
Causes of German Reunification

By Kristina Spohr

A consideration of the short-, medium- and long-term factors leading to reunification.

East and West Germany officially united on 3 October 1990 – three weeks after they had signed the 'Treaty on Final Settlement' with the four victor powers of 1945 (the US, USSR, UK and France). After four decades of division Germany's unity and full sovereignty had been re-established. The Cold War had ended in Europe.   5

How could German (re)unification happen so suddenly and yet peacefully? Why was West German chancellor Helmut Kohl able to realise a goal that had eluded all his predecessors, despite it being the stated aim of every Bonn government since 1949?

After Soviet leader Mikhail Gorbachev loosened the USSR's grip over   10
its satellite states after 1987, people power first shook and then toppled Communist regimes in Poland and Hungary. The East German regime under Erich Honecker shut itself away from any reforms as introduced in the USSR and recommended by Gorbachev to his Communist allies. But in summer 1989 the pressures escalated.   15

The opening of the border with Austria by the Hungarian reform Communists triggered a mass flight of East Germans via Hungary to the West. This flight reflected people's loss of loyalty and trust in the East German state, but also the appeal of the wealthy, democratic Western Germany.   20

Among those who stayed, there was growing opposition. The 'forty years GDR' celebrations in early October ended in farce, with ordinary citizens in the streets of East Berlin begging the visiting Gorbachev for help. Huge demonstrations for democracy and reforms followed. Significantly, unlike in Beijing, the people's uprising was not crushed by force – either by Soviet   25
forces or the East German army. Gorbachev could not risk his new *détente* with America.

The Berlin Wall fell on 9 November: this was a crucial turning point. The East German leadership had merely intended to liberalise the travel law, but its hasty implementation resulted in thousands of people taking the   30
opportunity to walk into West Berlin.

The Wall had been the prime symbol of the iron curtain and the East–West divide had gone. But initially few people anticipated rapid unification – more a gradual growing together of the two Germanys.

The ensuing mass migration from East to West, however, undermined *35*
such assumptions. Its motors were the desire for greater wealth and
more political freedoms, rather than a resurgent nationalism, as many of
Germany's neighbours feared. But it forced the question of German unity
onto the international agenda.

As the GDR bled people, so the social fabric increasingly dissolved. More *40*
critically, the East German economy was by winter on the brink of collapse
and no more western loans were forthcoming.

Almost as soon as the Wall came down, West German Chancellor Helmut
Kohl envisaged rapid reunification. On 28 November he presented a
10 Point Programme for achieving unity to the *Bundestag* in Bonn. The *55*
world was stunned. In the new year Kohl pushed for early East German
elections (held in spring), for intra-German unification via article 23 of the
West German Basic Law (in effect stipulating an absorption of eastern
Germany within the Federal Republic), and for an economic and currency
union. It was decisive that the first free elections in the GDR on 18 March *50*
1990 became dominated by West Germany, politically and financially.
The election result endorsed the chancellor's line thanks to the victory
of the sister party of Kohl's Christian Democrats, namely the *Allianz für
Deutschland*. From now on internal unification was almost self-propelling
and would be carried out essentially under West German (in other words, *55*
Kohl's) terms.

Solving the international aspects of reunification was a more complicated
process. Indeed the reception for Kohl's 10 points had been hostile in the
USSR, Britain and France – mindful of Germany's role in two world wars.
Only the USA had come out in favour of unification. But American support *60*
for Kohl eventually ensured that their reservations were brushed aside.
And the residual Allied occupation rights were negotiated away within the
2+4 framework: two Germanies and the four former occupying powers. The
Soviets agreed to a rapid withdrawal of their troops and continued German
membership of NATO after Kohl's skilful use of chequebook diplomacy. *65*

East Germany had been an artificial state – its existence based on
military, economic and political guarantees provided by the USSR. It
was furthermore held together by closed borders and intense police
surveillance. Gorbachev's reforms challenged the GDR's whole ethos
and the opening of the borders in 1989 destroyed its viability. The pace *70*
and shape of unification, however, was determined by Chancellor Kohl,
with crucial American support. This was a story of people power, skilful
statecraft and, at times, sheer luck.

**Kristina Spohr is Associate Professor in International
History at the London School of Economics.**

ACTIVITY

1 Using this essay, and the material in Section 3 of
this chapter (pages 267–77), produce your own
mind map of the causes of German unification in
1990. Ensure that you differentiate between
long-, medium- and short-term factors.

2 Below is an example of an A-level practice
question on this topic for you to attempt:

**To what extent were external factors in
the years 1961–90 responsible for German
reunification?** (25 marks)

(Note: this question focuses on causation)

Working on essay technique

Remember that breadth essays will cover a minimum of 20–25 years of the specification, and that each individual question will have a different principal focus: cause or consequence, change or continuity, similarity or difference, or significance.

Below is an A-level practice question related to the content of this chapter:

To what extent was the Cold War responsible for shaping the process of German unification in the years 1961–90? (25 marks)

It is easy to begin answering a question without fully understanding its demands. *Always study the wording of the question carefully to clarify its focus.* This seems obvious but can be forgotten under timed conditions in an examination. This question is a 'how far' question focusing on significance. It is asking you to balance the importance of the Cold War in relation to other factors responsible for reunification.

Consider the start and end dates. This is often an obvious signpost for fixing the context of the question.

Consider your overall argument. This will be clearly stated in your opening paragraph and will provide the thread linking your subsequent paragraphs together, leading to your judgement in your final, concluding paragraph.

A-LEVEL PRACTICE QUESTION

Now try writing an answer to this additional practice question:

'Willy Brandt set in motion the process of German reunification, Helmut Kohl merely completed what Brandt had begun.'

Assess the validity of this view. (25 marks)

Key questions 2: Germany 1871–1991

All breadth units cover a period of at least 100 years and each question set in your examination will cover at least 20–25 years. Examination questions might span the end of Part 1 of the specification and the beginning of Part 2. All will reflect one or more of the six key questions set out in the specification. The main aim of this 120-year study of German history, therefore, is to introduce you to broader issues of social, economic and political developments and trends in Germany, and to avoid a narrow question focus.

It is important, therefore, to take time to address these key questions and to consider the broader issues of cause and consequence, patterns of change and continuity, similarity and difference, and the significant impact of key individuals and groups on the events through which they lived. The sub-text of this specification is to develop your ability to reflect on events with a broad sense of historical perspective; after all, a sense of perspective is something all of us need in our own lives.

Questions to consider

- Was Weimar democracy doomed from the beginning? Did the Nazis seize power or was it gifted to them? Why did the Nazis come to power in 1933 and not another group or party? Why 1933?
- What was the source of Hitler's power? Did all political authority rest in the hands of the Nazis? To what extent was Hitler a strong ruler?
- Why did the Allies retain political authority in the immediate post-war years? Did the West Germans choose democracy or was it forced on them?
- How liberal was West German democracy? Was West German democracy in 1989 much different than it had been in 1949? Was West Germany a model democracy?

Working in groups

It has been suggested that the collapse of the Weimar Republic and the rise of the Nazis are evidence that the Germans were fundamentally anti-democratic. Yet it has also been suggested that by 1989 West Germany was a model democracy.

- Work together to discuss this issue. Can both views be correct?
- Identify arguments for and against these seemingly contradictory statements.
- Discuss the extent to which the German elites maintained their dominant political authority over the entire period covered by the specification.
- Compare the constitutions of 1871, 1919 and 1949. What are the key changes? Are there any significant continuities?

Questions to consider

- Was left-wing opposition to the Weimar government stronger than right-wing opposition? What grievances motivated Weimar's opponents? Were the Nazis the most important oppositional group?
- What was the extent of popular support for the Nazis? Why was Hitler a lesser target for opposition than the Party? Was fear the reason for the limited opposition against the Nazis? Are bystanders as guilty as perpetrators, or can reluctant loyalty be considered a form of opposition in itself?
- Why was the SPD unsuccessful in opposing Adenauer's policy of Western integration? Had parliamentary opposition effectively disappeared in West Germany by the mid-1960s? Why did extra-parliamentary opposition emerge in the 1960s?
- Was the RAF a genuine threat to Bonn democracy? Was opposition in West Germany in the 1960s and 1970s socially or politically motivated? How effective was the Green movement in the 1980s? Was West Germany effectively a conformist society?

Working in groups

The nature of political opposition is very broad, ranging from apathetic tolerance and reluctant loyalty, through non-conformity and civil disobedience, to actual acts of resistance, either political or violent. Discuss the following broad statements, designed to elicit thinking about the nature and effectiveness of opposition throughout the period:

- Opposition to the Nazis was ineffective because it had no clear outlet or organisational means through which to express its views.
- Adenauer faced little political opposition because people were materially satisfied.
- West German terrorism in the 1970s and 1980s posed no real threat to democracy.
- The environmental movement in the 1980s was idealistic but ultimately too unrealistic to succeed in its aims.

Consider the effectiveness of parliamentary opposition over the period of the specification as a whole. Can you find evidence for and against the view that opposition in parliament has generally failed to limit or influence government policy?

Discuss the effectiveness of extra-parliamentary opposition over the years 1871–1991.

KEY QUESTION 3
How and with what results did the economy develop and change?

Questions to consider

- To what extent did economic factors cause the collapse of the Weimar Republic?
- Did the Nazis achieve an economic miracle? Was Hitler's primary aim 'guns or butter'? Did the defence economy succeed? To what extent did economic failings cause Germany's defeat in the Second World War?
- Why was the issue of reparations such a major problem for the Allies? To what extent were economic disagreements between the Allies responsible for Germany's division in 1949?
- How far was Erhard responsible for West Germany's economic miracle? Why did economic stability matter so much to West Germans? How did the SPD change the management of the West German economy from 1967? To what extent were West German governments undermined by economic factors?

Working in groups

- Historians try to identify patterns of development and often suggest that political change is primarily prompted by economic success and failure. Consider the main changes of regime or government across the period 1929–91. What evidence can you find to support or challenge this view?
- Discuss the reasons why Germany has largely maintained its position as one of Europe's dominant economic powers.
- Consider the view that Germany's economic strength has been the key factor in its political development over the years 1871–1991.

. . . .

KEY QUESTION 4
What was the extent of social and cultural change?

Questions to consider

- Why did the Nazis despise Weimar society and culture? How successful were the Nazis in creating a new kind of German? To what extent did the German people support the concept of a *Volksgemeinschaft*? Was there social conformity in Nazi Germany? Was there such a thing as Nazi culture? Did Nazi social and racial policy inevitably lead to the Holocaust?
- How successful was denazification? Did defeat strengthen or weaken notions of German identity?
- Did West Germany become a more classless society? Was the pursuit of materialism a continuous social trend throughout the years of West Germany's existence? Why was the 1960s such a period of turbulent social change? How non-conformist was West German society?
- Was there a distinctive West German culture? To what extent did the role of men and women change in West Germany after 1949? Was sporting success a barometer of political maturity?

Working in groups

- Consider the statement: 'After 1945 everything changed.' Discuss how important 1945 was as a watershed in German social and cultural development. What continuities were there? What were the main changes?
- Consider other chronological turning points: 1933, 1968, 1990. Were these equally momentous years of change in Germany?
- How far have ideas of German identity changed over the period as a whole? Is it possible to identify common social and cultural trends influencing the ways Germans have viewed their national development over the years 1871–1991?
- To what extent was the cultural richness of German life in the Wilhelmine and Weimar periods lost after 1933?

Questions to consider

- Was the Weimar Republic doomed because it was too liberal?
- How coherent was Nazi ideology? Were the Nazis popular because of their ideology? How did the Nazis differentiate national community from social class? To what extent was Nazi ideology backward looking?
- To what extent was post-war German division caused by ideological differences?
- Why was there a conservative ascendancy in West Germany in the 1950s? Why had the SPD emerged as the dominant political grouping by the late 1960s? What caused *die Wende* in the early 1980s? How different were the ideologies of right and left in West Germany?

Working in groups

- Consider the ideological legacy of Nazism. Discuss the extent to which Nazi ideas re-surfaced in West Germany in the years 1949–89.
- To what extent have German political ideas and ideology over the period of this specification been largely backward looking and often based on an idealised view of the German past?

KEY QUESTION 6
How important was the role of key individuals and groups and how were they affected by developments?

Questions to consider

- To what extent did key individuals and groups conspire to bring down the Weimar Republic?
- To what extent was Hitler's position and political authority under threat in the years 1932–34? Why was Hitler virtually untouchable after 1934? Which groups were the Nazis unable to co-ordinate fully? Who were the decision-makers in Nazi Germany?
- To what extent were the Germans in control of their own fate in the years 1945–49? Who was responsible for the division of Germany? Why was Adenauer favoured by the Western Allies?
- Was Adenauer a Western puppet? Was Adenauer good for the development of West German democracy? Why was there an *ohne mich* attitude in West Germany in the 1950s? Why did this change in the 1960s? How important was the RAF? Why did Green activists emerge in the late 1970s and 1980s?

Working in groups

- Draw two timelines covering the years 1929–91. Label one 'individuals', and the other 'groups'. Mark key individuals and groups on the appropriate timeline. Can you draw any conclusions from this? Which have the biggest impact? Which have the longest impact?
- Discuss the idea of legacy. Which individuals or groups can be said to have had a legacy, either for what they did or the ideas they bequeathed?
- Discuss who you consider to be the greatest German in the years 1929–91. Define 'greatest'. Who might be the contenders: Hitler, Adenauer, Erhard, Brandt, Kohl, others?
- Consider whether the role played by and the impact of key individuals suggest that the importance of leadership has been a key, continuous theme of German political development in the years 1871–1991.

Further research

There are scores of excellent books on German history in the period covered by this book. It is impossible for most students to consult more than a few of these. However, it is vital that you read some. It is a common complaint of all history examiners that candidates do not read widely enough. The following suggestions are meant to serve as a guide.

Also listed in this further research are novels, films and places to visit which are recommendations intended to extend your overall sense of the period.

General recommendations

There are plenty to choose from. These are among the best.

A History of Germany 1815–1990 by W. Carr, (Edward Arnold), 1991.

This remains one of the best general histories of the period.

A History of Modern Germany 1800–2000 by M. Kitchen, (Blackwell), 2006.

Probably the best general textbook now available on modern Germany.

The Fontana History of Germany 1780–1918 by D. Blackbourn, (Fontana), 1997.

Another excellent book on the entire period.

German History Since 1800 by M. Fulbrook, (Edward Arnold), 1997.

An excellent collection of essays which provide a solid and reliable introduction to German history.

Iron Kingdom: The Rise and Downfall of Prussia 1600–1947 by C. Clark, (Penguin), 2007.

The definitive history of Prussia.

Nineteenth-Century Germany: Politics, Culture and Society 1780–1918 J. Breilly (ed.), (Bloomsbury Academic), 2001.

A useful collection of essays.

German History in Modern Times: Four Lives of the Nation by William W. Hagen, (Cambridge), 2012.

Covers German history from the seventeenth century. Not a starter text but full of insights; offers breadth.

A History of Germany 1918–2014: The Divided Nation by Mary Fulbrook, (Wiley Blackwell), 2015.

A superb, cogent overview brought right up to date.

Germany, Memories of a Nation by Neil MacGregor, (Allen Lane), 2014 (hardback).

Written as an accompaniment to the BBC Radio 4 series of the same title; a cross between a coffee table book and a splendid wide-ranging, thoughtful series of thirty essays; wonderful illustrations.

Books on particular periods

Texts on Bismarck

There are scores. Try some, if not all, of these.

Bismarck by E. Crankshaw, (Macmillan), 1981.

This is not a straightforward narrative and needs a basic knowledge and understanding of Bismarck's life for it to make sense.

Bismarck by E. Feuchtwanger, (Routledge), 2002.

Tautly written and thoroughly researched.

Bismarck: A Life by J. Steinberg, (Oxford University Press), 2012.

A deeply researched but still accessible guide to Bismarck.

Bismarck by B. Waller, (Blackwell), 1997.

This is a very useful review of Bismarck's life and achievements.

Bismarck and Germany, 1862–1890 by D. G. Williamson, (Routledge), 1995.

A good introduction to Bismarck's career.

Bismarck and the German Empire 1871–1918 by L. Abrams, (Routledge), 1995.

A recommended read on Bismarck post-unification.

Texts on Imperial Germany

Imperial Germany 1871–1914 by V. R. Berghahn, (Oxford University Press), 1994.

This deals largely with social, economic and cultural developments.

Imperial Germany 1871–1918: The Short Oxford History of Germany by J. Retallack, (Oxford University Press), 2008.

A useful introduction to the *Kaiserreich*.

Kaiser Wilhelm II: A Life in Power by C. Clark, (Penguin), 2009.

A critical and illuminating review of Wilhelm's life.

Imperial Germany 1871–1918 by S. Lee, (Routledge), 1998.

A good introduction.

Imperial Germany 1867–1918 by W. J. Mommsen, (Edward Arnold), 1995.

Another well-written and comprehensive text.

Kaiser Wilhelm II by J. C. G. Rohl, (Cambridge University Press), 2014.

Easily the best short history of Wilhelm II's life.

Wilhelm II, The Kaiser's Personal Monarchy by J. C. G. Rohl, (Cambridge University Press), 2001.

Useful, although possibly a little too detailed for most readers.

Germany 1914–19

Ring of Steel: Germany and Austria-Hungary in World War 1 1914–1918 by A. Watson, (Basic Civitas Books), 2014.

An authoritative and splendidly written account of Germany's experiences in the First World War.

The First World War: Germany and Austria-Hungary 1914–1918 by H. H. Herwig, (Bloomsbury Academic), 1996.

Fascinatingly detailed and lucidly written.

Imperial Germany and the Great War by R. Chickering, (Cambridge University Press), 2014.

A comprehensive survey of Germany's experiences in the First World War.

Weimar Germany 1919–29

A Short History of the Weimar Republic by C.Storer, (I. B. Tauris), 2013.

A balanced and reliable overview of the period.

The Weimar Republic by R. Henig, (Routledge), 1998.

A short, useful introduction to the short-lived Weimar Republic.

Germany After The First World War by R. Bessel, (Clarendon Press), 1993.

A wide-ranging survey of German society after 1918.

The Weimar Years: A Culture Cut Short by J. Willett, (Thames and Hudson), 1987.

A readable and informative visual introduction to the richness and complexities of Weimar culture.

Weimar Germany: Promise and Tragedy by E. D. Weitz, (Princeton University Press), 2013.

Spendidly illustrated and splendidly informative.

Weimar Germany (Short Oxford History of Germany) by A. McElligott, (Oxford University Press), 2009.

A very good introduction to the Weimar Republic.

The Weimar Republic by J. Hiden, (Pearson Education), 1996.

This remains a reliable book and contains some useful documents.

The Nazi experiment 1929–45

It would be possible to spend every minute of every day for a year reading about this period and still not exhaust the many thousands of texts and essays produced. The following list is, by its very nature therefore, selective and subjective.

Nazism 1919–45 J. Noakes and G. Pridham, eds, (University of Exeter Press), 1983.

Still the best documentary reader on the market; produced in four separate volumes.

The Coming of the Third Reich by Richard J. Evans, (Penguin), 2004.

Highly readable, detailed but not overwhelming. Fast becoming a standard text, as are the two further volumes in the series: *The Third Reich in Power and The Third Reich at War.*

Hitler by Ian Kershaw, (Penguin), 2009.

There are numerous biographies of Hitler available, but this is a masterpiece of research and insight. Also written by Kershaw, and useful to have at hand are:

The Nazi Dictatorship, (Arnold), 1993.

The End, Germany 1944–45, (Penguin), 2012.

Life in the Third Reich by Richard Bessel, (Oxford University Press), 2001.

This book contains eight essays originally published in *History Today* in 1985–86, which have been up-dated. This is a particularly good starting point for a broad survey of life in Nazi Germany.

The Third Reich, Between Vision and Reality by Hans Mommsen, (Berg), 2002.

Again a series of essays, more challenging than Bessel's text but good for students who wish to broaden and deepen their understanding. The essay on the 'People's Community' by Norbert Frei, and 'The Nazi Boom: An Economic Cul-de-Sac' by Christoph Buchheim are particularly useful.

Backing Hitler by Robert Gellately, (Oxford University Press), 2001.

An excellent survey of consent and coercion in the Nazi state from 1933 to 1945.

Nazi Germany by Tim Kirk, (Palgrave Macmillan), 2007.

A very good, clear, general history covering the rise of the Nazis in the 1920s, life and government in the Third

Reich, the economy, racism and anti-Semitism, and the main course of the Second World War.

The Third Reich, Politics and Propaganda by David Welch, (Routledge), 2002.

One of the best texts on the nature of Nazi propaganda and the manipulation of popular opinion.

The Nazi Economic Recovery, 1932–38 by Richard Overy, (Cambridge University Press), 1996.

A brief but highly detailed story of the German economy from the Great Depression to the eve of war.

Division, 1945–49

After the Reich, From the Liberation of Vienna to the Berlin Airlift by Giles MacDonogh, (John Murray), 2008.

Contains a wealth of detail; an excellent survey of the immediate post-war years.

The Making of the GDR, 1945–53 by Gareth Pritchard, (Manchester University Press), 2000.

Although focused on developments in the East, this is a useful companion to understanding broader post-war developments.

Germany 1945, From War to Peace by Richard Bessel, (Simon and Schuster), 2009.

Another very good text from this author who writes with great clarity and breadth.

The Federal Republic, 1949–89

Many of the books below cover both East and West Germany but are included for the quality of the relevant text.

Interpretations of the Two Germanies, 1945–90 by Mary Fulbrook, (Macmillan), 2000.

An excellent short text offering sharp analysis of West German development; good on the reunification process.

Germany Since 1945 by Lothar Kettenacker, (Oxford University Press), 1997.

Another solid analytical study of both Germanies.

Germany Since 1945 by Pol O'Dochertaigh, (Palgrave Macmillan), 2004.

A very good starter text; clear and straightforward.

German Politics, 1945–1995 by Peter Pulzer, (Oxford University Press), 1996.

A detailed text; good for a broad awareness of German political development.

The Making of German Democracy: West Germany During the Adenauer Era (Documents in Modern History) by Armin Grunbacher, (Manchester University Press), 2010.

An outstanding range of documentary material; probably the best on this period.

West Germany under Construction: Politics, Society and Culture in the Adenauer Era by Richard G. Moeller, (University of Michigan Press), 1997.

Contains a good selection of essays on a broad range of topics.

West Germany and the Global Sixties: The Anti-Authoritarian Revolt, 1962–78 by Timothy Scott Brown, (Cambridge University Press), 2013.

A strong new study of activism and terrorism. Well written.

Terror and Democracy in West Germany by Karrin Hanshew, (Cambridge University Press), 2012.

Another recent work analysing the turbulent years of student revolt and terrorism. Similar in scope to Scott Brown's book and of equal value.

The Miracle Years, A Cultural History of West Germany Hanna Schissler, ed., (Princeton University Press), 2001.

A good selection of essays, adding excellent detail to broader, more general surveys of this period.

Reunification, 1989–91

The Rush to German Unity by Konrad H. Jarausch, (Oxford University Press), 1994.

Splendid. Possibly the best, most thorough treatment of the years 1989 onwards. Masterly scholarship.

The People's State, East German Society from Hitler to Honecker by Mary Fulbrook, (Yale University Press), 2005.

The beginning of Chapter 2 of this text offers a number of insights for understanding what was happening in the Eastern zone of Germany under the Soviet occupation, and the conclusion is a good complement to understanding the reasons for the collapse of the East German state.

Exit-Voice Dynamics by Steven Pfaff, (Duke University Press), 2006.

Though more of a sociologist than a historian, Pfaff's concluding paragraph contributes to our understanding of the motivation of the German people for unity.

Novels, films and locations

Novels

The following list of suggested reading is not intended to be a 'best of', but is an indication of a range of fictional writing that offers a number of insights about the period covered in Part 2 of this A-level specification.

The British author Philip Kerr has written a series of nine, wonderfully researched historical crime thrillers largely set in 1930s Berlin. The central character is Bernie Gunther, a sardonic, world-weary former SPD voter whose career brings him into contact with a range of 'actual' and fictitious Nazis. Start with the first three, collected under one title:

Berlin Noir by Philip Kerr, (Penguin), 1993.

The novels of Christopher Isherwood, *Mr Norris Changes Trains* and *Goodbye to Berlin*, first published in 1935 in Britain, also terrifically evoke the atmosphere of pre-war Berlin and are based on the author's first-hand experience. The wonderful musical *Cabaret* was inspired by Isherwood's Berlin novels. You can obtain both novels together:

The Berlin Novels by Christopher Isherwood, (Vintage), 1999.

The 'Station' series of novels by David Downing are also excellent reads, set in Nazi Germany and the wartime period. Start with:

Zoo Station by David Downing, (Old Street Publishing), 2008.

The Second World War spy novels by Alan Furst have a committed readership. Try his fourth 'spy' novel set in Paris in 1940:

The World at Night by Alan Furst, (Random House), 2002.

Fatherland, What if Hitler had Won? by Robert Harris, (Arrow Books), 2009.

Set in April 1964, one week before Hitler's seventy-fifth birthday, Harris creates a world in which Hitler won the Second World War. Harris presents fascinating ideas and images of a Nazi state as it might have developed almost twenty years after 1945.

Alone in Berlin by Hans Fallada, (Penguin), 2009.

First published in 1947, this is a superb account of opposition against the Nazis. Primo Levi, the Italian Holocaust survivor, called this 'the greatest book ever written about German resistance to the Nazis'.

The Tin Drum by Günter Grass, 1959 (English translation by Breon Mitchell, Harcourt, 2009).

A long and starkly written vision of post-war Germany, which received praise and criticism in equal measure when first published. Try also: *Dog Years*, a novel set in three parts, starting in Weimar Germany in the 1920s and ending in the 1950s.

The Lost Honour of Katharina Blum by Heinrich Böll, (Vintage), 1993.

Set in West Germany in 1974, Böll's novel explores the role of the tabloid press and the continuing tendency to authoritarian government at the time of the terror attacks by the Red Army Faction.

Films

Once again, the following list is not a 'must see' of the best films produced on this period, but it is intended to provide a starting point for a cinematic review of some of the events covered in this part of the specification. A number of these films are critically acclaimed, others have received mixed reviews, and many focus on the events of the Holocaust. The films are listed in order of production.

Cabaret Bob Fosse (dir.), 1972, (15).

The Lost Honour of Katharina Blum Volker Schlöndorff and Margarethe von Trotta (dir.), 1975, (15).

The Bunker George Schaefer (dir.), 1981.

Sophie's Choice Alan J. Pakula (dir.), 1982, (15).

Schindler's List Steven Spielberg (dir.), 1993, (15).

Life is Beautiful Roberto Benigni (dir.), 1997, (PG).

The Devil's Arithmetic Donna Deitch (dir.), 1999, (12).

The Pianist Roman Polanski (dir.), 2002, (15).

The Miracle of Bern Sönke Wortmann (dir.), 2003.

Downfall Oliver Hirschbiegel (dir.), 2004, (15).

Munich Steven Spielberg (dir.), 2005, (15).

The Boy in the Striped Pyjamas Mark Herman (dir.), 2008, (12A).

Valkyrie Bryan Singer (dir.), 2008, (12A).

The Reader Stephen Daldry (dir.), 2008, (15).

Defiance Edward Zwick (dir.), 2008, (15).

Esther's Diary Mariusz Kotowski (dir.), 2010.

Locations

Fieldwork is an important component of any historical study, and this is particularly true of modern German history. The following is not intended to be a travelogue, nor have I included exhaustive lists of art galleries, exhibitions and museums but the cities listed offer extensive scope for student visits.

Berlin

A visit to this city offers enormous opportunities for anyone studying this breadth specification. Perhaps the most prominent focus of a visit might target Cold War sites, but there are numerous locations for visits linked to the Wilhelmine, Weimar and Nazi periods.

- The best location to study the Berlin Wall is at Bernauerstrasse. The development and reconstruction here is remarkable and continuing.
- Visit 'Topography of Terror' for the most detailed and visual exhibition of the Nazi terror apparatus.
- The Resistance Museum has recently been re-vamped and focused visits here can work very well.
- The Jewish Museum is excellent, and the area around Hackescher Markt and the New Synagogue offers many echoes of the city's Jewish past and present.

- For a student of the Holocaust, the memorial sites in the city centre, and a visit to the Wannsee Conference memorial site are hugely valuable.
- Weimar, Dresden and Leipzig are all beginning to re-discover elements of their past glory.

Nuremberg

A visit to the remains of the rally grounds and to the Museum of Fascination and Terror will reinforce the scale of the Nazi's one-thousand year vision.

Munich

Munich has been slow to acknowledge its Nazi past, but there is much to do here. A new Nazi Documentation Centre was due to open in 2015; there are a number of iconic buildings remaining here from the Nazi period, and much to see that gives a vivid impression of how different Bavaria is compared to Prussian Berlin.

The concentration camp system

A number of memorial sites exist. Perhaps the most visited are the camps at Dachau in Munich, Buchenwald in Weimar and Sachsenhausen in Berlin.

Glossary of terms

Absolute monarchy A monarchy in which the king or emperor has virtually absolute or total power and his will and decisions alone make the law.

Allied Control Council (ACC) The body responsible for day-to-day government in post-war Germany; it was composed of the military commanders of the four Allied occupying powers.

Anarchist A person whose ideal society is one without government of any kind. Late nineteenth-century anarchists often sought to bring about such a condition by terrorism.

Anti-Semitism A hatred of – or hostility to – Jews.

Aryan The ideology of Nazism was based on the belief that the Aryan race was the master race. Nazi racial theorists identified the northern European, or Nordic, Aryan racial grouping as superior to all other races.

Autarky Economic self-sufficiency.

Avant-garde Those who create or support the newest ideas and techniques, especially in art, music, literature, drama and architecture.

Axel Springer Press One of the largest digital and news publishing houses in Europe, its titles include the popular newspaper *Bild* and the German edition of *Rolling Stone*.

Bad Godesberg Programme At its 1959 Party conference in the German town of Bad Godesberg, the SPD abandoned its socialist economic policies and adopted the principles of the social market economy. It also abandoned its anti-Americanism and espoused the CDU's Western position. The SPD now also presented itself as a catch-all party, albeit of the left.

Bi-cameral A democratic constitution operated through two chambers, or houses, of parliament.

Blood and Soil (*Blut und Boden*) A part of Nazi ideology which promoted an intimate and mystical relationship between the blood of the German people and the soil of the German Fatherland.

Bundestag The Federal German Council which was a conference of representatives from all the states within the German Confederation from 1815 to 1866.

Bundeswehr This is the name given to the German armed forces established on 12 November 1955 as part of the FRG's admission to NATO. German rearmament was a controversial issue, both within and outside of Germany, but accepted as a necessity by the occupying powers as the Cold War deepened. The *Bundeswehr* was portrayed as a citizens' army to emphasise that it remained under political control.

Cartel An association of manufacturers who come to a contractual agreement about the level of production and the scale of prices and maintain a monopoly.

Catch 22 A contradictory or self-defeating situation or course of action.

Co-determination Shared decision making between management and labour, through their union representatives; designed to promote good industrial relations through co-operation rather than confrontation.

Collective farms Privately owned farms merged into very large state-controlled farms.

Command economy A command, or planned, economy, as existed in the Soviet Union, is one in which the state rather than the free market or private business organises all aspects of the economy.

The Council of Europe Founded in 1949, the Council was set up to promote legal and judicial co-operation between all countries of Europe. Perhaps its best known institution is the European Court of Human Rights.

Council of Ministers The Council was composed of the Foreign Ministers of Great Britain, the Soviet Union, the United States, France and China. Its purpose was to agree peace treaties with the defeated European states and to settle outstanding territorial disputes. It met five times, the last of which broke up in acrimony in London in December 1947 without any agreement on a peace settlement with Germany.

Cult of Motherhood The belief that a woman's main role in life was as wife and mother; the Honour Cross of German Motherhood was awarded to women for giving birth to four or more children. Motherhood was elevated to the highest national status to which a woman could aspire.

Death marches As Russian troops advanced westwards, the extermination camps and labour camps in the East were abandoned. Those camp inmates still alive and capable of walking were evacuated by their guards, ostensibly to reach camps deeper within Germany. In the brutal winter of 1944–45, thousands died of exposure, starvation and exhaustion; many hundreds more, incapable of keeping up, were murdered by their guards. It seemed to the prisoners that the evacuations were simply another means of extermination.

Deficit spending The spending of public funds raised by borrowing rather than by taxation.

Democratisation of the army Left-wing socialists believed that the army was a right-wing force which might be used against them. They thus proposed that army officers should be elected by the men and the regular army should be replaced by a people's militia.

Diet An assembly or parliament.

Diktat A dictated settlement allowing for no negotiations.

Divine right of kings The belief that a monarch rules by the authority of God rather than by the consent of the people.

Doppelverdiener This translates as second wage earner. It was a term of abuse aimed at married women who went out to work.

'Economic miracle' The term used to describe West Germany's astonishing economic boom of the 1950s and early 1960s (see Chapter 8, pages 255–56).

Elites The officer class, *Junker* landowners, industrial and business leaders, senior civil servants and judges.

Embargo A ban or prohibition on trade with a particular nation.

Ersatz An artificial or synthetic substitute for something natural or genuine; usually of inferior quality.

Eugenics A branch of science which, in simple terms, justifies the view that the purity of races can be preserved through selective breeding. Eugenics had a strong body of scientific support not only in Hitler's Germany, but throughout Western Europe and the United States.

The European Coal and Steel Community (ECSC) Set up by the Treaty of Paris in 1951 by Belgium, France, Italy, Luxemburg, the Netherlands and West Germany, the ECSC was the first step towards the creation of the European Union.

Fait accompli An accomplished fact.

Federal A government in which several states, while independent in domestic affairs, combine for general purposes.

Federal Republic of Germany This is the formal title of the West German state which existed from 1949 until the reunification of Germany on 3 October 1990.

Fourteen Points These were President Wilson's main war aims. Wilson hoped to prevent future wars by eliminating secret alliances and frustrated nationalism, and by establishing a League of Nations.

Franchise The right to vote for a representative in a national election.

Fraternisation Associating with others in a friendly way, especially with an enemy.

Free trade Unrestricted trade without protective import duties. Protective duties – or tariffs – are levied in order to protect a nation's own industries and/or farming from cheap foreign competition. Free trade allows people to purchase goods cheaply but it can endanger a country's industrial and agricultural production.

Führerprinzip Literally, the '*Führer* principle', the *Führerprinzip* was the operating principle for the Nazi state when Hitler was in power; the belief that Hitler possessed all power and authority within the Nazi Party; sometimes referred to as the 'leadership principle'. (*Führer* translates as 'the leader'.)

Gastarbeiter Literally 'guest worker'. The term refers to the foreign and migrant workers who moved to West Germany in the late 1950s and early 1960s as manual, unqualified labour to fill the employment shortages created by the economic miracle. Turkish workers, for example, arrived in large numbers after 1961.

German Democratic Republic (GDR) The formal title of the East German state which existed from 1949 until the reunification of Germany on 3 October 1990.

German Christians The German Faith Movement was set up in 1932. Led by Ludwig Mueller, they called themselves German Christians. They were fanatical in their desire to Nazify the Protestant Church.

Gross Domestic Product (GDP) The total value of all the goods and services produced by a nation's economy in one year.

Gross National Product The total value of all goods and services produced within a country.

Hottentot election SPD leader Babel labelled the 1907 election the Hottentot election. The Hottentots were one of the native rebel tribes in south-west Africa.

Hyperinflation An economic event where a country experiences very high and very rapid rates of inflation, which diminishes the real value of that country's currency.

Indirect taxation Taxation placed on the sale of goods rather than collected directly from the taxpayer.

Inflation Inflation means that prices of goods and services go up. This usually results from governments issuing too much paper money. Inflation results in a decline in the purchasing power of money. This is bad news for consumers and for people who have or depend on savings. It can be good news for those in debt.

Junkers The landowning nobility in Prussia. They had their own rules of conduct based on an elaborate code of honour, devotion to the military life, a strong sense of service to the Prussian state and an even stronger sense of their own importance. Most were deeply conservative.

Keynesian John Maynard Keynes, a professor of economics at Cambridge, argued that governments should spend their way out of recession. His ideas contradicted orthodox economic thinking in the 1930s but gained considerable support after 1945.

Kulturkampf This translates as a struggle for culture or a struggle for civilisation. In Germany, after 1871 the struggle was essentially between the state and the Catholic Church.

Laissez-faire A political doctrine which argues that government should intervene as little as possible in economic affairs and in the affairs of the individual; non-interference.

Land (plural, *Länder*) A state of the Federal Republic of Germany.

Left-wing A political point of view that supports social equality, and typically promotes progressive social values.

Living space Living space, or *Lebensraum*, was one of Hitler's key ideological goals: territory in the East was needed not only for economic exploitation, but primarily for settlement; 'superior' Germans needed room to expand, evicting their 'inferior' Slav neighbours

Lobby groups These were people, often belonging to particular organisations, who campaigned to persuade politicians to pass legislation favouring particular interests.

Machiavellian Machiavelli (1469–1527) was an Italian diplomat, political theorist and writer. His book, *The Prince*, is renowned for its portrayal of an amoral, opportunistic and deceitful political leader. 'Machiavellian' suggests cynical and unscrupulous political behaviour and strategy.

Marxist programme Those who supported such a plan supported the ideas of Karl Marx. Marx believed that leaders of the proletariat must work to overthrow the capitalist system by (violent) revolution.

Marxist–Leninism The communist ideology of Karl Marx as adapted by Lenin. Its goal was the creation of a classless society and the public ownership of all land and natural resources and production for the benefit of all members of society, not just the privileged few.

Meritocracy A system of promotion or advancement based on individual ability or merit rather than birth or privilege.

Minimum programme The name given to the plans of moderate socialists who were opposed to violent revolution. They wanted to bring about government ownership of banks, coal mines and industry, and called for social equality.

Monopoly A situation when someone or a particular firm has total control over something. In industrial terms, this often means a firm has control over the production of a particular product.

National Democratic Party of Germany (NPD) Founded in 1964, the NPD was the most neo-Nazi party to emerge since 1945.

Nationalisation Government ownership.

NATO A collective Western defence alliance formed on 4 April 1949 intended primarily to safeguard the West from Soviet aggression. Its original members were: Belgium, Canada, Denmark, France, Iceland, Italy, Luxemburg, the Netherlands, Norway, the United Kingdom and the United States.

Negroid The word 'negroid' was used in the nineteenth century as a racial classification for people with brown / black skin who generally originated in sub-Saharan Africa; it was adopted by the Nazis as part of their 'racial classification' ideology. It is now a term considered offensive and is no longer in scientific or common usage

Neue Sachlichkeit This translates as matter-of-factness or objectivity. *Neue Sachlichkeit* became a major undercurrent in all of the arts during the Weimar Republic.

Ohne mich Literally meaning 'without me', this term reflects the view of many Germans throughout the 1950s that political activism was unnecessary as long as the federal government delivered on its social and economic promises. In many respects, it was a reaction against the deeply politicised Nazi era.

Ostalgia A German term referring to the wave of sentimental nostalgia in recent years for aspects of life in the former East Germany.

Pacifism Pacifists are people who are opposed to war. Many socialists were pacifists in 1914.

Pan-German League Formed in 1893, the League was a powerful right-wing nationalist movement. It supported German expansion both in Europe and worldwide.

Papal Encyclical In its most basic meaning, an encyclical is a letter written by the Pope on matters of significant concern to the Catholic Church. The Papal Encyclical written by Pope Pius XI, entitled *Mit brennender Sorge* (With burning concern),

was smuggled into Germany and read from the pulpit on Palm Sunday, 21 March 1937 in all Catholic churches in Germany. It condemned Nazi breaches of the 1933 Concordat, accusing the Nazis of breaking their promises.

Party of Democratic Socialism (PDS) Founded on 16 December 1989, this party was the legal successor to the SED.

Plebiscite A vote on a single issue on which the whole electorate is asked a yes / no question; an old-fashioned term for a referendum.

Pocket-battleship A small battleship, built to the specifications laid down by the Treaty of Versailles.

Presidential government Government dependent on the President using his powers under Article 48 of the Weimar constitution to pass legislation through the *Reichstag*; government coalitions reliant on the President, not on parliamentary majorities. Presidential government became the norm from the fall of Müller's government in 1929.

Proletariat The proletariat comprised the growing numbers of industrial workers – men and women who worked in factories, mills and mines. Those belonging to political left-wing parties claimed the proletariat were exploited by the factory, mill and mine owners. The German philosopher Karl Marx (who is usually regarded as the founder of Communism) claimed that the proletariat would eventually rise up and seize power.

Proportional representation This system of voting ensures that a party receives the same percentage of seats as votes received.

Pulp fiction Popular fiction that is often not well written.

Realpolitik The term is used to describe the ruthless and cynical policies of politicians, like Bismarck whose main aim was to increase the power of the Prussian and later German state by whatever means were available to him.

Reich **Labour Service (RAD)** From June 1935 all men aged 18–25 had to do six months' labour, mostly in agriculture or on public works schemes. It was extended to women in 1939.

Reichsbank A national German bank, similar to the Bank of England.

Reichswehr The name for the German army after 1919.

Reserved status Reserved occupations were jobs considered essential to the war effort; men employed in these jobs were exempt from conscription.

Revolutionary Shop Stewards These were working-class activists who tried to organise mass action in the factories to end the war.

Right-wing A political point of view that sees social inequality as inevitable, and typically promotes traditional social values.

Schutzstaffel **(SS)** The SS was set up in April 1925 as a section of the SA, and acted as Hitler's personal bodyguard. Fanatically loyal to Hitler and his ideas, by 1934 the SS, under the leadership of Heinrich Himmler, had expanded to become the main agency of terror in Nazi Germany.

Secede To leave or quit.

Second German Empire The first German Empire (or *Reich*) was the Holy Roman Empire, established in AD800. Napoleon Bonaparte brought the Holy Roman Empire – described by the writer Voltaire as neither holy, nor Roman, nor an empire – to an end in 1806. The Second German Empire was the one established by Bismarck. It lasted until 1918.

Secretary of State The American equivalent of Foreign Secretary.

Self-determination The right of people to decide their own form of government.

Septennates The arrangement whereby military spending was agreed in the *Reichstag* for seven years. This greatly reduced the *Reichstag*'s financial power because it could only vote on military spending, the main government expense, every seven years.

Social Darwinist At its simplest, Social Darwinism is a political philosophy which argues that the strong survive at the expense of the weak; it is an idea derived from Charles Darwin's theory of evolution, and used by the Nazis as the cornerstone of their ideological belief in racial hierarchies.

Social market economy A mix of free market capitalism, guided by strong government regulation, and comprehensive social welfare policies; a middle way between socialist planning and laissez-faire economics a political doctrine which argues that government should intervene as little as possible in economic affairs.

Solidarity Founded in September 1980 in Gdansk, Poland by Lech Walesa, Solidarity was the first free trade union in a Warsaw Pact country. Solidarity led the opposition to Soviet Communist control in Poland throughout the 1980s.

Soviet Soviets were councils of workers, peasants and soldiers. Such councils had been created in Russia in 1917, eventually allowing the Bolsheviks to come to power.

Stahlhelm This translates as 'steel helmet'. This was a right-wing organisation – strongly nationalist, monarchist and anti-Communist. Most of its members were ex-soldiers.

Stasi The Socialist Unity Party of Germany (SED) governed the GDR for 40 years without ever being legitimised in a democratic election. The SED maintained its position of power through a huge security apparatus. The cornerstone of this system was the Ministry for State Security (MfS), better known as the *Stasi*, which was founded in 1950.

Structural unemployment A more permanent form of unemployment caused by underlying changes in the economy.

Tiergarten A former royal hunting ground, the *Tiergarten* is Berlin's most popular and largest inner-city park. The Reichstag and the Brandenburg Gate lie at the eastern edge of the park.

Total war A war which is not restricted to the warfront and where the economy and lives of citizens are bound up in prosecuting the war.

Veto The power or right to reject or forbid a proposed measure.

Volkisch groups These groups had their roots in the *Kaiserreich*. Their members were nationalist, racist and anti-Semitic. They demanded strong, authoritarian government.

War credits These were financial bills which were passed by the *Reichstag*. Without these measures, the German government could not have funded the war.

Weltpolitik This translates as 'world policy'. The term is used to describe Wilhelm's world power ambitions.

Zeitgeist Literally meaning the 'spirit of the times', it refers to the outlook, tastes and characteristics of a particular period or generation. In this context, Adenauer's political outlook no longer represented the dominant mood of a new generation as Germany entered the 1960s.

Zollverein This was a free trade union which had been established by Prussia in 1834. By 1844 it included most German states – with the important exception of Austria. It had done much to unify both the currency and system of weights and measures across Germany before unification in 1871.

The 25 Point Programme The NSDAP party programme, announced by Hitler on 24 February 1920 to a packed audience of about 2,000 people in the function room of the Hofbräuhaus, Munich's most famous and prestigious beer hall.

Index